NEILL'S "BLUE CAPS"

NEILL'S "BLUE CAPS"

Being the Record of the Antecedents and early History of the Regiment variously known as the East India Company's European Regiment, the Madras European Regiment, the 1st Madras European Regiment, the 1st Madras European Fuziliers, the 1st Madras Fuziliers, the 102nd Royal Madras Fuziliers, and the 1st Battalion Royal Dublin Fusiliers.

COMPILED FROM THE WORKS OF BRIGADIER NEILL, COLONELS HARCOURT AND BIRD, AND FROM THE NOTES AND MANUSCRIPT OF MAJOR DALE.

Vol. 1
1639–1826

by

COLONEL H. C. WYLLY, C.B.

The Naval & Military Press Ltd

in association with

The Imperial War Museum
Department of Printed Books

Published jointly by
The Naval & Military Press Ltd
Unit 10 Ridgewood Industrial Park,
Uckfield, East Sussex,
TN22 5QE England
Tel: +44 (0) 1825 749494
Fax: +44 (0) 1825 765701
www.naval-military-press.com

and

The Imperial War Museum, London
Department of Printed Books
www.iwm.org.uk

In reprinting in facsimile from the original, any imperfections are inevitably reproduced and the quality may fall short of modern type and cartographic standards.

GENERAL JAMES GEORGE SMITH NEILL, C.B.,
A.D.C. to the Queen.

Born May 26th, 1810, near Ayr; Lieutenant in Regiment, 1833; C.O., April 29th, 1857; Brig.-General, July 13th, 1857; Killed at the head of the Brigade in which the "Blue Caps" were serving at the Relief of Lucknow on September 25th, 1857 (aged 47). A London Gazette records that he would have been granted the K.C.B. had he survived. The title was, however, given by H.M. Queen Victoria to his widow.

Dedicated

BY HIS "BLUE CAPS"
ON THE EVE OF THEIR DISBANDMENT
TO THE GLORIOUS AND IMPERISHABLE MEMORY OF
GENERAL J. G. S. NEILL, C.B.
IN EVER GRATEFUL RECOGNITION OF THE
FACT THAT THEY EARNED THIS IMMORTAL
NICKNAME DURING THE PERIOD OF HIS
COMMAND OF THE BATTALION AND IN
ADMIRATION OF HIS HEROIC DEATH WHILST
LEADING HIS BRIGADE AT THE RELIEF OF
LUCKNOW

———

SPECTAMUR AGENDO

MAJOR-GENERAL STRINGER LAWRENCE,
The Regiment's first Colonel, 1748.
(From an oil painting by Sir J. Reynolds, in the possession of the Oriental Club, Hanover Square)

FOREWORD

As Colonel of the Regiment I wish to express to Colonel H. C. Wylly, C.B., the grateful thanks of all ranks of the "Blue Caps" for giving them such an excellent, clear, and most interesting history of the 1st Madras European Regiment from the year 1662 to the end of the First Burmese War. It must have entailed a great deal of careful work, and we all much appreciate the very kindly interest he has taken in giving the Regiment such a good history, which was very much needed.

Our thanks are also due to the late Major Dale who took an immense deal of trouble in collecting documents, and all the information he possibly could, and I understand it was a good deal from his manuscript and General Neill's book that Colonel Wylly worked on.

Messrs. Gale & Polden, Ltd., the publishers, are to be congratulated on their admirable work.

Colonel,
"The Royal Dublin Fusiliers."

CONTENTS

CHAPTER.		PAGE
I.	1639–1747: The Beginnings of the Regiment	1
II.	1748–1751: Siege of Pondicherry—Capture of Devicotah—Action at Volconda—Capture and Siege of Arcot—Action of Arnee	26
III.	1751–1754: Siege of Trichinopoly—Action of Cauverypauk—Surrender of D'Auteuil and Law—Battle of Bahoor—Relief of Trichinopoly—Actions of the Golden Rock and Sugar Loaf Rock	52
IV.	The Battle of Plassey	87
V.	1757–1760: The Defence of Fort St. George—Wandewash: "The Battle which gave us India"	113
VI.	1760–1767: Siege and Capture of Pondicherry—Colonel Joseph Smith's Operations	142
VII.	1767–1781: The Opening of the Mysore War	166
VIII.	1781: The Battles of Porto Novo, Pollilore and Sholinghur, and the Relief of Vellore	189
IX.	1782–1793: Battle of Arnee—The Siege of Cuddalore—The First War with Tippoo Sultan	215
X.	1793–1819: The Mysore, Mahratta and Pindari Wars	245
XI.	1821–1826: The First Burma War	277
Appendices		303

LIST OF ILLUSTRATIONS

GENERAL J. G. S. NEILL, C.B.	*Frontispiece*
	FACING PAGE
MAJOR-GENERAL STRINGER LAWRENCE	vii
JOSEPH-FRANÇOIS, MARQUIS DUPLEIX	16
FORT ST. GEORGE, MADRAS	22
ROBERT, LORD CLIVE	42
THE ROCK OF TRICHINOPOLY	52
PLASSEY COMMEMORATION MEDAL	108
ARMS, COLOURS, ACCOUTREMENTS AND TROPHIES	165
REDUCTION OF SAVENDROOG	238
MAJOR-GENERAL SIR THOMAS MUNRO	255
CAPTURE OF ISLAND OF BANDA	260
BATTLE OF MEHIDPUR FROM RIGHT BANK OF SEEPRA	268
FORT TALNEIR	270
MAJOR-GENERAL SIR JOHN MALCOLM	276
HORN SNUFF BOX	278
VIEW OF THE LANDING AT RANGOON OF PART OF THE COMBINED FORCES, MAY 11TH, 1824	280
THE STORMING OF THE FORT OF SYRIAM BY THE COMBINED FORCES, AUGUST 5TH, 1824	284
CAPTURE OF SITTANG	294

The coloured plates in this Naval and Military Press reprint are placed after this page.

LIST OF MAPS

	FACING PAGE
MADRAS AND FORT ST. GEORGE	18
TRICHINOPOLY	82
PLASSEY	104
PONDICHERRY	148
SERINGAPATAM	240
SOUTHERN INDIA	274

[From a Coloured Print in the Royal United Service Institution

VIEW OF THE LANDING AT RANGOON

Of part of the combined forces from Bengal and Madras, under the orders of Sir Archibald Campbell, K.C.B., on May 11th, 1824.

[From a Coloured Print in the Royal United Service Institution

THE STORMING OF THE FORT OF SYRIAM
By the combined force of Sailors and European and Native Troops on August 5th, 1824.

NEILL'S "BLUE CAPS"

CHAPTER I

1639—1747.

THE BEGINNINGS OF THE REGIMENT.

FROM the days of King Charles I until a very much later period the British factories established upon different parts of the coast-line of Hindustan maintained companies of European infantrymen for purposes of local defence; and by the Charter of Charles II, dated April 3rd, 1661, he gave power " to erect fortifications and provide men for their defence, as also to establish martial law if necessary." It would appear, therefore, that the " Madras Europeans " are entitled to consider themselves the first military force constituted for service with the East India Company, in other words that counting from its formation in independent *companies*, the 1st Battalion Royal Dublin Fusiliers was the oldest of the old Indian regiments, although the 2nd Battalion may equally claim to be the longest in existence dating from its formation as a *battalion*.

1639 " In 1639 a British merchant named Day bought a strip of territory on the Coromandel coast, about 30 miles to the south of Masulipatam. It was within the dominions of a Hindu raja, and was about 6 miles long and one mile inland. It included a small island which faced the sea and was defended on the land side by a river. Mr. Day agreed to pay the raja a rent of £500 a year in native coin known as pagodas and the transaction was duly engraved on a plate of gold. A factory of brick was built upon the island, mounted with cannon and called Fort St. George. . . . This factory was the germ of the city of Madras."*

* Wheeler, *India under British Rule*, p. 7.

"Though not the earliest British settlement in the Indian peninsula, Madras possesses a peculiar interest as constituting . . . the first territorial acquisition by the English in Hindustan. It enjoys the distinction, moreover, of being the oldest of the three presidential cities, and for a considerable period it was the only fortified stronghold belonging to the East India Company."*

From Fort St. George detachments of troops were sent to the different factories on the Coromandel coast as well as to others more distant such as Bantam and Java. The president of each factory appears to have been, *ex officio*, the commander-in-chief of the forces garrisoning his particular factory, and the guards consisted in the early days of English soldiers sent out to India in the Company's ships, of men who enlisted or deserted from the settlements of other Powers established in the Peninsula, or of natives either of India or belonging to the Company's possessions on the African coast who could be induced to take service.

1644 On September 8th, 1644, a letter was written to the Company in England from "the factors" at Fort St. George as follows :
—"The names of all the English soldiers will be found in a list enclosed." (Missing.) "Disposal of the 21 men belonging to Courten's *William*†—two are dead, two are at Masulipatam at their own charge, William Hall has gone thither to get a passage to Achin. . . . 7 have joined the garrison here. . . . Geoffrey Bradford who was shipped out corporal of the *Discoverie*, 1632, at 25s. per month and taken ashore at Armagon the same year, hath lived there and here since as sergeant of the souldiers."‡

On the same date the Company's representatives at Fort St. George wrote to their "honourable masters" stating the cost of building the fort and maintaining the garrison of fifty men, pointing out that when the work is fully "compleated" it will need a garrison of not less than a hundred men, "when we need not fear any inland enemy more unto us in these parts"; and it may perhaps be

* Love, *Vestiges of Old Madras*, Vol. I, p. 1.
† Of 140 tons, lost near the Cape of Good Hope *en route* to Acheen in 1644.
‡ Foster, *English Factories*, 1644-45.

THE BEGINNINGS OF THE REGIMENT

accepted that these fifty men were the nucleus of the Madras European Regiment.

1646 The authorities at Fort St. George having apparently been able to increase their garrison to the establishment desired, in 1646 lent a number of men to the Native potentate then engaged in besieging the Portuguese possession of St. Thomé—a proceeding which not unnaturally aroused the ire of and provoked reprisals from the Portuguese; and in a letter of October 27th, complaining of the action of the rival European Power, we read for the first time of commissioned officers as forming part of the garrison of Fort St. George: these were a "captaine of arms" and a "leiftenant." By October, 1647, the "number of **1647** souldiers," wrote the factors in bitter complaint, "are no more than 33, which is too few by 17 in this troublesome and distracted countrye."

1649 The first commander of the troops in Madras appears to have been a Lieutenant Jermin, who retained command until his death some time in 1649. His successor, a Captain Martin, **1650** though nominated in March, 1650, did not reach Fort St. George until September, 1651, and pending his arrival an **1651** officer named Minors, who happened to be in Madras, was temporarily appointed to the command of the garrison, and on the death of Martin in 1654 Minors again filled the post.

1652 In 1652 the garrison had fallen to no more than 26 European soldiers and a number of West Indian natives, and then in 1662–63, in consequence of the formation of a new African company and the transfer of the East India Company's rights in Africa to the new body, the Guinea trade was wound up and a great many Africans were introduced into the different factories in India as labourers and were trained to the use of arms. A large number of Portuguese had also been enlisted in Madras, but they were not found to be satisfactory, and orders were received from the Court of Directors that all those serving were to be discharged and that no more men of that nation were thenceforth to be accepted.

1664

1665

The garrison of Fort St. George was increased in 1664 and 1665 by some 45 men sent out from England; the privates, who were shipped as "landmen," were assigned pay at the rate of 13s. 4d. per month, sergeants at 25s., while armourers received £1. Accompanying these "landmen" was one James Bett who afterwards rose to the command of the garrison, while among the 1665 draft was Philip Bradford "Chirurgion to the Fort."*

The wastage from deaths was very high and in January, 1665, in letters to England the fear is expressed that "though the men have been sent out most of them will die. . . . You may be pleased also to take notice in what want we are of Englishmen for soldiers by the mortality that hath happened among those sent out as per list of dead men here with sent. . . . Shoemakers, tailors, carpenters, smiths and such like" are asked for since "they would be very useful here and in a capacity of getting more than their wages." The list of dead included Captain Thomas Axtile, whose successor was Lieutenant Francis Cheeseman, 1 sergeant, 2 armourers and 5 other ranks; all but two of these died within six months of their arrival.

The authorities at Fort St. George had occasion to complain of the quality of the arms supplied to their troops; they wrote† :— "It did lately happen that several of our soldiers have received great mischief by the breaking of their muskets, whereupon one ended his life, so that we made a general search and trial of them all and there was no less than 53 of them that would not endure the same but break to pieces." Complaint was at the same time made of the swords sent out, "for what they have now are little better than butchers' knives." But the "factors" at Fort St. George were not only anxious as to the arming of their guards, which indeed was a matter affecting the security of the settlement generally, but it is pleasant to find that they displayed equal solicitude about the care of the troops when sick; and at the end of 1664 the men complaining "that the wages are not sufficient to supply them now in

* Love, Vol. I, p. 214.
† *Ibid.*, Vol. I, p. 215.

this time of their sickness. So, rather than to see Englishmen drop away like dogs in that manner for want of Christian charity towards them, we have thought it very convenient that they might have an house on purpose for them, and people appointed to look after them and see that nothing comes into them, neither of meat nor drink, but what the doctor alloweth."

Accordingly the house of a Mr. Cogan was rented to serve as a military hospital at two pagodas a month.

About this time the troops appear to have been " daily troublesome about their pay," complaining, it would seem, of the arrangement under which part of their pay was kept back for issue to their families in England. The major part of them, we are told, " are such Blades of fortune that they care not much whether ever they return to their country or no "; they complained also of the insufficiency of their rations and the difficulty of obtaining liquor, and declared " they would rather desert and leave the Fort to go into the Moors' service than to continue here and not to receive what is due to them."

In 1665 an armed ship arrived in Madras with a number of recruits.

1671 In 1671 the garrison of Fort St. George being much reduced by detachments, deaths, and the service of many men coming to an end at the same time, the Madras authorities received sanction to engage from the ships sufficient men to complete the garrison. But it was realized that these haphazard arrangements did not fulfil the needs of the growing settlement, and in

1672 February, 1672, a serious consultation took place regarding the fortifications themselves and the number of troops necessary to man them. It seems to have been agreed that " less than 300 Europeans could not suffice for the well-keeping of this garrison." The French occupation of St. Thomé in this year naturally led to a substantial augmentation of the garrison of Fort St. George, and from an undated letter which reached London

1673 in June, 1673, it appears that the military force in Madras comprised 241 British infantry and 14 artillerymen with 163

Portuguese soldiers. This paper does not give the number of native soldiers, but a nearly contemporaneous document puts it at 550.

The British infantry was divided into four companies which took the guard duty as follows:—One Company in the Inner Fort, one in the Outer Fort or Christian Town, a third, known as the Free Guard, remained as a reserve in the town, while the greater part of the fourth company were at liberty to go to their homes in the native city; barracks were not at this time provided.

Here follows a "state" or, as it is called, "Repartition of the Garrison Soldiers to the Points."

Companies, or, as they seem then to have been called, "squadrons," contained 60 men each, that is 55 other ranks and 5 officers, sergeants and corporals.

One squadron on guard every night in the Fort	60
At the South-west Bastion of the Outer Fort	9
At the South-east Bastion of the Outer Fort	9
At the North-east Bastion of the Outer Fort	9
At the Middle Gate in the North Curtain	8
At Caldera Point	8
At the Choultry Gate	17
The Free Guard or Reserve Company in the Outer Fort	60
At the Half Moon Point	11
At the Land Gate of the Inner Fort	6
	197

The 163 Portuguese were also distributed among the "points" in like manner, as were the 14 artillerymen.

The troops in garrison seem to have been as innocent of uniform as of barracks, and in December, 1672, it occurred to the Company that, were uniforms to be provided, the native princes might be inspired to dress their troops in the same style, whereby a market would be established for the Company's woollen goods; the following quaint letter was accordingly written to the president at Fort St. George:—

THE FIRST UNIFORM

"It being found here in Europe very necessary and convenient for the soldiers to have coats of one colour, not only for the handsome representation of them in their exercise but for the greater awe to the adversary, besides the encouragement to themselves, we have thought requisite that our soldiers with you should be put into the like habit, for though it be hot in the daytime, yet the night being cool (and in time of rain) it may be a measure to preserve their health.

"And this example probably may beget a vent of our cloth if the practice will take with the Princes of the country to put their Regiments and Companies into cloth coats of several Colours...."

About this time sanction seems to have been asked and granted for the practice when necessary of Martial Law. The Directors at home and the Factors in India appear to have now begun to take increased interest in their troops, and in 1676 and 1677 a

1676 Major William Puckle was detailed to conduct something of the nature of a military investigation, and he proposed,

1677 *inter alia*, that one of the two European companies, to which the original four had now been reduced, should be called "the Governor's Own Company" being officered by a Captain-Lieutenant, an Ensign and a "Bringer-up," the other Company having a Captain-Lieutenant and an Ensign; this, so Major Puckle considered, "will render them complete companies and be for the honour of the Honourable East India Company whom they serve. That the captain, etc., be continued in their old pay; 'tis only the title which is more than the pay with true-spirited soldiers."

It was now enacted by the Directors that the garrison of Fort St. George was for the future to consist wholly of Englishmen; the pay of the soldier was to be raised to 21s. per mensem; while the custom of training civil servants to the use of arms was prohibited, as also the transfer of any officer from a civil to a military appointment.

In 1678 Streynsham Master became President of the Council

1678 at Madras and at once inaugurated several changes in the garrison; the two companies were reduced to 80 men and the numbers of the black soldiers were ordered to be gradually reduced "to no more than should appear to be absolutely necessary." Shortly after this the officers petitioned for the grant of commissions, relative rank and increase of pay; the two first requests were granted, the other was referred home; by virtue of his own commission as Governor and Commander-in-Chief of Fort St. George—a dual appointment which caused much trouble in later days between Macartney and Coote—Master issued commissions to :

    Philip O'Neale as captain of a Company.
    James Bett as lieutenant of the Governor's Company.
    William Richardson as lieutenant of O'Neale's Company
    Nathaniel Bonus as ensign of the Governor's Company.
    Tilman Holt as ensign of O'Neale's Company.

Further these officers were given relative rank as under :—

    Captains to rank with senior merchants.
    Lieutenants with merchants.
    Ensigns with Factors.
    Sergeants with Writers.

The Directors of the Honourable Company, however, disapproved of this issue of commissions, and in November, 1681, Master having by then returned to England, wrote to Fort St. George :—" Our late Agent's giving commissions to the officers of our Garrison we look upon as a vain ostentatious thing and to no good purpose. We therefore hereby revoke and annul all Commissions from receipt of this letter, and order expressly that no Commission be given any officer in our Garrison of Fort St. George, or at least that new ones be given them under the hands of all, or four at least, of our Council there."

During the year 1677 the great Mahratta General, Sivagee, appeared within a short distance of Madras which he intended surprising, and the improvement of the defences of the north front was undertaken. He contented himself with the seizure of Gingee and Nellore from the Nawab, and shortly after left the Carnatic at the head of his cavalry, leaving the rest of his army behind with orders to surprise and plunder Madras at the first favourable opportunity. At the same time he confirmed the possession of

Pondicherry to the French, who had settled at and fortified that place in 1672.

In 1678 an order arrived from the Court of Directors allowing ten fanams* monthly to every soldier on completion of seven years' service: this was intended to encourage re-enlistment after seven years' service.

In this year one Lingappa, the native governor of Poonamallee, gave much trouble, stopping all paddy coming to Madras except through Poonamallee, so that he might sell his grain at an exorbitant rate. He virtually blockaded Madras and threatened active hostilities, whereupon the Portuguese militia in Madras was called out and the native inhabitants offered to raise a corps at their own expense.

1679 In the year following we find that the proposals as to putting the troops into uniform had borne fruit, and are able from the following to determine that the garrison appear at this period to have worn red uniforms with green facings :—" Fort St. George Consultation dated July 14th, 1679 :—

" And whereas there was some Perpetuanoes sent out last year and some this year which will not sell, it is thought fit to clothe the soldiers with the red ones at 7 fanams per yard and line the said clothes with calico dyed green, and the money for the said clothing to be stopped out of their pay, the English in four months and the Portuguese in six months."†

1681-82 In 1681–82 an Act of Parliament authorized the Company to seize and send home all British subjects trading irregularly to the East Indies; these persons were styled " interlopers " and one of the most notorious of them was Thomas Pitt, afterwards Governor of Madras and grandfather of the Earl of Chatham. Certain of these adventurers had assembled at Hooghly in Bengal and threatened the agent of the factory. " An ensign of tried courage and fidelity " was sent from Fort St. George with 30

---

* A division of the pagoda, worth about threepence.
† Love, Vol. I, p. 439.

soldiers for his protection, and these were the first European troops sent to Bengal from Madras.

1683 A year later the Court of Directors constituted the agency of Fort St. George a governorship, Mr. Gyfford being nominated the first governor, and he was also directed to proceed to Bengal and assume the supreme command there. He took with him as his escort a company of soldiers from Fort St. George with Lieutenants Richardson and Lesley; this now left *three* companies in Madras, so the number must have recently been augmented; these three were commanded by Lieutenants Bett, Child and Landey.

1684 Now at last, in 1684, temporary barracks were provided and were erected on the west side of the town opposite the gate of the Inner Fort; three years later they were made permanent and handed over for the use of the "Free Guard."

1685 Instructions were received from the Company in 1685, sanctioned by His Majesty, for their servants to take action against the Native Powers in retaliation for injuries sustained **1686** and for their loss of privileges in Bengal, and war was in 1686 declared against the Nawab of Dacca and equally against the Great Moghul, Aurungzebe. An expedition had been fitted out in England by the Company consisting of ten ships of from 12 to 70 guns, under the command of Captain Nicholson, who was to have the rank of vice-admiral until his arrival in the Ganges, when the President of Bengal was to assume the office and titles of admiral and commander-in-chief of the land forces. On board this fleet were embarked nearly 800[*] men in 6 companies under subaltern officers only, the Company desiring that the captains and other superior officers should be supplied from their civil servants, " for they did not think it safe to have soldiers by profession in any post higher than that of lieutenant." This force was to be joined by a detachment from Fort St. George and by a company from Priaman in Sumatra; by this means an effective regiment of one thousand men in ten companies was formed.

[*] Wilson, *History of the Madras Army*, Vol. I, p. 3, says "600 soldiers."

"It may be remarked, in connection with the above, that this great expedition failed from want of discipline in the soldiers employed. Some of them went into the bazar to make purchases; there they got into a squabble with the natives; this grew to a riot, and the riot to a battle. In this the English had the best of it, but the affair gave the alarm to the Native government which concentrated its forces before the English could do the same, and thus defeated and drove them out of Bengal. It is reasonable to suppose that had the soldiers been under the command of *officers*, that is, men trained to the business and not taken from civil employment for the occasion, they would have been under better control."

During the detachment in Bengal of so large a force the Governor of Madras was under great anxiety for the safety of Fort St. George which was constantly threatened by the army of Aurungzebe.

1687 Early in 1687 a new battery was constructed to hinder any hostile advance across the Island, and steps were taken to place the native contingent on an improved footing; the following seems to refute the oft-repeated statement that no organized native force existed before the days of Stringer Lawrence :—

"There being 280 Peons in pay for the watch and guard of the suburbs, who in the disorder they are scattered about be of little credit or force to the place, the Governor therefore formed them into three regular companies, each two divisions of musquets and one of lances, their commanders and most of their officers English natives of the town. Each company to march under a red Beteelae* ensign. . . . and for the encouragement of the officers it is ordered that their pay have a small advance, and that they exercise and drill the Peons twice a week, which will make them formidable and serviceable upon occasion."†

A Mahratta army of 2,000 Horse and 5,000 Foot now attacked and destroyed Conjeveram and plundered Poonamallee, causing much military activity in the Madras settlement. The Company's servants and all English freemen were formed into a company of

* A kind of muslin.
† Love, Vol. I, p. 528.

Train Bands, and these, with the three companies of regulars then in garrison, attended a general parade when "the methods of the military exercises were shown them round the garrison. Afterwards marched over the river to the campaigne where they did form and order them in a battalion." In August, 1688, mention is made of the arrival in the *Defence* and *James* of a " seasonable and brave supply of soldiers to the number of 140 lusty men," and these were reinforced in the March following by the men brought down from Bengal when the British were forced to leave their settlements in that part of the country. The troops now formed four companies commanded respectively by Captain-Lieutenant James Bett and Lieutenants Francis Seaton, Zouch Troughton and Henry Sinclare. Each company had an ensign, 4 sergeants, 4 corporals and 4 " rounders " and two companies were on duty daily. The messing of the men seems at this time to have been put out to contract at 60 fanams per man per mensem " to provide them with sufficient good provisions, beef, mutton, pork, fish, pilao and rice," with a dram and punch sometimes, " 2 meals each day " ; dinner was at 11 and supper at 6 p.m.

A little later Seaton's company was converted into one of " Granodeers " with extra pay and the sole duty of guarding the Inner Fort.

During 1688–89 more recruits arrived from England, the *Chandos* bringing out a draft of 60 and large quantities of much-needed military stores; the fort had further been strengthened, and to these causes the president and council of Fort St. George attributed the backwardness of the enemy to attack. The factory at Vizagapatam had not been so fortunate, for one of Aurungzebe's armies appeared before it and took it by surprise, every person belonging to the factory being killed.

In 1690–91 a company of European artillery and a troop of cavalry formed part of the garrison of Fort St. George; at the time, however, there were only three infantry companies and one of these was ordered to be disbanded, the men being permitted to transfer to the artillery or cavalry or to the

THE GRANTING OF COMMISSIONS

Company's Bombay Regiment. A year later this order for disbandment was cancelled, but it was laid down that the infantry companies were to be commanded by lieutenants only, the higher ranks being filled by the president and officers next to him in seniority, but only to draw pay in time of war. A staff officer or adjutant was at this time allowed, to draw pay at the rate of 4s. a day *plus* a maintenance allowance of 20s. a month.

1698-99 In the winter of 1698-99 the old question as to the authority whereby commissions should be granted to officers of the garrison was settled in the following resolution: " It is unanimously agreed and resolved that the Governor alone do sign the commissions, it being absolutely necessary that a sufficient power be lodged in one person whereby he may be enabled to ask for the defence of the place upon emergent occasions. But no person to have a commission given him but by joint consent of Council, which commissions are understood to be revokeable at any time (when reason shall appear for it) by majority of Council."

1701 Daud Khan, the newly-appointed Nawab of the Carnatic, visited Fort St. George in July, 1701, but does not appear to have been particularly well pleased with his reception, and
1702 returning to the neighbourhood in February, 1702, established a strict blockade, which was, however, raised in May. It is possible that the Nawab was deterred from making himself more actively disagreeable by the strength of Fort St. George, of which a contemporary writer* gives the following account :—" The garrison consists of 250 European soldiers . . . . and 200 Topasses or black mongrel Portuguese ; they have also 200 Peons in constant pay, a company or two of Portuguese Train Bands, with the Merchants' servants and other inhabitants, a singular decorum, good fortifications, plenty of guns and much ammunition, render it a bugbear to the Moors and a sanctuary to the fortunate people living in it."

About this time there is recorded a curious instance of the enlistment of a woman : under date of June 10th, 1703, in Public Consultations there appears the entry :—" Mr. Adrian Plymour

* Lockyer, *An Account of the Trade in India.*

pays into the Rt. Honble. Companys Cash Fifty six Pagodas, being on account of a Souldier listed by the Company in England, proved to be a female, which he co-habited with on board and marryed here; so, to disburse the Company for her Passage, etc., he payes the aforesaid sume." The entry in the register of marriages at St. Mary's Church runs :—" Adrian Playmer and Anne Duccer, married by George Lewis, June 5th, 1703."

1703
1704
During 1703 and 1704 Madras was besieged by the Mahommedans who were repulsed, but in consequence of urgent representations from the governor and council of the need for more troops to resist aggression and prevent insult, drafts were sent out from home. There was unfortunately great mortality among them, 12 recruits dying out of one batch of 16.

At this time the Madras authorities began to manufacture their own gunpowder.

1705-6
Complaints went home in 1705-6 that very few recruits were being sent out, while the French at Pondicherry were constantly receiving reinforcements. Some of the time-expired British soldiers are described as pressing for their discharge, which, if a writer of that day may be believed, was not easily obtainable : " another hardship the soldiers complain of is," he says, " that though they have served 40 years they shall not be released or suffered to return to their native country; and if they are so hardy to petition for it, a dungeon probably will be their portion."

1706-7
Thomas Pitt, the one-time " interloper," now governor of Fort St. George, was in 1706-7 threatened with attack by the Arab fleet, and made very strong representations regarding the weakness of the garrisons on the Coromandel coast, stating that both Forts St. George and St. David required 400 European soldiers each to complete them to a proper strength.

Whether these suggestions were approved or negatived cannot be stated, but the faulty principle seems always to have been followed of regulating the strength of the garrisons from England, the Court of Directors frequently issuing orders in a time of peace which not infrequently had changed to a time of war when the instructions reached those who had the carrying of them into **1719** execution. Thus in July, 1719, the Directors' orders reached Madras ordaining that the garrison of Fort St. George be reduced to 360 men and that of Fort St. David to 340. On the arrival of these orders the country was in a very disturbed state, moreover there was famine in the land, so that any sudden reduction of garrison would certainly have driven a large body of trained men into the service of some one or other of the Native Powers. It was decided that the disbandment "of the worst of the Topasses" should be very gradual, no more than 20 to 40 being discharged in any one month; but the garrison officers pointed out that the number of guards was as many as 16 or even 19, that the main guard took 50 and each of the others 20 men, exclusive of sergeants and corporals, so that if the number of duty men was materially reduced, it would be impossible to find proper and regular reliefs. This petition is signed by Alex. Fullerton, Edward O'Neill, Alex. Sutherland, company commanders; Thomas Ogden, Peter Eckman, Hugh Boyd, lieutenants; Ralph Clark, Arthur Crew, James Harrington, Peter Nangle, Benjamin Brewster and James Adaire, ensigns.

From now onwards the attitude of the Country Powers
1732 caused the Company's officials in India no small anxiety; in 1732 the government was greatly annoyed by the exactions
1736 and oppression of the Nawab's servants; four years later Chanda Sahib, the Nawab's Dewan, seized Trichinopoly;
1737 while in 1737 the Court of Directors began to realize that the French were their most powerful European rivals in India and called for detailed information regarding the activities of the representatives of that nation, by the ships of the next season sending out reinforcements, ordnance and military stores of all kinds. Nothing appears to have been immediately put in hand to strengthen Madras or to add to its all-too-few defenders. In February,
1741 1741, we find the Council of Fort St. George writing home to the Honourable Company pointing out the low proportion

of European to Indian soldiers, suggesting " whether it might not be proper to have the most part of our Standing Garrison European," and asking that particular orders be given " that the Recruits sent us be good men. It is not uncommon to have them out of Newgate, as several have confessed ; however, those we can keep pretty well in order ; but of late we have had some out of Bedlam " !

The ships of that season brought the distant Council good news and made it clear that the Directors had now thoroughly appreciated the gravity of the situation in their far posses-

1742 sions. In January, 1742, orders went out for the proper and thorough repair of the fortifications of Fort St. George; while at the end of March the Company wrote that it had been decided to increase the garrison to 600 Europeans divided into four companies, and further that a Major Charles Knipe, an able and experienced officer, who had served upwards of thirty years in the Army, abroad and at home, was to take command of the military forces; he was to have command of a company and a Mr. Rudolph de Gingins accompanied him as his lieutenant, and a Mr. Moses Stephen Holland as ensign. Major Knipe was to receive pay at the rate of £250 per annum. All these three officers had special knowledge of fortification and were to have particular charge of the works.

Major Knipe died within four months of his arrival and Ensign Holland never reached Fort St. George at all ; but before he died Major Knipe had taken the initial steps to bring Fort St. George to its present outline.

The Home Government early in 1742 sent out more recruits from England, and directed the Governor of Madras to put the fort in the best posture for defence and to give assistance to neither Moors nor Mahrattas.

War having been declared between England and France in
1744 March, 1744, an English squadron of four small ships of war under command of Commodore Barnett, appeared off the Coromandel Coast in July, 1745, and landed a few recruits
1745 at Fort St. David. The French garrison at Pondicherry at this time contained 436 Europeans, while those of the English

JOSEPH-FRANÇOIS, MARQUIS DUPLEIX, Commandeur de l'Ordre Royal et Milit.^{re} de St Louis, Commandant Général des Etablissemens françois dans l'Inde, Gouv.^r pour le Roy des Ville et fort de Pondichery, né à Landrecy en 1697, mort à Paris le 11 9.bre 1763.

at Forts St. George and St. David were no more than 150 men each. M. Dupleix, the Governor of Pondicherry, managed to induce the Nawab to forbid the English committing any hostile act against his government by land, on pain of his instantly attacking Madras and other English possessions.

(The ship *Winchester* arrived this spring having on board Robert Clive, who is thus described in the Fort St. George Diary:—" Robert Clive, Time of Arrival, 31st May, 1744. Station at arrival, Writer. Salary at arrival £5 per annum. Present employment, Under the Secretary. Age, 19.")

Barnett remained in Indian waters, harrying the French **1746** trade and taking many good prizes; but on April 19th, 1746, he died at Fort St. David and was succeeded in naval command by Captain Edward Peyton, whose qualifications were far inferior to those of the deceased.

In June a French fleet of nine ships arrived on the coast under M. de la Bourdonnais, Governor of Bourbon and Mauritius, carrying 3,300 soldiers, of whom 700 were lascars. The two fleets came to action on June 25th when the result was indecisive, but the British commander decided to take his ships to Trincomallee for repair and sailed thither leaving Madras to its fate. La Bourdonnais proceeded to Pondicherry and shortly after sailed with a large armament for the reduction of Madras. The only troops which the English had at this time on the coast were the immobile garrisons of Forts St. George and St. David, each of some 200 men. Fort St. George, although strong enough to resist any native enemy, was quite unfitted to stand a siege from a large and well-found European force. It was in other respects also unprepared; the garrison, though composed of good enough material, was weak and insufficient in numbers to man the line of works.

Love gives* the complete muster-roll of the Madras garrison, from the *East Indian Chronologist* published in Calcutta in 1802, and from this it appears that there were 300 men on the rolls, but after deducting 100 of these as in hospital, " vagabonds," deserters, etc.,

* Vol. II, pp. 351-352.

there remain the following :—" Lieutenants 3, Ensigns 7, Drums 6, Sergeants, Corporals and Sentinels 184, total 200.

"First-Lieutenant, Peter Eckman,* an ignorant superannuated Swede, was a common soldier 50 years ago; became afterwards a sergeant at Fort St. David and for certain services got an ensign's commission, then a lieutenant's; and by length of service became the first.

"Second-Lieutenant, John Holland,† a gentleman about 40 years of age, of great honour and spirit and many other amiable qualities, but never saw any other service than upon the (hitherto) peaceable parades of Madras and St. David.

"Third-Lieutenant, Adolphus Gingen,‡ a Swiss gentleman, and as brave a one I believe as any of his nation, of great honour and some experience, having seen actions in the service of the Princes of Europe.

"One Ensign was a sergeant in the troops here, came out from the Company six or seven years ago as an ensign, and I believe may be a good garrison officer.

"Three ensigns were a few years ago common soldiers, rose to be sergeants, and were chosen out of that rank as vacancies fell, but never saw other service than that of relieving the guards.

"One Ensign§ had been sent to England since the loss of Madras on suspicion of having correspondence with the enemy.

"One Ensign had been a common soldier many years back under the Duke of Marlborough and since in India, quite superannuated.

"One Ensign,¶ a very promising youth.

"The sergeants and corporals cannot be supposed to be very well qualified since the second and third Lieutenants have often

---

* According to his own account, Eckman had served 56 years, of which upwards of 40 were under the Company.

† Commanded as Major at Calcutta, and died there before the attack on that place by Surajah Dowlah.

‡ Served on the coast with great credit, as Orme testifies.

§ Ensign Van Franken " was very busy among the French after the Surrendry of Madras, and did certainly give M. de la Bourdonnais a plan of the Town."

¶ Afterwards General Joseph Smith, a most gallant officer.

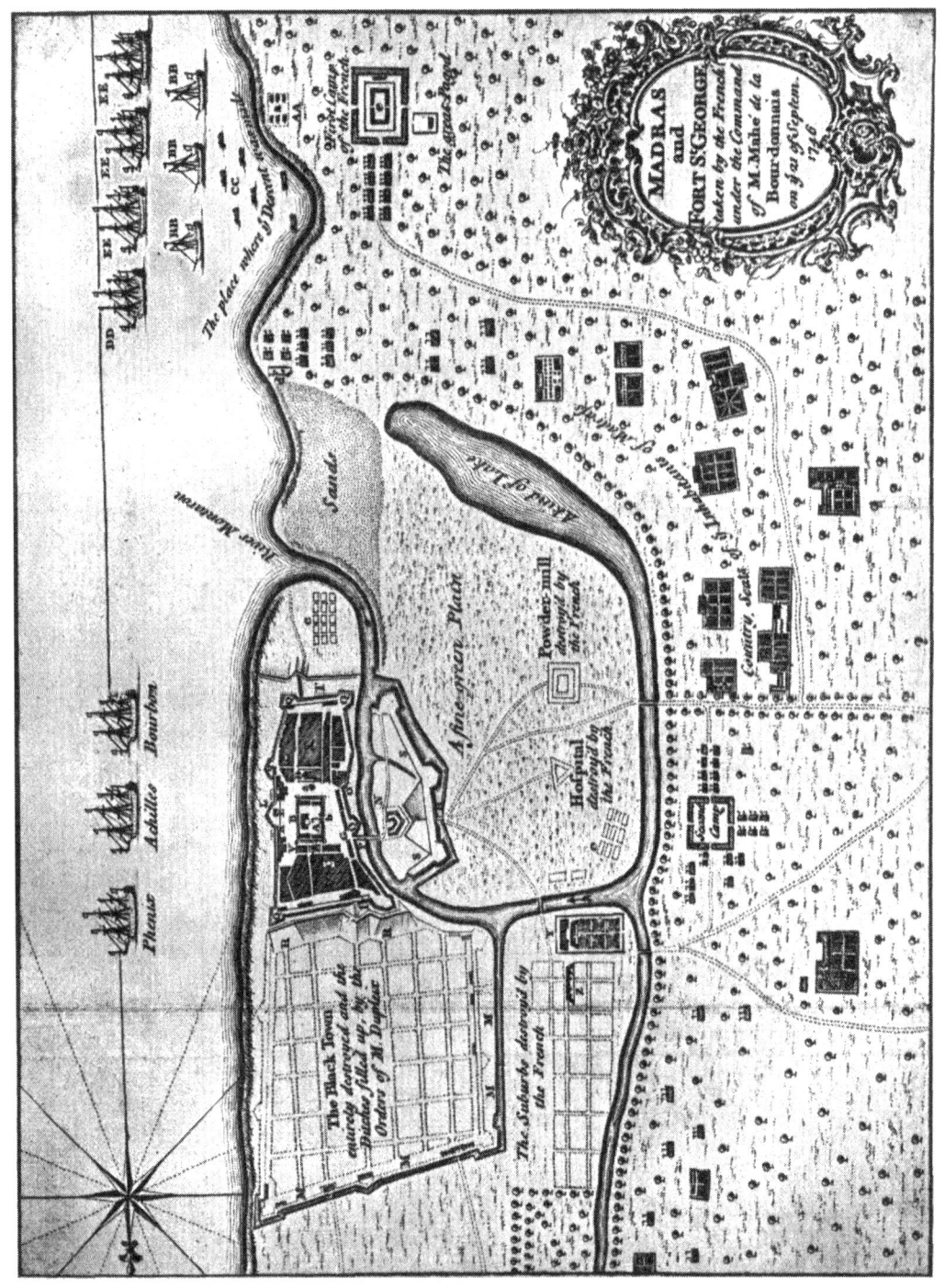

complained that they could scarce pick a man out of their companies fit for either trust.

"The Topasses, of which the major part of the garrison consisted, everyone that knows Madras knows to be a black, degenerate, wretched race of the ancient Portuguese, as proud and bigotted as their ancestors, lazy, idle and vicious withal, and for the most part as weak and feeble in body as base in mind. Not one in ten possessed of any of the necessary requisites of a soldier."

The French, on the other hand, had at this time nearly 3,000 troops in India.

On September 3rd, 1746, the French squadron anchored a short distance to the south of Madras, having on board about 1,700 seamen, 1,000 soldiers, 400 caffries and 400 natives of India disciplined after the European fashion. The troops with their guns and stores were landed, and on the 7th bombarded the fort from a battery of ten mortars, erected to the westward and within 500 yards of the walls, while in the evening some of the ships drew closer in and cannonaded the town. On the following day a second battery of five mortars was erected to the south and opened fire. The bombardment was maintained until September 10th, when Fort St. George surrendered and Madras was given up to the French, having been in British possession for upwards of a century.

The enemy sustained little or no loss, the English had only seven men killed and wounded. The officers were parolled, the other ranks becoming prisoners of war ; but the French not having observed the terms agreed upon on the surrender of Fort St. George, the majority of the English officers and merchants, considering their parole cancelled, contrived with some of the soldiers to make their escape to Fort St. David, whither the seat of government on the Coromandel Coast had been transferred.

Robert Clive had become a prisoner of war, but afterwards escaped, with his friend, Mr. Edmund Maskelyne, disguised as natives, to Fort St. David.

On December 8th a French force consisting of 1,700 men, nearly all of whom were Europeans, fifty being cavalry, with two companies of caffries, six field pieces and six mortars, appeared before Fort St. David, the garrison of which is said not to have exceeded 200 Europeans and 100 Topasses, inclusive of those who had escaped thither from Madras, but there were also some 3,000 peons among whom a few hundred muskets had been distributed and who were intended to protect the Company's territory outside the Fort.

1747 The most important attack was delivered on March 1st and 2nd, 1747, when the garrison was very hard pressed, but a British squadron of eight ships arriving opportunely in the Bay, the enemy fell back and raised the siege.

One hundred European recruits were landed from the squadron, twenty had previously arrived in February; in May 100* trained soldiers of the Bombay Regiment arrived from Tellicherry, and in September another hundred recruits were landed from England, bringing the number of the European troops up to the respectable total of 500.

In the actions at Fort St. David the officers and men of the garrison did excellent service; the senior officers were John de Morgan, John Holland, John Crompton, and Rudolph de Gingins; while in the reports of the period we read the following† :—" Mr. Robert Clive having behaved as a volunteer in the late engagement and requesting to be entertained as Ensign, the same is granted him and a commission ordered to be drawn out accordingly. . . . Mr. Robert Clive, writer in the service, being of a martial disposition, and having acted as volunteer in our late engagement, we have granted him an ensign's commission upon his application for the same. . . . Be sure to encourage Ensign Clive in his martial pursuits. According to his merit, any improvement he shall make therein shall be duly regarded by us."

Fort St. George thus passed out of the hands of the English for some three years, not being restored until the Peace of Aix-la-Chapelle. There does not appear to be extant any wholly contemporary description of the Fort, but the following is taken from that

---

* In *Crown and Company*, p. 110, the number is given as 300.
† Love, pp. 384, 385.

made by one Salmon who was resident in Madras some five and forty years previous to the siege, and during that time, although improvements in and additions to the defences had been projected and some indeed taken in hand, they do not appear to have involved any material change in the earlier design.

"The fort," writes Salmon, "is a regular square, about a hundred yards on each side, with four bastions built with what they call iron-stone, being of the colour of unwrought iron, and very rough on the outside like honeycomb. There is no ditch about the fort and the walls are arched and hollow within, so that I question if they are cannon proof. It has two gates, one to the east and the other to the west. The western gate which looks towards the land is pretty large, and here the main guard is kept, the soldiers of the guard lying on the right and left of it under the wall, which being hollow serves them instead of a guard house. The east gate towards the sea is but small and guarded only with a file of musketry. . . . The fort stands pretty near the middle of the White Town where the Europeans inhabit; this is an oblong square about a quarter of a mile in length, but not half so much in breadth. . . . Over against the west gate of the fort is a barrack, or rather one long room where all the Company's soldiers are obliged to lodge when they are off the guard; and adjoining to it on the north is a very commodious hospital where they are taken care of when they are sick. . . .

"On the west part of the Town runs a river close to the buildings; but on this side there is no wall, only one large battery of guns upon the river which commands the plain beyond it. On the east there is a slight stone wall pretty high, and appears something grand to the shipping in the Road; but here is very little occasion for any fortification, the sea coming up close to the Town, and no large vessels can ride within 2 miles of the place, the sea is so very shallow; nor is there any landing but in the country boats, the surf runs so high and breaks so far from the shore. The north and south ends of the Town are each of them defended by a stone wall moderately thick; but then, like the fort walls they are hollow within and would hardly hold out one day's battery. There is a little suburb to the southward of the White Town, inhabited only by the black watermen and fishermen, and consists of little, low, thatched cottages, which hardly deserve the name of buildings. Beyond this is an outguard of Blacks who serve to give intelligence to the fort; but there is no other fortification on this side.

"To the northward, adjoining to the White Town, stands a much larger, called the Black Town, where the Portuguese, Indians, Armenians, and a great variety of other people inhabit. This is built in the form of a square and is better than a mile and a half in circumference, being surrounded with a brick wall 17 foot thick, with bastions at proper distances after the modern way of fortification; it has also a river on the west and the sea on the east, and to the northward a canal is cut from the river to the sea which serves for a moat on that side; so that now considering where it stands, might be reckoned a town of strength if the garrison was answerable to the fortifications, but it consists of no more than 3 companies of four-score or a hundred men each and one-third of these Topasses or Portuguese Indians. The Company indeed entertain 2 or 300 of native Blacks in their service and a body of men may be formed out of the inhabitants."

In May, 1743, the commandant of the garrison of Fort St. George, Major Knipe, had died, and no attempt seems to have been made by the Company to replace him for nearly four years, during which time Lieutenant Peter Eckman assumed command of the troops as senior officer, and appears to have commanded during the siege.

According to the record of the proceedings of the Court of Directors of the East India Company for December 17th, 1746, it was "Resolved, that the garrison of Fort St. George be strengthened with a number of recruits, sergeants and ensigns, and that an able officer be sent from hence, as Major thereof, at the salary of £250 per annum and one hundred guineas for his charges out. And Captain Lawrence being recommended as a person qualified for the post. Resolved by the ballot that the said Captain Lawrence be appointed Major of the Garrison on the terms above mentioned, and, being called in, he was acquainted therewith."

FORT ST. GEORGE, MADRAS.

(From a painting by George Lambert and Samuel Scott, now in the India Office)

APPOINTMENT OF STRINGER LAWRENCE

On February 18th following he took the usual oath and sailed in the *Winchelsea*, his appointment being notified to the Governor of Madras in the following terms :—

"Stringer Lawrence Esq. is entertained by us to be Major of our Garrison at Fort St. George upon the same terms as Major Knipe viz. : two hundred and fifty pounds stirling per annum and one of the Companies."

Stringer Lawrence was the son of John Lawrence and Mary his wife, of Hereford, where he was born on February 24th, 1697–8, so that he was 49 years of age when he sailed for India. "In December*, 1727, he received a commission as ensign in Major General Clayton's Regiment, the 14th now the West Yorkshire, and saw service with that Regiment in Spain and Flanders and during the Highland Rising in 1745. He became a lieutenant in March, 1735–6, captain in June, 1745, and retired on January 20th, 1746–7. The circumstances under which his services were transferred to the East India Company are not known ; but it was not until the Company had agreed to employ him that his name ceased to appear on the rolls of Clayton's Regiment."†

In notifying to the Madras Council the appointment of Stringer Lawrence, the Company announced that they had " also appointed James Cope, William Keene, Lawrence Donaldson, Edmund Pascall and John Brooke to be Ensigns of your Garrison."

The new commander's Table or Diet Money was fixed at ten pagodas a month. The total emoluments granted seem ridiculously small, but Wilson (vol. 1, p. 25) states that they would actually amount, with allowance as Member of Council, to about £820 per annum.

Four months after Lawrence's departure the news of the fall of Madras reached London, whereupon the Directors appointed a new Governor and a Council, of which Lawrence was made the third member ; but it was ordered that his work in Council was to be confined to military advice and duties.

* December 22nd was the actual date.
† Biddulph, *Stringer Lawrence*, p. 17.

The *Winchelsea* was nearly eleven months prosecuting her voyage, going for some reason first to Batavia before making the Coromandel Coast, and it was not until January, 1748, that **1748** Lawrence landed at Fort St. David, then momentarily expecting an attack by the French; here Lawrence assumed charge from Captain George Gibson, a naval officer lent by the commodore to command the garrison.

When Lawrence joined the little force at Fort St. David " very little was wanting to deprive the English of their last foothold in Southern India. Two attacks, since the fall of Madras, had been foiled rather than defeated. Lawrence's first care was to form a camp outside the walls. This led to the detection of a plot among the native officers of peons who were in secret correspondence with Dupleix, the presence of the English fleet on the coast prevented any French movement against the place for a time.

" Lawrence employed the interval in reorganising the companies of Europeans and in introducing a system of military law. The reorganised companies were seven in number, consisting each of one captain, one lieutenant, one ensign, four sergeants, four corporals, three drummers and seventy privates. The lieutenant of Lawrence's company was called captain-lieutenant and ranked as a captain. In the field these companies acted together as a battalion, but ten years elapsed before they were formed into an administrative battalion in quarters."*

During the next ten years, however, these European troops were almost continuously in the field.

The following are some of the officers who, from the date of the arrival in India of Major Stringer Lawrence, and for some time after, were serving with the Company's troops in Madras :—

Captains John de Morgan, John Crompton, Rudolphus de Gingins, John Usgate, John Holland, Thomas Andrews, William Brown, Robert Saunderson and William Henry Southby.

Lieutenants John Scrimsour, Thomas Langford, Daniel Murry, John Williams and Joseph Chesborough.

* Biddulph. pp. 19-20.

Ensigns Ralph Wardlow, Lawrence Donaldson, James Cope, William Keene, Edmund Pascall, John Brooke, Philip Buckley, Robert Clive, Edmund Maskelyne—(sometimes spelled Masculine)—Samuel Smith, Francis Hamilton, John Harden, Hyde Parker, Edward Lewis, Benjamin Pigou, John Clarke, William Mathews, Thomas Langford, John Turnbull, Samuel Sampson and Thomas Grenvill.

CHAPTER II

1748—1751.

SIEGE OF PONDICHERRY—CAPTURE OF DEVICOTAH—ACTION AT VOLCONDA—CAPTURE AND SIEGE OF ARCOT—ACTION OF ARNEE.

WITHIN some six months of the arrival at Fort St. David of the new English commander, Dupleix took advantage of the absence of the squadron, now under Commodore Griffin, to make an attempt to surprise Cuddalore, a settlement about one mile to the south of Fort St. David. By a sudden march a force of 800 Europeans and 1,000 sepoys from Pondicherry, appeared within three miles of Cuddalore on the morning of June 17th. The force halted during the day on the hills of Bandapolam, intending to attack at night.

Lawrence obtained intelligence of the enemy's design and openly withdrew the guns and garrison to Fort St. David, hoping by this movement to cause the French to believe that he did not consider the place tenable; but as soon as darkness came on the garrison, made up to 400 Europeans, marched back to Cuddalore taking their guns with them. The French were completely deceived; advancing with their scaling ladders at midnight they were received with a heavy fire of musketry together with that of four or five guns loaded with grape, upon which, seized with a panic, "most of the men flung away their arms without firing a shot; but the precipitation of their flight prevented the English fire from doing much execution amongst them; nor did their fears quit them when arrived at the place of their encampment; for expecting to be followed, they marched on without halting until they came to the bounds of Pondicherry."*

* Orme, *Military Transactions*, Vol. I, p. 91.

On receipt of the news of the loss of Madras, the Directors in London were roused to action, and made to the Crown an application for assistance which met with a ready response. An expedition against Pondicherry was fitted out under Admiral Boscawen; the fleet consisted of nine ships of war with a hospital ship, while eleven of the East India Company's own vessels were employed to carry the stores and a force of 1,200 infantry soldiers, volunteers from various regiments in England, with 200 artillery men.

The *Evening Post* of May 30th, 1747, contains the following about the raising of these 1,200 men for service in India :—" The 12 Independent companies to be raised are to be draughted six out of the regiments on the Irish Establishment, and six out of the regiments in England, and are to have each a captain, three lieutenants and an ensign, and the officers, we hear, will be appointed out of those regiments lately disbanded."

The names of the officers belonging to these Companies appear in the Army List for 1755, p. 94, under " 12 Indep. Com. from the E. Indies under Admiral Boscawen"; they are as under :—Captains Patrick Lyon, James Dalrymple, John Ramsay, John Noble, Archibald Grant, First-Lieutenants Colin Campbell, Lauchlan MacPherson, Dugald Campbell, John Dalton, Matthew Walker, Second-Lieutenants Thomas Ilderton, Stephen Nevinson, Edward Jacobs, William Lewis, Robert Duncanson, Daniel Campbell, Erskine Mackenzie, Peter Gwibal, John Speed, James Ogilvie, Godfred Knuttall, Jasper Saunders, Joseph Chesborough, Hugh Fraser, John Grant and George Coke; Surgeons William Stukely, John Hammond, John Raworth and James Brodie.

"This fleet left England in November and the greatest part arrived at the Cape of Good Hope the latter end of March, but five ships not until April 15th. They were joined at the Cape by six ships belonging to the Dutch East India Company, on board of which were 400 soldiers. The troops having been landed to refresh, were all re-embarked before April 26th when it was intended to sail; but contrary winds and weather detained the fleet until May 8th, when they left the Cape, bound to the island of Mauritius which

Mr. Boscawen was ordered to attack in his way to the coast of Coromandel."*

1748 Boscawen arrived off Mauritius early in July, 1748, but found it too strongly defended to attack; and, pushing on, joined Griffin a month later off Fort St. David, when the troops and marines of the two fleets, with the Company's soldiers, made up a total strength of 3,700 Europeans.†

On the arrival at Fort St. David of the English fleet, the troops were put on shore and on August 8th began their march to Pondicherry. The Admiral was in chief command of the land forces and Major Lawrence's authority extended to the Company's troops only, stated by Orme to have "consisted of a battalion of 750 men of which 300 were Topasses, together with 70 artillerymen," and amounting altogether to about one-fifth of the total force assembled.

Dupleix had not been idle; he had greatly strengthened the actual defences of Pondicherry and had added a strong fort at Ariancopang, of the design or even existence of which little seems then to have been known, while spies reported that it was but very slenderly garrisoned. The following is the text of the report sent to the Directors in England‡ :—

"As soon as our forces were landed from the Fleet, they immediately encamped to the eastward of the Garden House, where they continued till all the baggage and the Train was landed, when your Honours' Troops, under the command of Major Lawrence, joined them and the 8th ultimo they set out for Pondicherry, but were obliged to make very short marches on account of their baggage, so that it was 12th before they got to a very small fort of the enemy's named Areocopang, about 3 miles to the southward of Pondicherry, which was so well fortified by fascine batteries and other works they had thrown up there that it was the 19th before they got possession thereof.

"Whilst they were before this place the enemy one morning attacked our trenches, upon which our people gave way and very

---

* Orme, p. 92.
† Fortescue, *History of the British Army*, Vol. II, p. 188.
‡ Love, Vol. II, p. 387.

unfortunately our brave Major and one Captain Bruce of the Independent Companies, by their people leaving them, were made prisoners; and we should have suffered considerably had not Captain Holland (from whom we are afraid we shall have no more service this season, as he has received a musket shot in his shoulder) with a great deal of briskness rallied our people, who, upon giving one smart fire, drove the enemy quite away and took several prisoners. We have since received a letter from the Major, who says he received no hurt in the action, and that they meet with extreme good treatment.

"We have also been so unfortunate as to lose Mr. John Haliburton, to whom, as we before acquainted your Honours, we had given a commission to be lieutenant of the Troop of Horse. . . . It was by one of our own Sepoys that he had the misfortune to be killed, who shot him upon his reprimanding him for some offence, of which the poor Gentleman died the next day; and the villain did not live so long for his comrades that stood by him cut him to pieces immediately.

"When we had got possession of Areocopang, after a stay there of a few days, they marched round to the westward, and are since gone to the northward, where they are landing their heavy artillery and carrying on their approaches."

On August 30th ground was opened before Pondicherry; two sorties were made by the enemy, in repulsing which the Battalion companies were engaged, inflicting much loss on the enemy.

The Orme MSS. in the India Office contain Clive's own account of the progress of the siege, and his description of one of these sorties is as under:—

"At about 1 o'clock we could perceive the enemy advancing with a large body of men and field pieces to drive us out of the trenches; notice was immediately sent to the general but before succours came the sally was decided. Paradis, who commanded, ordered the French Grenadier Company and some seapoys to attack the lesser trench, whilst he with the main body advanced to attack the large one. Fortunately for us, whilst he was advancing with his field pieces to enfilade the Grand Trench, he was mortally wounded in the head by a random shot; this put an end to the design, and the detachment retreated back to the town unobserved by the French Grenadier Company and seapoys, who according to orders attacked the front trench, where Captain Brown, who commanded, was mortally wounded, and his platoon fled and abandoned the trench, so that there remained only one platoon consisting of about 30 men belonging to the Independents with Ensign Clive. The French Grenadier Company could approach under cover of the huts to within 10 yards of the trench, which they did, and fired upon the men in the trenches for about 3 or 4 minutes, when they attempted to force the trench, but were received with such a heavy fire from Ensign Clive's platoon that they immediately went to the right about. In this affair Captain Le Roche and 27 French were killed upon the spot; of Ensign Clive's platoon 8 men were shot through the head."*

Fire was opened against Pondicherry from the land batteries and from the guns of the fleet, but as the ships were prevented by shoal water from approaching nearer than 1,000 yards, their fire was ineffective. For three days the bombardment continued, but the rainy season commenced earlier than usual, the trenches were flooded, and sickness set in among the besiegers. Finally on October 11th Boscawen raised the siege and the British retired, leaving over one thousand Europeans dead behind them.

In November, 1748, intelligence reached India of a cessation of arms between Great Britain and France, since in April of this year peace had been made at Aix-la-Chapelle. Under the terms of the treaty Madras was given back to the English, but still the war did not end. "As in Europe French and English could fight fiercely as auxiliaries of an Elector of Bavaria and a Queen of Hungary, so in Asia they could carry on, as allies of native princes, the contest which was to determine the fate of India."†

Pending ratification of the treaty Lawrence returned to Fort

* Forrest, *Life of Lord Clive*, Vol. I, p. 73.
† Fortescue, Vol. II, p. 191.

St. David on parole; and the amenities of military life there may be judged from the following extract from a letter written thence in January, 1749, by an artillery officer to a friend in England:—" We have no business here but looking after our men and no pleasure but waiting on the General; for by-the-bye this is as damned a place as ever men were troop'd in; black women instead of white; boiled rice instead of bread, and the punch houses such cut-throats that a man need have the Indies to pay their bills. I warrant you think we have rack punch for nothing, but it is a confounded mistake, for in ordering some they brought us so much to pay, in saying it came from Goa or Batavia, that we have been forced ever since to content ourselves with a drink made of Toddy—a liquor which would not go down with you at Woolwich. However, we are all cheerful. . . ."

1749

The first of the native states in whose internal affairs the Madras officials now decided to interest themselves, was the Kingdom of Tanjore. Here the ruler, Sauhojee, had some years before been deposed by the French, and he had ever since been living under the protection of the Company. Sauhojee now sought English assistance in regaining his throne, and offered to pay the expenses of the operations and to hand over the fort and territory of Devicotah, assuring the English that his appearance in Tanjore territory, supported by European troops, would be the signal for thousands to flock to his standard.

A force of 430 of the European Battalion, with 1,000 sepoys and a small siege train, was assembled at Fort St. David at the end of March, 1749, and, accompanied by Sauhojee in person and under the command of Captain Cope of the European Battalion, it marched for Tanjore. On the way the small force suffered greatly from a storm and its progress was much delayed; but crossing the Coleroon River it entered the Tanjore country driving the enemy before it. The promised local support was not, however, forthcoming, and after some rather blundering operations, Captain Cope returned to Fort St. David, having effected nothing.

The possession of Devicotah was, however, considered of special importance and another and larger expeditionary force was got together; it consisted of the Madras European Battalion, a detachment of the Bombay Regiment and some artillery—in all about 800 Europeans with 1,500 sepoys; Major Lawrence was placed in command. The operations were carried on with vigour and the following is the commander's account of all that took place.

"May 27th.—Embarked the Company's troops at 5 this morning.

"May 29th.—Anchored off Devicotah at half-an-hour past 5 p.m. I ordered my own, Captain Scrimsour's and Captain Dalton's companies with all the Lascars that were in the ships *Exeter* and *Harwich* to disembark in the Roads that Captain Powlett appointed for them, in order to land as soon as the signal was made with 2 field pieces, which were to follow the boats that landed the soldiers.

"May 30th.—At 1 p.m. we put off from the ships in 4 armed long-boats and several muscolas. Landed on the northern shore at 5 o'clock and drew up about 70 yards from the river, with our front to the westward, our left flank secured by the river and 1 field piece, the right by some bushes and the other field piece. We lay upon our arms all night and sent out small parties of Rangapah's sepoys which came by land, in front, and on our right flank advanced between one and two hundred yards before the main body, to give timely notice of the approach of the enemy.

"May 31st.—The remaining part of our soldiers, with some of the sepoys, landed on the opposite shore at 8 a.m. and then sent their boats to carry over the men I landed before, to join them, which we did about 12 o'clock the same day. I ordered Captain Dalton with his company to attack a redoubt of the enemy's, but finding a deep river between it and him, and it not appearing to be of any great advantage, I ordered him back again, but at the same time sent 2 field pieces to dislodge the enemy from thence, so that they might not disturb us on the ground we proposed encamping on. We removed some distance from the river side and encamped with our front to the Southward; our flanks secured, the right by a thick wood and an unpassable river, the left by some high sandhills with parties of sepoys lodged behind them.

"June 2nd.—Began to make fascines.

"June 5th.—Began to open ground with all our officers and men off duty, and a covering party of 1 captain, 2 subs., 4 sergeants, 4 corporals, 2 drums, and 60 private men, who were all ordered to observe the greatest silence for fear of drawing the enemy's fire upon them. Upon hearing our men at work, the enemy gave a general discharge round the whole garrison without doing the least execution, the work going slowly on. The covering party and Lascars voluntarily offered to work in the daytime which I ordered them to do and had only 3 men wounded."

On June 8th at daybreak the battery opened fire and Lawrence then caused a "Chamade" to be beat and summoned the garrison. No reply was returned, so fire was reopened, and on the 9th the native governor made answer that he had 5,000 men and would "not sully the small remains of life by surrendering a place he thought impregnable."

"June 11th.—I applied to Captain Powlett to land a body of marines for the security of our camp while we attacked the place. Accordingly he landed 3 officers and 100 marines, and we marched at sunset from our camp to the battery and lay upon our arms, expecting to pass the river that night, but was prevented by a heavy shower of rain which wetted all our ammunition and rendered it impracticable. Mr. Moore, the carpenter of the Train, passed the river the same night, and made fast the rope on the other side to pass our float; as our battery was upon marshy ground I was apprehensive that another day's rain would have made it impossible to attempt anything, I therefore determined to attack the place in the day, which we did on the 12th at 10 o'clock a.m., and performed it in the following order. As soon as we had all passed the river to the number of 700 sepoys and 400 military upon the float made by Mr. Moore for that purpose, I first ordered Lieutenant Clive, with a volunteer platoon of 30 men at the head of 400 sepoys, to drive the enemy from an entrenchment which must flank our left on storming the breach, and 300 more sepoys on the right to secure the right flank from a large body of horse, which were posted there for that purpose. Lieutenant Clive accordingly set out for the attack and met with a deep slough which we knew nothing of; however, passed it with the major part of his platoon and attacked the entrenchment, but not being seconded by the sepoys and being charged in the rear by the Horse at the same time that he was attacking the entrenchment in front was obliged to retreat to the slough again, upon which I ordered Sergeant Brown* with the forlorn hope to attack the entrenchment, and, in case of need, Captain Dalton, at head of Grenadier Company, to support him; but there being no occasion I immediately ordered Captain Dalton and his company, followed by the main body, to attack the breach, which he did, and being joined by Lieutenant Clive and the remainder of his platoon was in full possession by 5 o'clock, and I, at the head of the main body, wheeled one platoon to the right and faced the Horse in order to prevent them from flanking Dalton's company, and gave them a fire which was so successful that it killed some and put the rest in such disorder that they went off immediately. We all of us lay that night upon our arms."

Devicotah Fort being now secured, Lawrence, on June 20th, sent Captain Cope with his company, two guns and a body of sepoys against a place called Atchavaram; this was seized without opposition, but Cope's party was attacked in the night in considerable strength. He repulsed the enemy, losing four men killed and five wounded, and was next day reinforced by Lawrence, who later withdrew the troops, as possession of the place did not appear to be of any real military importance.

Of Clive's military qualities, as revealed in the operations now concluded, Lawrence afterwards wrote as follows† :—" This young man's early genius surprised and engaged my attention as well before as at the siege of Devicotah, where he behaved in courage and judgment much beyond what could be expected from his years, and

---
* Promoted Ensign for gallant conduct on this occasion.
† Cambridge, *Account of the War in India*, p. 14.

his success afterwards confirmed what I had said to many people concerning him."

The Madras authorities were now fully convinced that Sauhojee had no real following in Tanjore territory, and peace was therefore speedily made with the reigning monarch on the following terms: the surrender of Devicotah and surrounding lands to the Company, the defrayal of all the expenses of the expedition, and the grant of an allowance to Sauhojee on the understanding that the English accepted responsibility for his refraining from causing any further disturbance in Tanjore.

The force under Lawrence now returned to Fort St. David leaving a sufficient garrison in Devicotah.

At the Peace of Aix-la-Chapelle, Fort St. George was restored to the East India Company, and in August, 1749, Admiral Boscawen sailed thither with part of his squadron to take possession, Major Lawrence, and certain civilian members of the Council, being associated with him for the purpose as Commissioners; Clive accompanied Lawrence in the capacity of Quartermaster.

Fort St. George was found to have been left by the French in a very ruinous condition—" the walls and bastions round the Town being all undermined, the cannon to the number of 104 pieces all unserviceable, and very few stores remain in it."

" Boscawen, who had only waited on the coast till Madras was received over from the French, returned to England. . . . Many of the survivors of the troops Boscawen had brought out with him entered the service of the Company. Eleven subalterns were in this way transferred to the Company's service, their names being retained on the half-pay list in the event of their returning to England at a future date. Among them may be mentioned two officers, John Dalton and James Kilpatrick, who served in India with much distinction."*

" The scope of this work does not permit us to follow in detail the events of the struggle for power in the Carnatic. On one side were Muzaffar Jang and Chanda Sahib, supported vigorously by

* Biddulph, *Stringer Lawrence*, p. 26.

the French; on the other Nasir Jang and Muhammad Ali, **1750** aided feebly and fitfully by the English. ... In March, 1750, Muhammad Ali left Trichinopoly to join Nasir Jang at Valdore " (15 miles west-north-west of Pondicherry on the road to Gingee), " and was by him confirmed as Nawab of Arcot."[*] The English, seeing that Nasir Jang and Muhammad Ali were supported by many influential persons, and hearing that the former possessed an army of 300,000 men, largely composed of cavalry, were convinced that he was the real Subadar of the Deccan and decided to support him; and in March, 1750, Major Lawrence, with 600 Europeans, joined the camp of Nasir Jang, who was opposed by the rival pretenders to the Subahship and Nawabship of the Carnatic, supported by a force of 2,000 French under d'Auteuil, the brother-in-law of Dupleix. It was the first time since the establishment of peace that English and French troops had been opposed to each other, and d'Auteuil tried to intimidate Lawrence by a bit of bluff. Sending him a flag of truce, he expressed his desire that no European blood should be shed; as he did not know where the English were posted, he would not be to blame if any shot came in their direction.

"Lawrence replied that his post would be known by the English colours carried on his flag-gun; that he too was averse to spilling any European blood, but if any shot came his way he would certainly return them. In order to try Lawrence's mettle d'Auteuil fired a shot over the English camp. Lawrence at once answered it with three guns, ' and saw that they were well pointed.' "

Some of the French officers, dissatisfied with their pay and allowances, resigned their commissions, and d'Auteuil, afraid to trust his troops, retreated the same night, sacrificing his guns and gunners.

Lawrence on his side, finding his relations unsatisfactory with Nasir Jang, withdrew his troops and marched them back to Madras.

During the four months that followed Major Lawrence was officiating as governor of Fort St. David and was consequently unable himself to take the field, so that when in June Muhammad Ali wrote from Trichinopoly imploring the English to assist him, it

---

[*] Love, Vol. II, p. 427.

was under Captain Cope that 400 of the Battalion marched to Trichinopoly. On arrival Cope found Muhammad Ali's troops greatly disturbed, while the neighbouring country, particularly about Tinnevelly and Madura, was in open revolt. A force of 2,500 cavalry and 300 infantry, under the Nawab's brother, was dispatched to Tinnevelly, and with it went 300 Europeans under command of Lieutenant Innis, who proved of the greatest assistance in checking an incipient mutiny among the native troops. Madura having now openly revolted, Captain Cope marched thither with 150 Europeans, 6 guns and 600 native cavalry, and on arrival, being joined by the detachment under Innis, proceeded to invest the place.

Madura was surrounded by a double wall and ditch ; the outer wall being ruinous in many places the inner one was easily breached and might in two days have been rendered practicable had fascines been to hand. All the shot for the larger ordnance with Cope having been expended it became necessary either to storm or to raise the siege, and the Nawab's troops now showing a disposition to mutiny an immediate assault was ordered. The first wall was passed without opposition, and though the storming party was seriously annoyed by missiles of all kinds and the forlorn hope had some difficulty in despatching several men clad in armour, who for some time held the breach sword in hand, the bayonet in the end prevailed, the breach was mounted, and the parapet gained. Here, however, the enemy had raised a mound and laid the trunks of fallen trees along it, and thrusting their pikes through the spaces between the stems, they managed to wound severely nearly all the storming party. Further, within the breach and at the foot of the wall, a strong entrenchment with a deep ditch had been made, and from behind this some 4,000 of the enemy kept up a hot fire and seemed prepared to defend themselves to the last. Four of the Europeans were here killed and 90 wounded, while of the sepoys four officers had been mortally wounded and of other ranks more than two-thirds had fallen; further, not only did the Nawab's troops render no assistance, but of them 1,500, horse and foot, went over at once to the enemy, followed two days later by nearly 3,000 more. Captain

Cope now broke up his camp, destroyed his siege-guns and withdrew to Trichinopoly.

In the meantime Lawrence's relations with the provisional government at Madras had become strained. He had cause for annoyance in regard to several matters. Thus, in June, 1748, the right to convene courts martial had been granted to Lawrence by the Court of Directors, though a power to over-ride it was vested in the Governor and Council. In 1750 the Directors sent orders for the withdrawal of Lawrence's powers, but it was found to be impracticable to do this. He was also dissatisfied at the failure of the Company to enforce the measures necessary for the maintenance of discipline; he had no proper authority over his men; and his pay was very small for the position he held. On September 25th, 1750, he resigned the Company's service and sailed a month later for England, Captain de Gingins, as senior officer, assuming the command in his absence. The Directors acted with unusual decision and promptitude. Lawrence had hardly been two months in England when they sent him back to India with the appointment of Commander-in-Chief of all the Company's military forces in the East Indies, on a salary of £500 per annum, with a yearly allowance of £250 " in lieu of diet money, servants, horses, and all other privileges and perquisites whatever." He was also directed to go thoroughly into the question of a proper artillery establishment at Fort St. George. On March 14th, 1752, Lawrence again landed in Madras and at once took command of the Army.

While Lawrence was away news was received that Chanda Sahib and the French were marching from Arcot to besiege Trichinopoly, and Muhammad Ali at once begged for assistance from the Governor and Council of Madras, offering to cede a large extent of territory in exchange for the same and to pay the expenses of the opera-

1751 tions. In the beginning of April, 1751, this request was granted, and Captain de Gingins took the field with 400 of the European Battalion, 50 more mounted as dragoons, and 1,100 native soldiers with eight field guns, and in May this small force was joined by 1,600 of Muhammad Ali's troops. The combined force then marched to Vriddhachalam, a large and well fortified pagoda, garrisoned by 300 of Chanda Sahib's men, and this surrendered after some show of resistance. Leaving 30 Europeans and 50 sepoys as garrison at Vriddhachalam, de Gingins marched to the west and was joined *en route* by 100 Europeans sent by Captain Cope from Trichinopoly, and by 4,000 of the Nawab's cavalry and foot, and thus reinforced de Gingins came upon Chanda Sahib's army encamped near the town of Volconda, a considerable place 90 miles from the coast and 45 from Trichinopoly. " The citadel of Volconda, " wrote Dalton,[*] who was with the force under de Gingins, " has round towers and some small pieces of cannon mounted on it, and is surrounded by a pretty good stone wall of about 16 feet high, flank'd with round towers, but has no ditch. In this place the Moors and all the people of distinction reside, and without all is the *petta* or village, where the poorer sort have their habitations, inclos'd with a mud wall and a ditch."

De Gingins was not now very happily placed, with this strong place in his front and Chanda Sahib's army approaching, and does not appear to have acted with any decision. Some of his officers suggested seizing the *petta* where the English force would at least have been behind some sort of cover, but de Gingins being, as Dalton states, " of an unfortunately jealous temper which made him mistrust the good will of any who offered to give him advice," rejected this counsel and made an ineffective attack on the citadel, at the close of which the enemy was found to be close at hand marching to raise the siege.

" We then stood to our arms and the Commanding Officer asked the officers whether it was their opinion that we could prevent the enemy getting in by advancing upon them. I believe this beginning gave none a very extraordinary idea of our success. Notwithstanding which some gave it their opinion that a brisk push might still do it as the fire of the fort was very inconsiderable. In consequence of which the officer of the Cofferys, showing great readiness, was ordered to make what dispatch he could and engage their front, and if possible stop them till our main body could come up. I marched after him

---

[*] Dalton, *Memoir of Captain John Dalton*, p. 92.

as fast as I could, in any order, with the grenadiers, 3 companies of sepoys from the right, and a company of topasses belonging to the Nabob."

All for a time went well, the sepoys and the Europeans under Dalton attacked with great spirit and the French were at first thrown into confusion, but then they managed to get " 2 field pieces* up on the bank to bear upon our battalion which was marching down in all appearance with a great deal of resolution to support us, but on receiving about 20 shot which killed a lieutenant and 8 or 9 men, the whole went to the right about and marched towards camp in great disorder, without giving us who were advanced the least notice to retire in time."

Another historian† tells us that " the Captains Gingen, Dalton, Kirkpatrick and Lieutenant Clive endeavoured to rally them, but in vain," and Dalton in his journal sums up with—‡" In short we had no excuse for our bad behaviour. It was a scandalous affair on our side, and the French had nothing to boast of for they behaved to the full as ill as we."

As soon as it was dark de Gingins broke up his camp, and, marching with great expedition, arrived the next morning at Utatoor, about 20 miles from Volconda and the same distance from Trichinopoly, Captain Dalton with a small force and two guns being left in a village to guard the approach to the town, while the main body camped in the valley.

The account of all that here followed may well be supplied from the journal of Captain Dalton, who was in the best possible position to see all that took place. " We lay in this position," he writes, " about a week without seeing any appearance of the enemy, till one evening a small body of their Horse came down quite close to us, so near that we at first took them for deserters, but on seeing them draw their swords we made a company of sepoys give them a volley, and advancing on them with these and the 12 dragoons I had with me to patrol, we repulsed them a considerable distance beyond the advanced

* Orme says 14.
† Orme, Vol. I, p. 174.
‡ Dalton, p. 97.

guard." The sound of the firing brought up de Gingins and some other officers, and these with the few mounted men available seem to have unwisely pursued too far, fell into an ambush and made their way out only with great difficulty, some of the native soldiers being cut to pieces and others taken prisoners; with these last was Lieutenant Maskelyne. The commander of the mounted men on this occasion was Captain James Kilpatrick.

On July 15th the enemy advanced to force their way through the pass, but were checked by Captain Dalton's party, who were holding their ground well when orders came for them to retire—a difficult operation since Dalton's men were by then in the closest possible touch with a very superior force. "Our extraordinary retreat that day," he says, "may be principally ascribed to the gallantry and steady behaviour of that company who have never failed to distinguish themselves in every action that happened during the war.... We lost in all but 15 killed and wounded, most of which we brought with us."

The British continued their retreat next day and reached the river near Trichinopoly at 2 p.m. after a march of 18 miles, in the heat of the day at the hottest season of the year, followed up by an overwhelming body of enemy horsemen who were, however, dispirited at the loss they had experienced on the previous day. "We never halted," writes Dalton, "till 2 o'clock next day, when we arrived on the banks of the great Coleroon river about 3 or 4 miles from that place" (Trichinopoly), "with our poor people almost jaded to death. 'Tis astonishing how they were able to perform a march of 18 hours without refreshment, after the fatigue they had undergone in the action which kept them under arms from morning to 4 in the evening, and we marched off at 8 o'clock at night, yet they did it with great cheerfulness considering our situation at the time."

The English battalion being now reduced to some 400 men, and the Nawab's army not being to be depended on, it was decided, two days after crossing the Coleroon River, to encamp under the walls of the fort at Trichinopoly—the European troops on the west side and those of the Nawab on the south. The enemy followed and took possession of a fortified pagoda on the island of Seringham, between the Coleroon and Cauvery Rivers.

The only post besides Trichinopoly which still held out for the Nawab was the small fort of Coilady, and this was now captured by a strong force sent against it, in spite of the very gallant defence made by Lieutenant or Ensign Trusler. Reinforcements were now sent from Fort St. David to Trichinopoly, but the European battalion was still barely 600 strong, while the French could muster 900 Europeans, and the army of Chanda Sahib outnumbered that of the Nawab by ten to one.

It was at this time, in July, 1751, that Clive suggested that a diversion should be made, and that an expedition be sent against Arcot, the capital of the dominions of Chanda Sahib, and the following documents * show the readiness with which the authorities at Fort St. David accepted both his proposals and the offer of his services in carrying them out. The first is dated July 27th and reads as follows :—" Mr. Robert Clive, who has lately been very serviceable in conducting several parties to camp, offering now to go without any consideration of pay, provided we will give him a brevet to entitle him to the rank of a captain, as he was an officer at the siege of Pondicherry and almost the whole time of the war, and distinguished himself on many occasions, it is conceived that his offer may be of some service ; and therefore now ordered that a brevet may be drawn out and given him. . . ."

The second is dated August 19th and runs :—" The Board, being of opinion that a diversion in the Arcot country will oblige the enemy to withdraw part of their forces from Trichinopoly, and put it in our power to attempt something that way, now agree that Captain Clive be sent with a party of all the Europeans we can possibly spare and some sepoys for this purpose. And that he proceed on the *Wager* to Fort St. George, where he is to be reinforced by all the men they can any ways furnish, and march immediately towards Arcot. And the President is now desired to write to the Deputy Governor to acquaint them with the intent of their coming."

* Love, Vol. II, pp. 427, 428.

LORD CLIVE.
Joined Regiment in 1747.
(From an oil painting by N. Dance, in the possession of the Oriental Club, Hanover Square)

On August 26th Clive marched out of Fort St. George for Arcot; he himself had then attained the mature age of 27, and his little force consisted of 200 Europeans and 300 sepoys with eight officers, "six of whom had never before been in action, and 4 of these 6 were young men in the mercantile service of the Company who, inflamed by his (Clive's) example, took up the sword to follow him "*; for guns Clive had three field pieces. The names should be recorded of those eight youngsters who marched under Clive to lay the first stone of our Indian Empire; they were Lieutenants Bulkley, Revel, Pybus and Trenwith with Ensigns Glass, Morrice, Dawson and Turner.†

The town of Arcot lies 64 miles to the south of Madras. Surrounded by a barren country and granite hills, it was chosen by the Muhammedan Nawabs of the Carnatic to be their capital on account of its healthy climate and its great strategic situation. It was only 15 miles from Vellore, the strongest fortress in India, which commanded the main communication from and to Mysore, then a powerful Hindu kingdom. The city stands upon the left bank of the River Palar, whose bed at the dry season of the year is a stretch of sand some 3,000 feet wide. It had a population of 100,000 and was believed to be garrisoned by 1,100 soldiers, and on arrival at Conjeveram, two days' march from Madras, Clive, hearing of the strength of the garrison, sent back to Fort St. George for two 18-pounders.

He did not, however, wait for them to come up, but pushed on again on the 31st through a violent rain storm, and on September 1st, so records one who accompanied the expedition,‡ "the enemy in possession of Arcot hearing of our approach, abandoned the fort about 2 in the morning, and at 10 we marched without opposition through the town amidst a million spectators, whose looks betrayed them traitors, notwithstanding their pretended friendship and dirty presents. We then took possession of the fort, where we found

* Orme, Vol. I, p. 187.
† Love, Vol. I, p. 428, note 3.
‡ *Siege and Defence of Arcot, by a Sergeant*, Orme MSS., India, Vol. II.

great quantities of rockets and lead with some gun powder, which afterwards was of infinite service to us."

Clive restored confidence among the population, assured them of protection, thus securing their neutrality, and began at once to collect provisions and materials for the siege which he envisaged. He had no intention, however, of merely remaining immobile behind his defences awaiting attack, and on the 4th he moved out towards Timmery, a fort at some 6 miles distance, where early in the afternoon he came upon an enemy force 500 strong, both infantry and cavalry; sending forward a gun escorted by Lieutenant Bulkley's platoon, while he himself advanced against them with the sepoys, Clive quickly drove them off with some loss, his own troops having only one sepoy wounded.

On the 6th Clive encountered the enemy again on the same ground, and had three of his few Europeans killed, attacking the enemy's flank with a platoon under Lieutenant Glass, while Bulkley assailed them in front; but " as we could do nothing by bullying, were sensible nothing could be attempted with hopes of success by force of arms, having no battering cannon with us and our force short of one platoon (left in Arcot) of the number brought out with us, we returned to Arcot in the evening, attended great part of the way by the enemy's Horse, who carefully avoided coming within cannon-shot of us."

During the next few days Clive was employed in repairing the works and constructing new defences, while the enemy's forces were increasing in numbers, and an assault was threatened. On the night of September 14th–15th Clive stole out of the fort " with 3 platoons and the sepoys, observing the most profound silence, well knowing the success of a handful of men against such numbers entirely depended on not being discovered. The attempt succeeded to wish, for, unobserved, we arrived in their camp and alarmed them by firing platoons." Considerable loss was inflicted on the besiegers, while " alarm and despondency " was created amongst them, and the little party returned to the fort having suffered no casualties of any kind. The Sergeant mentions with regret that " as our people were strictly ordered to keep their ranks, less plunder was got than perhaps might have been expected from such an exploit!"

The two 18-pounders and some stores were now on their way from Madras, under only a small escort of sepoys, and it was feared that the enemy would endeavour to intercept these. Clive consequently sent out the greater part of his garrison to strengthen the escort, Lieutenant Bulkley being in command and having with him Revel, Trenwith and Dawson; and on this occasion we learn that Clive was "somewhat dissatisfied with the proceedings of Lieutenant Trenwith."

The enemy did not, however, pay any attention to this party, but, realizing how greatly Arcot Fort was denuded of its garrison, came into the town and attacked the fort about 10 p.m. on the 18th, "flushed with hopes of our non-resistance and of an insurrection amongst their friends within. The number of our men would not admit even of centries upon the proper posts round the walls, so that we were oblidged to divide into parties and keep moving round. The enemy did little else but pop at us from the houses on the side of the ditch, by which we had 1 or 2 wounded."

The attack was beaten off, but Chanda Sahib, relaxing his hold on Trichinopoly, hurriedly sent off 4,000 of his best troops under his son, Razia Sahib, to recover Arcot, assisted by 150 French soldiers from Pondicherry, and on the night of the 23rd these entered the town of Arcot and took possession of the palace and streets adjacent to the fort.

The following is the Sergeant's account of the events of the next day:—" Captain Clive with the whole garrison sallied forth, only a few were left in the fort. The enemy began firing on us before we got 50 yards from the gate, but we kept so brisk a fire from our musketry and field-pieces with grape as obliged them to retire into the palace and houses, from whence they kept up a continual fire, wounding many of our people. The only people of theirs remaining in the street were the French artillery who played their guns upon us with great execution. Our people got into a Choultry which proved a good shelter from the enemy's shot. Our train by this time had advanced their foremost gun within 10 yards of the enemy's two and obliged them to desert them (having killed most of the gunners) upon which Captain Clive ordered Lieutenant Trenwith's platoon to bring off the guns, but the men not showing the greatest readiness, and the loss it must necessarily be attended with, made us decline it as the taking of guns is at best but a nominal victory and dearly purchased by the loss of even a few Europeans where they are so scarce. Lieutenant Glass with his platoon was stationed at a street on the other side of the palace and was ordered to come upon the enemy's rear, but by some mistake the order miscarried. The enemy, not a man of them to be seen in the street and their shot falling in great quantities, was the only reason we had to think they were not gone, for they were all in the palace and house windows under cover. How to retreat now became the question, and as the doing it in a regular manner must have been attended with the loss of many, Captain Clive ordered the field-pieces to be fired till they ran back to the corner of a street when the men followed and carried them off. The loss on our side was very considerable, having a great number both Europeans and blacks wounded, of whom some afterwards died, viz., Lieutenant Trenwith and some 1 or 2 of the train, besides blacks. The loss of the enemy must likewise be great, most of their train being killed or wounded, as were a good many blacks by Mr. Glass, who ordered his platoon to fire over a wall into a square where 200 of them were."

Orme* gives the casualties suffered by the besieged this day as "15 Europeans who were either killed on the spot or died afterwards of their wounds; amongst them was Lieutenant Trenwith, who perceiving a sepoy from a window taking aim at Captain Clive, pulled him on one side, upon which the sepoy, changing his aim, shot Lieutenant Trenwith through the body. Lieutenant Revel, the only artillery officer, with 16 other men, was likewise disabled."

The enemy was now able to prevent the entry of all supplies into the fort while he also stopped the water supply, and it seemed that the defences were in no condition to stand against heavy ordnance—

* Vol. I, p. 187.

the parapet gave little cover, the bastions were ill contrived, the ditch where not altogether dry was easily fordable, while the houses, being close up against the walls, gave ready cover to the attackers; "we had nothing before our eyes," writes the Sergeant diarist, " but the dismal prospect of either being starved out by blockade or being obliged to stand a storm in case of their bringing battering cannon to make a breach, which the unshaken fortitude of our officers made us cheerfully resolve upon rather than meanly to submit to any terms could be proposed to us."

Razia Sahib had now been joined by Murtaza Ali Khan with a reinforcement of 2,000 men, bringing up the numbers of the besiegers to 10,000 horse and foot with 150 Europeans, while Clive's force was by this reduced to 120 Europeans and 200 sepoys fit for duty, and of the original eight officers, four only were now left. Orme tells us that "three sergeants were killed who at different times singly accompanied Captain Clive in visiting the works."

Nothing very important occurred until October 7th when the enemy brought up and opened fire with some siege guns; Clive managed to get a letter through to Fort St. David reporting his situation and this was laid before the Board on October 21st. In this Clive stated that two of his 18-pounders had been disabled by the enemy's fire, that he was about to mount the last he had, that he had three months' provisions, and considered himself able to defend a breach should the enemy make one, that his people were "falling down through fatigue," and that unless a relieving force of 200 Europeans and 1,000 natives could be sent, he had better "evacuate the place as soon as possible."

The military resources of the Company in India were, however, at this time especially meagre, and it was not until some recruits had been received from Europe, that a relieving party of no more than 100 Europeans and 200 sepoys set out from Madras under command of Lieutenant Innis. This small force was surrounded and attacked *en route* at Trivatore by 2,000 of the enemy with several guns, but Innis cut his way through, losing several men, and threw himself into the fort of Poonamallee, 15 miles west of Madras. Spies brought to

Clive the news of the ill-success of the measures for his relief and he now sought to draw on other resources. A body of 6,000 Mahrattas, under Morari Rao, "had lain for some time encamped at the foot of the western mountains, about 30 miles from Arcot; they had been hired to assist Muhammad Ali by the King of Mysore; but the retreat of the English and Nawab's troops to Trichinopoly had been represented in the neighbouring countries so much to their prejudice, that the Nawab's affairs were thought to be desperate. . . . Captain Clive had found means to send a messenger to inform them of his situation and to request their approach to his relief; the messenger . . . brought a letter from Morari Rao, in which he said he would not delay a moment to send a detachment of his troops to the assistance of such brave men as the defenders of Arcot, whose behaviour had now first convinced him that the English could fight."*

Chanda Sahib now offered terms for the surrender of Arcot, but Clive, returning a defiant answer, the besiegers, hearing of the approach of the Mahratta cavalry, determined upon an immediate storm, which took place on November 14th. Two columns advanced on the gates, two others to the breaches, while numerous attempts were elsewhere made to escalade the walls. The columns attacking the gates drove before them elephants to push the gates open; but these were wounded, became unmanageable and fled, trampling down many of the attackers. The N.W. breach was surmounted, but the defenders held their fire until the enemy were massed together, when their fire was delivered with great effect. But so soon as one body was destroyed another came on, until the intrepid garrison drove them at last back with bomb, butt and bayonet.

The assault of the S.W. breach where the ditch was still unfordable was more easily beaten off, and then for two hours the fighting ceased, though firing was maintained with guns and muskets. In the afternoon there was a two hours' truce while both sides collected and carried off their dead, and then the firing broke out again, continuing until 2 a.m. on the 15th, when it suddenly and entirely ceased, and at daybreak it was discovered that the enemy

* Orme, Vol. I, p. 192.

THE "BLUE CAPS'" FIRST BATTLE HONOUR

had retreated, whereupon the garrison, sallying forth, seized eight guns and a large quantity of ammunition which, in the hurry of withdrawal, had been abandoned.

And in such manner, and after 50 days, ended the siege of Arcot, maintained under every disadvantage, by a small body of men with the utmost resolution and the most undaunted courage. During the siege 45 Europeans and 30 sepoys were killed and very many wounded, and when the assault was delivered there were no more than 80 Europeans, including officers, and 120 sepoys available to withstand it. In those last desperate hours upwards of 400 of the enemy were killed, while Clive's party had happily only 4 Europeans killed and 2 Indian soldiers wounded.

Among the numerous and desperate services in which any part of the European Corps has ever at any period of its existence been engaged, the defence of Arcot must always rank as one reflecting the most honour upon it, and it entitled the Regiment to the first of the many distinctions or Battle Honours emblazoned on its Colours— "Arcot" having been granted to the Regiment in General Order No. 48 dated Fort St. George, March 12th, 1841.

The resources employed by Clive, the talent, activity and courage displayed by him on every occasion in the successful defence of one untenable post, were nobly seconded by the devoted gallantry and loyalty of the little body of heroes under his command.

On the evening of the day on which the siege was raised, Lieutenant Innis's party, made up to 150 Europeans and having four field guns, came in under Captain Kilpatrick; and on the 19th Clive, leaving a garrison in the fort under Kilpatrick, marched towards Vellore, taking with him 200 Europeans, 700 sepoys and three guns. That day the force reached Timmery, which at once surrendered, and, marching on, reinforced by a body of Mahrattas, Clive came up with the enemy as they were preparing to cross the river to the north of Arnee. The enemy, confident of their superiority, numbering as they did 4,500 with 300 Europeans and four guns, advanced to the attack. Clive drew up his little army, the sepoys on the right, the Mahratta Horse on the left, and the Europeans and guns in the centre, the front being covered by wet rice-fields across which the only approach to the English position was by a narrow causeway on the right. Across this the French advanced with their guns and Indian allies, their cavalry moving round to attack the Mahratta cavalry on the left, where a hot mounted action ensued.

The French advancing by the causeway received so heavy and galling a fire that all, except the guns, deployed across the rice fields, and Clive moving forward, caused them to retire, and following them up rapidly, drove them from one position after another, finally causing them to seek shelter under the walls of Arnee, whence at midnight they fled precipitately to Gingee. The French casualties amounted to 200 in killed alone, while the English lost eight sepoys only.*

The Mahratta cavalry followed in headlong pursuit, making many captures of men, horses, and of the enemy treasure chest; while great numbers of the enemy came in and offered their services to Clive, and 600 of the most promising and the better armed were promptly enlisted by him for the Company's service.

While the siege of Arcot was in progress, the French had occupied Conjeveram with 30 Europeans and 300 sepoys; here they cut the communications with Madras and had captured many sick and wounded officers and men returning from Arcot; among these were Lieutenants Revel and Glass and six Europeans. The officers' lives were spared but the six soldiers were murdered. Three days after the action at Arnee Clive marched on Conjeveram at the head of a punitive force, but on summoning the place the French commandant, not understanding English, " ordered his prisoners, Revel and Glass, to write a letter and acquaint Captain Clive that he intended to expose them on the walls if the pagoda was attacked. They wrote this, but added, that they hoped no regard for their safety would induce him to discontinue his operations against the place."†

Clive waited two days until two 18-pounders had arrived from Madras and then opened fire against the walls from a range of 200

---

* The following officers are mentioned in the Sergeant's *Journal* as present at Arnee—viz., Bulkley, Morrice, Dawson, and Turner.

† Orme, Vol. I, p. 192.

yards; "the enemy had no cannon but fired very smartly with their musketry, which killed several men at the battery, and Lieutenant Bulkley, reconnoitering the pagoda over a garden wall in company with Captain Clive, was shot through the head by his side. The wall resisted three days before it began to give way, when the garrison conscious of their demerits, and dreading the just resentment of the English, abandoned the pagoda in the night but left behind the two prisoners.

"After ruining the defences of Conjeveram, Captain Clive sent 200 Europeans and 500 sepoys to Arcot and returned in the middle of December with the rest to Madras; from whence he went to Fort St. David to give an account of his campaign to the presidency."*

* Orme, Vol. I, p. 200.

CHAPTER III

1751—1754.

SIEGE OF TRICHINOPOLY—ACTION OF CAUVERYPAUK—SURRENDER OF D'AUTEUIL AND LAW—BATTLE OF BAHOOR—RELIEF OF TRICHINOPOLY—ACTIONS OF THE GOLDEN ROCK AND SUGAR-LOAF ROCK.

WHILE one part of the Battalion was carrying on the war in the Arcot provinces, another, though the service upon which it **1751** was employed did not offer equal opportunity for distinction, was upholding the honour of British arms in a number of gallant combats in the neighbourhood of Trichinopoly, which the French and Chanda Sahib had continued to invest.

The city of Trichinopoly is situated upon a plain, which, prior to the wars between the French and English, was highly cultivated and covered with villages and crops. The fort is in the shape of an oblong, the longest sides facing east and west. On the north runs the Cauvery River, less than half-a-mile from the city walls which are nearly four miles in circumference; a ditch thirty feet wide, but not very deep, surrounds the whole. Some of the towers had been improved as far as possible by the English, who had mounted guns upon them, while an old projecting gateway had been formed into an outwork, with several guns, by Captain Dalton and had received the name of Dalton's Battery. A rock about 300 feet high stands in the middle of the city commanding a view of the country as far as Tanjore; this post was of the greatest use to the English during the course of the operations and a sentry was constantly stationed there and reported all enemy movements.

Seringham, 15 miles east of Trichinopoly, is so narrow an island that the Coleroon and Cauvery Rivers, which it separates, would

THE ROCK OF TRICHINOPOLY.

(From a painting by F. S. Ward, now in the India Office)

join were they not prevented by a high embankment whereby the waters of the Cauvery are conducted into Tanjore to irrigate that country, and for this advantage the King of Tanjore paid tribute to him who held Trichinopoly. This bank was known by the British as " the Pass " from the good defensive position it afforded for a small body of men. About a mile to the east was the small but strong fort of Coilady.

On the island is the famous pagoda of Seringham and others known by the name of Jambukeswaram, and these were occupied by the enemy during his operations against the city. The plain round Trichinopoly is 19 miles by 7 to 12; on the plain are several groups of rocks—the Golden and Sugar Loaf Rocks to the south and French Rock to the west—and these were repeatedly the scenes of hard-fought actions. The plain itself was much cut up by hollows, water-courses and ravines, as was also the Island of Seringham.

The army of Chanda Sahib and that of his French allies was camped on the south bank of the Cauvery at a place known as " Dalaway's Choultry," and in September, 1751, they erected three batteries wherewith to cannonade the city. One, 1,200 yards distant, called the Grand Battery, was placed to the east of the north-east angle of the fort and mounted three 18-pounders and three mortars; it was defended on all sides by a wall and was garrisoned by 100 Europeans and 400 sepoys; a second battery of two 18-pounders on the north bank of the river fired across the stream at the north gate; while two other 18-pounders were placed on the summit of French Rock 2,000 yards east of the south-east angle of the city. These batteries were all too distant for the fire from them to be really effective, and the small impression made by them upon the works only roused a feeling of contempt in the minds of the besieged.

Captain de Gingins, who was here in command, was a brave, but withal a very careful, officer, and his aim was to save his men as much as possible while letting the enemy exhaust his means of offence and his military resources generally. " To save," says Orme, " that part of the wall against which the enemy's principal battery fired, a glacis was raised to such a height as left nothing but the parapet exposed, and the Grenadiers, commanded by Captain Dalton, were posted behind this glacis. An entrenchment was flung up between the French Rock and the south-east angle of the town, in which the company of Caffres was posted to prevent from surprises the Nawab's cavalry encamped to the south; and to oppose the enemy's battery in the island, two guns were mounted close to the south bank of the river. To enfilade these, the French mounted two guns on the same side of the river, but were one night driven from this post by Captain Dalton. . . . The enemy's batteries fired indeed constantly and smartly every day and damaged some houses, but made no impression on the defences of the town; they supplied the defenders with a great number of cannon balls, all of which had the English mark, being the same which the ships had fired against Pondicherry, with as little effect as they were now thrown away against Trichinopoly."*

Muhammad Ali's troops were now greatly distressed from want of pay, but having made terms with the Regent of Mysore a large amount of treasure was sent to Trichinopoly escorted by 70 Mysore Horse. On the day of their arrival a small skirmish took place, which raised the native opinion of the English. A small party of Europeans and some sepoys had been sent out some distance from the city to cut and bring in wood; on their way back the French sought to intercept them and sent out a considerable body of cavalry for the purpose. This having been noticed from the high vantage ground within the walls, Captain Dalton, with the Grenadier Company and a gun, went out to cover the withdrawal of the party. On coming up with the wood-carts he sent them off to the city by another road and with his combined force marched against the enemy, the small body of Mysore Horse accompanying him. The enemy charged more than once up to the British bayonets, but were repulsed and put to flight, leaving many dead and wounded behind.

The Mysore horsemen who had witnessed this action took back so good an account of it, that towards the end of November the

* Orme, Vol. I, pp. 201, 202.

Mysore King marched to assist Muhammad Ali, who had, however, already taken 6,000 Mahrattas into his pay.

An advance party of these latter, 500 strong, arrived at Trichinopoly in December, and at once began to harass Chanda Sahib's light troops, whose *morale* was quickly and appreciably lowered. In the meantime the army of Mysore, with 4,000 Mahratta cavalry, had arrived within a few marches, and the enemy sent a strong force of French and native soldiers to occupy Kistnavaram, a strong post on the high road from Mysore, and from here, having strengthened and improved the post, they threatened to attack the Mysore army or to enter and plunder the country. The Mysore commander, alarmed at the situation, halted and sent an urgent appeal to Trichinopoly for help. In response to this call a force of 100 Europeans, 100 sepoys and two small field guns, marched out under Captain Cope and Lieutenant Taishan of the European Battalion, but found the enemy very strong both as regards numbers and position, the defences of Kistnavaram consisting, as they did, of a double wall, flanked by towers, with the Cauvery on one side and a morass on the other; moreover the place was approachable by one road only and that defended by a strong outwork.

Cope at once assaulted the place hoping to carry it by a *coup de main*; but his party was forced to retire, having lost many killed and wounded, Lieutenant Felix being shot through the body and Cope himself being mortally wounded; he died on February 3rd, 1752.*

Captain Dalton was ordered from Trichinopoly to take command of Cope's party, but on arrival he found that Muhammad Ali had been so very considerably reinforced from Mysore, that further help was scarcely needed, and he accordingly withdrew his men **1752** to Trichinopoly, where they arrived on February 6th, 1752.

"Considerable difficulty having been experienced about this time in procuring recruits, the Court of Directors took the following

---

* In the *Records of Fort St. George*, 1752, it is stated that " we had lost only 2 men and had 6 wounded, beside Mr. Lieutenant Felix, a volunteer " which seems an under-estimate of the loss this day incurred.

steps to supply the deficiency. Early in 1750 they authorised the payment of £10 to every soldier who would re-enlist for the period of five years, and in 1751 they sanctioned the purchase of 600 slaves in Madagascar. In July of the same year they made arrangements for raising two companies of Swiss in the Protestant Cantons, and entered into an agreement for that purpose with Sir Luke Schaub, of Old Bond Street, and Mr. Jasper Sellon, of Austin Friars . . . the men to be from 20 to 25 years of age. Each company to consist of 1 captain, 2 lieutenants, 1 ensign, 6 sergeants, 6 corporals, 1 drum-major, 2 drummers, 1 fife and 120 private centinels. The engagement to last for seven years.

"During November and December, 1751, 8 officers and 231 non-commissioned officers and men embarked for Madras. . . . A few of the men were from Hanover and Alsace, but the great majority belonged to Zurich, Geneva and Basle. The officers were Captain John Chabbert, Lieutenants George Frederick Gaupp and Rodolph Wagner and Ensign John Conrad Heidigger, 1st Company; Captain John Henry Schaub, Lieutenants Frederick Gurtler and John Francis de Beck and Ensign John Lewis Provost, 2nd Company."*

We shall meet some of these names again in the course of this narrative.

During the ensuing three years further detachments of Swiss, amounting in the aggregate to 279 men, were sent out to Madras, but none were enlisted after the end of 1754. The experiment did not prove entirely satisfactory, and after 1756 the Swiss companies were gradually absorbed in the British. Both Gaupp and Gurtler became captains in the Madras European Battalion, while de Beck rose to be lieutenant-colonel; Gaupp, as we shall see, commanded the Madras troops at Plassey.

Razia Sahib, now, at the suggestion of Dupleix, determined to relieve the pressure on Trichinopoly by threatening Madras, and he accordingly invaded the Company's territory, burnt several villages, and plundered the country up to St. Thomas's Mount and the gates of Poonamallee. It was therefore determined to try to disperse

* Wilson, *History of the Madras Army*, Vol. I, pp. 61-63.

ACTION OF CAUVERYPAUK

this hostile force before moving again on Trichinopoly, and Clive was ordered to return at once to Madras and assume command.

On February 10th and 11th, 1752, Clive wrote to the Board acquainting them that he had assumed command of the army at Madras and had been joined by a detachment arrived from Bengal in the *Fort St. David*, but that he required muskets to arm 500 sepoys whom he had raised; and that he was encamped in a very strong position at the Little Mount with the enemy about seven miles distant from him, their numbers being about 2,800 horse and foot with 30 Europeans and eight small field pieces.

He wrote again on the 15th and 20th saying he had had a letter from de Gingins begging him to advance on Trichinopoly, and that he had been joined by Captain Kilpatrick, from Arcot, thus bringing up his numbers to " 400 Military and Train, 1,300 sepoys, besides matchlocks, and 120 Horse "; he expressed a hope of bringing the enemy to action, and stated that he proposed " leaving behind him for the protection of Madras about 60 Military, some Horse and Sepoys."

The enemy was in an entrenched camp at Vendalore, about 17 miles south-west of Madras, and had a force far superior to that of Clive and greater in number than Clive estimated; it contained 400 Europeans, 2,000 sepoys, 2,500 cavalry and a large train of artillery

Clive marched round on February 22nd to attack the enemy in rear, whereupon they precipitately broke up their camp which he then occupied, but twelve hours later hearing that they were at Conjeveram, he realized that their object was Arcot, and making a forced march of 20 miles reached Conjeveram that evening. Having rested and refreshed his men Clive pushed on for Arcot and about 6 p.m. on the 23rd, when near the village of Cauverypauk, his force was suddenly fired on from a range of only 250 yards, his deficiency in cavalry having prevented his receiving timely notice of the near presence of the enemy.

The baggage was sent to the rear under escort and Clive drew up his men in a water-course under cover. The night was a bright moonlight one; a heavy fire was maintained by either side for two hours, the enemy's cavalry repeatedly charged and was as often repulsed; but the enemy's superiority in guns caused considerable loss among Clive's few artillerymen, and there was no choice but to retreat or charge upon and capture the opposing artillery.

A sergeant of the Battalion named Shawlum,* who spoke the language of the country, was sent with two sepoys to reconnoitre. He returned reporting that no troops were posted in rear of the enemy's guns, and thereupon 200 Europeans and 400 sepoys were at once detached under Lieutenant Keene, with the sergeant as their guide, to penetrate to the rear of the enemy and take the guns in reverse. Keene's party approached unnoticed to within 300 yards of the rear of the guns, when Ensign Simmons was sent forward to scout; suddenly coming on a nullah full of sepoys he was challenged, but replied in French and was allowed to pass. He saw that the guns had an escort of 100 Europeans who were looking out to their front only, and returning to his party led them unperceived to within 30 yards of the guns, when a sudden and well-directed volley swept away the escort of Frenchmen and entirely routed them; a few took shelter in a building close at hand where they soon surrendered. The party in the nullah, who were making a good front against Keene's men, no sooner saw their artillery silenced than they dispersed.

The English remained all night under arms, and as a result of the action took nine guns, " an Aid Major, 39 French and 18 topasses made prisoners . . . had it not been late in the evening not a single man would have escaped . . . our loss had been pretty considerable, besides Ensign Keene and Mr. Preston, a volunteer, wounded."†
Of the European Battalion 40 were killed and upwards of 60 wounded, while 31 sepoys were killed and several wounded.

" The battle of Coverepauk," says Forrest, " won by the skill and insight of Clive, deserves the dignity of an historical event. It destroyed the organised force which Dupleix had raised with so

---

* In the Orme MSS. described as " Shaulur, a Mustee "—*e.g.*, Portuguese half-caste.

† Fort St. George Records.

much difficulty; it increased the reputation of British arms, and it changed the balance of French and English influence in Southern India."

By their late successes the officers and men of the Battalion engaged had mainly contributed to recover for Muhammad Ali an extent of country 60 miles by 30, providing a yearly revenue of 400,000 pagodas.

On the afternoon of March 11th the force under Clive returned to and encamped within the bounds of Fort St. David. Three days later it was ready to take the field again under Clive, when on March 14th Major Lawrence arrived from England, and at a consultation held on the 16th it was determined that " the military being very well refreshed and the stores for the Camp all ready, ordered that the forces march to-morrow evening to join the army at Trichinopoly, and Major Lawrence acquainting the Board that if agreeable to them he purposes proceeding with the troops and taking upon him the command of the troops when he gets there, the Board entirely concur therein. . . ."

When Lawrence took over command of the forces again things do not appear to have been in a very satisfactory state; in the year previous a dangerous spirit of discontent had arisen among the officers owing to a dispute with Government on the subject of *batta*, and Captains John Dalton, William Richards, James Kilpatrick and several others had written letters the terms of which were considered mutinous. Government regarded Captains Richards and Kilpatrick and Captain-Lieutenant Murray as the ringleaders, and these were sent for to Fort St. David and there placed in arrest. Captain Richards died, Murray appears to have deserted to Pondicherry, where he obtained a commission, while Kilpatrick made submission, was pardoned and reinstated. The discontent among the officers was not without its effect upon the subordinate ranks, whose discipline in 1751 does not appear to have been all that it should have been. The whole subject is discussed and the correspondence is given in Wilson's *History of the Madras Army*, Vol. I, pp. 32–36.

The force with which Lawrence set out on March 18th consisted of 400 Europeans, 1,100 sepoys and eight field guns, and, escorting a large quantity of military stores, it marched through the Tanjore country towards Trichinopoly, where the Mysore and Mahratta troops were rather sore with Captain de Gingins, whose cautious tactics had, they considered, deprived them of opportunities for plunder.

On March 27th Lawrence and his troops arrived at a small fort in the Tanjore country about 20 miles from Trichinopoly, and here some of the stores were left. On the following morning he moved along the main road which passed under the guns of the fort of Coilady, where the Cauvery divides into several branches, and received information that an enemy force provided with artillery was there awaiting him. He decided to evade this ambush by following another road, but his guides, either by design or ignorance, led him to the very place he wished to avoid and he was fired on by six guns on the further side of the Cauvery River. Before he could withdraw Lawrence's force had suffered a loss of 20 Europeans.

The convoy continued its march and that night arrived unopposed within ten miles of Trichinopoly, and was met by a reinforcement of 100 Europeans and 50 Horse, sent out by de Gingins.

At daybreak Captain Dalton, with his own Grenadiers and another company under Captain Clarke, 400 sepoys and four guns, was ordered to march to Sugar Loaf Rock, to remain there till the convoy appeared and then join it. The French and their allies were drawn up in order of battle between the fortified posts of Elmiseram and French Rock, while the rest of their army was in a line extending from French Rock to Chuckleypollam by the river side; thus the northern approach to Trichinopoly was barred.

Major Lawrence, hearing of these dispositions, marched to the south of Elmiseram, and near Sugar Loaf Rock effected a junction with Dalton's party and the forces of the native allies. It was noon and the heat very great, but the brief halt which was now made was ended by the enemy advancing to the attack. A small *serai*, in front of the French infantry, was at once occupied by Dalton's grenadiers and two guns, and the French advancing to dislodge them were very severely handled and kept in check until the main body came up under Lawrence with the Mysore and Mahratta soldiers. The enemy had 22 guns opposed to 9 of the English, but those of the latter were under cover, while the French artillery was exposed on the open plain, and after a time the French battalion began to waver and then fell back followed by all their allied troops.

Captains Clive and Dalton pursued until recalled by their commander, who was unwilling longer to expose his scanty and overworked force to the excessive heat. Seven men of the Battalion were struck dead by the sun, 14 were killed and 30 wounded. Orme gives the enemy casualties as follows:—" The French lost about 40 men and 300 of Chanda Sahib's troops with 285 horses and an elephant were found dead on the plain," while Clive in a letter also mentions the elephant, but as to the remainder gives no details—" on the plain lay dead one elephant and 297 Horse, Allam Cawn, the Second-in-Command, was killed with abundance of sepoys, besides the number of wounded is very considerable."

The Mahrattas proved themselves on this occasion but lukewarm allies, and neither entreaties nor threats could induce them to make even a single charge.

The same night Lawrence marched on to Trichinopoly and there handed over his convoy, and at once put measures in hand to harass and weaken the enemy. On the night of April 1st he sent Dalton with 400 men to beat up and set fire to the French camp, but this usually very careful and enterprising officer lost his way in the dark, managing however to regain Trichinopoly without loss, though the morning of the 2nd surprised him in the French lines. The mere attempt, however, alarmed Law, the French commander, to such an extent that he precipitately withdrew across the south branch of the Cauvery on to the Island of Seringham, destroying such stores as he was unable to remove.

A French detachment was still holding the Elmiseram Rock to the south-east of the city, and on the 3rd Captain Dalton, with 100 grenadiers, some Mahrattas and sepoys, was sent against it, capturing it with a loss of five men only. The garrison, 15 Frenchmen and 30 sepoys, was taken with two guns, one of them an 18-pounder.*

Two days later Dalton and his grenadiers, soldiers ever remarkable for dash and gallantry, captured another gun from the enemy. Law had placed a gun in a small building on the island, and Dalton, concealing his men behind a wall on the river bank, waited until noon when the gun escort were asleep or engaged in cooking their food, and then forded the river and rushed the gun before it had been twice discharged, bringing it across the river under cover of the fire of some field pieces. The boldness and success of these achievements made an impression on both sides, out of all proportion to their importance, and the native allies of the English, particularly Morari Rao, were greatly elated.

Law's position on the island was very strong, indeed, practically unassailable, while the great stone-walled temples, of which there were many, were easily convertible into defensible posts. It was above all things necessary that Law should be able to keep open his communications with Pondicherry, and in order to sever these Clive now proposed to Lawrence that half the army should be sent north of the Cauvery; to this Lawrence at once agreed, for he had accurately gauged Law's want of enterprise, while he (Lawrence) was at the moment unusually well off for cavalry.

"Promising myself great success from the activity and vigilance of Captain Clive, I detached him with 400 of my best Europeans, 1,200 sepoys and 4,000 Horse to take post on the other side," states Lawrence in his narrative. "He crossed the two rivers about 7 miles below Seringham." Clive was the junior Captain of the Battalion, and his seniors had to be reconciled to his being appointed to an independent command. The matter, however, was soon settled; "the Nawab, the Mahrattas and Mysoreans demanded Captain Clive to command the Army sent to Samiavaram."†

Samiaveram, 7 miles to the north of the river, was occupied on April 6th and here two pagodas were strongly entrenched, and on

---

* The Nawab presented Captain Dalton with a horse worth £100 for this capture.
† Forrest, Vol. I, p. 176.

the 7th the post at Munserpet, whither Law had sent a party as a counter-move, was attacked, and though the enemy drove back the English at first, they eventually withdrew, and on the 8th Clive captured Lalgudi and a large supply depot.

Meanwhile Dupleix, greatly alarmed at the situation produced by Law's retreat to Seringham, had collected all the men he could spare from Pondicherry, and sent them under d'Auteuil* to reinforce Law. D'Auteuil reached Uttatur, 13 miles north-east of Samiaveram, on April 14th, and sent messengers to Law advising him of his intention to reach the Cauvery by a circuitous night march. One of his messengers was captured by Clive who marched the same night to intercept him, but d'Auteuil, hearing of his movements, fell back again on Uttatur, when Clive returned to his post arriving early on the 15th, having covered 26 miles during the night. On the afternoon of this day the French, knowing only of Clive's departure, and hearing nothing of his rapid return, thought to surprise the post at Samiaveram, and sent a force of 80 Europeans, forty of whom were deserters from the English,† and 500 sepoys to attack it. These arrived at midnight and on being challenged stated they were a party sent by Lawrence to reinforce Clive, and were actually supplied with a guide to the part of the post where were Clive's quarters.

It should be stated that the defensive position consisted of two pagodas, one large and one small; in the larger was the whole body of Europeans with the greater part of the sepoys, while the smaller one contained only Clive's personal guard, he himself sleeping in an adjoining choultry or *serai*. On approaching the small pagoda, the enemy party was challenged, and at once opened fire both on the pagoda and on Clive's sleeping quarters.

Clive, starting from his sleep, imagined that his sepoys had been alarmed at some attack on the outskirts of the camp, and hastened to the larger pagoda where he found the Europeans there quartered were all under arms. As he drew near he saw a large body of sepoys

---

* Forrest describes d'Auteuil as " disabled by age and gout."
† Clive adds in his account " with an English officer at their head."

firing in a direction away from the camp and believing them consequently to be his own men, went forward ordering them to cease fire. " But one of the officers who understood something of the French language found out Captain Clive to be an enemy and cut him in two places with his sword and then ran into the little pagoda where Captain Clive immediately followed him to the entrance of the gate, when to his very great astonishment he found himself in the midst of six French. He made use of presence of mind upon that occasion and told them if they would look out they would find they were all surrounded and would certainly be cut to pieces if they did not surrender immediately. This had such an effect that three of the men ran into the pagoda to give the intelligence and the other three surrendered to Captain Clive, who was returning with a full design to demolish the sepoys whom he now knew for the first time to be enemies, but they finding out their error likewise had stolen off. . . . Captain Clive was making the proper disposition for the attack of the pagoda. Accordingly Captain Clive, judging it of the utmost consequence to dislodge the enemy before they could be reinforced perhaps from the whole French army, resolved to storm the pagoda, but the entrance of the gateway being so narrow that not even two men could enter abreast, an officer and 12 or 15 men were killed in the attempt, which proved impracticable. . . . The French commander finding the situation desperate, made a sally at the head of his men, who was killed with the like number of men by the platoon stationed there for that purpose. After this Captain Clive went to the gate of the pagoda, and being weak with loss of blood, leaned upon two soldiers' shoulders with his body projected and summoned the officer to surrender on pain of having no quarter. The English officer made no answer but fired his piece at Captain Clive, which luckily missed him, but shot the two men who supported him both through the body."* The remainder of the enemy in the pagoda then " all surrendered prisoners at discretion to Captain Clive, in number 2 officers and 64 private men Europeans, besides

* From Clive's own account quoted by Forrest, Vol. I, pp. 180-2, from the Orme MSS.

which 500 of their sepoys and several Europeans were cut to pieces by the Mahrattas in attempting to escape . . . 600 stand of arms and 2 Colours were taken."*

Biddulph gives the name of the leader of the deserters as *Kelsey*, but in a letter to Clive of April 16th Lawrence writes :—" As *Kelsall* was taken in arms against us after he had deserted our service, no commission of any kind whatsoever from any nation can be a protection to him ; so let him be hanged immediately for an example and keep the other English deserters strictly guarded as I intend they shall soon share the same fate. . . . The gunner who deserted yesterday and showed the enemy the way to the pagoda you will likewise order to be hanged immediately."

Clive adds the following information :—" Kelsall had been a pay sergeant in the Independents and deserted to Pondicherry with the pay of his company. This man Dupleix made an officer. He with three other Englishmen were hanged the next day." This drastic action produced lively complaints from Dupleix.

On April 26th the English captured Coilady, the loss of the large magazine of stores in which was seriously felt by Law ; and on May 9th Lawrence sent Dalton across the river with 150 of the Battalion, 400 sepoys, 500 Mahratta Horse and four guns to attack d'Auteuil at Uttatur. Arriving within two miles of the place at five in the afternoon, Dalton sent forward a party to occupy the *serai* intending to defer attack until night, but the *serai* being found to be occupied by the enemy, fighting ensued in which success was gained first by one side and then by the other ; but eventually the French were driven back into the fort which they evacuated in the night, making a hasty retreat to Volconda. Dalton's detachment was now ordered to return to Trichinopoly, " but a sudden swelling of the Coleroon rendered that impracticable. Clive determined to take advantage of the state of the river to take the French post of Pitchandah, on its northern bank, which Mr. Law could not now succour. Captain Dalton being informed of his resolution, and not wishing to interfere

* Fort St. George Records.

with his command, immediately placed his corps under Clive's orders and requested to be employed as a volunteer."*

The attack on Pitchandah was made on the 13th, Clive's guns breaking up Law's camp and forcing him and his allies to take shelter in the Jumbakistna Pagoda, and Pitchandah fell after two days' bombardment. During the operations one of the English guns burst, killing three Europeans and wounding Captain Dalton, who was on crutches for a month after.

The investment of the island of Seringham was now complete, every part of it being exposed to artillery fire. Lawrence's next move was to cross over to the island at Chuckleypollam and throw an entrenchment right across the island, east of the Jumbakistna Pagoda, forcing Law and Chanda Sahib to take post at the Seringham Pagoda, which was now, on May 18th, at once invested by Lawrence though the enemy was twice his strength. Having no battering guns a train was sent for to Devicotah, but while awaiting the arrival of these Lawrence dispatched Clive on May 27th with 100 Europeans, 6 guns and 200 natives in search of d'Auteuil, whom he came upon a few miles south of Volconda. The English sepoys who had outmarched the Europeans, and many of whom were men Clive had enlisted after Arnee, were now so full of ardour that they attacked impetuously and drove the French into the town. The Europeans then coming up, carried a gateway by assault, and before morning on the 29th, d'Auteuil surrendered with 100 Europeans, 400 sepoys, 340 horse, 3 guns and quantities of stores of all kinds.

Already before this Chanda Sahib's people, seeing which way the affair was going and straitened for provisions, had begun to leave him, and Chanda Sahib entered into negotiations, but was treacherously made prisoner by the Tanjore general and put to death the same day. On June 3rd Law surrendered with 35 officers, 785 Europeans, 2,000 sepoys and 45 pieces of artillery. Four hundred of the French prisoners were escorted to Madras by Captain Campbell of the Battalion, while the remainder with the captured guns and stores were sent to Trichinopoly.

* Malcolm, *Life of Clive*, Vol. I, p. 119.

THE FIGHT NEAR BAHOOR

On the 28th the Battalion, leaving Captain Dalton to garrison Trichinopoly with 200 Europeans and 1,500 sepoys, marched with 2,500 sepoys and 2,000 of the Nawab's Horse for Volconda, where the Governor paid tribute and swore allegiance, and the force then marched to Trivady where, the garrison having surrendered, the troops encamped. Here, Major Lawrence, handing over command to Captain de Gingins, went to Fort St. George, his health being somewhat impaired.

Two months after Law's surrender, the French inflicted a severe repulse on an English force. The Madras Council, wholly against the advice, and indeed in spite of the protestations of Lawrence, resolved to reduce Gingee, an exceptionally strong fortress held by the French, about 40 miles from Pondicherry and 75 from Madras, and moved thither on July 26th a force of 200 Europeans and 2,000 of the Nawab's troops under a Major Kinneer, an officer quite new to the country. Dupleix sent a force of equal strength against him commanded by M. de Kerjean, and the two met some 20 miles south-east of Gingee. The English guns, commanded by a French deserter, were badly fought, the English attack was repulsed, Kinneer was wounded and many of his officers and men were killed; but his party managed to withdraw in good order to Fort St. David, which de Kerjean, following up, proceeded to blockade. Lawrence, still in anything but restored health, then embarked at Madras for Fort St. David with 400 Europeans, among whom were some of the newly-arrived Swiss troops, 1,700 sepoys, and 8 or 9 field guns, together with 3,000–4,000 of the Nawab's soldiers. Upon this de Kerjean broke up his camp and retreated, closely followed by Lawrence, until he was close to Pondicherry and on French soil, where Lawrence's orders forbade him to make any attack. The English commander then, hoping to induce the Frenchman to follow him, retreated precipitately to Bahoor, two miles from Fort St. David. The opposing commander fell into the trap, advanced in pursuit, and at 3 o'clock on the morning of August 26th was attacked by Lawrence, the sepoys being, contrary to the custom hitherto pursued, in the first line, the European Battalion being kept in reserve.

The British sepoys found themselves opposed to those serving with the French, but when day dawned the European battalions on either side discovered themselves to be face to face, the French battalion being by some fifty men the stronger and drawn up between a high bank and a pond. " The British halted to extend their front to equal that of the French, a French battery of eight guns playing upon them vigorously as they executed the movement, and then advanced firing, platoon after platoon. Closer and closer they came, still firing; but the French never shrank for a moment until, rarest of rare incidents, the bayonets crossed and the two battalions engaged each other fiercely hand to hand. At length, however, a company of British grenadiers, the choicest troops in India, forced their way through the French centre; upon which the whole of the French gave way, flung down their arms and fled."* Kerjean and fifteen other officers with a hundred men were taken prisoners, upwards of a hundred of the enemy fell by the bayonet, and many were killed and wounded by gun and musket fire. The British Battalion lost 4 officers and 78 men killed and wounded, and the Fort St. David records tell us that " Messrs. Repington and Kirk behaved very gallantly in the late action with the enemy and that the success we gained over them was greatly owing thereto, and that Sergeant Nelson has also signalised himself both in that and every other action he has been in."

It will be remembered that Captain Dalton had been left in command at Trichinopoly, on the possession of which depended the future equally of the Nawab and of the East India Company. Dalton had no easy task to keep order and maintain discipline, filled as was the city with a numerous rabble in the Nawab's pay; within the fortress were also many French prisoners, while outside the walls treachery and deceit were rife. No sooner had the Battalion left Trichinopoly to take part in the operations just described, than the people of Mysore made many treacherous attempts to obtain possession of the city; 500 of the Nawab's men had been gained over and were to make common cause with 700 Mysoreans at a parade

* Fortescue, *History of the British Army*, Vol. II, p. 217.

that had been arranged. Dalton got wind of the scheme and ordered the flints to be removed from these men's muskets on pretence that he proposed giving them better ones; the ringleaders, however, took the alarm, confessed their guilt and begged for pardon, handing over the money they had received as the price of their treachery. Dalton then sent these men off next day to join Lawrence. This plot having thus been frustrated, the Mysore Regent now bribed two men to murder Dalton, but the plot was happily discovered in time. Five days later two Mysore men attempted to suborn a Jemadar, who commanded the guard at one of the gates, but he seized them and on their being brought before Dalton, the orders to murder him signed by the Regent were found on them; they confessed and were blown away from a gun; their fate had an immense effect on the men of Mysore and no more could be found to carry out the Regent's murder schemes. He now evinced a more open and active enmity, and so Captain Dalton, having received orders from Madras to treat him as an enemy of the Company, marched out against him on the night of December 23rd, crossed the river, entered the camp, bayoneted the sentries, and threw the whole force into the utmost confusion. The enemy took refuge inside the pagoda and on January 4th, 1753, Dalton determined to cannonade it from a position on the banks of the river, but a party of eighty of the Regiment and 500 sepoys were exposed to a sudden attack* by a body of nearly 4,000 Horse who " made a third charge and our rascally sepoys gave way, which discouraged the Europeans so much that though they had but 2 or 3 wounded and close entrenched, they quitted their officers and ran out of the post, the natural consequence of which was that the Horse instantly charged them in their disorder and killed or wounded almost the whole. . . . Lieutenants Wilkey and Crow, with about 60 men as near as I can compute, are missing. When the enemy retreated I brought off the wounded, in all about 19 men with Lieutenant Wood, who I hope will do well."

* Dalton's despatch is given in full in *Memoir of Captain Dalton*, pp. 176-179.

This hope was not realized for Lieutenant Wood died of his wounds shortly afterwards, and a lieutenant's commission was bestowed on Sergeant Dickinson, who had distinguished himself in the action.

We must now leave for a time the consideration of affairs in Trichinopoly, its garrison reduced to a handful of men and unable to risk any sorties against the enemy, and the city so strictly blockaded that no supplies could come in from the surrounding country, while we see what has been occurring elsewhere and what were the measures that Major Lawrence finally took for the relief of Captain Dalton and his hard-pressed garrison.

After the success at Bahoor Major Lawrence recommended the reduction of Chingleput and Covelong, and a force of 200 European recruits lately landed and 500 recently raised sepoys was accordingly sent from Madras for this purpose, Clive being placed in command. On September 10th the force marched against Covelong, but before the four 24-pounders of the Train had even been placed in battery, the place surrendered, just prior to the arrival of a relieving force. This was immediately attacked by Clive and dispersed, the commander, eight Europeans and 150 sepoys being captured, while the rest, flinging away their arms, fled towards Chingleput, closely pursued by Clive. Here again there was but feeble opposition, the fort surrendering on October 1st.

The capture of these two places, held by a superior enemy, by a party of raw recruits of the Battalion and a handful of freshly-raised sepoys, made a great impression on the native powers, while these successes completed the reduction of the whole country to the north of the Palar River, between Sadras and Arcot. The works at Covelong were destroyed, while Chingleput was strengthened and garrisoned by the English, and, marching by Trivady, the troops reached Fort St. David again on November 15th.

The Directors of the Company in London knew so little of the very serious condition of affairs in and about Madras, that about this time they actually sent instructions for Lawrence to proceed to Calcutta to inspect and advise on the fortifications there, but

Lawrence naturally could not be spared. Just now he seems to have again been considering the question of relinquishing his command. There was recurrent discontent among the troops owing to their pay being constantly in arrears, while the men were worn out with harassing service; Lawrence's plans too for the prosecution of the war were disregarded, he could not exercise the not especially liberal powers conferred upon him without constant interference, while the Governor sent him orders for military operations and made promotions and appointments without even going through the form of consulting him. In November then Lawrence gave up his command but at the end of three weeks was induced to resume it.

In January, 1753, Lawrence was again in the field engaged in harassing operations in the neighbourhood of Cuddalore. In this month the French equipped a force of 500 European infantry, a troop of 60 European cavalry, 2,000 regularly trained and disciplined sepoys, and a fine body of Mahratta Horse under Morari Rao, the Mahrattas having now definitely declared themselves against Muhammad Ali and the English. This force marched to within sight of Trivady, under the walls of which the English, to the number of 700 of the Battalion, 2,000 sepoys, and 1,500 very inferior Horse belonging to the Nawab, were then encamped. On January 9th a large body of Mahratta cavalry, with two companies of native infantry and three guns, came close to Trivady and cannonaded the fort. The grenadier company of the Battalion, supported by some sepoys, advanced rapidly, captured their guns which they turned against them, and drove them with much loss back on their main body. The Mahratta Horse rallied and charged, but the Grenadiers held their fire until the enemy were close upon them, when every shot took effect, and with the assistance of the guns the enemy were finally beaten off having suffered casualties in men and horses to the number of one hundred.

During four months now the two armies remained within sight of one another, and a number of minor engagements took place; in these, however, the want of cavalry on the English side placed Lawrence at a serious disadvantage. Only on one occasion had the

Mahrattas, for the French were generally held back in reserve, any measure of success. In February a cavalry body galloped up to within a short distance of a work at the western boundary of the hedge of Fort St. David—for the Mahrattas, it must be remembered, now overran the whole country between the Palar and Coleroon rivers; the post was held by a brave but inexperienced sergeant of the corps, and he, irritated at their insolent and defiant gestures, and thinking by chastising them to gain reputation and promotion for himself, marched out into the open against them with 25 men of the Battalion and 50 sepoys. The enemy fell back, drawing the sergeant and his party on until they were half a mile from cover, then wheeled about and charged home. The fire of the English, delivered at close quarters, was very effective, but before they could reload the Mahrattas were upon them, and the party was cut down to a man.

On April 1st, while bringing up a convoy from Fort St. David, Lawrence was attacked by a large force of Mahrattas supported by a French battalion and a brisk engagement ensued. Impeded by the presence of the convoy the English could only advance very slowly, charged into at every opportunity by the enemy's cavalry; the weather moreover, was excessively hot and several men of the Corps fell down dead from the sun and want of water. When within three miles of Trivady the enemy made a general attack on all sides; in this the Mahratta leader was killed and his death dispirited his troops who retreated. The English pressing on found the French battalion drawn up close to Trivady, and both lines advancing, it seemed as if it would come to push of bayonet, but on the European Battalion continuing to advance, the French halted and then broke and fled. Lawrence now brought the convoy safely into Trivady.

Lawrence was not unmindful of the desperate situation of Dalton at Trichinopoly; on April 19th he wrote to the Governor and Council, saying that, " if Captain Dalton is to be reinforced, and his situation seems to cry aloud for it, 'tis high time to determine something, for the rising of the rivers (and that season is approaching) will put it out of our power to assist him." On the very next night Lawrence received a letter from Dalton, dated the 13th, in which he said that he was so closely invested that no supplies could be passed in to him, that he had only thirty days' provisions in hand, and then winding up with the stout-hearted assurance that " whatever distress we are driven to, you'll find that while I have my life I will not render myself unworthy of my charge."*

Stirred by this intelligence Lawrence marched out of Trivady early on the 21st, leaving behind a garrison of 150 men of the Corps and 400 sepoys under Captain Chase,† moving first to Fort St. David to collect what military stores he required for the relief of Trichinopoly, and arranging to march thither through Tanjore, where he hoped to obtain the assistance of a mounted force of which he stood greatly in need.

In the meantime Dalton at Trichinopoly continued strenuously to do all that was possible to annoy the enemy, and with so much success that just prior to the arrival of the relieving body he had driven off the force immediately investing him, had captured much baggage and grain, and had made it possible for the people of the country round once again to bring in their produce to replenish his magazines.

Lawrence entered Trichinopoly without opposition on May 6th, only seventeen days from the receipt of Dalton's message. Sickness and desertion on the march had considerably reduced the strength of his force; 100 of his Europeans were carried to hospital on the day of his arrival, and his whole force now, including the original garrison of Trichinopoly, consisted only of 500 Europeans, 2,000 sepoys, 3,000 of the Nawab's Horse, ten field guns and one or two 18-pounders manned by 80 artillerymen. The day after the English marched in a reinforcement of 200 Europeans, 500 sepoys and four guns under M. Astruc, a general of considerable ability, joined the Mysoreans at Seringham and he assumed command of the whole force.

The English were badly off for supplies. Lawrence's sole chances of success against an enemy superior in numbers and operating

* This correspondence is in the *Memoir of Captain Dalton*, pp. 187-191.
† Trivady surrendered on May 4th.

in favourable country, lay in an active defence and in gaining over the Tanjore chief, who was still neutral, for his mounted troops were quite unable to face the Mysore and Mahratta horsemen, led by Hyder Ali and Morari Rao. Having given his men three days' rest, Lawrence on the night of May 10th passed his infantry and guns over to the island, the Nawab's cavalry refusing to move, and offered battle on the next morning. The enemy attacked at once and at first threw the front line of British sepoys into confusion; these then recovering, stood their ground well, and being promptly supported by the European corps and by the close fire of the English guns, they drove back the enemy with loss, and then withdrew at nightfall with a loss of 2 officers killed and 3 wounded and a few casualties among the other ranks. Having been nearly twenty hours under arms in the sun, without water or provisions, the troops were greatly exhausted.

Lawrence now, recognizing Astruc's ability, abandoned for the time any idea of dislodging the enemy from Seringham and devoted himself to the collection of supplies; to this end, and to prevent a complete investment, he moved out to and encamped at the Faquir's Tope, $2\frac{1}{2}$ miles from the city, and sent out parties to bring in provisions. At this spot he remained five weeks during which time the enemy received a further substantial reinforcement of Europeans and sepoys, and Lawrence found himself obliged to leave his post at the Faquir's Tope and encamp nearer the city. Here his communications with the open country were cut, his surrender for want of supplies seemed only a matter of time, and the spirits of the English were at a low ebb.

Half a mile from Lawrence's camp, and nearly a mile from that of Astruc, was the Golden Rock where Lawrence maintained a guard of 200 sepoys. Astruc saw that if he could gain possession of this post he would force the English back into the city and shorten the investment. On June 26th at daybreak the Frenchman attacked the Golden Rock with a mixed force of Europeans and sepoys, and captured it after a very gallant resistance in which the whole garrison was killed or taken prisoners.

THE REGIMENT RECAPTURES THE GOLDEN ROCK 75

Lawrence at once ordered all his troops under arms, and leaving 100 men of the Battalion to protect his camp, instantly marched with the rest, consisting of 300 of the Corps, 80 gunners and 1,300 sepoys, and hurried off to try to reach the Golden Rock before the enemy's main body could come up. The French Battalion, however, arrived there the first and formed in line, the right resting on the rock held by their sepoys, supported by the French Grenadiers; their guns were divided, some to the right of the rock, the remainder on the left of the French battalion; the Mysore troops were in masses on the flanks, while the Mahratta cavalry threatened the flank and rear of the English.

The British continued to move forward, immutably serene; the Grenadiers, under Captains Kilpatrick and Kirk, and about 400 sepoys were directed to carry the rock with the bayonet, while Lawrence led on the rest of the little force to the attack on the French battalion. " Seldom in war has such a sight been seen as this little band of British soldiers moving to the attack, surrounded by many thousands of enemies. Scrambling up the rock with fixed bayonets and without pulling trigger, cheering as they moved, the unexpected onset of the grenadiers struck the French defenders with panic. Not daring to stand the shock they fled headlong down the reverse side. Meanwhile, Astruc, behind the rock, not seeing what was happening, had wheeled up his battalion to meet Lawrence, exposing its right flank to the fire of the English grenadiers from the rock, which was increased by some sepoys who had followed the grenadiers. At this moment Lawrence drew up his men directly opposite the French front at twenty yards distance. In spite of Astruc's efforts his men were struck with consternation at seeing themselves attacked by the foe that a few moments before had seemed in their power. Smitten by musketry fire in front and flank they fell into disorder, which a bayonet charge converted into panic, and they fled from the field leaving three guns in Lawrence's hands.

" In vain the Mahrattas strove to retrieve the fortunes of the day. Some of the grenadiers fell under their sabres, while in disorder taking possession of the guns. But they were soon forced to withdraw with the loss of many men. Among others fell Morari Rao's nephew. He had cut down one of the grenadiers when the man's comrade, who was loading his musket at the time, fired his ramrod through his body. . . . The French rallied on the Mysore army and contented themselves with keeping up an ineffective cannonade. For three hours Lawrence remained at the foot of the rock, in the expectation that they would renew the combat. Finding that the French would not advance, he formed his little army into a hollow square, with the captured guns and about seventy prisoners in the centre, and deliberately marched back towards his camp. Hardly had he got clear of the rock when the whole of the enemy's cavalry, upwards of 10,000 in number, charged furiously down. . . . The English Battalion and sepoys stood firm; not a trigger was pulled. The square was halted and the guns rapidly served, pouring in grape-shot into the dense masses, till they broke up and forsook the field, leaving the little band of heroes to march unmolested back to camp, bearing the trophies of victory. No finer feat of arms was ever performed."*

In his despatch dated July 7th, 1753, Lawrence wrote:—" I ought to mention, because it is due to their merit, the extraordinary gallant behaviour of Captains Kilpatrick and Kirk who forc'd up a Rock against four times their number of Europeans and in the face of 2,000 sepoys, and dislodg'd them and attack'd them in flank, whilst we did the same in front, a more extraordinary action I have never yet seen, in short, all the officers and people in general behav'd very bravely."

The enemy was so dispirited by his defeat that Lawrence was able undisturbed to bring in fifty days' supplies which had been collected, but he made no immediate attempt to engage the enemy again, and, leaving Dalton in command at Trichinopoly, he marched on July 2nd for Tanjore, hoping to induce the chief of that country to furnish him with cavalry; in this project he was successful, receiving a welcome reinforcement of 3,000 Horse and 200 matchlock men, while 170 Europeans and 300 sepoys joined him on

* Biddulph, pp. 65-67.

SECOND ACTION AT THE GOLDEN ROCK

August 1st from Fort St. David under Lieutenant Repington. With his force thus increased, Lawrence set out again for Trichinopoly, but, on arriving within 10 miles of that city, he found his way barred by Brenier, who had now relieved Astruc, and who was in occupation of the whole of the strong positions south of the city from Weycondah to Elmiseram, the centre, where were the Golden and Sugar Loaf Rocks, being strongly held by the French infantry and artillery.

On August 9th Lawrence resumed his advance. The key of the position was the Golden Rock, but the English commander formed up as though he intended to attack the Sugar Loaf Rock, and Brenier foolishly denuded the vital point to strengthen the less important one apparently threatened. Lawrence then sent some of his grenadiers and sepoys under Lieutenant Repington to seize the Golden Rock, while Brenier dispatched 300 Europeans to reinforce the garrison and a thousand horse to hinder the English advance. But the British outmarched their opponents and drove the enemy from the rock, when the party sent by Brenier took post on some high ground and opened a galling gun fire on the Golden Rock, to the rear of which Lawrence moved his whole force; Brenier remained halted with his main body near the Sugar Loaf Rock.

An artillery duel now ensued in which the European Battalion suffered some loss, but Dalton issued from the city with two field pieces and fired on the enemy's cavalry which broke up and galloped off.

Seeing the French main body still stationary, Lawrence sent the grenadier company, 200 Europeans and 300 sepoys against it. The officer detailed for the attack sent back to ask for guns in aid, whereupon Lawrence galloped up and himself took command. Captain Kirk at the head of the grenadiers, Captain Kilpatrick with the picquet, and Lawrence with the four platoons, marched forward in line, keeping admirable order in spite of a very smart fire from the enemy's artillery. By this many casualties were caused, the brave

Captain Kirk* being killed at the head of his grenadiers by whom he was much and deservedly loved. Captain Kilpatrick put himself at the head of the grenadiers, desiring them if they loved their captain to follow him and avenge his death. " These things on the spot have generally a very great effect, when delivered from a person whose spirit and courage is known," as Lawrence afterwards wrote, describing the affair. " The fellows, roused in an instant, swore after their manner they would follow him to Hell," and avenge Kirk's death, and rushing on to the attack drove the enemy before them. The English main body moving up in support, joined in assailing the French battalion, which, not staying even to deliver its fire, left the field in great disorder.

The enemy lost upwards of 100 killed and wounded, and had three guns captured; the Battalion suffered in casualties at this second battle of the Golden Rock a loss of 1 officer killed and 40 men killed and wounded.

After this action the enemy retreated towards Weycondah, while the British marched to Trichinopoly, from whence, having reprovisioned the city, they moved out again. On their approach their opponents withdrew hurriedly to a position nearer Seringham and on the south bank of the river, leaving behind them a 9-pounder. Their position here was too strong to be lightly attacked, so Lawrence marched away to cover the arrival of some convoys from Tanjore, and on the same day the French were reinforced by 400 Europeans, 6 guns, 2,000 sepoys and 3,000 Mahratta Horse, the whole under M. Astruc, who had now resumed command.

On the night of September 18th Lawrence seized a small height between the two camps and opened fire with an 18-pounder on the French whose front was covered by entrenchments. A skirmish ensued, during which a small addition to Lawrence's force of 237

---

* According to regimental tradition, the sobriquet, " The Lambs," dates from the period of the command of the Grenadier Company by this officer, under whom it was known as " Kirk's Lambs," in humorous reference to the dash and spirit displayed under his leadership. And as the old " Tangier Regiment " became " the Lambs," so the nickname " Kirk's Lambs," abbreviated to " the Lambs," was for long applied to the whole of the Madras European Regiment.

Europeans and 300 sepoys under Captain Ridge, joined him unmolested. With Ridge also came Captain Caillaud, who was destined in time to succeed Lawrence. Having nothing to gain by further delay, while he had only three days' supplies in camp, Lawrence, his troops in the highest spirits, now decided on assuming the offensive, sent his impedimenta into the city, drew up his little army at the Faquir's Tope at daybreak on the 20th and offered battle. The challenge was not immediately accepted, so very early on the morning of the 21st Lawrence formed his column of attack and marched out.

The Madras European Battalion, 600 strong, was formed in three divisions and marched at sufficient distance to wheel into line to either flank as required; 2,000 sepoys marched in support of the flanks; the cavalry followed in reserve; while the guns were on either flank. The leading division of the Battalion—the grenadiers, the picquets and two platoons—was ordered to advance against and carry the Golden Rock. The whole left camp in deep silence and, the morning being very dark, the column was close up to the Rock before it was detected. The defenders—100 Frenchmen, 600 sepoys, two guns and two companies of topasses—were taken so greatly by surprise that they fired their muskets at random and omitted to fire their guns at all, although these were standing ready loaded with grape. The Rock was taken at a rush, its defenders flying with the greatest precipitation towards the French camp.

The post was secured, the leading division reformed, and the advance now resumed against the main camp, which was entered on the left where the defence works were incomplete. Here the enemy was drawn up in readiness, and fire was opened by them from both guns and muskets, but though brisk it was ill-aimed. The British sepoys engaged those of the French with great ardour and success, and the former, pushing on, attacked and carried Sugar Loaf Rock. During the advance of the Battalion Captain Kilpatrick was severely wounded and several officers and men fell; but Captain Caillaud, seeing the French flank exposed, wheeled his men to the left, drove in upon it, and after a short melée hurled the Frenchmen back in disorder in their centre. The other two divisions, now advancing at the charge, completed the rout, and the enemy, defeated at all points, broke and fled, abandoning their camp and leaving eleven guns in the hands of the victors.

The French battalion had 100 men killed and 100 wounded and prisoners, among the latter being M. Astruc and nine officers, while their native allies lost 1,000 men in killed and wounded. The Tanjore cavalry for a time did good service in the pursuit, but forsook it to plunder. As the fugitives fled past Trichinopoly on their way to Seringham, Dalton sallied out and captured nearly thirty Frenchmen who had become detached from their corps.

In this action, known as the Battle of Sugar Loaf Rock, the Battalion had 6 officers and 70 men killed and wounded; Lawrence himself was slightly wounded in the arm; Kilpatrick was shot through the body, and believing it mortal he forbade any of his men to stay by him, but sent them in pursuit of the enemy. Some straggling Mahratta cavalry, having worked round to the rear of the Battalion, came upon him lying on the ground helpless and alone, and as they rode by cut at him with their *tulwars* inflicting several wounds; he would doubtless have been killed had not the Surgeon of the Regiment come up and, with the few men he had with him, dispersed the cowardly assailants.

On the evening of the same day Lawrence laid siege to Weycondah. Early on September 23rd, before the breach was ready for assault, the English sepoys, seeing some of the garrison escaping, broke from their officers and tried to mount the breach. Finding this impracticable they made for the gateway. A sergeant of sepoys, "a resolute Englishman," whose name has not been preserved, clambered up by the carved work and planted the Colours of his company on the parapet. Joined then by others of his men the gate was forced, and those outside rushed in with bayonets fixed when the garrison flung down their arms and surrendered.

The winter rains now setting in Lawrence left 150 men of the Battalion to augment the garrison of Trichinopoly, where Kilpatrick relieved Dalton,* and on October 18th marched his troops to Coilady, leaving a small garrison at Elmiseram to keep open his communications with the Tanjore country.

About this time a very gallant action was fought near Tirupati by forty men of the Battalion, two companies of sepoys and three guns, under Lieutenant Holt and Ensign Mackenzie. These were on the march from Madras to succour Tirupati, which was threatened by a powerful chief, and were suddenly attacked by him in great force near Trivady. The attack was beaten off, the chief, his standard, guns and baggage being captured, but the detachment suffered heavily and Lieutenant Holt was severely wounded.

In November a French reinforcement of 300 Europeans and 1,200 sepoys under M. Maissin arrived unnoticed at Seringham, and at 3 a.m. on the 28th a determined effort was made to surprise Trichinopoly. A chosen body of 600 Frenchmen, led by an English deserter, crossed the ditch, and seized a detached battery without alarming the main garrison. A very little more and the attack might have been wholly successful, but the French lost their heads, disobeyed orders and commenced firing. The alarm was given; Kilpatrick was still confined to bed by his wounds, but his orders to his subaltern, Lieutenant Harrison, were coolly obeyed. The picquet and reserve doubled to the ramparts and opened a fire by which some of the French leaders were killed, and the remainder of the party, shut in between the outer and inner walls, were so exposed to fire that they were only too glad to surrender. Eight officers and 364 men were taken prisoners, 1 officer and 24 men were killed and many were wounded. Thus, "French petulance," as Lawrence styled it, saved Trichinopoly from the greatest risk it had run during the war.†

* Captain John Dalton actually left Trichinopoly November 14th, 1753, resigned the Service from March 1st, 1754, and sailed for England on the 10th in the *Durrington* in very bad health. He was only 28, and had been eleven years on foreign service. He was given a handsome sword by the Nawab of Arcot for his defence of Trichinopoly.

† The above is largely drawn from Biddulph, pp. 78-80. Lieutenant Harrison died not long after these happenings; he was a young officer of great promise.

Lawrence returned on December 5th to the neighbourhood of Trichinopoly, which now contained so many prisoners that it was necessary to increase the garrison to 300 Europeans and 1,500 sepoys. At the time there were 150 of the Battalion in hospital and the numbers of Lawrence's mobile troops were 600 Europeans and 1,800 sepoys. The French were equal in Europeans and greatly superior in the number of their native allies, but none the less they remained within their entrenched camp.

1754 Dupleix was now at the end of his resources and sought to come to terms with the English; in January, 1754, commissioners of both nations met at the Dutch settlement of Sadras, but no arrangement was arrived at, and the negotiations which at the same time had been opened with Mysore were equally fruitless. While these negotiations were going on Lawrence was encamped at Trichinopoly, confronting the French force in Seringham under M. de Mainville. The country for some distance round had been swept bare of supplies during two years of war, and provisions for Lawrence's men were only brought in with great difficulty and risk from Tanjore. In the middle of February a more important convoy than usual was on its way from Tricatopoly, 18 miles east of Trichinopoly, and a party of 230 Europeans, 500 sepoys* and four guns, under Captain Grenville, had been sent out to help it in. Grenville was ordered to keep his force in hand and, if attacked, to take up and defend a position until Lawrence could come to his assistance. De Mainville knew of the approach of the convoy and sent 400 Europeans, 8,000 sepoys, 8,000 Mahratta Horse and seven guns to intercept it. On February 15th Grenville was attacked in the morning between Elmiseram and the river. Contrary to the orders he had received, his men were strung out all along the length of his supply column, and he neither attempted to concentrate his force nor to take up a position. As a result he was overwhelmed by the Horse, and men, guns, supplies and £7,000 in treasure were lost, Grenville himself being killed; of eight officers of the Battalion

---

* These are the numbers given by Lawrence writing ten days after the event. In a later narrative he gives the same figures as Orme—viz., 180 and 800.

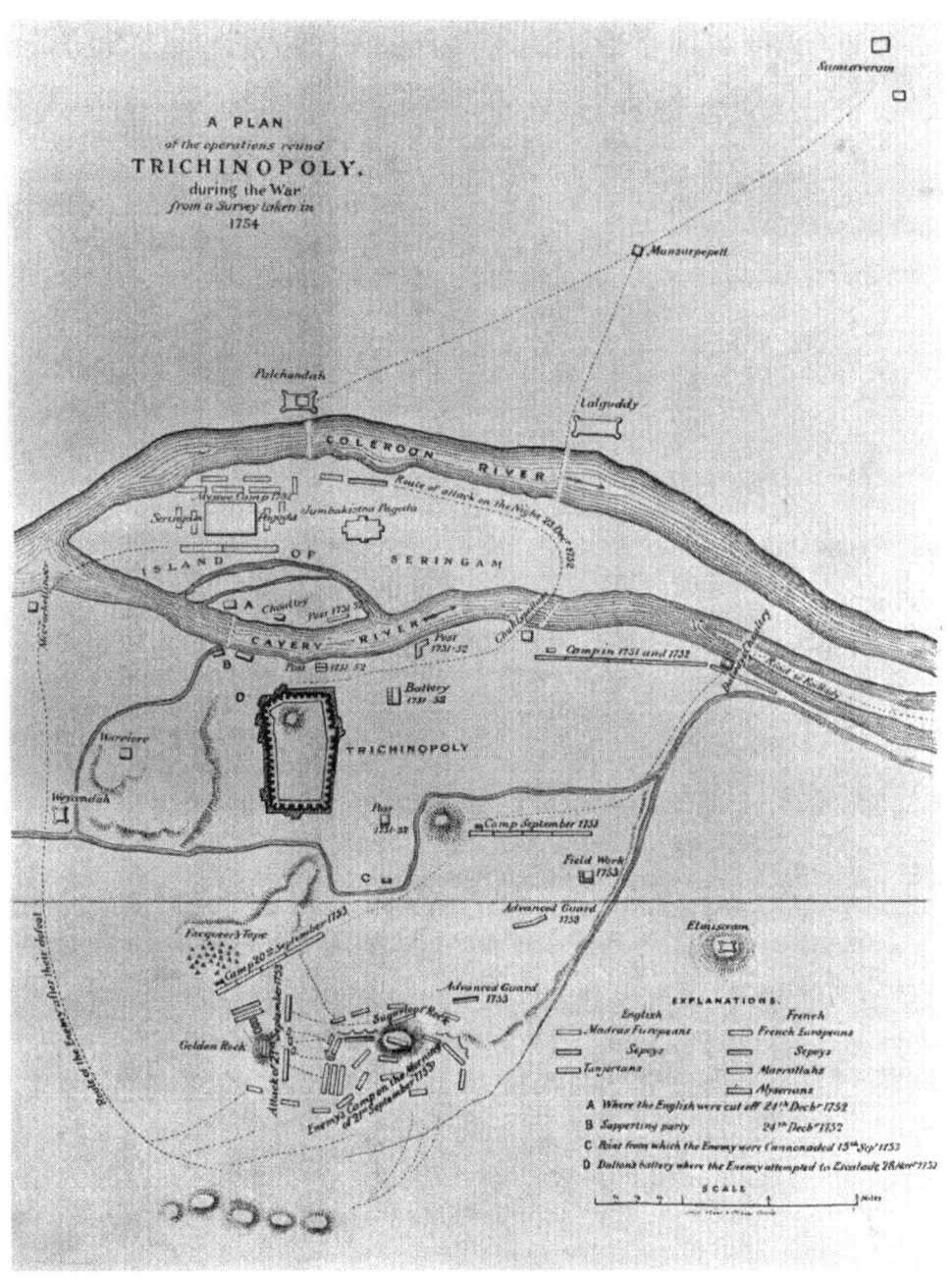

present four were killed and the rest wounded. Lieutenant Revel, who had served with distinction at Arcot under Clive, was cut down serving one of his guns. One-third of the Battalion was swept away, and with it was lost that splendid company of Grenadiers whose courage and discipline had saved the day in so many desperate actions.

In spite of this very serious reverse Lawrence held his ground, and gathered in a precarious supply of provisions, being greatly assisted by Muhammad Yusuf Khan, an excellent partizan officer and the commander of the sepoys in the Company's service. On the news of this disaster reaching Madras 180 Europeans under Captain Pigou were sent by sea to Devicotah, where they were to halt until joined by some mounted men.

On May 12th, 1754, Lawrence detached, under Captain Caillaud, 120 Europeans with 500 sepoys and two guns to bring in another convoy. Again did de Mainville send a small force to intercept it at the spot where Caillaud was to meet and take it over. The escort left its camp at 4 a.m. and on the march, while it was yet dark, the column was fired into by a party of French under cover of a bank. Caillaud pushed out skirmishers on both flanks and the enemy were driven from their cover with the loss of some men and a tumbril of ammunition. Orders were then sent back to halt the convoy, while Caillaud waited where he was for the day to break. Reinforcements now reached both sides; Captain Polier* joined Caillaud with a party which brought their joint force up to 360 Europeans, 1,500 sepoys, 11 English dragoons and 5 guns, and Polier, who appears to have been the senior officer, then took command, and commenced to retreat in face of the overpowering strength of the enemy, who had now at disposal 700 Europeans, 50 dragoons, 5,000 sepoys, 10,000 Mysore Horse and 7 guns.

Two of the English guns were disabled but were brought off; Polier was wounded, and Caillaud took his place. The French advanced to attack the English, who were drawn up to receive them,

* A Swiss, his name being Polier de Bottens; killed at the Siege of Madras, December, 1758.

and were met by so hot a fire that they were thrown into some confusion. Perceiving this, Caillaud advanced at the charge and drove the enemy back; the whole then retreated to their camp on the island having suffered in all some 500 casualties. Caillaud had 56 of his Europeans killed and wounded, six out of nine officers hit, and 150 sepoys *hors de combat*.

The French now, despairing of any substantial success in the field, devoted their energies to ravaging the country, Lawrence not being able to offer any serious hindrance to these measures, especially as he was able to get little or no assistance from his Tanjore allies. At the end of May Lawrence marched to Tanjore where he was joined by Pigou, and remained there until August, finally succeeding in obtaining at least promises of military help from the Tanjore chief, and being joined by two companies of the Bombay Regiment, 80 of the Battalion and 200 topasses from Madras. On August 15th Lawrence's whole army—1,000 Europeans, 14 guns, 3,000 sepoys and 200 topasses—were reviewed by the King of Tanjore.

On August 16th Maissin, who had relieved de Mainville, marched against the English, who, with their native allies, were encamped 6 miles west of Elmiseram.

The British force was in a position here of some strength, but the French attacked confidently; they were, however, so warmly received that they fell back after sustaining considerable loss, though Lawrence was prevented from turning their retreat into a rout owing to a sudden attack made by Hyder Ali upon his baggage, much of which was taken, and the French retreated to Seringham. A separate attack which had been attempted from Seringham, was met by a sortie from Trichinopoly under Kilpatrick and driven back.

The loss occasioned to the troops under Lawrence amounted to one officer, Captain Pigou, and 15 men killed, while of the French battalion 160 were killed and wounded.

Further operations were now suspended on account of the rainy season, and in October news was received of a truce having been established between the English and French preparatory to a definite peace; it was further announced that Dupleix had been recalled.

At the same time Lawrence received notice of the grant to him of a sword of honour, of the value of £750, by the Court of Directors, who wrote :—" The behaviour of Major Stringer Lawrence as Commander of our Forces having been greatly to our satisfaction, we came to an unanimous Resolution to present him with a sword enriched with Diamonds, of about seven hundred and fifty pounds Value, in Order to express our grateful sense of his Signal services to the Company in the Chief Command of their Forces in the field."

A similar presentation was made to Clive and was announced as follows :—" We have likewise agreed to make a present to Captain Robert Clive of a Sword set with Diamonds, to the value of Five Hundred Pounds, as a Token of our esteem for him and Sense of his signal military services to the Company on the Coast of Choromandel."

This letter is dated February 15th, 1754, and under date of July 25th of the same year Kilpatrick was given the brevet of major.

When the negotiations for peace were first opened between the rival Companies, it did not appear that any satisfactory and enduring settlement would result, and the Governor and Council at Madras represented to the Court of Directors in London the urgent necessity of sending out a reinforcement of troops to enable them to obtain a solid advantage over the French. The Court of Directors applied to the Crown for aid, and in answer to their appeal it was decided to send to the East Indies a small squadron of men-of-war, under Rear-Admiral Charles Watson, and the 39th Regiment, commanded by Colonel Adlercron. A small detachment of artillery accompanied the Regiment, and 200 recruits for the East India Company's forces were also embarked. The fleet and transports left port on March 29th, 1754, and arrived at Madras on September 10th.

For something like a century the Madras European Regiment and its forebears had been engaged, and had borne the chief share, in all the actions fought in Southern India ; and it is not too great a claim to prefer that the early services of the Corps, up to the arrival of the first Royal Regiment at Madras, laid the foundation of the

British power in the south of the Peninsula. During the past eight years of fighting against the French, in which the Battalion had taken a very active and prominent part, nearly 2,000 Frenchmen had been killed in action, upwards of 2,000, including 62 officers, had been taken prisoners, and 105 guns had been captured.

CHAPTER IV

THE BATTLE OF PLASSEY.

DURING the past two or three years the directors of the East India Company seem to have been impressed with the increasing military importance of their commitments in Bengal and Madras, and they appointed certain senior officers to their forces in addition to Major Lawrence. In December, 1752, the Company wrote to Fort St. George stating that they had appointed Lieutenant-Colonel Caroline Frederick Scott of the 29th Foot to be their Engineer-General of and in Fort St. George, Fort William and Bombay, and that in the event of anything happening to Lawrence, Scott would take command of all the Company's forces in India.

Colonel Scott reached Madras early in August, 1753, and sailed for Bengal within ten days; he returned, however, in the following April, when it seemed likely that Lawrence's health might oblige him to resign the command, but as a matter of fact Scott was in a worse state than Lawrence, and "his feaver increased and proved fatal to him" on May 12th, 1754. In his place the Company sent out one Alexander Heron,* who was permitted to enter their service "on condition of his delivering up his commission as Lieutenant-Colonel and resigning his rank in the army." He entered the Company's service as second in command and third in Council with the rank of Major, and of this officer it may be enough here to say that early in 1755 he was given the command of a small force sent to Madras and Tinnevelly, but being careless and having omitted to take the most ordinary military precautions, he was attacked in very wooded country, and lost most of his baggage and stores, while his force would have suffered very severely had it not been for the skill

---

* Formerly of General Oglethorpe's, the old 42nd or Georgia Regiment.

and energy of Captain Joseph Smith, commanding the rearguard. Heron was tried for disobedience of orders and on other charges and was sentenced to be dismissed, but fled to Sadras and then to Pondicherry, where he sought the protection of the French, before his sentence was promulgated. Orme says of him—" His crimes will almost sanctify any punishment."

The Court of Directors intimated to the Madras Government at this time, with reference to the expected arrival in India of the 39th Regiment, that the King's officers were to rank before the Company's officers of the same degree. By virtue of this order a King's captain of one day's standing became senior to the oldest captain in the Company's service. Wilson* quotes two cases of the hardship and absurdity of the seniority enjoyed by King's officers ; one, where a lieutenant, fourteen years of *age*, took command in face of the enemy of a picquet of native troops under a Company's lieutenant of fourteen years' *service* ; and another, where a captain of the Company's forces of seventeen years' standing had to yield precedence to a captain of a King's regiment who had only just arrived in India and who had no more than twenty-six months' service all told ! Under the circumstances the directors were perhaps wise in issuing the following order to the Council at Fort St. George :—" You are to carry it with great respect to Colonel Adlercron, who is appointed by His Majesty Commander-in-Chief, and you are to treat all the officers of His Majesty's Forces in a gentleman-like and friendly manner, and take the utmost care to promote and cultivate a good understanding and harmony between the King's and our own troops, as the general good of the service depends so greatly thereupon."

The order as to precedence was not amended until 1788.

With the arrival in India of the 39th Regiment, Lawrence received notice that the King had bestowed on him the commission of a lieutenant-colonel in the East Indies, but this did not save him from the loss of the chief command of troops in the field, which passed to Adlercron. Lawrence, however, refused to serve under this officer—described by General James Wolfe as " a very poor

* *History of the Madras Army*, Vol. II, p. 121.

OPERATIONS AGAINST ANGRIA

insignificant officer "*—and since he retained command of the Company's troops only, his duties during the next two years were chiefly administrative.

1755 During the year 1755, in addition to the operations already mentioned in Madura and Tinnevelly, there was a good deal of trouble at Trichinopoly, of which the Regent of Mysore was anxious to gain possession, but all his attempts were frustrated by the vigilance and determination of that part of the Battalion by which it was garrisoned. Then in November of this year Clive arrived at Bombay on his return from leave in England to Madras, and there found the ships of Admiral Watson's squadron which had repaired thither after the transports it had escorted had landed the troops contained in them at Madras. In March a decision had been come to in England to attack and subdue certain forts and strongholds belonging to the Pirate Angria on the Malabar Coast. Clive was given the command of the troops employed, which consisted for the most part of the Bombay Regiment and of drafts of recruits which had come out in Clive's ship and which were intended to reinforce the Battalion at Madras.

1756 On February 11th, 1756, the expeditionary force arrived off Angria's main fort of Gheriah, and after a severe bombardment the troops were landed and all the forts captured. In April the force was back in Bombay and the fleet then sailed for Madras arriving off Fort St. David on May 14th. Here, on June 20th, Clive assumed office as Deputy-Governor.

M. Godeheu was now Governor of the French settlements in India in the room of Dupleix.

The truce which had been made between the English and French companies in the East did not promise to be one of very long duration, and already at this time the Directors in London had sent word to their representatives in Madras, that 3,000 French had embarked at French ports in six ships of the line and in the same number of vessels belonging to the French East India Company ; and that as soon as this fleet reached Mauritius the Indiamen were to be converted into ships of war. Admiral Watson had himself received no confirmation

* Wright, *Life of Wolfe*, p. 318.

of these tidings from the Admiralty, but the news was to a large extent corroborated by the French and Dutch residents in India. It was therefore determined to prepare to receive the French on their arrival on the coast in the most effective manner possible, and the 39th Regiment, which had been up to this at Fort St. David, was now brought round to Madras.

But another and more pressing danger to English interests in India now arose in a wholly unexpected quarter, and, in order properly to understand what had lately been happening in Bengal, some account must be given of recent events in that part of India.

Ali Verdy Khan, the Nawab of Bengal, who had always been friendly to the English, died in April, 1756, and was succeeded by his grand-nephew, Surajah Dowlah, who was known to be hostile to the English. This animosity was encouraged by all those about him, who pointed out the booty to be obtained by the capture of Calcutta, and the honour which the defeat of the English would confer upon him. These arguments took effect, and an excuse for hostilities was soon found. The factory at Cossimbazar was attacked and surrendered on June 4th; on the 9th the Nawab commenced an advance upon Calcutta; and on the 16th his advance guard appeared before the walls of the fort and the siege commenced. The garrison made a spirited defence, but having been deserted by the Governor and by the Commander of the troops, it surrendered on June 20th, on the night of which day occurred the tragedy of the Black Hole. Such of the garrison as were able to effect their escape took refuge at Fulta, forty miles down the river, and were here joined by all the English who could reach that haven from the out-factories.

News of the capture of Cossimbazar reached Madras on July 15th, and on the 20th Major Kilpatrick* sailed for Calcutta in the *Delaware*, taking with him a small force variously estimated at from 230 to 250 Europeans, of whom probably forty belonged to the artillery and not less than 100 were drawn from the Madras European Battalion. The officers of the Corps who sailed with Kilpatrick

* Was transferred to the Bengal Establishment in October, 1756, and died twelve months later.

were Captain William Lin,* Lieutenants Dugald Campbell† and Samuel Samson, Ensigns John Vouga‡ and Francis Flaction.§ Three artillery officers were also embarked on the *Delaware*—Captain-Lieutenant Godwin, Lieutenants Paschoud and Erdman. This detachment was happily ready to move, having been prepared in obedience to orders from home, where it had been anticipated that disturbance might arise in Bengal on the death of the aged Ali Verdy Khan, and it had been directed that the force in Bengal should be reinforced from Madras.

The intelligence of the loss of Calcutta was conveyed in a letter from Messrs. Watts and Collet, dated Chandernagore, July 2nd, and arrived on August 16th at Madras where it created the greatest consternation. The Board had already on August 3rd resolved to send a further detachment to Calcutta, but it was now realized that the Company must put forward its full strength, and on the 18th resolutions were passed " ordering the whole squadron and all the land forces to the relief of Calcutta." The news, however, from Europe seemed to point to the re-opening of the war with France, and Admiral Watson advised that the expedition to Bengal be postponed until the last week in September.

Ships from England were at this time daily expected and it was decided to wait and see what news these might bring. The *Chesterfield* and the *Walpole* came in on September 10th, but brought no news of any war with France, and on the 21st the Madras Council discussed " whether upon the news received from Europe it is proper to undertake the expedition to Bengal," and it was unanimously decided that it should be undertaken. The question of a commander was then debated ; as might only have been expected, Lawrence at once offered his services, " but when we considered the unhealthiness of the Bengal climate at that season, his time of life and state of health, we thought the chance of his surviving it greatly against him, and therefore desired he would waive his motion."

The Council had apparently made up their mind that the commander of the expeditionary force should be an officer in the

* Died in 1757. † Killed December 29th, 1756.
‡ Died in 1756. § Transferred to Bengal Establishment in 1758.

service of the Company, and " as Colonel Clive " (who had arrived from Fort St. David on August 24th) " has before offered his services, he is now desired on many considerations to accept the command which he very readily does." He was thereupon appointed " commander-in-chief of all the troops sent and to be sent on the expedition to Bengal," while in the event of anything happening to him he was to be succeeded by Major Kilpatrick.*

" The appointment of Clive gave satisfaction to the troops, but not to Colonel Adlercron, who as senior officer claimed the command, but would not bind himself to obey orders from Madras, nor to repay the Company's losses out of the expected booty. He now refused to allow any of the King's troops to proceed to Bengal. ' Surely gentlemen,' he wrote to the Board, ' you are not so unreasonable as to expect that I will send away any part of His Majesty's Train or Regiment (who are so immediately under my direction) and leave to you the nomination.' He demanded that His Majesty's artillery with the stores be immediately disembarked. ' The Select Committee agreed to order immediate landing of the King's Train, but to request of Colonel Adlercron to spare the train appurtenances, stores, etc., for the present expedition, upon the Committee's promise to replace the same for the use of His Majesty's Train.' But the sullen and perverse Adlercron refused to spare the King's stores unless he were satisfied of the Committee's ability to replace them, and the Committee then ordered the Company's stores to take the place of the King's stores."†

Eventually Colonel Adlercron most reluctantly agreed that three companies of the 39th should accompany the expedition, but only on the condition that they should serve as marines on board Admiral Watson's squadron.

The composition of the force was finally settled as under; it comprised five ships of war, the *Kent, Tiger, Cumberland, Salisbury* and *Bridgewater*, with five Indiamen, while the troops were composed of about 900 Europeans, of whom 250 belonged to the 39th, while

---

* Kilpatrick had actually resigned the Service when ordered to Bengal with the advance detachment, but withdrew his resignation on nomination to command it.

† Forrest, Vol. I, p. 274.

THE EXPEDITION TO CALCUTTA

there were five companies of the Madras European Regiment, 650 strong, 80 artillerymen, 1,200 Madras sepoys, 12 field pieces and 1 howitzer.*

Captain Briggs of the Battalion was appointed aide-de-camp to Clive.

All being completed, the expedition sailed on October 16th.†

The following are the names of the officers of the Battalion who embarked at Madras for the Plassey Campaign :—Captains Gaupp, Bridge and Pye ; Lieutenants Wagner, Fischer, Rumbold, Fraser, Robert Campbell and Joecher ; Ensigns Scotney, Knox, Tait or Tuite, Kerr, Oswald, Wiecks, Stenger and Tabby. As junior captain of the 39th detachment embarked Eyre Coote, under whom in years to come the Madras European Battalion was to gain some of the most important of its victories.

The following " Return of the Strength of the Troops order'd for Bengal " is in the India Office in the " Records of Fort St. George, Diary and Consultation Book, Mil. Dept., 1756."

Fort St. George, Oct. 8th, 1756.	Lt.-Colonel.	Captains.	Capt.-Lieuts.	Lieutenants.	Ensigns.	Volunteers.	Sergeants.	Corporals.	Drummers.	Centinels.	Bombardiers.	Gunners.	Matrosses.	Total.
Train of Artillery	0	0	1	5	0	0	5	5	3	0	21	21	48	103
Grenadiers	0	1	0	1	2	2	8	6	4	94	0	0	0	112
Capt. Maskelyne's	0	1	0	1	2	2	6	6	4	73	0	0	0	89
Capt. Gaupp's	0	1	0	2	1	2	4	6	4	77	0	0	0	91
Capt. Campbell's	0	1	0	1	2	1	6	6	4	73	0	0	0	89
Capt. Callender's	0	1	0	0	3	1	6	6	4	73	0	0	0	89
Total	0	5	1	10	10	8	35	35	23	390	21	21	48	573

(Sd.) ROBERT CLIVE, Lieut.-Coln.

N.B.—2 Captains, 2 Lieutenants 4
      2 Sergeant-Majors, 1 Qr. Master Sergt., 1 Corporal ... 4
      and 12 Camp Colourmen not returned in the Body of the Return 12
                                                                                 593

---

* Wilson, Vol. I, p. 87, gives the numbers as 39th, 250 ; Madras Europeans 528 ; Artillery, 109 ; Lascars, 160 ; and Sepoys, 940 ; and states that a further party of 250 more sepoys embarked on October 28th.

† Coote, in his Diary, says 17th.

(It will be seen that this does not seem entirely in agreement with the foregoing.)

The start did not promise well. During the first twelve days the ships of the fleet were driven down as far as Ceylon by strong currents, and it was not until November 30th that the fleet came to an anchor in Ballasore Roads, and on December 15th two ships of war and one of the Indiamen reached Fulta. Two vessels had parted company, the *Salisbury* having sprung a leak and being only able to proceed on her journey under easy sail, while the *Marlborough*, Indiaman, had been obliged to bear away for Vizagapatam. As one of these ships carried 300 Europeans, mostly of the 39th, and the other the greater part of the field guns and stores, their absence rather impaired the efficiency of the force. At Fulta were the fugitives from Fort William and other parts of Bengal, with the detachment under Kilpatrick which had arrived on August 2nd, and of which Orme tells us, " that of the whole detachment, which was 230 when sent, one-half were dead, and of the remainder not more than 30 men were able to do duty when Admiral Watson arrived."

On December 27th the fleet proceeded up the Hooghly River, the sepoys marching overland and keeping the ships in view. The following day the fleet reached Mayapur, when as Orme states, " all the men of Adlercron's regiment who were arrived, being 120, remained on board the ships of war. The rest of the Battalion, 500, with all the sepoys and two field pieces landed and at sunset marched from Mayapur under the command of Colonel Clive, and under the conduct of Indian guides." It had been arranged at a Council of War that the ships were to bombard the fort of Budge Budge on the river, while Clive and his troops marched north to intercept the garrison when, driven out by the cannonade, they should retreat along the Calcutta road. The road lay through a swampy country and it was after sunrise on the 29th when the troops reached the place where they were to lie in ambush—the dry bed of a tank about a mile from the river, a mile and a half north-east of Budge Budge and half a mile east of the high road to Calcutta. The commander of the sepoys, one Keshar Singh, was sent forward with 200 of his men to reconnoitre, being supported by Captain Pye at the head of the grenadier company and the remainder of the sepoys, while Captain Gaupp with his company was so placed as to give timely notice of the approach of any of the enemy by the Calcutta road.

Captain Pye, finding no sign of any enemy in his front, joined the party of sepoys and then put himself under the orders of Captain Coote, who had just landed from the ships with some of the 39th; " upon this," says Coote in his diary, " I formed the King's troops into platoons, the Company's grenadiers in the rear of me, and divided the sepoys into the advanced and rear guards. I immediately advanced and took possession of two out forts the enemy had evacuated," and was preparing to storm an inner fort, when Captain Weller, who was Coote's senior in the 39th and had just then landed from the *Salisbury*, came up, and news now arriving that Clive had been attacked by a large body of horse and foot, it was decided to go to his assistance. " After three miles' march we joined him," wrote Coote. " He was then drawn up in a plain, and had a smart skirmish with the enemy before he could disengage himself from some enclosures and houses that the enemy had possessed themselves of."

There is a journal extant written by " one of Clive's family " —possibly by his aide-de-camp, Captain Briggs of the Battalion, for in those days the staff officers of a commander were usually described as his " family,"—and in this it is stated that, " the skirmish lasted half an hour, in which time we had Ensign Kerr and 9 private men killed and 8 wounded." In a letter from Clive himself to the Governor of Madras he wrote :—" Our two field pieces were of little or no service to us, having neither tubes nor port-fires, and wrong carriages sent with them from Fort St. David; indeed, we still labour under every disadvantage in the world for want of the *Marlborough*."

The enemy being dispersed, Clive now went on board the flag-ship to consult with Admiral Watson, while Coote and Weller with " the troops, as well King's as Company's, were ordered to march down to the fort, where the men-of-war had silenced the guns but had made no breach in the wall further than destroying the parapet over which the enemy kept firing their musketry; but, as the military were under cover of a high bank they did no execution. At 4 in the afternoon two 9-pounders were brought on shore from the ships to be mounted on the advanced battery of the enemy (of which we had possession) in order to make a breach in the curtain nigh the gate, as well as to cover the party that were ordered to storm the place at daybreak, which consisted of the King's troops, the grenadier company and one hundred seamen." (Coote was now in command here for, as he relates in his diary, " the Colonel and Major Kilpatrick were retired to rest as they had a very fatiguing march all the night before, and Captain Weller was gone sick on board.") " At 8 in the evening a drunken seaman straggling from his command pushed into the fort, when finding no resistance gave three cheers and was followed by the whole body without any orders, scarce any being found to oppose them as the garrison had begun to leave the fort at sunset. In the confusion Captain Campbell " (of the Battalion) " was killed upon one of the bastions (giving orders for posting sentinels upon a magazine that was there) by the seamen or sepoys."*

1757 On January 1st, 1757, the fleet arrived before Alighar, which, with Thana, was found abandoned, and on the next morning Clive, having landed with the Company's European troops and some sepoys, marched on Calcutta. The ships, however, arrived there before him and after a smart cannonade the enemy evacuated the fort, when it was taken possession of by Captain Eyre Coote and a detachment of the 39th.

Under date of January 4th Coote notes in his journal :—" I received orders to embark with the King's troops on board the 20-gun ship and sloop of war, and the rest of our detachment that was on board the *Salisbury* all joined, except Captain Weller who was left sick on board. Major Kilpatrick with the Company's Grenadiers

---

* *Journal of the Military Proceedings of the Honourable Company's Troops sent on the Expedition to Bengal, commanded by Lieut.-Colonel Clive.* Given in Wilson, Vol. I, pp. 78-81.

and 170 Sepoys were also embarked; we were in all about 200 Europeans and 170 sepoys.

"9th.—The ships came to anchor off Hooghly."

As to the capture of the fort at Hooghly on the 11th, the "Madras Records" say:—"The reduction thereof by the *Bridgewater*, *Kingfisher*, and a detachment of land forces under Major Kilpatrick was executed with the loss of but very few, but a great number of the enemy," the actual casualties incurred being 3 European soldiers and 10 sepoys killed and several wounded, while there were 30 or more of the naval forces engaged killed and wounded. On the next day a party of Europeans and sepoys was sent under Coote to destroy certain granaries 3 miles to the north, and Coote encountered considerable opposition from a very superior force; Kilpatrick moved out in support on hearing the firing, but Coote had managed to extricate his party with small loss before Kilpatrick arrived upon the scene.

The fort at Hooghly was now demolished, and the troops all re-embarked and sailed for Calcutta, where they arrived on January 19th.

Meanwhile the authorities at Madras had become gravely disturbed at the news which reached them from Europe. On November 12th, 1756, accounts had come to hand of the outbreak of war between England and France; the intelligence was at once transmitted to Clive, and the Governor and Council of Madras, after suggesting an attack upon the French settlement of Chandernagore, besought Clive to return southward with as many troops as could be spared to protect the settlement from the dangers likely to result from the expected arrival of a French expedition from Europe. These messages reached Calcutta and Clive while the operations against Hooghly were in progress.

There being at this time a considerable body of French troops at Chandernagore, it was determined to open negotiations with the Nawab, and so prevent any alliance of the French with him; the attempt, however, was unsuccessful, and the Nawab, Surajah Dowlah, moreover, irritated at the capture and plunder of Hooghly, had commenced his march on Calcutta, his army coming within sight of that place on February 2nd. In his journal Coote estimates the hostile force as " consisting of 40,000 horse and 60,000 foot, 50 elephants, and 30 pieces of cannon; our body, for I cannot call it our army, consisted of 711 men in battalion, about 100 artillery with 14 field-pieces—6-pounders—besides the cannon on our batteries, and 1,300 sepoys." There was some skirmishing this day, and a few men were killed and wounded.

On the 4th Clive determined to attack the Nawab's camp, and some 600 seamen having been landed from the fleet, Clive moved out at midnight with a force of 650 Europeans, 6 guns with 100 artillerymen, and 800 sepoys. At daybreak the enemy's outposts were encountered and quickly driven in, and the advance was resumed in a dense fog, under cover of which the enemy's horse executed a very bold and tolerably successful charge. All hope of a surprise had now been dissipated, and the troops under Clive returned to camp very greatly fatigued and having suffered serious loss: 27 European soldiers, 12 sailors, and 18 sepoys had been killed; 70 Europeans, 12 seamen, and 35 sepoys wounded. Captains Pye and Bridge of the corps were killed, as was also Mr. Belcher, Clive's secretary, while Captain Gaupp and Lieutenant Rumbold were wounded. The enemy's loss was also very considerable, but the moral effect of the action was even greater. In his report to the Madras Government of February 6th, Clive wrote:—" Now the consequences of this blow. The Nawab has decamped with his whole army; has wrote me a letter that he will comply with all our demands except a sum of money for the inhabitants—viz., that he will put us in possession of everything granted by the Royal Firmaund, liberty to fortify Fort William as we please, and the liberty of a mint. . . ."

In the month of February the small body of Europeans under Clive had sustained 170 casualties; in the Madras European Battalion these amounted to 126—viz., died, 43; killed, 26; wounded, 51; and deserted, 6.

During the first half of March reinforcements had reached

CAPTURE OF CHANDERNAGORE

Clive, the missing men of the 39th Foot had been landed in Bengal, while 400 of the Bombay European Regiment had arrived under Captains Buchanan and Armstrong, as also some artillery, and it was now determined to attack the French settlement of Chandernagore The place was summoned on the 13th, and fire was opened on the 19th from the shore batteries, while the ships of war dropping anchor off the fort on the morning of the 23rd, a furious cannonade was maintained until nine o'clock, when the white flag went up, the place finally surrendering at three in the afternoon. The losses sustained by the besiegers were chiefly among the Navy. " During the engagement," records Coote in his Diary, " the *Kent* had 3 of her 32-pounders dismounted, 19 men were killed and 74 wounded ; among the former was Mr. Perreau, first lieutenant, and among the latter Captain Speke : Mr. Hay, third lieutenant, Captain Speke's son and 4 or 5 petty officers ; my detachment, consisting of 30 rank and file, had 9 men killed and 5 wounded. . . . The *Tyger* had 14 men killed and 56 wounded, the master being the only person of rank among the former ; among the latter, Admiral Pocock, slightly hurt, of the King's detachment under Captain Grant 1 man killed and 2 wounded. . . . The enemy was so much employed against the ships that the Army ashore under Colonel Clive had but 1 man killed and 10 wounded."

Clive had by this definitely made up his mind to turn a deaf ear to the entreaties of the Madras Government, and to remain in Bengal with his whole force, being convinced that, in the absence of any substantial body of English troops, no treaties would be binding with the Nawab of Bengal, or would prevent him from attacking the Company's possessions in these provinces on the very first favourable opportunity ; the army therefore remained for the present encamped on the plain to the north of Hooghly, a position well suited either to overawe or from which to act against the Nawab.

In April Clive wrote to the Nawab demanding, as an outward and visible sign of his goodwill towards the English, permission to attack the French at Cossimbazar, where M. Law, the chief of the French factory, had been joined by some adventurers who had escaped from Chandernagore. But the Nawab blew hot and cold, at one moment professing the utmost cordiality towards the English and directing M. Law to depart; at another driving the English emissary from his presence with insult and abuse. On May 19th, therefore, Clive made an agreement with Mir Jaffier, the Nawab's Commander-in-Chief, to dethrone the Nawab and set up Mir Jaffier in his place.

All necessary preparations had been made to attack the Nawab, and the garrison of Chandernagore having been supplied by the Navy, the whole of the military force was thus available for field service. On June 18th the army arrived at Palta, and Coote, who had recently been accorded the local rank of Major, was sent off with a small body of 700 men—200 Europeans drawn from the 39th Foot, the Madras and Bombay Regiments, and 500 sepoys—to seize the fort of Katwa about 12 miles distant. This surrendered the next day after a comparatively feeble resistance. That evening the main body arrived and camped near the fort, and on the 21st Clive summoned the only Council of War which he ever called together, and, as he stated in after years before the Select Committee of the House of Commons, "had he abided by the votes of the majority, he would have caused the ruin of the East India Company."

The situation at the moment was a sufficiently serious one. At Katwa Clive was to have been joined by Mir Jaffier, but that arch-intriguer did not appear, and though he had written explaining his position, his letter had been delayed in transit. What had happened was that the Nawab was now thoroughly alarmed at the advance of the English, the apparent weakness of the French support, and the defection of his own adherents. He opened negotiations with Mir Jaffier, and a reconciliation of a kind was patched up; but before Mir Jaffier was able to establish communication with Clive assuring him of his intention to abide by the treaty made between them, in spite of his apparent renewal of friendly relations with his former master, intelligence had reached Clive that the whole plot was at an end. It had never been contemplated that Clive's small force should engage, unsupported, the Nawab's huge army; the rainy season was at hand; and if Clive now advanced across the River Baggirruttee, he would find himself in the presence of overwhelming enemy forces before which there could be no retreat, neither with honour nor with life.

Coote's journal contains a complete record of this historic Council, and it may here be given in full:—

"A Council of War was held composed of the following members, viz. :—

Lieutenant Colonel Robert Clive: against an immediate action.

Majors
- James Kilpatrick: against.
- Archibald Grant: against.
- Eyre Coote: for immediate action.
- Frederick Gaupp: against.
- Alexander Grant: for.
- John Cudmore: against.
- Thomas Rumbold: against.
- Christian Fisher: against.
- Charles Palmer: against.
- Andrew Armstrong: for.
- Grainger Muir: for.
- M. le Beaume: against.
- Robert Campbell: for.
- Rudolph Waggener: against.
- John Corneille: against.

Richard Hater, lieutenant in the Navy, did not give his opinion because he thought he had not his proper seat in Council.

Captain-Lieutenant Peter Casters: for.

Wm. Jennings: for.

John Francis Paschoud: against.

——. Molitor: against.

"The Colonel informed the Council that he found he could not depend on Meer Jaffier for anything more than his standing neuter in case we came to an action with the Nawab; that Monsieur Law with a body of French was then within three days' march of joining the Nawab, whose army (by the best intelligence he could get) consisted of about 50,000 men; and that he called us together to desire our opinions, whether in those circumstances it would be prudent to come to immediate action with the Nawab, or fortify ourselves where we were and remain till the monsoon was over, and the Mahrattas could be brought into the country to join us.

"The question being then put began with the president and the eldest members whose opinions are opposite to their names. And I, being the first that dissented, thought it necessary to give my reasons for doing so, which were that, as we had hitherto met with nothing but success, which consequently had given great spirits to our men, I was of opinion that any delay might cast damp. Secondly, that the arrival of Monsieur Law would not only strengthen the Nawab's army and add vigour to their councils, but likewise weaken our force considerably as the number of Frenchmen we had entered into our service after the capture of Chandernagore would undoubtedly desert to him upon every opportunity. Thirdly, that our distance from Calcutta was so great that our communication from thence would certainly be cut off, and therefore gave us no room to hope for supplies, and consequently that we must be soon reduced to the greatest distress. Therefore gave it as my opinion that we should come to an immediate action, or if that was thought entirely impracticable, that we should return to Calcutta, the consequence of which must be our own disgrace and the inevitable destruction of the Company's affairs.

"About an hour after we had broken up, the Colonel informed me that, notwithstanding the resolution of the Council of War, he intended to march the next morning, and accordingly gave orders for the army to hold themselves in readiness, leaving a subaltern officer's command, together with all our sick, in the fort at Katwa."

Later, in his evidence before the Parliamentary Committee, Coote stated that when Clive gave him the above information "Captain Robert Campbell, to the best of my recollection, was with me at the time," which seems by no means unlikely since Campbell had voted as had Coote.

CLIVE'S COUNCIL OF WAR

It should be stated that Forrest gives (Vol. 1, p. 443) what purports to be an exact transcription of the original record of the Proceedings of the Council of War signed by the officers present and now in the Powis MSS., and this does not wholly agree with the account given by Coote in his contemporary diary; it runs as follows:—

"At a Council of War held at Cuttawa, June 21st, 1757:—
Colonel Clive, President

Major Kilpatrick ⎫
Major Coote ⎬ Members. ⎧ Major Grant.
Captain Armstrong ⎪ ⎨ Captain Gaupp.
Captain Rumbold ⎭ ⎪ Captain Grant.
  ⎩ Captain Cudmore.
Captain Mieur Captain Fisher.
Captain Corneille Captain Palmer.
Captain Campbell Captain Hater.
Capt.-Lieut. Passhaud Captain Castiers.
Capt.-Lieut. Jennings.

"When the following question was proposed by Colonel Clive.

"Whether in our present situation without assistance and on our own bottom it would be prudent to attack the Nabob, or whether we should wait till joined by some Country Power and was carried in the negative.

Robert Clive.   Eyre Coote.
James Kilpatrick.   G. Alex^r· Grant.
Arch^d· Grant.   G. Muir.
George Frederick Gaupp.   Chr. Palmer.
Andrew Armstrong.   Robert Campbell.
Thos. Rumbold.   Peter Carstairs.
S. Cudmore.   W. Jenings.
Christian Fischer.
John Corneille.
J. S. Paschoud.
            John Power, aid du Camp."

It will be seen that these lists in the Powis MSS. contain some curious inconsistencies; only eight of those present are described as "members," yet all appear to have given their votes, and while Coote's list contains twenty-one names, those in the Powis MSS. contain each only eighteen, while further the names are not identical, that of Hater in the one being replaced by that of Power in the other; it is also noticeable that the voting of Armstrong and Palmer as given in Coote's diary is reversed in the Powis MSS.

On June 22nd Clive's little army crossed the Baggirruttee River, and moving on again before sunset the same evening, the troops marched on in the darkness, and at 1 a.m. on the 23rd, after a very fatiguing march in heavy rain and through mud which in places was up to the soldiers' middles, the force reached a tope or grove of mango trees, known locally as the Laksha Bagh. The grove was surrounded by a low mud wall and ran almost due north and south, being some 800 yards long by 300 wide; it lay at an angle to the river, the north corner being within 50 yards of the bank, the south angle being some four times that distance away from it. To the north of the grove and on the river bank was a hunting lodge of the Nawab enclosed by a garden wall. About a mile to the north of this lodge the river bends to the south-west, and here there was an entrenchment, the right of which rested on the river, then ran for 200 yards westward parallel with the grove at Plassey, and then made a bend to the north-east. At the angle of this entrenchment there was a redoubt; to the left front, and outside the entrenchment, was a tree-crowned hillock, and further still to the south and nearer the north-west angle of Plassey Grove, were two tanks about one hundred yards apart, and both surrounded by mounds of earth.

On arrival here Clive received information that the Nawab's advance guard was then within three miles, and he now caused the house at Plassey to be occupied by the advance guard of 200 Europeans and 300 sepoys with two guns, while several picquets of native soldiers were posted on the outskirts of the grove.

At daybreak on June 23rd the enemy was observed marching towards the grove of Plassey with the evident intention of surrounding it, and the small handful of troops under Clive viewed with wonder this numerous and imposing army advancing slowly towards

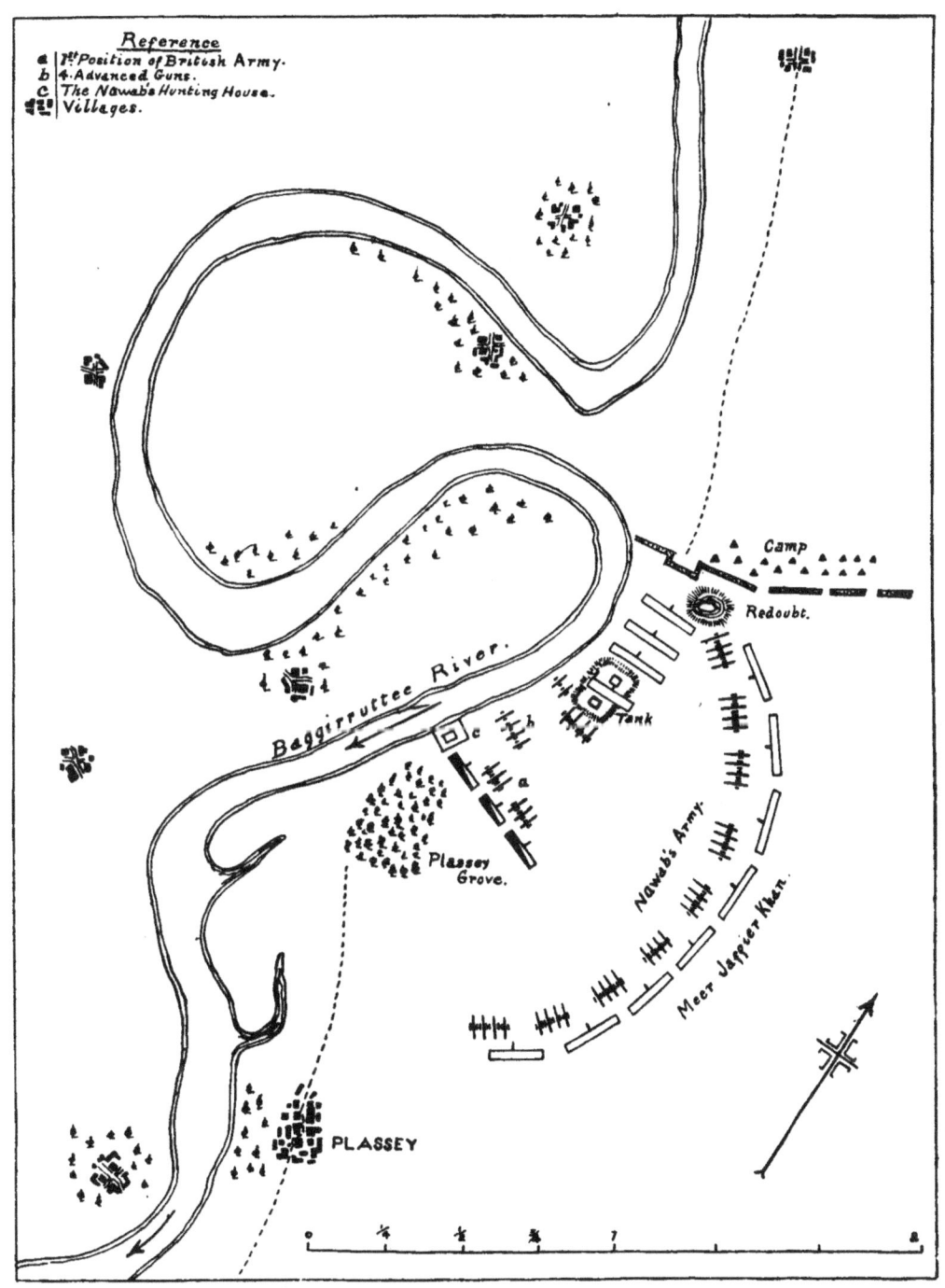

THE BATTLE OF PLASSEY, JUNE 23RD, 1757.

them, and consisting of at least 50,000 foot, 18,000 horse and 50 pieces of artillery. The infantry were for the most part armed with matchlocks, pikes, swords and bows and arrows; the cavalry were especially fine, the men of a very superior warlike class, and their horses larger and better bred than any which the British had before met with in India, and far superior as a cavalry force to any seen in the late wars in the Carnatic. The guns were chiefly 18, 24 and 32-pounders, and each of these, with its carriage and tumbril, was raised on a large wooden stage on wheels about six feet from the ground and carrying the gun detachment as well. These machines were drawn by forty or fifty yoke of large white bullocks, and in rear of each gun marched an elephant trained to help on the gun in heavy ground by pushing it from behind. A party of forty Frenchmen under M. de St. Frais manned four French field guns attached to the Nawab's army.

On the approach of this army Clive formed his force outside the bank surrounding the grove; the Europeans composed four divisions—one under Major Kilpatrick contained 300 men of the Madras Regiment, the second under Major Grant was made up of 200 men of the Madras and 30 of the Bengal Regiment, the third under Major Coote consisted of 170 soldiers of the 39th only, while the fourth division was commanded by Captain Gaupp and contained 200 men of the Bombay Europeans. The sepoys were formed on either flank; three field pieces were on each wing of the Europeans, and these, and the two guns with the advanced guard, were manned by 100 artillerymen and 50 sailors. In all the army under Clive had in it no more than 1,020 Europeans and 2,100 sepoys.

The formation of the enemy on this occasion differed materially from that usually adopted, the position of his artillery being very much more judicious, for instead of the guns being all disposed in one long line, as had been the usual practice, they were dispersed in detachments or sections of from two to four guns between the divisions of the troops which were formed in deep columns; an attack upon any one part of the enemy artillery could not well thus be decisive.

Finding that the proximity of the river made any encirclement of the British impossible, the enemy now halted and St. Frais advancing with his four guns to the front of the native infantry, placed them in battery on the *bund* of a tank near the grove, and at about 8 a.m. opened a brisk cannonade, the very first round of which killed one and wounded another of the grenadiers of the Madras Battalion.

The British, drawn up outside the grove, their left resting on Plassey House and the river, and their right on the grove, remained for some time exposed to the fire of all the enemy's guns, and after a short period, having lost some Europeans and sepoys by the cannonade, Clive withdrew them within the grove and behind the cover of the bank and ditch. This was done leisurely and in order, the left flank remaining covered by Plassey House and the river. At sight of this retirement the enemy were greatly elated and pushed their guns up to a closer range. The English field pieces were, however, admirably served and continued a heavy fire on those of the enemy.

In this situation both armies remained until mid-day when some of the enemy's tumbrils were blown up and their fire slackened. Their cavalry then made as though they would charge, but being received with a well-directed fire they broke up and withdrew out of range. The cannon-fire was maintained on either side until 3 p.m., by which time the enemy had lost many men and some of their best leaders, and then began to retire within their lines. St. Frais maintained his position for some time longer with his four guns, but on his withdrawal Major Kilpatrick at once pushed forward with his division and occupied the ground, and Clive, now joining him, ordered a general advance, the British guns forming up in the place just vacated by the French artillery and maintaining a heavy and galling fire upon the enemy now crowded together within their camp.

Being now ordered to storm, the British charged forward in two columns, one of the Madras Europeans headed by Kilpatrick, the other formed of the Grenadiers of the 39th and the men of the Bombay Regiment under Coote. The former bore down upon and captured St. Frais' guns and drove the enemy there out of the camp, while Coote's party was opposed by a large body of the opposing infantry which was dispersed and routed. Cavalry, artillery and infantry now took to their heels and fled in one large disorderly mass, the fugitives throwing away their arms and everything that could impede their flight. All their guns were abandoned, many of the elephants had been wounded and became unmanageable, while great numbers of the gun-bullocks had been killed and wounded.

Clive sent forward a detachment under Coote to pursue the flying foe, who were followed up for six miles, a halt being finally called at Daudpore, "where," wrote Coote, "the rest of the army under Major Kilpatrick joined us."

That evening (June 23rd) Clive sent the following brief note to Admiral Watson and the Gentlemen of the Committee of Fort William :—

"Gentlemen.—This morning at one o'clock we arrived at Placis Grove, and early in the morning the Nabob's whole army appeared in sight and cannonaded us for several hours, and about noon returned to a very strong camp in sight, lately Roydoolub's, upon which we advanced and stormed the Nabob's camp, which we have taken with all his cannon and pursued him six miles, being now at Doudpoor and shall proceed for Muxadavad to-morrow. Meer Jaffeir, Roydoolub and Luttee Cawn gave us no other assistance than standing neuter. They are with me with a large force. Meer Muddun and 500 horse are killed and three elephants. Our loss is trifling, not above twenty Europeans killed and wounded."

In the Battle of Plassey the victors lost only 4 Europeans and 14 sepoys killed ; 17 Europeans and 31 sepoys wounded. It is not easy accurately to distribute the loss nor do we know exactly what was the " present strength " of each corps which fought at Plassey, for there is no " state " forthcoming ; there are, however, in existence two " states " which throw some light upon the subject and extracts from them are here given :—

The one is dated Camp near Chinsura, April 7th, 1757, and gives as " present and doing duty " :

39th: 3 captains, 4 lieutenants, 5 ensigns, 8 sergeants, 10 corporals, 7 drummers and 213 privates.

Madras Infantry: 1 major, 5 captains, 5 lieutenants, 4 ensigns, 5 volunteers, 41 sergeants, 26 corporals, 14 drummers, 271 privates.

Bengal Infantry: 4 captains, 1 captain-lieutenant, 2 lieutenants, 9 ensigns, 12 volunteers, 18 sergeants, 14 corporals, 10 drummers and 105 privates.

Bombay Infantry: 2 captains, 2 lieutenants, 2 ensigns, 2 volunteers, 21 sergeants, 19 corporals, 6 drummers and 113 privates.

In this return the names of the Madras officers are stated as follows:—Major Kilpatrick, Captains Lin, Maskelyne, Callender, Gaupp, with Captains Rumbold, Wagner and Fischer as supernumeraries and Fraser as adjutant; Lieutenants Campbell, quartermaster, Knox, Tuite, Scotney, lieutenant and adjutant, and Joecher; Ensigns Stenger, Tabby, Oswald and Wiecks.

The other "state" is dated Sydabad, August 3rd, 1757, and gives the following:—

39th: 1 lieutenant, 1 ensign, 1 adjutant, 1 quartermaster, 1 sergeant, 5 corporals, 4 drummers and 26 privates.

Madras Infantry: 3 captains, 3 lieutenants, 4 ensigns, 4 volunteers, 28 sergeants, 14 corporals, 8 drummers and 135 privates.

Bengal Infantry: 2 captains, 1 lieutenant, 4 ensigns, 1 adjutant, 1 quartermaster, 3 volunteers, 11 sergeants, 8 corporals, 10 drummers and 109 privates.

Bombay Infantry: 1 captain, 1 lieutenant, 2 ensigns, 1 quartermaster, 7 sergeants, 4 corporals, 3 drummers and 57 privates.

This return also gives the casualties "since June 10th" presumably up to the end of July—as "dead, 9; deserted, 10; killed, 2; wounded, 11; and entertained, 5"; and the casualties during that period in the Madras Infantry are:—

Deceased: June 10th, Captain Lin; June 13th, Daniel Murry, centinel in the Grenadier Company; June 24th, Peter Pegler, drummer in Captain Gaupp's Company.

Killed: June 23rd, John Raison, corporal in the Grenadier Company.

MEDAL STRUCK IN COMMEMORATION OF THE VICTORY AT PLASSEY.

Wounded: David Pridmore, sergeant in Captain Gaupp's Company; John Pringle and John Dyson, sergeants in the Supernumeraries.

Consequently if we may take this " state " as correct, the casualties of the Madras Battalion at Plassey were one killed and three wounded.

The losses of individual corps at Plassey were as follows :—

39th : *Killed*, none ; *wounded*, 1 sergeant and 3 privates.

Madras Battalion : *Killed*, 1 corporal ; *wounded*, 3 sergeants.

Bengal Battalion : *Killed*, 1 private ; *wounded*, 1 lieutenant, 1 sergeant, 1 private.

Bombay Battalion : *Killed*, none ; *wounded*, 1 private.

Madras Artillery : *Killed*, 1 corporal, 1 gunner, 1 matross ; *wounded*, 1 lieutenant, 1 corporal, 2 bombardiers, 1 gunner.

Bengal Artillery : *Killed*, none ; *wounded*, 1 lieutenant, 1 matross.

Madras Sepoys : *Killed*, 4 ; *wounded*, 19.

Bengal Sepoys : *Killed*, 9 ; *wounded*, 11.

The total loss incurred by the British force was, as Fortescue remarks,* " a small price to pay for dominion over the provinces of Bengal, Orissa and Behar, for such and no less were the fruits of victory. Yet it is not by the mere tale of the slaughtered and maimed that such successes must be judged. The victory may have been easily won when the moment came for the actual clash of arms ; but the main point is that the British were there to win it. The campaign of Plassey is less a study of military skill than of the iron will and unshaken nerve that could lead 3,000 men against a host of unknown strength, and hold them undaunted, a single slender line, within a ring of 50,000 enemies."

On June 25th at daybreak the British army resumed its march and arrived at Maidapore, and on the same day, at Murshedabad, Mir Jaffier was proclaimed Nawab in the place of Surajah Dowlah, who had, by his enemies, been put to death. On the 28th the army reached Cossimbazar ; and on the 30th Clive made his public entry

* *History of the British Army*, Vol. II, p. 430.

into Murshedabad, escorted by 100 of the 39th, the Grenadier Company of the Madras Regiment, 500 Sepoys and two guns; and so ended the connection in the field of the Madras Battalion and its distinguished leader, Robert Clive.

The European troops with Clive were, after Plassey and the various manœuvres and marchings which followed upon that battle, concentrated in the first instance at Chandernagore and later at Cossimbazar. On September 17th the *Revenge*, Commodore James, brought news to Calcutta of the arrival on the Madras coast of a powerful French fleet, with a large military force on board. Further advices speedily followed, accompanied by urgent solicitations from the Madras Government for the immediate return of the troops which had been sent to Bengal under Clive; but to these the state of affairs in the northern province did not incline Clive to listen, and the Madras Europeans remained in the vicinity of Calcutta.

In June, 1757, the *Hardwicke*, East Indiaman, had brought from England orders for the return home of the 39th Foot, but permission was given for those officers and men who might wish to do so to enter the Company's service. As a result nearly all the men of the detachment serving in Bengal joined the Bengal European Regiment, while of those who had remained behind in the south with Adlercron 334 transferred to the Madras Battalion, receiving a bounty of ten pagodas each. In September, 1758, the **1758** Madras and Bombay Europeans serving in Bengal were transferred to that establishment, and the officers having been allowed the option of accompanying the men, the majority of them appear to have done so; consequently but very few of those who came north with Clive, returned again to Madras.

The substantial transfer of officers and men of the 39th to the Madras Battalion greatly augmented its strength, while in November, 1757, the Court of Directors advised the Madras Government that drafts from certain newly-raised regiments in England, to the number of 1,100 men, had been granted them by the Home Government; and though nothing has been found to determine the manner and date of their formation, it seems likely that the creation of two battalions of the Madras European Regiment dates from the accession of the volunteers from the 39th Foot and of the large drafts above mentioned.

However this may be, it appears from certain " Proceedings of Government" dated July 17th, 1758, that there were then in existence two battalions, commanded, the one by a Captain Gardner, the other by a Captain Maskelyne. The first particulars discovered appear in the following Garrison Order by Colonel Lawrence, dated Fort St. George, October 20th, 1758, in which the officers are posted to the Battalion companies as under :—

" The two battalions having been regulated are to consist of the following officers :—

	1st Battalion.	*2nd Battalion.*
	Grenadiers. Captain Beaver.	Grenadiers, Captain Charles Campbell.
	Lieutenant Elliot.	Lieutenant Robson.
	Lieutenant Smith.	Lieutenant Blair.
1st.	Major Polier.	1st. Major Caillaud.
	Lieutenant Parrott.	Lieutenant Clarke.
	Ensign Desplan.	Ensign Willson.
2nd.	Captain Schaub.	2nd. Captain Pascall.
	Lieutenant Fletcher.	Lieutenant Darke.
	Ensign Bellingham.	Ensign Faizan.
3rd.	Captain Innis.	3rd. Captain Richard Smith.
	Lieutenant Hart.	Lieutenant Frischman.
	Ensign Croley.	Ensign Harper.
4th.	Captain Joseph Smith.	4th. Captain Gurtler.
	Lieutenant Flint.	Lieutenant Lang.
	Ensign Beaver.	Ensign Wynn.
5th.	Captain Preston.	5th. Captain Greig.
	Lieutenant Elivy.	Lieutenant Meyers.
	Ensign Deegman.	Ensign Phillips.

6th. Captain Donald Campbell.　　6th. Captain Lieutenant Bilhock.
　　　Lieutenant Bates.　　　　　　　Lieutenant Little.
　　　Ensign Villeret.　　　　　　　　Ensign Bonjour.
Lieutenant Minns, Adjutant.　　Lieutenant Orton, Adjutant.
Mr. Hopwood, Quartermaster.　　Lieutenant Lang, Quartermaster
Supernumeraries to the 1st Battalion, Captains Black and Wood.
Supernumeraries to the 2nd Battalion, Captains De Beck and
　　Ogilvie, Ensigns Fitzpatrick and Kilpatrick."

It will be noticed that the above list does not contain the name of any officer who sailed from Madras to Calcutta with Clive, so the inference is that all survivors transferred to the Bengal European Regiment.

Early in 1757 the Swiss Companies had been placed in all respects on the same footing as the English Infantry in the service of the Company, and were made subject to the same courts martial.

In thus bringing the narration up to October, 1758, events have necessarily been somewhat anticipated, and we must now return to Madras and describe what had there been happening while the detachment of the Battalion was serving in Bengal.

CHAPTER V

1757—1760.

THE DEFENCE OF FORT ST. GEORGE.

WANDEWASH—"THE BATTLE WHICH GAVE US INDIA."

1757 WHILE the events recorded in the last chapter had been transpiring in Bengal, that portion of the Madras European Battalion which had remained in the neighbourhood of Madras had been engaged, in detachments of varying strength, in operations in the south.

Thus, about the end of March, 1757, a detachment was placed under the command of Major Forde of the 39th Foot, for the purpose of coercing the Governor of the district of Nellore who had evaded compliance with certain demands of the Nawab of Arcot in the matter of tribute. The European portion of the force placed under Forde appears to have consisted, in part at least, of the Madras Battalion and contained 8 officers and 112 other ranks, while there were in addition 300 sepoys, 56 coffrees and some 20 gunners with three guns.

The sepoys proceeded Nellore-wards by land, while the remainder of the force embarked on April 1st from Madras in two vessels which anchored the next afternoon off a salt-water inlet, seven miles to the north of Kistnapatam. Here much delay was met with in the collection of supplies and transport, and it was not until April 27th that the little army joined the forces of the Nawab before Nellore. The fort was bombarded for several days and then on May 5th Forde assaulted, sending forward first the coffrees under Ensign Elliot, then the sepoys, holding back his Europeans in reserve. In a few minutes the coffrees had seventeen men killed and wounded, Elliot being among the latter, while the sepoys, having advanced to within sixty paces of the breach, then lay down in the ditch and could not be induced to advance further. The Europeans now moved forward and, joining the coffrees, a very hot fight ensued on the top of the breach, but further the assault could not get and Forde now withdrew his party. Captains Hunt, Callender and Richard Smith and Ensign Elliot were wounded, the latter dangerously, and the casualties among the other ranks numbered close upon one hundred, of the Europeans four being killed and twenty-one wounded.*

It is recorded of Captain Richard Smith that one of the guns having been abandoned he, bringing up the rear, " halted with a few of his own Company, and afterwards with the assistance of some of the Nawab's horsemen, who were near, dragged the field-piece to the battery; during which two of his sergeants and two of the horsemen were wounded from the walls."†

While the siege was in progress the Madras authorities had more than once intimated to Forde that the long-expected French armament had arrived off the coast and that it might be necessary to recall him and his troops to the presidency, and on May 15th, receiving express orders to return with the utmost expedition to Madras, he gave up all idea of prosecuting the siege of Nellore, and embarked his troops at once for Fort St. George.

From the beginning of this same year part of the Battalion had been employed from Trichinopoly under Captain Caillaud in reducing the country about Madura, which had been seized by one Mahfoos Khan, and in the beginning of May Caillaud was making preparations for the attack of the place when he too received advices from Madras acquainting him that the French were in motion, then that they were actually in sight and evidently proposing to attack Trichinopoly—then 100 miles distant; Caillaud therefore, leaving a force sufficient to blockade Madura, set out for Trichinopoly taking with him all his Europeans, amounting to some 150 only, and 1,000 of his best sepoys

* There is a very full account of these operations in Forde's *Lord Clive's Right Hand Man*, pp. 1-13. Callender, Richard Smith, and Elliot are all names that appear in the Battalion Lists, while Hunt does not seem to have been a 39th officer.

† Orme, Vol. II, p. 205.

On May 12th a French force of 1,000 Europeans, 150 Hussars, 3,000 sepoys and 10 field guns under d'Auteuil, arrived at Seringham, and three days later commenced to bombard the city of Trichinopoly which was held by only 165 Europeans and 700 sepoys under Captain Joseph Smith, who had assumed command *vice* Caillaud absent at Madura. The garrison was greatly hampered by the presence in the fort of some 500 French prisoners of war, the release of whom was one of d'Auteuil's objects of attack. For ten days Smith and his men were harassed by continual bombardment and threatened assaults, when the news of Caillaud's approach caused d'Auteuil to draw off and dispose his army to intercept him by occupying the old positions at the Five Rocks, Fakir's Tope and others. Caillaud, marching without guns, tents or baggage, had arrived within twelve miles of his goal, when he was met by Smith's messengers telling him of the disposal of the enemy force. Setting off in the evening he marched as though to pass by the road where d'Auteuil was awaiting him, and then, when darkness fell, he changed the direction of his march, struck eastwards through deep rice fields, which the Frenchman had deemed impassable, and after a terribly trying march of seven hours entered the defences and joined his force to that of Smith. "A salute of twenty-one guns at daybreak announced to d'Auteuil that he had been outwitted. He at once broke up his camp and marched for Pondicherry."

Intelligence of the French being before Trichinopoly was received in Madras on May 15th, and on the 26th Colonel Adlercron marched out from Fort St. George with 300 of the 39th, 4 guns, 30 gunners and 500 sepoys with the object of relieving Trichinopoly. His movements were, however, so slow that he took six days to cover thirty miles and had got no further than Uttramalur when the news reached him of Caillaud having joined Smith. He then marched on Wandewash, but seeing no prospect of its capture before the French, who were rapidly advancing, could come up, he fell back on Uttramalur, where orders reached him from the Council to return to Madras.

The French, under Saubinet, an enterprising officer, followed

Adlercron, but failing to bring him to action, advanced upon and burnt Conjeveram; upon this the Madras Council, regretting their mistake in leaving all the fertile country open to French depredations, ordered Adlercron to take the field again, distrustful though they now were of his capacity for command. In this crisis, Lawrence, who had hitherto refused to serve under Adlercron, now offered to accompany him as a volunteer. Making his way to Fort St. David he took a hundred men from there, landed at Sadras and joined Adlercron, who had now advanced again and had reached Chingleput. On June 29th the English were at Uttramalur, " where an uncommon sickness broke out in the camp, men being suddenly seized and dying in twelve hours, and as many died as recovered. The mortality continued four days, but the camp having moved on July 5th five miles beyond Uttramalur, fewer men fell down the next, and in two days more the sickness entirely ceased."

For forty days the French and English armies remained within a few hours' march of each other but did not come to action, and on Lawrence's advice the English fell back at the end of July on Conjeveram, where 500 Europeans and 1,500 sepoys had remained in garrison under Colonel Forde by whom Adlercron had been joined on his first setting out from Madras. From here the remainder of the force returned to the garrisons and stations whence its component parts had been drawn.

In September, 1757, the French received a small but welcome reinforcement of regular troops, but in compliance with the very definite orders from Paris little was attempted and less effected, with the result that at the close of this year's campaign in the south, the troops of each nation had wrested one small place from the forces of the other.

In November Colonel Adlercron returned to England with such officers and men of the 39th Regiment as had not transferred to the Company's forces, and Lawrence now once again became the senior officer and Commander-in-Chief in India.

ARRIVAL OF LALLY IN INDIA

1758 On April 28th, 1758, the great French armament so long and so anxiously expected, arrived in Madras waters and anchored off Cuddalore, and Count de Lally, the commander-in-chief and commissary of the King for all French possessions in the East, proceeded with two vessels to Pondicherry.

Thomas Arthur, Count de Lally and Baron de Tollendal, was now in his fifty-ninth year, and had been engaged in the study and practice of war for nearly half-a-century. He came of the O'Mallalys of Tullendaly near Tuam, and his father, Sir Gerard, who had entered the service of France after the capture of Limerick in 1691, had risen in that army to the rank of Brigadier-General. Young Lally was entered to war early in life; before he was in his teens he had smelt powder at Gerona and Barcelona; he was a captain in Dillon's Regiment of the famous Irish Brigade at eighteen; he fought at Kehl and Phillipsburg and Fontenoy; he served under the Young Pretender at Falkirk; he was engaged at Lauffeldt and Bergen-op-Zoom; he had shown himself, when the opportunity was afforded him, as no mean diplomatist; and Voltaire has recorded of Lally that he possessed " a stubborn fierceness of soul accompanied by great gentleness of manners." Such was the man to whom was now entrusted the decision as to which nation should be paramount in the Peninsula, and with him sailed men who bore some of the great names of France—a d'Estaing, a Crillon, a Montmorency, a Conflans; but while Lally's great military qualities were marred by intolerance, and by a contempt, shared by an even greater French commander than he, for Sepoy Generals, he was indifferently supported by his second in command, de Soupire, who was indolent and unenterprising, and by his naval colleague, d'Aché, who was the weakest of admirals.

When, nineteen months previously, the expedition had been projected, 6,000,000 livres had been allotted for its cost, and it was to have been composed of six battalions and three men-of-war with such other ships as the French East India Company might be able to fit out; but the delay in dispatching the expedition had been very great, some of the troops intended to accompany it had later been withdrawn, and although Lally eventually sailed from Brest with his own Irish regiment, 1,000 strong, and 50 artillerymen, he had lost over 300 of these before his journey was more than half completed.

"At a time when the presence of every British soldier was worth his weight in gold, the Company had been forced to move the Crown to recall the 39th Regiment, merely to get rid of Adlercron."* But the Directors of the East India Company were none the less persuaded of the need for a larger leaven of European troops among their forces in Madras and in Bengal; and owing to certain representations which they made to the Home Government, two new regiments were raised at home for service in India. The first of these, known as Draper's Regiment and numbered the 79th, was raised in November, 1757, and the greater part of it landed in Madras in September, 1758, only some five months after the appearance off the coast of Lally's expedition; the second, raised by Eyre Coote in January, 1759, and numbered the 84th, was actually intended for Bengal, but circumstances induced its being diverted to Madras, where it landed in October, 1759.

The arrival of Lally and his forces was announced to the Court of Directors at home by the Madras Council in a letter saying:—"We dispatch this by the way of China and Bombay to advise you of the arrival of a French fleet of eleven sail under the command of M. D'Asche, having on board the Count de Lally in quality of Commander-in-Chief of their forces in India. This Fleet appeared at Fort St. David the 28th ultimo, 7 of them anchored in that Road, 2 laid off to the eastward and 2 passed by to Pondicherry."

Lally landed in Pondicherry on April 28th, and on the same evening he sent 1,000 Europeans and as many sepoys under Count d'Estaing against Fort St. David, but the party had no proper guides, and after much wandering about in the dark, only arrived there after daylight on the 29th, hungry and exhausted. On the 30th reinforcements, guns and supplies came up, but D'Aché, who was to have brought more men by sea, came in sight of the English

* Biddulph, p. 100.

squadron under Pocock and stood out to sea again carrying his troops with him. In the action which ensued no ships were captured or destroyed on either side, but the French losses in killed and wounded greatly exceeded those of the British, and the French were further obliged to run the *Bien Aimé* ashore at Alamparva.

Lally, who in the meantime had arrived near Fort St. David from Pondicherry, heard of the action, and now at once sent D'Estaing against Cuddalore, the defences of which were in a very ruinous condition, while the garrison was composed of 30 Europeans, 25 European gunners, 400 sepoys and some lascars, who had also to guard a very large number of French prisoners of war; on May 4th Cuddalore surrendered, the garrison being permitted to retire to Fort St. David with arms and ammunition, and the French prisoners being released and allowed to proceed to any of the neutral ports in the south, pending the fate of Fort St. David.

For the attack upon this place Lally had immediately available 1,600 Europeans and some 600 natives, while the garrison of Fort St. David consisted of 619 Europeans, of whom 83 were pensioners, 250 recently landed sailors and about 1,600 sepoys and lascars. Major Polier de Bottens, who commanded in Fort St. David, was a brave officer but showed himself a poor tactician, attempting to defend the place by holding a number of small outworks. The enemy's fire, moreover, destroyed the reservoir and filled in many of the wells so that the only water obtainable was from the ditch, which was brackish. The discipline of the garrison was not of a high standard, and it is worthy of notice that at the time Polier was promoted major, about the end of 1757, Orme, then a member of Council, had objected on the grounds that, being a foreigner, Polier would be unable to maintain proper discipline among English troops.*

The garrison seems to have hoped for relief from the arrival of the English fleet; on June 1st some ships of war were noticed making for Fort St. David, but it was soon seen that they belonged to d'Aché's squadron, and on June 2nd, the defence abandoned all idea of further resistance and hung out a flag of truce. " At six in

* Wilson, Vol. I, p. 100, *note*.

the evening, a company of French grenadiers were admitted into the Fort, and the garrison marched with drums and Colours to the foot of the glacis where they grounded their arms, and surrendered themselves and their ensigns to the French line drawn up to receive them," the garrison yielding themselves prisoners of war to be exchanged on the first opportunity.

Clive was furious at the surrender and expressed himself thereon in unmeasured terms :—" I could wish," he wrote, " for the honour and welfare of our nation that court martial would make the severest example of the guilty in such cases." Here there was no question of bringing anybody to trial, but a court of inquiry convened at Madras held that, while there was no question of Polier's personal bravery, his measures had been injudicious. The court considered that the place should have held out much longer and they reflected in strong terms on what they regarded as its premature surrender. The Directors concurred, and in a letter from the Company in London to Fort St. George, dated March 13th, 1761, they wrote :—" Fort St. David was given up for want of economy in the management of the stores, ammunition and provisions, and this absolutely owing to most shameful neglect and dissipation. The whole siege was one scene of disorder, confusion, mismanagement, and a total inattention to every important branch ; and after the strictest examination, we cannot yet trace who had the care and delivery of the stores and ammunition."

Lally blew up the works of Fort St. David and reduced the place to ruins ; on the day that Fort St. David surrendered, he sent a force against Devicotah, the garrison of which abandoned the place on June 4th on the approach of the enemy, retreating to Trichinopoly, while shortly afterwards the troops in Arcot and Carangoly were withdrawn to Madras.

Lally was now very anxious to attack and possess himself of Madras—on the capture of Fort St. David he had written to Bussy : " It is the whole of British India which it now remains for us to attack " ; but he was at this time greatly in want of funds, while he was without naval support as d'Aché was cruising in the south.

A means of obtaining money was now suggested to Lally, viz., to demand payment of an ancient bond for fifty-six lakhs of rupees executed by the King of Tanjore in favour of Chanda Sahib, and which Chanda Sahib's son had handed over to Dupleix. Sauhojee was found resident in Fort St. David and Lally determined to march into Tanjore territory, using Sauhojee as a lever to extract payment of the bond from the reigning king.

He set out with 1,600 Europeans and a large army of sepoys, but met with many difficulties both for carriage and supply; the King of Tanjore was willing to come to terms but was quite unable to produce the enormous sum demanded by Lally, and Caillaud now sent from Trichinopoly to aid the Tanjore ruler 500 trained sepoys, 10 English artillerymen and 300 "colleries." As Lally advanced the Tanjore army fell back slowly, covered by clouds of mounted men, while the "colleries" hung upon his rear, cutting off his foraging parties and capturing his supplies. On August 2nd Lally's batteries opened fire against Tanjore, but the French lost many men by the fire from the walls, and on the 6th Caillaud sent a further reinforcement of 500 sepoys, with two sergeants and 27 men from the Battalion. On the 7th the French guns had made a practicable breach and the end seemed very near, when, on the 8th, news came in of the arrival of the English fleet off Karical, and Lally decided to raise the siege and sent away his sick and wounded preparatory to retiring.

On the morning of the 10th, however, the Tanjore general with his English allies beat up the French camp, and Lally himself was wounded and his whole force thrown into the greatest confusion; on the following night he spiked his guns and fell back via Trivellore on Karical where he arrived on August 18th and there found the English squadron at anchor off the mouth of the river. There can be no doubt that Tanjore would have fallen to the French had it not been for the useful and timely help sent thither by Caillaud.

On September 15th several Indiamen and two men-of-war arrived at Madras with the first division of Draper's Regiment, while shortly after 100 more were landed, and it was then found possible to augment the garrison of Chingleput, one of the few small posts near Madras which still held out, and its defenders were made up to nine companies of sepoys, with thirty European infantrymen and twelve gunners. These were placed under the command of Captain Richard Smith of the Madras Europeans, and he was ordered to defend Chingleput to the last.

Lally's expedition against Tanjore had been very far from replenishing his treasury—on the contrary it had increased the financial pressure, and he was at his wits' end to obtain sufficient money for the needs of his army and the payment of his troops. In September then he made up his mind to obtain possession of Arcot, the capital of the Carnatic, where he hoped to find an overflowing treasury and abundance of provisions. He sent out four small columns, under his best officers, to capture the various petty forts which lay on his route and which, if left unoccupied, might impede the advance of the main column, and this, under his immediate command, moved on Wandewash. Here, the country having been cleared, the army was to concentrate and advance on Arcot.

The operation was well conceived and ably executed. The several small forts fell one after another, and on October 4th Lally made his entry into Arcot and there made over charge to the eldest son of the late Chanda Sahib. But he found an empty treasury, and when he wished to march on Chingleput—a strategic position of immense importance, since, situated on the Palar River, it commanded the road to Pondicherry and dominated the country whence Madras drew its supplies—his troops refused to move unless they first received their arrears of pay, and Lally was obliged to give up any idea of attacking Chingleput and to return to Pondicherry. He was, however, still without the funds to carry out his cherished scheme of besieging Madras, but at this crisis a ship laden with treasure reached him from Mauritius with a small but welcome reinforcement of 250 Europeans and 500 sepoys, while Lally himself and several of his officers advanced money for the expedition from their own purses. "Better," said Count d'Estaing, "Better to die storming the glacis of Madras than of hunger behind the walls of Pondicherry!"

DEFENCE OF FORT ST. GEORGE

Lally now again took the field with 2,000 European infantry, 300 cavalry, and 5,000 sepoys, and hoped to reach Madras before the middle of November; but he was delayed by heavy storms and bad roads, and it was December 12th before Lally appeared before Madras, occupying the town two days later.

"The Government of Madras had early realized that Lally was determined to lay siege to Fort St. George, and had accordingly made active preparations for defence. Provisions of all kinds were brought from the surrounding country and stored. Stringer Lawrence, with a sense of sound strategy, abandoned all the less important forts, and concentrated his forces on two vital points—Fort St. George and its barrier post, Chingleput. He recalled Captain Caillaud with all the 180 Europeans in garrison at Trichinopoly. Marching through the Tanjore country, they embarked at Negapatam, and landed at Madras on September 25th, 1758. Eleven days before a small reinforcement had arrived from England."* Some of Draper's Regiment, as we have seen, had already landed, and before Lally had altogether invested Fort St. George, Ensign Croley brought in his small European garrison from Poonamallee. The total number of European troops available for the defence of Fort St. George was consequently as under :—

Troop of Horse	3 officers	35	N.C.Os. and Men.
Royal Artillery	16 ,,	132	,, ,,
Company's Artillery	6 ,,	64	,, ,,
H.M.'s 79th or Draper's	16 ,,	195	,, ,,
Detachment of Marines	2 ,,	100	,, ,,
Company's 1st Battalion	23 ,,	625	,, ,,
Company's 2nd Battalion	23 ,,	575	,, ,,
Supernumeraries	5 ,,	32	,, ,,
	94	1,758†	

Besides these, there were the 1st and 2nd Battalions of Madras Native Infantry, numbering together 2,213.

* Forrest, Vol. II, p. 89.
† The above is Love's list (Vol. II, p. 540); Wilson (Vol. I, p. 103) adds the Madras sepoys, and makes the total of Madras Europeans 3 less.

At daybreak on December 14th the French entered the Black Town, the English picquets retiring to the fort, and the regiment of Lally then took up its quarters near the breach, the regiment of Lorraine and the regiment of India on the rising ground to the west, but behind buildings which screened them from fire from the walls of the fort.

Lally took up his residence in the Governor's country house, and his men, proceeding to plunder the town, got drunk, which being reported by spies to the defence, Colonel Draper proposed that a sally should be made, and offered to lead it. This was accepted, and at 8.30 a.m.* he marched out by the west gate with 600 men and 2 field guns, detaching Major Brereton of his regiment to protect his right flank. Their march was quite undetected, but the drummers with Draper's party began to beat the "Grenadiers' March," the men cheered, and the French, thus warned, drew up the regiments of Lorraine and India across the head of the street up which the English were advancing, placed four guns in position, and posted platoons in the cross lanes opening on to the main street. On the appearance of the head of the British column, the French opened fire and did some execution; but Draper, pushing on, wheeled round a corner and came upon the flank of the Lorraine regiment and India battalion. The British opened a fire of musketry and guns, whereupon the enemy, taken by surprise, fell into confusion, abandoned their guns, and took shelter in the houses lining the street.

Draper ordered his men to cease firing and to charge; "he even set the example himself and advanced; but was followed only by four brave fellows, two of whom were killed and the other two dangerously wounded. The Colonel had several balls through his coat, but was not wounded. He advanced, and exchanged a pistol with the French officer of artillery, who immediately surrendered, but the Colonel had the mortification to find that he had no men to carry off the guns."†

* Forrest accepts the French account, and says 11 p.m., which is obviously ncorrect (*vide* Lieutenant Smith's letter and Colonel Lawrence's Order).

† Forrest, Vol. II, p. 93.

The French soldiers, finding their assailants had ceased fire, now streamed back out of the houses, and a stiff contest ensued which lasted for twenty minutes, and then Draper, seeing that the French were being reinforced and fearing that his retreat would be cut off, abandoned the guns and gave the order to retire. This was not heard by the grenadiers of the Madras Battalion, who were hotly engaged in an enclosure, and eighty of these, " the prime men of the garrison," were taken prisoners.

Draper drew off, rejoined Brereton's detached party, and, after a nasty rear guard action, managed to regain the town.

The following account of the sally was written to Orme, the historian, in 1776 by Lieutenant Stephen Smith of the Madras Europeans :—

". . . I was then a lieutenant in the first company of Granadiers commanded by Captain Beaver with Lieutenant Elliot. Early in the morning of the 14th the two companies Granadiers paraded and we marched to the North Gate but did not goe out. The enemy were facing us, firing their musketry very briskly, but the glassey (glacis) covered us. Myself, and many more I make no dout, were looking, when a shot came in my direction, grounded on the top, and through the dust in my face, at the same time one of the men calling out with an oath I should not be kill'd that day. About 10 o'clock we were ordered back to the parade, were the remainder of troops for the sorty were drawn up. We fell in on the Right. The whole were served with a dram and biscuit. About 11 o'clock we marched out West Gate giving many joiful Cheers, the 1st Company in front and so on after us. The first street was clear till we came to the Cross Street were we halted a little, till the Count Destaing, mistaking us for Lally's regiment, rode up to us, but finding his mistake turned his horse about, but fell; when 2 of our Drumers were, as I imagined, going to run him through, when I stepped betwixt and saved him, and sent one of the men with him to Colonel Draper, when we were ordered down the Cross Street to the left, and in about 60 yards we met the Lorains, when a very brisk musketry commenced. Each stood their ground tho' very hot. After some little time 2 of our guns were up, six-pounders, when we sided to the right of the street to clear for the grape. After some time our Guns ceased, when Captain, now Colonel Charles Campbell, of 2nd Company Granadiers, ordered me to advance, when I replyed, ' You see we cant, Sir,' when he left me and in a few minutes the Lorrains mouved off, when some one turned and saw the street clear behind us, when we run off. I followed the men with my best speed, and they and self soon after got into a House were we remained near half an hour, when 2 or 3 of the enemy coming in that Street, our people beged me to goe out to them and surrender miself and them, witch I did out of compassion to the wounded, 9 in number, 3 or 4 of whom were badly wounded, miself a shott through my ribs. Captain Beaver headed the company though but was ill in health. Elliot was in the rear and wounded soon to the best of my Nowledge. I saw no other officer but Charles Campbell after turning to the left before the Action. . . ."

In a letter from Mr. Vansittart, dated Madras, December 15th, he wrote : " Colonel Draper made such a push as would astonish all who do not know him. . . . Captains Bilhock and Hume killed, Captain Pascall and Lieutenant Elliot wounded, thought mortally, 3 or 4 others taken. Men about 150 killed, wounded and taken. On the side of the enemy Count d'Estaing taken."

The loss in officers and men seems to have been for the most part among the Madras European Battalion : " Our loss was Major Polier mortally wounded ; Captain Pascall, shot through the body ; Captain Hume, mortally wounded and taken ; Captain-Lieutenant Bilhock, killed ; Lieutenant Elliot, shot through the body ; Lieutenant Smith, wounded and taken ; and Ensign Chase, mortally wounded and taken. Our loss of men was 103 taken, of which 19 were wounded, about 50 men left dead on the spot, and the same number came in wounded."*

The enemy's losses numbered 30 officers and 220 men ; Saubinet was among the slain.

* Cambridge, p. 145.

The following is an extract from Fort St. George orders of the day, dated 14th :—

"*Colonel Lawrence thanks officers and men for their behaviour this morning ; recommends to the soldiers a greater coolness and attention to the orders given them, as their repulse and misfortune has been entirely owing to that fault and not to any valour of the enemy.*"

The following day the besiegers commenced the construction of their batteries ; but their heavy guns had not yet been landed, and on the day of Draper's sally, a party under Lieutenant Airey from Chingleput captured on its way from Pondicherry the only mortar the French possessed ; while Captain Preston, commanding at Chingleput, endeavoured to intercept the escort taking to Pondicherry the prisoners whom Lally had captured from Draper's party, but unfortunately missed the escort during the night.

1759 On December 22nd the siege guns arrived on board the sloop *Harlem*, and at daybreak on January 2nd, 1759, the batteries opened fire. The British, however, had no idea of conducting an inactive defence ; on the night of the 16th a sortie was made by a party of volunteers under Ensign Croley ; on the night of the 19th Ensign Bonjour led out another ; on the afternoon of the 21st Captain Bannatyne, Town Major, conducted a reconnaissance ; on January 12th Major Brereton went out with 100 Europeans and 400 sepoys and captured two guns, but the result of this sally showing that the native commandants of sepoys were hardly equal to their responsibilities, Lieutenant Charles Todd of the Regiment was appointed to command them ; finally on January 17th a sortie was made by a party under Ensign Barnes, who was killed.

The siege had barely commenced when the Governor, Mr. Pigot, issued the following order :—" As soon as we have obliged the enemy to raise the siege, the Governor promises, in the name of the Company, to present the garrison with 50,000 rupees, which sum shall be divided among them within five days after the enemy's retreat."

On December 23rd the *Thames* ran the blockade successfully and came in with provisions and bringing also the news of the victory which Colonel Forde, who had been sent south by Clive from Bengal, had won at Condore; and on January 30th, 1759, the *Shaftesbury*, Indiaman, arrived with treasure, provisions and military stores and—best of all—news that she was one of a fleet, from which she had parted some three weeks earlier off Galle, conveying the remainder of Draper's Regiment.

Up to February 14th the fire on the defences of Fort St. George continued brisk and incessant and the trenches were advanced; but on the 16th the long-expected ships, with reinforcements from Europe and Bombay, appeared in the offing. That evening they anchored in the roads, and although a heavy fire was maintained all night from the batteries, early next morning the enemy set fire to the Company's powder mills at Egmore, abandoned their trenches and batteries and retreated to Pondicherry, leaving behind fifty-two guns and a large quantity of stores, besides forty-four sick and wounded men in their hospitals. By noon of the 17th the reinforcements, 600 men of the 79th Foot, were landed.

"The whole of our loss during the siege amounts to:—

Commissioned officers killed and dead of sickness ...	15
Commissioned officers wounded, some dangerously	14
	— 29
Non-commissioned officers and soldiers killed and died of sickness	257
Non-commissioned officers and soldiers wounded, some dangerously	182
Non-commissioned officers and soldiers taken prisoners	122
Non-commissioned officers and soldiers deserted ...	20
	— 581
Sepoys, officers and privates killed	105
Sepoys, officers and privates wounded	217
Sepoys, officers and privates deserted	440
	*— 762."

* Love, Vol. II, p. 552.

The casualties in the two battalions of the Madras European Regiment were :—

Killed ... 11 officers, 134 non-commissioned officers and men.
Wounded 10 ,, 82 ,, ,, ,, ,, ,,
Died ... 1 ,, 17 ,, ,, ,, ,, ,,
Prisoners 3 ,, 110 ,, ,, ,, ,, ,,

The names of the officers killed or died of wounds were Major Polier, Captains Hume, Monchanin, Bilhock, and Brooke; Lieutenants Robson, Little and Bates; Ensigns Barnes, Chase, Schomberg and Belton.

The siege had endured for fifty days, and although this was the most important event in the history of Southern India, and although, of the above-mentioned casualties, eighty per cent. in the case of the officers and sixty-three and a half per cent. in that of non-commissioned officers, rank and file were sustained by the Madras European Infantry Regiment, the defence remains uncommemorated by any honorary distinction upon the Colours. " Had Fort St. George fallen, the Fort of Trichinopoly, then our only remaining place of strength, could not have held out long unsupported and cut off from communication with the coast by the loss of our settlements at Fort St. David and Devicottah."*

The officers of the corps, who served during the siege under their old commander, Lawrence, were Major Polier, Captains Pascall, Hume, Charles Campbell, Monchanin, Brooke, Beaver, Richard Smith, Gurtler, Donald Campbell, de Beck, Greig and Black; Captain-Lieutenant Bilhock; Lieutenants Robson, Elliot, Little, Bates, Blair, Frischman and Todd; Ensigns Barnes, Cook, Chase, Croley, Bonjour, Schomberg and Belton. Lieutenant Vasserot commanded the small troop of cavalry.

" As in the siege of St. Thomé 85 years earlier, so in that of Fort St. George, the burial place of the fallen is unknown. The 272 Europeans who perished of wounds and sickness during the siege of 1758–59 are unmentioned in the Vestry Registers. . . . Wherever they were interred—and the likeliest spot is between the

* Wilson, Vol. I, p. 104.

Fort and the river bar—it is surprising that no monument was afterwards erected to their memory."*

Of the help afforded outside the walls by Major Caillaud and Captain Preston, the Madras authorities made acknowledgment as under in a letter of February 21st, 1759, to the Court of Directors :—
"An Army of Observation, consisting of about 50 Europeans from Chingleput, a considerable number of Seapoys from Trichinopoly, and some Country Horse, commanded first by Captain Preston and afterwards by Major Caillaud, jointly with Usoff Cawn, the Commandant of your Seapoys, were of great service during the Siege by drawing off a part of the attention of the Enemy, who four times sent considerable detachments against them, but were always repuls'd with loss."†

It is pleasant to find that the Governor did not forget the promise he had made to the garrison at the crisis of the siege, for in General Orders of February 20th he called for a return of the names of those entitled to share in the grant he had offered them, " solely as a mark of his regard, knowing they needed no spur to make them exert themselves against the common enemy."

During the operations before Madras, the French lost 700 Europeans by capture and death, left some wounded behind and took many away with them. Of the men of the Battalions of Lorraine, Lally and India who had marched from Chingleput to Madras, scarcely 2,000 returned, worn out, dispirited, in rags and all with their pay many months in arrears. Although the reinforcements brought out in the ships escorted by Admiral Pocock's squadron brought up the number of British soldiers to 1,500 effectives, yet, for want of transport of any description, the army under Lawrence was unable to move until March 6th, when, 200 more men of Draper's Regiment having joined, the force moved out towards Conjeveram where Lally was entrenched.

But while the opposing armies were actually in sight of one another, letters were received from Colonel Forde, who after his

* Love, Vol. II, p. 552.
† *Ibid.*, Vol. II, p. 559.

victory at Condore had marched to the siege of Masulipatam, despairing of success unless supported by men and money. The Council, however, feeling that their resources were not equal to keeping Lawrence's force in the field, suggested withdrawing it and sending 200 of his men to Forde. But Lawrence, while fully persuaded of the folly of attacking Masulipatam—a plan which had been adopted against his advice—was equally convinced of the impolicy of retreat. He accordingly proceeded to Madras on March 26th in order to try to dissuade the Council from this measure; he was successful, but while there the state of his health obliged him to relinquish the command on April 9th, and in that month he left for England, fully intending never again to return to India.

The command was then offered to Colonel Draper, but he was also ill and anxious to go home, and the command then devolved upon Major Brereton of the 79th, Major Caillaud succeeding to that of the Company's troops.

The two armies remained inactive for some days in front of one another, and Brereton then, hoping to bring the French to action, moved towards Wandewash and opened ground before that place. The French moved up to relieve it, and Brereton, being informed they had left only a small garrison in Conjeveram, made a forced march on the night of April 13th, reached Trivatore the next morning and, finding it deserted, destroyed the works. Continuing his march he arrived early on the 15th at Conjeveram and at once invested it. By 8 a.m. on the 16th the fortified pagoda seemed sufficiently battered to assault, and the grenadiers of the Madras European Regiment, led by Caillaud, stormed it and drove off the defenders. But while the party, having got inside the ravelin, was forming up for an attack on the gateway, a big gun, loaded to the muzzle with musket balls, was fired among them, eight men being killed and ten wounded. Of the officers of the Corps, Captains Stewart and Bannatyne, Lieutenant Robinson and Ensign Hurter were killed, Major Caillaud, Captain Vaughan, Lieutenant Brown, Ensigns Flint and Smith were wounded.

In his despatch on this action Major Brereton spoke very highly of Ensign Airey of the Regiment, who seems to have behaved well on more than one occasion. " . . I should think myself guilty of great injustice," he wrote, " if I did not inform you of those officers in your service who have so greatly distinguished themselves. Mr. Airey has done it twice since I have had the command of the Army; after Captain Preston had taken possession of Outramalore, he detached Mr. Airey with the Seapoys to lye in the village of Carangoly. The Garrison, which was more numerous in Seapoys than his Party besides Europeans, made a sally upon him and were driven back by him with a very considerable loss. When we stormed the Pagoda yesterday, he brought the Seapoys up to the Wall and climbed over it on to the opposite side to the Gateway, in short, upon every occasion no man can show more readiness or be more indefatigable than he is."

During the month of April an exchange of prisoners took place, and 100 men of the Corps, who were captured when Fort St. David surrendered, rejoined their regiment. In the latter end of June 200 recruits for the Madras European Corps arrived from England, while about this time the same number of European prisoners were received from Pondicherry, who had been exchanged for an equal number of Frenchmen released from Trichinopoly. Then, early in September the first party of the 84th Regiment— 300 men in three companies, under command of Major Robert Gordon—landed in Madras, and was immediately sent off to join the army with Brereton at Conjeveram.

Thus strengthened, Brereton was very anxious to endeavour to possess himself of Wandewash; the Madras Government at first agreed to this project, then later asked that its execution might be deferred; but finally, at Brereton's very earnest solicitation, he was permitted to advance, and on September 26th his force marched out of cantonments at a strength of 1,500 European infantry, 100 of the Madras Corps mounted and serving as dragoons, 80 Coffries, 2,500 sepoys, 700 native cavalry, and 10 field guns.

Trivatore surrendered to Brereton on the 27th, and he then pushed rapidly on to Wandewash, where he arrived on the 30th. He had very seriously underestimated the force there opposed to him, and at once attacked in the dark on three sides, hoping to carry both pettah and fort by a *coup de main*. Fighting went on all through the night, but the attack failed, though all the troops engaged behaved with signal gallantry, and in the morning of October 1st he retired in good order, having lost 12 officers and 195 other ranks in killed, wounded, and prisoners.

Of the Corps, Lieutenant Minns, Ensign Latour, and 30 non-commissioned officers and men were killed; Captain Greig, Lieutenants Whitman and Fitzpatrick were wounded; and Ensign Hamilton was taken prisoner.

The Madras Government was by no means pleased with the loss incurred in the operations which Major Brereton had been conducting, and came to the following resolution: "The Board have often times cautioned Major Brereton against attacking the enemy in strong posts, as our force is not sufficiently superior to admit of our running such risques, although we have no objection to meeting them on terms of equality, and the Board think it their duty on this occasion to enforce that point to his serious consideration.

"Ordered that a letter to Major Brereton be accordingly wrote and dispatched."

"To CHOLMONDELY BRERETON, ESQ.,
    Commander-in-Chief of the
        Land Forces of the Coast.

"SIR,

"The President has laid before us your letter to him of the 30th September, containing the account of the attack made that morning on the pettah of Wandiwash, and that our troops after having taken post there, were obliged to quit it again with the loss of 12 officers and 195 men killed, wounded and missing. We are extremely glad our loss is not greater, as we think our superiority over the enemy is not sufficient to attack them in Forts or strong Posts, although we have no objection to meeting them on terms of equality. So much caution we think it necessary again to recommend to you, and remain with great esteem.

(Signed) "GEORGE PIGOT
"AND COUNCIL."

Major Brereton was, however, to have no more opportunities of this kind, for on October 27th Colonel Eyre Coote reached Madras with the remaining companies of the 84th and assumed command of the army.

A few days later—on November 2nd—Major Caillaud sailed for Calcutta to take command of the troops in Bengal; he took with him 200 of the Madras Europeans and 9 officers, and at the same time 60 men of the Corps were sent to Masulipatam.

With these 200 men of the Regiment went the following officers:—Captains Hart and Blake; Lieutenants Blair, Hooper, Lang, Hamilton, and Bellingham; Ensigns Vaughan and Stables.

About the end of October, 170 men of the Regiment, the last of the prisoners remaining for exchange at Pondicherry, rejoined their corps, while the prisons at Trichinopoly had also been cleared of 670 French non-commissioned officers and men who had been captured during Lawrence's last campaign. Trichinopoly was now garrisoned by 250 of the Madras Europeans and 3,000 sepoys.

*The choice of operations had been left to Coote, who on November 21st assembled a Council of War, at which it was agreed that the distance by which the enemy's forces were now separated offered a reasonable chance of reducing the fort of Wandewash, and this it was determined to attempt. Two days later Captain Preston, of the Madras Regiment, went off with his own company, the Pioneers, and all the Horse that could be spared from Madras, to remain at Chingleput in readiness to proceed to Wandewash when called for.

* This account of the operations up to the Battle of Wandewash is wholly drawn from the author's *Life of Sir Eyre Coote*, p. 69 *et seq.*

With the view of puzzling the enemy, Coote, on the 25th, moved with his main body in the direction of Arcot, while Brereton with a strong detachment proceeded to Trivatore, which he assaulted and captured, the garrison, however, effecting their escape. On the next day, the 26th, Brereton arrived before the fort of Wandewash, and captured the pettah after but a slight resistance; and Coote then pushed on with his few mounted men to join Brereton, leaving Major Monson to follow with the main body. On arrival before Wandewash, Coote found that Brereton was erecting a battery for his two 18-pounders, and the construction was at once commenced of another for the guns which Preston should have brought up from Chingleput, but as these were not yet come up, the battery, when ready, was armed with 12-pounders. On the 29th Coote's whole force having arrived, the big guns opened against the south-east tower of the fort, which was soon silenced and a breach made; at noon the place was summoned, but Lieutenant Mahony,[*] who commanded, then refused, but on the afternoon of November 30th the fort was delivered up. "The garrison," writes the victor in his journal, "consisted of 5 subaltern officers, 63 private men, and between 800 and 900 sepoys. We found in the fort 49 pieces of cannon and a great quantity of ammunition. During the siege one officer of artillery was wounded and a sepoy, and a lascar's arm broke."

From Wandewash the British force marched on December 4th 35 miles to Carangoly, the town of which had already been seized by the Company's Grenadiers and some cavalry. On the 6th a battery of two 18-pounders opened against the north-west bastion of the fort, on the 7th another battery was ready, and later a howitzer was placed in position and approaches were opened; on the 10th Colonel O'Kennely, the commandant, surrendered with 3 officers, 96 Europeans of lower rank, 500 sepoys, and 9 guns. The

---

[*] Wilson, Vol. I, p. 137, draws attention to the number of French officers with Irish names taken during this campaign: Butler, Creagh, Inniskilling, Geohagan, Henegan, Heguerty, Kearney, Kelly, Kennedy, O'Donnel, O'Kennely, Mahony, Murphy, Plunkett, and Walsh; also two Scotch names—Macdonald and Macgregor.

British losses amounted to no more than four—two among the artillery, and two among the sepoys.

On December 12th the army under Coote received a welcome reinforcement of 180 Europeans, 160 native cavalry, and 1205 sepoys under Captain Moore; this was urgently needed by reason of the reports which reached Coote almost daily of the strength of the different French detachments, and of the efforts which these were making to oppose the English commander. Thus, under date of December 15th, we read in his journal:—" Received intelligence that 600 Patan Horse, part of Bussy's forces, was arrived at Arcot, and that he had with him 2,000 sepoys and 500 Arabs. Got account of 1,000 Mahrattas arriving at Arcot, and that 2,000 more were expected."

On December 18th heavy rain set in; the army, wrote its commander, was in a " dreadful situation," and on the 19th the troops moved into cantonments at Cauverypauk, on the north bank of the Palar River, with that river separating the two forces.

On the following day, Coote, who had had a sharp attack of fever, went into Madras, where he found the government disposed to indulge the Nawab of Arcot by reinforcing Trichinopoly in order to retake Seringham, which the French had captured late in November, and Uttatur. Coote, however, pointed out to the Council the error Lally had committed in sending out so many detachments, and the impropriety of diminishing the main army at a time when the French were collecting their whole force to risk the fate of the Carnatic in a general action. His arguments prevailed and he returned on the 27th to Cauverypauk.

1760 The two armies remained quietly in their respective camps during the early days of January, 1760; both were doing all they could to attract Innis Khan and his Mahrattas to their side; he, however, joined the French on January 8th with 3,000 Horse and many thousands of foot-men bent on the plunder of the English, and on the 9th the French army took the road to Trivatore.

The news that at this time reached Coote was alternately cheering and depressing; thus on January 4th a letter came from Captain

Joseph Smith of the Regiment at Trichinopoly, stating that he had intercepted a convoy from Uttatur and had captured a company of French grenadiers; the vicinity of the French to Wandewash made Coote anxious for the safety of that place; while the Madras Council were pressing him to bring the army nearer to Fort St. George.

On January 12th Lally, by a rapid night march, appeared before Conjeveram, where he hoped to find abundance of stores; he plundered the town and carried off 2,000 head of cattle, but having no guns with him he could effect nothing against the fort, ably defended by Lieutenant Chisholm. Coote, hearing of Lally's move, marched to meet him, reaching Conjeveram early on the 13th to find the French had gone, Bussy being left to observe the English while Lally had marched against Wandewash, the garrison of which was, however, on the alert. Lally's movements did not pass unnoticed and on the 15th the army had passed the river and by the 17th had taken up a position at Uttramalur, midway between Wandewash and Chingleput. Here Coote learnt that the enemy had effected the capture of the pettah at Wandewash with but small loss. Hearing of the approach of the English, Lally directed Bussy to join him at once with every man and gun he could gather.

What follows is taken from Colonel Coote's Journal:—

"Monday, January 21st.—Went out from Outramalore with all the cavalry to reconnoitre the enemy. Having received a letter from Captain Sherlock that they had made a breach, I was determined to engage them the next morning, therefore sent the Major of Brigade back to the army with the following orders: 'The tents of the line, except six per company and the bell tents are to be struck immediately and packed up in order to be sent to Carangolly under an escort of one company of sepoys, and are to move off at General Beating. The *General* to beat at 2 in the afternoon and the *Assembly* half an hour after, and the whole to march off at 3 in order to join the Colonel at Trimborough. It is recommended to the officers to keep with them only what baggage is absolutely necessary.'

"After the arrival of the army gave out the following orders:—

"'Trimborough Village, 7 o'clock in the evening.

"'The army to march off to-morrow morning at 6 o'clock by the left upon the Taps beating. . . . It is to form and be ready to march immediately after. All the cavalry and five companies of sepoys to form the van of the army, except 200 Black Horse, who, together with three companies of sepoys, are to cover the baggage in the rear. The army to observe the orders given out the 27th December which were :—that the first line consist of Colonel Draper's Regiment on the right, Colonel Coote's on the left, and the Company's in the centre. The artillery to be divided as follows :—Four pieces on the right, four on the left, and two pieces between each interval, making in all twelve in the first line. The second line to consist of the grenadiers of Colonel Draper's, Colonel Coote's and the Company's, with one piece of cannon on each flank, who are to form 200 paces in rear of the first line ; an 8-inch Howitz to be between the two lines. Major Brereton to command the right of the first line, Major William Gordon the left and Major Robert Gordon the centre, Major Monson to command the second line. The cavalry to be divided into five squadrons, the European* to make the centre squadron. . . . When the line forms, the cavalry will have orders to form about fifty paces in the rear of the second line, leaving a proper interval between each squadron. At the same time the five companies of sepoys that supported the cavalry are to form upon the right of Colonel Draper's Regiment, and the five companies that were in the rear of the line of march to form on the left of Colonel Coote's Regiment. Five companies who were upon the left flank in the line of march are to form in the following manner : two on the right of the second line and two on the left, one in the rear with the cavalry. The whole army, as well European as black, are to have a green branch of the Tamarind tree fixed in their hats and turbans, likewise upon the tops of the Colours in order to distinguish them from the enemy. The commanding officers of corps are to take particular care that their respective corps are properly told off, and that the men know their right and left-hand men and leaders. They are to

* This was only 80 strong, 35 men drafted from the Madras European infantry battalions, probably under Lieutenant Vasserot, and a troop of 45 foreign deserters under Captain de Beck.

be cautioned not to give their fire till they are ordered by their respective officers.'"

At sunrise on January 22nd, 1760, the army marched to the south side of the hill of Wandewash, while Coote moved forward with the advance guard of 200 horse and two companies of sepoys to reconnoitre the enemy's position. This was what he saw: a hard, dry, wide plain, dotted with trees, admirably suited for the movements of cavalry, an arm in which Lally was strong while Coote was weak. On the north the plain was fringed by the rocky, serrated peaks of the low range known as Wandewash Hill, the drainage from which was caught in several tanks of varying size which occupied the centre of the low ground. To the right front was a village, and in the middle distance the fort of Wandewash with its pettah on three sides. To the east of it was the camp of the last army of French-India, from which the men were hurrying to take up their ground and fight out the question as to which, to England or to France, was to belong the Empire of India.

At sight of Coote's party some of the Mahratta Horse issued from camp, but the English brought up two guns, a 12 and a 6-pounder, and caused the enemy cavalry to retire precipitately, and the commander then sent back orders to his main body, some three-quarters of a mile in rear, to form in line of battle but not for the present to move forward. After a while Coote came back and led his army to the front, arriving about 9 a.m. at the tank which his advanced troops were holding, some two miles from Lally's camp.

The following was the disposition of the enemy: his army was drawn up in a single line, the regiment of Lally on the left, its left thrown rather forward and resting on a tank; in the centre was the battalion of India; on the right the regiment of Lorraine; further to the right was the whole of Lally's cavalry; in the battalion intervals were the guns; and in rear were the regiments of French sepoys.

Having watched the enemy for some little time and seeing no disposition on the part of the French to attack, Coote now moved his army to the right in order to gain for that flank the protection afforded by the hills three miles distant; this movement caused Lally to alter his dispositions, and while still keeping his left on the tank and entrenchment held by his marines and sailors, he wheeled forward his right so as to maintain a line parallel to that of the British. An artillery duel had begun and was still in progress, and there was skirmishing with Lally's Mahratta Horse.

It was now midday; the French made a short advance and Coote's regiments marched joyously to meet the foe; the cannonade became very sharp; the French hussars, attacking the English flank and rear, were smitten in flank by guns and musketry and charged by Vasserot, when they fled back to the shelter of their own lines.

The Lorraine Regiment charged forward against the 84th "resolved to break us, being as they said a raw young regiment," so wrote Major William Gordon, "but we had not fired above 4 rounds when they went to the right about in the utmost confusion." At this moment a shot from one of the British guns blew up a tumbril of ammunition near the tank, killing many of the French and throwing the enemy into the utmost confusion. The European regiments of the rival Companies were contending fiercely in the centre, and, the whole line now advancing at the charge, the enemy's entrenchment was stormed and occupied, and from here the English opened so hot a musketry fire on the guns that the artillerymen abandoned them. The Marquis de Bussy, coming up at this crisis of the battle, endeavoured to retake the position and restore the fight with the regiment of Lally, but his horse was shot under him and he was taken prisoner, his men leaving him and retreating.

Major Monson now brought up the second line and about 2 p.m. the whole of Lally's army gave way, his sepoys refusing to move forward, while his Mahratta allies left the field when they saw how things were going; and only the devotion of the French hussars, who covered the retreat, saved the army from annihilation.

The French carried off three small guns but they left on the field twenty-two of varying calibres; besides Bussy, thirteen officers were captured and the French admitted a loss of 800 killed and wounded, of the former 200 being buried on the field by the English, who took 200 wounded and 40 unwounded prisoners.

The loss of the army under Coote was almost wholly confined to the European troops of whom 53 were killed and 139 wounded, the casualties in the Madras Regiment being Ensign Evans and 18 privates killed, Cornet Kuhn and 29 privates wounded.*

"During the whole engagement," wrote Coote in his despatch, "and ever since I have had the honour of commanding the army, the officers and men have shown the greatest spirit."

One may imagine with what deep interest the garrison of the fort of Wandewash must have followed so much as could be seen from its walls of the course of the action. There is in existence a journal† kept during the siege by Cotsford, a young officer of Engineers. On January 22nd we find the entry: "About 7 this morning a great fire of cannon was heard to the westward of the Hill, which we may reasonably expect to be the Army coming to our relief"; adding, with a rare prescience: "Then followed the Battle which gave us India!"

* These are Coote's figures; Wilson's (Vol. I, p. 133) are different.
† Orme MSS., 63-10, p. 81.

CHAPTER VI

1760–1767.

SIEGE AND CAPTURE OF PONDICHERRY—COLONEL JOSEPH SMITH'S OPERATIONS.

1760 THE news of the victory at Wandewash reached Madras by one of the English spies on the morning after the battle, and later in the day another messenger arrived bringing with him a couple of lines written on the field by Coote himself announcing his success. Eyewitnesses soon after reached Fort St. George giving details of the action, and the joy evinced by the inhabitants of Madras on receiving intelligence of the victory is said to have equalled that felt at Calcutta when the tidings of Plassey reached that place.

It has been stated that "it is more than probable that had the English immediately fallen upon Pondicherry, they would have carried that place in eight days." It was not, however, then known to Coote that the place was very short of supplies, while though the French army had been defeated it was in no sense annihilated, and Coote no doubt considered it best to seize one by one the smaller posts held by the French, trusting that Pondicherry would fall when he had cut off all the sources whence it drew its supplies.

On the day of the battle Lally fell back on Chittapet, and on the 23rd, without reinforcing the garrison of this place, he retired to Gingee.

Coote's cavalry was too few in number and too fatigued to pursue the French very vigorously, but on the 23rd the following dispositions were made and orders given. Two bodies of horse were sent out to harass the enemy; Captain Wood, of the Madras Europeans, commanding at Cauverypauk, was ordered to invest Arcot, and all the men who had been left sick at Conjeveram were directed to join him; the authorities at Madras were asked to send to Conjeveram all men of the 79th and 84th who had been discharged from hospital, together with the guns and stores needed for the siege of Arcot; the baggage which had remained in rear was ordered up to the army; and on the 26th Vasserot was sent off with 1,000 horse and three companies of sepoys to ravage the country between Alamparva and Pondicherry.

Colonel Coote was greatly concerned about the condition of the wounded in the late battle; from the outset of the campaign the medical arrangements had caused him great anxiety, and already in December he had urged the appointment of a surgeon-general to the staff of his army; and in consequence of the representations now made, a Mr. Briggs was appointed surgeon-general, and was placed in medical charge of the King's and Company's services.

Learning of the weakness of the garrison of Chittapet, it was decided to reduce this place before attempting anything against Arcot, and on the 26th a force moved thither from Wandewash, Chittapet surrendering three days later.

News now came in from Vasserot that he had raided up to within 8 miles of Pondicherry, had burnt 24 villages and captured 4,000 head of cattle; and from Captain Wood that he had taken possession of the *pettah* of Arcot, driving out the native auxiliaries who were holding it for the French. On the 31st the army marched to Arnee, where Captain Stephen Smith, of the Madras Europeans, who had been detached to try to cut off some of the enemy, came in bringing 10 captured Frenchmen, 50 sepoys, and 2 brass field-pieces. Part of the army under Major Monson was now directed to march on and summon the fort of Timmery, which surrendered on February 1st, while Coote moved on to Arcot, where he arrived on the 2nd.

The fortifications of this place had been greatly improved and added to since its defence by Clive in 1752. The English had done something, as had also the French; the ditch had been deepened and a glacis and covered way carried all round; from the centre of the north face projected a strong ravelin carrying six guns; in the interior the walls had been strengthened and raised; the towers or bastions at each angle mounted three guns, and each of the others along the faces one. "Began," wrote Coote in his diary, "to erect batteries against the fort—viz., one of five 18-pounders against the curtain between the north-west corner tower of the gateway, one of two 18- and one 24-pounder against the tower and curtain west of the south-west corner tower, and one of one 12-pounder against the north gate to enfilade the west front."

Fire was opened from all these batteries on the 5th, on the 6th and 7th the approaches were advanced, and by the 9th the walls were breached in two places, whereupon the garrison surrendered; but it seems likely that the place might well have held out longer had the commandant only realized the straits to which the attacking force was reduced. Shells were sent from Madras unaccompanied by gunpowder, those sent were unsuited for siege guns, while the stock of ammunition in camp became so low that it seemed likely to be exhausted before the breaches were practicable.

Coote placed Captain John Wood, of the Madras Regiment, in command of Arcot, and this appointment was questioned by Mr. Pigot, the Governor of Madras, who demanded that the post should be given to Captain Cheshyre, of the 79th; Coote, however, stood his ground, and, on the matter being pressed by Pigot, threatened to resign if any such unwarrantable interference were repeated—and Captain Wood retained the command of Arcot!

The news of the victory of the English at Wandewash reached Captain Joseph Smith, of the Regiment, at Trichinopoly on January 30th, while at the same time Lally sent peremptory orders to the French at Seringham to evacuate that place and join him as soon as possible. This movement did not escape Smith's notice. "As I had certain intelligence," he wrote in a letter of February 18th, "of the enemy's intention to abandon Seringham, I deferred sending my escort till their business was over, and as they had again employed a partizan named Hussein Cawn to give disturbance to our frontiers, and who was in Totcum fort with 400 men, I thought it best immediately to drive this rabble out of the dependent countries. . . . I therefore ordered Lieutenant Horn with a considerable detachment to march and reduce the forts of Catallum and Totcum; the first was abandoned, at the second the enemy obliged us to raise batteries, the appearance of which, together with some Cohorn shells thrown into the fort, induced them to abandon it in the night."

Those two small forts were the only posts which then remained in the possession of the enemy, and with their capture the neighbourhood of Trichinopoly was, for the first time, wholly freed from the presence of the French.

The army had not restored its equipment sufficiently to be in condition to move from Arcot until February 20th, and even then three heavy guns, the carriages of which had been broken, could not be repaired in time and had to be left behind. Of the start Coote records in his diary:—"February 20th: Marched and encamped near Timmery. . . . Detached Captain S. Smith with 500 sepoys and 100 Black Horse to take Trinomally with orders to join me at Chittaput . . . 23rd: near Chittaput received a letter from Captain Smith that he had taken possession of the *pettah* of Trinomally, but that the garrison seemed determined to hold out, upon which I detached the Volunteers of France,* consisting of 50 men and two 12-pounders, to join him."

On February 29th the army reached Tindavanum, and Colonel Coote went forward with an escort to reconnoitre the rock fortress of Permacoil, coming under a heavy fire from the walls. The *pettah* was captured by Ensign Carty and a company of sepoys, losing one sepoy killed, and having three of the Volunteers and nine sepoys wounded. Four guns were here found, but they had been spiked and their carriages set on fire. The fort itself was on so high a hill

* Some eighteen months previously all deserters from the enemy had been formed into a special company under officers of their nation or speaking their language; the first officers of this company were Captain de Monchanin, Ensigns Faizan, Bonjour, and Villeret. Later a special body called "Volunteers" was raised by Coote from this company under Sergeant, later Ensign, Rudolph Marchand.

that the British guns could not be sufficiently elevated to reach it with their fire, so Coote decided to storm. Accordingly, at eight on the night of March 2nd, having secured two guides, he sent two companies of sepoys to mount the hill by a little known track and seize a pagoda near a tank just under the fort ; these were followed by a party carrying ladders, gabions, and fascines, and as soon as all were in position a number of the grenadiers of the 84th, with a company of sepoys, were ordered to make a false attack on the main gate.

Coote himself joined the assaulting party and hoped to have carried the fort by escalade, but the ladders were found to be too short. The attackers, however, held on all night, longer ladders were made ready, and the commander was preparing to storm, when the commandant expressed a desire to treat. The negotiations were, however, fruitless and a 6-pounder was with infinite difficulty brought up and opened on the gate and parapet, and then at last on the 5th the fort surrendered with 20 guns and 150 Europeans and natives under a Colonel O'Kennedy.

"I have the pleasure to acquaint you that Permacoil surrendered to me last night," wrote Colonel Coote to the Madras Government. " I had Ensign Blakeney killed and three Europeans, I was wounded myself and Captain Adams, my aid de camp, Ensign Carty, 12 Europeans and one Volunteer ; of the sepoys one subedar, two jemadars and 40 killed and nearly 70 wounded."

On March 7th Coote, taking the whole of his cavalry and four companies of sepoys, moved towards Pondicherry to reconnoitre, but after proceeding for some ten miles he left the infantry behind and pushed on another ten miles to the outskirts of the town. Here three squadrons of the enemy's Horse made their appearance on the side of the Red Hill, but these were driven back by the mounted men under Captain de Beck.

The following is Orme's description of the ground about Pondicherry :—

" A large collection of sand-hills, of which the whole together is called the Red Hill, rises about half a mile from the seashore and a mile and a half to the north of the town; they extend four miles to the west and the last hill, where they cease on this side, is called Perimbé; across from north to south they extend two miles and have passable dales between; directly opposite to the side of Perimbé stands the fort of Villenore, a strong outpost, situated near the north bank of the river of Ariancopang, which falls into the sea about 500 yards from the wall of Pondicherry, and in its course from Villenore forms a curve to the south. The Red Hill, on the other side of the plain, recedes to the north-east from Perimbé to its end towards the sea. So that the interval between Villenore and Perimbé is the narrowest part of the plain between the river and the Red Hill, being here scarcely more than a mile, whereas farther back it is three. The plain as far as the bound-hedge was occupied by country houses, enclosures, avenues and arable land."*

On the 9th, having moved his army forward, Coote marched at daylight to scan the northern defences, approaching them slowly so as to draw fire and cause the defenders to disclose the positions of their batteries, but without result. On this day Major Monson was detached with a considerable force to invest Alamparva which surrendered on the 12th, and on April 5th the same officer effected the capture of Karical, 70 miles to the south of Pondicherry. On April 17th Valdore, nine miles north-north-west of Pondicherry also fell to the English, and before the month was out Trivady, Cuddalore and Fort St. David were all in our hands. On April 25th Admiral Cornish announced his arrival at Cuddalore with his squadron to co-operate with the army in the reduction of Pondicherry.

Early in May the French garrison of Pondicherry had retired within the " bound-hedge," a thick cactus fence encircling Pondicherry on the landward side and strengthened by four redoubts at regular intervals; and Coote, having received from England a small but welcome draft of nearly 200 artillery men, was hoping to be able actively to prosecute the siege, when news of a disquieting character reached him. This was to the effect that Lally had concluded an alliance with Hyder Ali and that the Mysore chief

* Orme, Vol. III, p. 610.

was to bring 3,000 horse and 5,000 foot into the field to the assistance of the French. It was for Coote an anxious time, but he remained undismayed; the season promised to be a sickly one, the army had been greatly tried, many men were in hospital, many had died; but the commander kept up the spirits of his men by constantly beating up the enemy's outposts, cutting off stragglers, making captures, and preventing supplies, urgently needed by the garrison, from being swept into Pondicherry from the surrounding country. Admirable work was done in this way by Ensign Turner of the Company's service.

About this time—in June, 1760, " Government with a view of improving the discipline of their European Infantry, which up to that time had been commanded by captains, appointed a field officer to each battalion. The officers selected were Captain Joseph Smith, who had become senior officer of the Company's troops on the departure of Major Caillaud, and Captain Achilles Preston, both of whom were promoted to the rank of major."*

For some weeks nothing of any consequence transpired except that the communications of Pondicherry, both by land and sea, became daily more and more constricted; until, on July 17th, Coote, having heard that the Mysore reinforcements, already received by Lally, were likely shortly to be further augmented, decided to adopt more active measures.

During the early part of the 17th Major Monson with a strong detachment took possession of Perambeck; the rest of the army followed in the afternoon, and a company of grenadiers with a gun and six companies of sepoys occupied the *pettah* of Villenore Fort; later a 13-inch mortar was sent down and preparations made to erect batteries against the fort. Then follows in Coote's diary the entry :—" 18th July.—Threw up a redoubt leading into the village of Villenore, and another about half a mile to the front of our right on the Pondicherry road. Received intelligence that Major Moore† had had an engagement with the Mysoreans, which ended to his disadvantage."

* Wilson, Vol. I, p. 141.
† Of the 79th Foot.

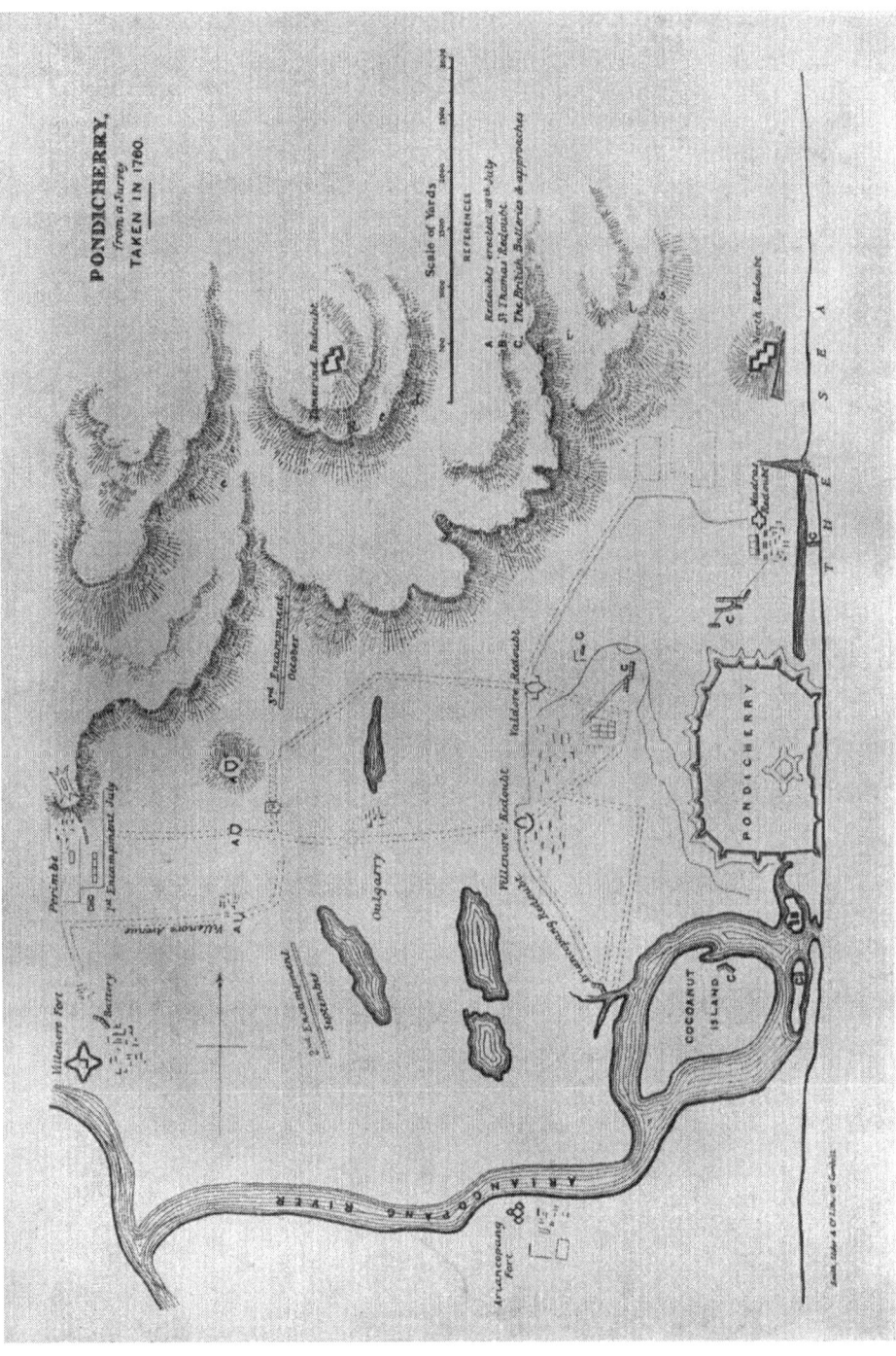

What had happened was that Coote had detached under Major Moore a force of cavalry and infantry to intercept a body of Mysore troops commanded by one Mukdoom Ali, which was escorting a convoy of provisions into Pondicherry. Moore's force was met on July 17th near Trivady by Mukdoom Ali's troops and completely routed; the native horse and foot were entirely dispersed, while the Europeans escaped into Trivady having suffered many casualties.

In the early days of the siege the investing army was thus distributed: the left rested on the foot of the hill of Perimbé, the right extending 1,500 yards across the plain towards Villenore; to the right and centre of this position two elevated roads led to Pondicherry from Trichinopoly and Tanjore. Across these two roads Coote had thrown up entrenchments, and in line with them a field work mounting three guns was constructed on a small detached hill in front of the left of the line; the plain between the right of the British position and Villenore was open, but it was secured by the detachment holding the villages near that fort and the party engaged in bombarding it.

When on July 20th fire was opened against Villenore, the enemy, considering no doubt that the garrison was likely to be hard pressed, marched out in force to endeavour to raise the siege. Upon this Coote reinforced his troops in Villenore village with infantry and guns, got the whole army under arms, redoubled the fire of his batteries, and sent his men forward to storm. The fort was triangular, of solid masonry, surrounded by a ditch with covered way and glacis; the fortifications were strong and laid out after the modern style of those days. When, however, the storming party got into the covered way the garrison at Villenore at once surrendered, and the batteries were then turned upon the relieving party of the enemy, who fell back under the guns of the Ariancopang Redoubt.

From this date Lally probably realized that the net was being drawn more closely round him, while the ardour of his allies was cooling owing to the scarcity of supplies and the growing conviction that they had espoused a losing cause; and while Coote had hitherto been hardly strong enough actually to besiege Pondicherry, he had by this established a very effective blockade, and in all affairs of outposts his troops had proved their superiority.

On August 13th the Mysore troops left the French camp, and while passing near the British lines they were severely handled by a party under Lieutenant Kirker of the Madras Europeans, consisting of 30 of the Corps, 400 sepoys, and 100 Horse, 60 of the enemy being killed and several prisoners, much baggage and cattle being captured; on the 14th drafts to the number of 600 arrived for Draper's and Coote's regiments; on the 30th the Admiral landed 422 marines and placed them at Coote's disposal; while finally on September 2nd a wing of the 89th Foot, Colonel Morris's Highlanders, joined under Major Hector Munro.

Coote now felt himself sufficiently strong to prosecute the siege more actively, and on the evening of September 2nd he issued orders for the investment of the redoubt of Ariancopang, but these orders were later cancelled. Lally had received information about Coote's plans, but had heard nothing of their being countermanded, so he now resolved to make a determined effort to hurl back the besieging army, and arranged for a sortie from his works in three columns, to surprise the Perimbé redoubt, and its detached post known as the Tamarind redoubt, and also the fortified garden house in the British centre; another force, advancing from the Ariancopang direction, was to cross the river behind the English camp and fall upon its rear. The French right attack succeeded, the enemy penetrating into the redoubt, carrying off a brass 3-pounder and setting the battery on fire; the Tamarind redoubt was also assailed, but held out gallantly. The detached column lost its way and never came into action at all, but in the centre the fighting was very severe, "the French never fought better," and Coote himself brought down reinforcements to the garden house and led a vigorous counter-attack. The French fell back, having lost between 20 and 30 Europeans killed, chiefly of the Regiment of Lally, while 5 prisoners were taken, one of them being M. d'Auteuil, who had commanded the French at Amboor in 1749, and had surrendered to Clive at Volconda.

On the day following this success letters were received from home granting the rank of Colonel to Coote and Monson, but dating that of Monson the earlier, whereby Coote was superseded, and he accordingly left the Army before Pondicherry and withdrew to Madras. Monson then, burning to distinguish himself, decided to make an attack by night upon four separate redoubts held by the enemy—the Madras redoubt on the north, the Valdore and Villenore on the west, and the Ariancopang to the south—all of which were strongly fortified and well garrisoned. He made up two strong columns of attack, and with the second were 800 men of the Madras European Regiment; this column was led by Major Joseph Smith, of the Corps, and was to carry the village of Oulgaret and then attack the Villenore redoubt. The advance of this column was early detected on arrival at a village in front of Oulgaret, which was held in strength; the grenadiers, however, led by, amongst others, Ensign Cosby, cleared the village with the bayonet, driving out the garrison composed of Lally's and the Lorraine regiment, and taking 100 prisoners and 10 guns. The defenders then fell back and drew up in front of the Villenore redoubt, but, being again assailed by Smith and his men, they made no attempt to reinforce the garrison, and retired, accompanied by the defenders of the redoubt, to the main works.

In the meantime the other column, led by Monson in person, had captured the Valdore redoubt, but with considerable loss, Monson himself being badly wounded, and having to resign the command to Coote, who was urgently pressed by the Madras authorities to resume it. He was back again with the army on September 20th, and at once took the necessary steps to secure the gorges of the three captured redoubts.

On the 23rd a piece of rising ground to the north of the town and opposite the Madras redoubt was fortified and occupied, and on the 27th Coote approached Ariancopang with his usual escort, meaning merely to reconnoitre it; but the garrison was seized with a panic and abandoned the work, which was at once taken possession of by a small body of Madras Europeans and some sepoys under

Cosby. Two days later the enemy attempted to recover it, but were repulsed, and Cosby held this post throughout the siege.

It was now noticed that the French were strengthening their posts to the north, so on October 1st Coote took three companies of sepoys in that direction, drove in the enemy, and captured and occupied the Madras redoubt. The French, however, returned in strength at midnight and retook it, Ensign MacMahon being killed, when the commandant of sepoys, a Dane, abandoned the post. A subadar, named Coven Naik, then assumed command, rallied his men, led them back to the assault and retook the redoubt, causing the French 54 casualties. The capture of this work completed the investment of Pondicherry, from the sea on the north, all round on the land side, to the Ariancopang River on the south-west, between which and the seashore to the south there remained an opening, secured by a redoubt called St. Thomas's, on a small sandy island in the river about 500 yards due south of the main defences.

At midnight on December 8th the newly-erected English batteries opened fire; one to the north, at about 1,500 yards, enfiladed the east face of the works; another, of two 24-pounders and three mortars, was situated to the west, and bore upon the north-west angle; then of two others to the south, one, on the edge of the large island formed by the river, fired on the south-west angle of the fort and on St. Thomas's redoubt, while the other fired from another island in the same direction. On the 25th another battery, armed with eight heavy guns and two mortars, opened fire, and now intelligence came from within the beleaguered town that there was no more than eight days' supplies in the magazines, and that Lally was ill and harassed by intrigue and disaffection.

1761 On the night of January 1st, 1761, a sudden and violent storm arose, and brought something of a respite to the besieged; it endured for several hours, and was responsible for much damage. The batteries of the besiegers were almost ruined and many men were killed, several ships of the British Fleet ran ashore and others were blown out to sea, the country round was inundated, much of the powder in the lines was ruined, tents and huts overturned, and the army very much scattered. But happily the enemy were unable to take advantage of the misfortunes of the English.

Coote acted under this disaster with commendable decision; he ordered ships up to Pondicherry from all parts of the coast to replace those sunk, ashore, or dismasted; he wrote to Madras for fresh supplies of ordnance stores; he sent out native boats to help the storm-beaten vessels; and he collected supplies of food for the crews of the three war-ships which had run ashore.

Further, as he wrote in his diary, " thinking it necessary at this critical time to push everything to the utmost against the enemy, I went this night " (on January 5th) " to attack St. Thomas' Redoubt, a place of great consequence to the enemy. Between 11 and 12 we took it," but the garrison left there—170 strong—was surprised at daylight on the 6th, and the post reverted to the French, who, however, immediately sent back the prisoners they had taken, being unable to feed them.

On the 10th Coote's aide-de-camp, Lieutenant Duespe, was killed by a cannon shot, fired by some misunderstanding as he was receiving a flag of truce.

On January 12th a large battery named the Hanover Battery opened against the west face of the works; on the next night 700 Europeans, taken from every corps in the besieging force, assembled, and before daylight on the 14th had not only constructed a battery within 500 yards of the town, but two long parallels; and in the course of this day the Hanover Battery succeeded in silencing those opposed to it. Another work had been marked out near the north side and even closer to the walls, but about 6 p.m. on the 15th Lieutenant-Colonel Durre, of the Artillery, Père Louvoir, the head of the Jesuits, and three other civilian officials came out of the lines to open negotiations, and on the same day the articles of capitulation were signed.

Between seven and eight o'clock on the morning of January 16th the Grenadiers of the 79th and 84th occupied the main gates, and in the afternoon the whole garrison paraded—the regiments of Lorraine and Lally, the India battalion, the Marines, the Volunteers of Bourbon, the King's and the French East India Company's artillery—and laid down their arms in the Citadel. No more than 1,100 French soldiers appeared under arms, and these were worn down from famine, fatigue, wounds, and disease, the most impaired and feeble being the grenadiers of the regiments of Lorraine and Lally, the finest body of French troops that had ever landed in India, and whose conduct on all occasions had been distinguished by the most devoted gallantry.

On the following day the white flag with the golden lilies fluttered down from the flagstaff and the English colours were hoisted in its place, their appearance being saluted with a thousand rounds from the guns.

With Pondicherry there surrendered Lieutenant-General Count de Lally, 3 brigadiers, 169 subordinate officers and 1,264 other ranks, while the captures included 567 guns, brass and iron, 17 howitzers, 96 mortars, vast stores of military supplies and 12,750 stand of arms.

During the siege the British casualties amounted to 32 officers and 500 non-commissioned officers and men killed and wounded.

The forts of Gingee and Thiaghur still held out, but the former was attacked by Captain Stephen Smith with a detachment of Europeans from the Regiment and a large body of sepoys, and was taken after but a slight resistance on April 5th; on the same date, after a forty-five days' bombardment, the strong fort of Thiaghur surrendered to a force under Major Achilles Preston, who had with him a detachment of his own regiment, a large body of artillerymen, a strong party of sepoys and some native horse; and with these captures the French flag had ceased to wave over any strong place in Coromandel.

Thus, after a war of nearly fifteen years' duration, in every action or affair of which the Madras European Regiment, or some portion of it, had been engaged, the important fortress of Trichinopoly remained in British possession, French commerce and power in India were wholly destroyed, and the policy and ambitious projects of Dupleix and Lally were altogether frustrated.

The fortifications of Pondicherry were now razed to the ground, and arrangements for the reduction of the army were put in hand; the Highlanders were sent to Madras, the Marines returned to their ships, the Bombay troops prepared to embark for Bombay, and on February 3rd the rest of the army went into cantonments at Cuddalore. On the 9th Colonel Coote sailed from Madras to take up at Calcutta the command in Bengal to which he had originally been appointed, leaving his regiment to follow as transport could be provided, and on the same day Lally left India for Europe.

"On October 3rd, 1761, Lawrence again took his seat in the Madras Council, having returned to India in the *Fox* packet, yielding, apparently, to the solicitations of the Directors. . . . He was again made Commander-in-Chief of all the Company's forces in India, and, to ensure that he should not be superseded in the field by any colonel of King's troops, he received the commission of major-general in the East Indies from the King. . . . His salary was fixed at £1,500 a year, and it was ordered that in the event of his visiting Bengal or any other place where there was a Council he was to be granted a seat on the Council Board. Hitherto no personal staff had been granted to the senior military officer, except in the field. Lawrence was now granted an aide-de-camp and a brigade-major. From this time his work was wholly administrative. The power of the French in India had been broken; Caillaud, Carnac, Coote and Adams were dealing effectively with the situation in Bengal."*

1762 In June, 1762, it became known in Madras that England had declared war against Spain and preparations were made to send an expedition against Manilla. The force detailed left Madras on August 1st, but it does not appear to have contained any detachment of the Madras European Regiment, and for that reason no account of the expedition will here be given. The European infantry of the force employed was wholly drawn from the 79th Foot, and the only connection the Madras European Regiment had with

* Biddulph, pp. 109, 110.

it was that Captain Wood, of the Corps, accompanied the expedition in command of the Company's troops, composed of 650 sepoys made up of details from the seven battalions of sepoys which were at that time in existence.

"Shortly after the expedition sailed for Manilla, orders were issued directing the formation of the whole of the Company's European infantry into one battalion of thirteen companies, viz., two companies of grenadiers, nine battalion companies, one company of foreigners, and one of coffrees, each company to consist of 6 sergeants, 6 corporals, 3 drummers and 85 privates."* At this time there were already a large number of Frenchmen in the service of the Madras Government and it was considered that their presence constituted something of a danger; these were therefore later sent to Bengal under command of Ensign Claud Martin who had deserted to the English during the siege of Pondicherry.

Southern India enjoyed a season of general tranquillity until **1763** August, 1763, when a force of some 9,900 men was assembled at Trichinopoly under Colonel Monson, 79th, to march on Madura. The occasion for the employment of troops arose in this way. One Mahomed Yusaf, who had served as commandant of sepoys under Clive, Caillaud and Preston, had been appointed in 1761 Governor of Madura and Tinnevelly by the Nawab of the Carnatic. Before long it became evident that he was aiming at independence, for he collected arms and men, invaded Travancore territory at the end of 1762 and proclaimed himself on the side of the French, taking into his service a small corps of 200 Europeans under a French officer. General Lawrence, on being consulted, advised immediate action whereupon the following force was assembled:—

European Cavalry	about 163
Artillery (10 guns and 2 howitzers)	,, 50
European Infantry	,, 600
Coffrees or Topasses	,, 100
5 Battalions of sepoys	,, 5,000
Nawab's Infantry	,, 2,000
Nawab's Horse	,, 2,000

* Wilson, Vol. I, p. 173.

EXPEDITION AGAINST MADURA

To these were later added 100 Europeans from Bombay, some artillery, and some few officers and men taken from the newly-raised and recently landed 96th Regiment. The following officers of the Madras European Regiment accompanied the expedition, the last six in command of the native infantry battalions :—Majors Charles Campbell, Achilles Preston and Wood, Captains Kirkpatrick and Bullock, Lieutenants Ware and Owen, Ensigns Vashon, Macdonald and Bruce, Captains Fitzgerald, Croley, Ross Lang, Hart, Airey and Harper.

Mahomed Yusaf's enterprising character quickly showed itself, for on August 11th a reconnoitring party was attacked by him with a superior force and compelled to retreat with a loss of 150 sepoys killed and wounded and 200 stand of arms taken, while on the 3rd of the month following another party sent out by Colonel Monson was driven back with a loss of nearly 20 Europeans, including an officer. In October operations commenced against Madura, but the enemy's artillery was the better and little impression was made, and in November, owing to the want of men and material, the siege was raised and the force fell back some six miles to Tirumboor to await reinforcements. Monson then returned to Trichinopoly leaving Preston in command of the force.

1764 Early in 1764 certain terms were offered to Mahomed Yusaf, but were not accepted and operations were resumed in April under the direction of Major Charles Campbell,* the senior officer of the Company's troops ; on the 29th five redoubts were taken by storm, batteries were opened on June 9th and Madura was assaulted on the 26th. But there had been heavy rain, the ditch was full and its passage very difficult, the men's ammunition was wetted and the assault was repulsed with loss.† Campbell wrote of the assault :—" They still went on in hopes of driving the enemy with their bayonets, and when Major Preston was gallantly leading them on to the right he was unfortunately wounded ; they, however, got up in several places to the top of the towers, but the

---

* Colonel Monson returned to England after the Peace of Paris.

† Campbell's despatch is in Wilson, Vol. I, p. 189 *et seq.*

enemy had under cover so many men with pikes which they kept pushing across one another and throwing large stones, hand grenades and shells down the breach, that our soldiers found it impossible, notwithstanding the spirited example of all the officers, to gain the top of any of the breaches, and therefore retreated ; our loss in this unfortunate affair is Captain Bullock and Ensign Vashon killed, Major Preston, Captains Kirkpatrick and Thomas Fitzgerald, and Lieutenants Ware and Owen, Ensigns Macdonald and Bruce wounded, and I guess about 120 Europeans killed and wounded, besides many others who have slight bruises with stones, but I have not yet been able to get an exact return of them or sepoys, though I suppose there are of the latter about 50 killed and wounded, but I hope from the report of the Surgeons that Captains Kirkpatrick and Fitzgerald and about 40 of the 120 Europeans above-mentioned will shortly be fit for duty, but upon Major Preston and the other officers wounds are very dangerous."

These fears were justified so far as concerned Major Preston, for he died of his wounds shortly afterwards.

Major Campbell, knowing that almost the whole available force in the Presidency was already with him, did not consider it prudent to run the risk of another assault and converted the siege into a blockade, which was maintained until October, when Mahomed Yusaf was seized by the commander of his French detachment and handed over to the Nawab by whom he was hanged, Madura surrendering on the 14th.

" At the end of 1763—by a letter from London, dated December 30th—the Company re-constituted their military establishment on the Coast. They ordered that the army should consist of 2,600 Europeans and 6,000 sepoys, including officers. The Europeans consisted of three battalions each of 700 men, each commanded by a major ; two companies of cavalry of 100 men each, and three of artillery of 100 each. . . . Colonel Caillaud, who was in England, was promoted Brigadier-General and appointed to command the forces in Bengal with succession to Lawrence as commander-in-chief. . . . Six months later these orders were amended. The three

European battalions were converted into regiments, each with a colonel, lieutenant-colonel and major, and John Caillaud, Charles Campbell and Achilles Preston were appointed the three colonels."*

From the end of 1764 up to June, 1767, detachments were employed against the Polygar chiefs of the Central and Southern Carnatic, all of whom, after a good deal of desultory fighting, were reduced to submission for a time at least. Colonel Charles Campbell commanded a force sent against the Polygars to the north of Trichinopoly; Major Thomas Fitzgerald commanded another which proceeded against the rajah of Ongole; while Major Flint was employed against Tinnevelly.

1766 In May, 1766, there arose what has been described as a mutiny of the officers of the Company's forces in Bengal over the question of certain allowances which were known as "Double Batta." Some 130 officers, chiefly those belonging to the brigades stationed at Patna and Monghyr, formed a combination, proposing by a simultaneous resignation of their commissions, to force the Government to grant their demands. The Bengal Council at once applied to Madras to send them as many captains and subalterns as could be spared, and this appeal was followed by an application for two companies of Europeans, it being feared that the mutiny might spread to the rank and file. Forty-two officers, two companies of the 1st Madras European Regiment and 240 recruits were sent to Calcutta in June, but the mutiny had been suppressed before they arrived.

Nineteen officers—Captains Fletcher, Marchand and Orton, Lieutenants Gravely, Duncanson, Shaw, Knox, Godfrey, Nield and Bilcliffe, Ensigns Watts, Moore, Nairne and Hammond, Quartermaster Patterson, Volunteers Dunn and Barton, Lieutenant Fireworkers Roberts and Carr—returned to Madras in September, the remaining officers and all the non-commissioned officers and men being transferred to the Bengal Establishment.

By the Treaty of Paris of February 10th, 1763, Pondicherry was restored to the French, and about the same time the Northern

* Love, Vol. II, p. 587, 588.

Circars were ceded to the Company by the Nizam. War having been declared by the Nizam, in alliance with the Mahrattas, against Hyder Ali, the ruler of Mysore, the British, as allies of the former, became embroiled in it. During the month of May, 1767, the Mahrattas invaded Mysore by its northern frontier, while the forces of the Nizam, together with a detachment of the Madras Army under Colonel Joseph Smith, penetrated into Mysore territory from the north-east, the two columns uniting at Seringapatam. Colonel Smith's detachment was composed of 763 Europeans, including officers, and five battalions of sepoys; the European infantry numbered 27 officers and 637 other ranks.

1767

Hyder Ali astutely bought off the Mahrattas and then managed to effect an alliance with the Nizam, so that when Smith reached the place of concentration, he found himself deserted by his allies and in the presence of two powerful enemy forces and himself far from reinforcement and supplies. Colonel Smith at once began slowly to fall back towards the Carnatic, being joined *en route* by a detachment which had been operating to the southward in the Baramahal and endeavouring to reduce certain small posts. During these operations a very gallant but fruitless attempt had been made to capture by storm the rock fort at Kistnagherry. It is mentioned by Wilks* that nearly the whole of the European grenadiers were killed by fragments of rock thrown from the summit. Colonel Smith in his report stated that, " In the successful attack of the rock of Kistnagherry the grenadiers of the 2nd Regiment behaved with remarkable spirit and firmness. The officer that led them, Captain Robert Villiers Fitzgerald, distinguished himself greatly as well as Messrs. Godfrey, Bandinel and Fitzgerald."

The Madras Council had not been able to bring themselves to believe in the ill-faith of their allies, and no preparations had been made, no magazines formed, nor any useful steps taken to repel the powerful invasion with which they were now threatened.

On August 25th the British force was encamped at the foot of the Ghats near Caveripatam, when it found itself suddenly

* *Historical Sketches of India*, Vol. II, p. 2.

surrounded by the enemy's cavalry which began driving off the transport cattle. The English Horse could do little or nothing against the superior numbers of the enemy, and were driven back with the loss of a third of their strength, while the loss in transport cattle prevented the British moving until the 28th, the enemy taking advantage of their immobility to capture Caveripatam defended gallantly by Captain McKain and two companies of sepoys, who managed, however, to effect their retreat.

For three days Colonel Smith continued his march towards Trinomallee, where a detachment of 400 of the Madras Regiment and 4,000 sepoys from Trichinopoly under Colonel Wood, of the Regiment, was to join him. The march was constantly harassed and impeded by clouds of the enemy's cavalry, and on September 2nd the road to be pursued led through the small pass of Changama at the exit from which was a river; a village and some high ground had been occupied by the enemy, whose infantry was coming up rapidly to seize the position, when Captain Cosby, commanding the 6th Battalion Sepoys, immediately attacked and drove them back. The advance guard, under Major Bonjour, then coming up, the position was strengthened by another sepoy battalion under Captain Cowley who held it until Colonel Smith arrived. A severe action now ensued, the enemy making repeated charges, but he was driven back, losing two guns and being finally completely routed.

The enemy in this action, known as Changama, lost more than 2,000 in killed alone, the British only 170, but while the troops were engaged the enemy's horse had plundered the baggage, and Smith was obliged to move on by reason of shortage of supplies, and finally on the afternoon of September 3rd the army reached Trinomallee, where, however, there was only so much provisions as supplied the immediate needs of the troops. On the 8th Colonel Wood joined Smith, having 400 of the Madras Europeans in his column, but the combined forces were obliged to march south in search of food.

For ten days or more Colonel Smith moved about the neighbourhood, collecting supplies and dispersing such small bodies of the enemy as he encountered; and then on the 14th he returned again to Trinomallee in the vicinity of which another action was fought on the 26th, resulting in the complete defeat of the enemy, who lost 64 guns. In his report of the encounter on the 2nd Smith specially mentions Captains Cook, Cosby, Cowley and Baillie, of the Madras Europeans. But in a postscript he adds :—" It is with great concern I inform the Honorable Board that Lieutenant Hitchcock deserted to the enemy on the 16th instant, an example, considering all circumstances, unexampled, and he is beheld with detestation and horror by all the officers of the army. Hyder Ally, I hear, has committed this traitor to prison." Reporting on the fighting of the 26th he spoke highly of Major Fitzgerald, Captains Brown and Baillie and Lieutenant Bowman.

When Tippoo Sultan, then engaged in plundering the outlying houses of Madras, heard of this last defeat of his father's army, he retired hastily to join him, calling in at the same time all the other enemy cavalry bodies then laying waste the Company's territories.

The Carnatic being for a time clear of the enemy, the British forces were withdrawn into cantonments there to recuperate and rest during the rainy season, and the Madras Europeans marched to Vellore, remaining there until the renewal of operations early in December.

Something must now be said about the Regiment and the various changes which during these operations above recounted had taken place in its constitution, and about the departure from India of the distinguished soldier whose connection with it was now finally severed.

When in 1764 all the King's troops serving in Madras were sent home, a number of each rank were permitted to volunteer for the Company's service, such lieutenants as could induce fifty men to volunteer with them being granted the rank of Captain ; Lieutenants William Baillie and Mathias Calvert, 89th, and Lieutenants Hooker and Madge and Ensign Painter, 96th, were among the officers who thus volunteered, with 586 other ranks—viz. :—

    From the 79th, 2 sergeants and 94 rank and file.
    From the 84th, 2 sergeants and 5 rank and file.

From the 89th, 7 sergeants, 60 rank and file, and 2 drummers.

From the 96th, 14 sergeants, 386 rank and file, and 14 drummers.

In October, 1765, a Board of Officers, composed of Major-General Lawrence, Brigadier-General Caillaud, Colonel Charles Campbell, and Major John Call, was convened to advise the Government as to the reorganization of the Army; and the Board having submitted their recommendations, the Government directed, on November 4th, that the European infantry should be formed in three battalions, each of nine companies, the grenadier companies having 6 sergeants, 6 corporals, 2 drummers, 1 fifer, and 94 privates, and each battalion company 4 sergeants, 4 corporals, 2 drummers, and 60 privates; the officers were to be 31 per battalion—viz., 1 colonel, 1 lieutenant-colonel, 1 major, 6 captains, 1 captain-lieutenant, 13 lieutenants, and 8 ensigns.

In April, 1766, Stringer Lawrence bade a final farewell to India, being succeeded as Commander-in-Chief by Caillaud, who retired in January, 1767, when Colonel Joseph Smith was appointed to the command of the army in Madras.

" Lawrence had that supreme gift of a great commander in being able to obtain great results from his men at critical moments, while he commanded their entire confidence at all times. . . . In front of the enemy his self-possession never deserted him at the most trying moments. On no occasion did he ever hesitate or convene a council of war. Never forcing a battle without necessity, he struck with all his force and with the greatest daring when the opportunity occurred. His decision once taken was carried out without faltering, and always with the best results. Especially had he the gift of misleading and confusing his enemy as to his intentions. In council his judgment was as sound as it was in the field. . . . He seems never to have made a personal enemy. Among the prominent men of that time he stands alone in having left no trace of personal ill-feeling attached to his name. . . . Since

Lawrence's day many illustrious names have been added to the roll of our Indian officers. None among them has a better claim to be remembered than Stringer Lawrence, the Father of the Indian Army.

"On his death,* the Directors of the East India Company voted a sum of £700 for the erection of a monument to his memory in Westminster Abbey, in testimony of their gratitude for his eminent services. It bears the following legend :—

DISCIPLINE ESTABLISHED.
FORTRESSES PROTECTED.
SETTLEMENTS EXTENDED.
FRENCH
AND INDIAN ARMIES
DEFEATED
AND
PEACE CONCLUDED
IN THE CARNATIC."†

The pay and allowances of officers and men in 1765 were as shown below :—

Field Officers.	Neat Pay per Day.	Batta of Each per Day.	Extra Allowances in Madras.
	£ s. d.	P. F. C.	P. F. C.
Colonel	1 5 0	6 0 0	2 1 0
Lieutenant-Colonel	1 0 0	5 0 0	2 1 0
Major	0 15 0	4 0 0	2 1 0

* On January 10th, 1775.
† Biddulph, pp. 114-119.

THE ARMS, COLOURS, ACCOUTREMENTS AND
TROPHIES OF THE REGIMENT

PAY OF CAPTAINS, SUBALTERNS, NON-COMMISSIONED OFFICERS, AND MEN.

Quality.	Neat Pay of each Officer per Day.	Stoppages of each Man per Month of 30 Days.	Full Pay of each per Month of 30 Days as issued from the Company.	Batta of each per Day.	Extra Allowances per Month in Madras for a Peon and Oil.	
	£ s. d.	P. F. C.	P. F. C.	P. F. C.	P. F.	
1 Captain ...	0 10 0	—	—	1 25 16	2 1	For oil & peon.
1 Lieutenant	0 5 0	—	—	1 2 64	0 15	For oil.
1 Ensign ...	0 4 0	—	—	0 33 48	0 15	Do
	Neat Pay of Each per Month.					
	P. F. C.	P. F. C.	P. F. C.			
4 Serjeants	5 0 0	1 10 60	6 10 60	Victualled in the Field by contract	—	
4 Corporals	3 14 0	1 1 60	4 15 60		—	
2 Drummers	3 14 0	1 1 60	4 15 60		—	
70-80 Privates	2 21 0	0 26 20	3 5 20		—	

PAY OF THE STAFF.

	Per Day.	Batta per Day.		Extra Allowances in Madras.	
	£ s. d.	P. F. C.		P. F. C.	
1 Adjutant ...	0 5 0	1 2 64	If they receive it in no other capacity	0 15 0	If they receive them in no other capacity.
1 Quartermaster	0 4 0	1 2 64		0 15 0	
	Per Month.				
	P. F. C.				
1 Serjeant-Major	4 0 0	Victualled in the field by contract.			
1 Quartermaster-Serjeant ...	4 0 0				
1 Drum-Major ...	1 28 0				

In March, 1767, the Court of Directors announced that, instead of sending out annually a number of officers, thus blocking promotion and causing discontent, cadets only would be sent to India in future, " who, by being trained up in the service will in time, no doubt, make good officers."

CHAPTER VII

1767–1781.

THE OPENING OF THE MYSORE WAR.

EARLY in November, 1767, Hyder Ali took the offensive, moved against and captured two petty forts held by the Company's troops, and then marched upon the more considerable rock-fortress of Amboor, garrisoned by fifteen Europeans of the Madras Regiment, several hundred men of the 10th, and a small party of the 3rd Native Infantry under Captain Calvert. These held the place for the best part of a month, Hyder retiring on the approach of Colonel Smith with a force from Vellore. Smith pursued and came up with the enemy in position near the fort of Vaniembaddy—one of the two captured in November by Hyder—and caused him to fall back, on which occasion a troop of French horse serving in Hyder's Army deserted to the English in a body under their commander, a Captain Aumont.

The combined armies of Hyder and the Nizam then retired to the fort of Caveripatam, and were followed up by Colonel Smith, who was now joined by a detachment from Trichinopoly under Colonel Wood, having with him nearly 500 of the Madras Regiment; but the enemy's position was too strongly entrenched to be attacked, while his powerful cavalry menaced the English communications, and supplies could only reach Smith if protected by unusually strong convoys. Against one of these convoys under Captain Robert Villiers Fitzgerald, which was expected by the Singarpetta Pass, Hyder moved in person with a carefully selected body of 4,000 horse, 2,000 infantry, and 6 guns, having sent his baggage and heavy guns into Mysore. Colonel Smith, having heard of these designs, dispatched Major Thomas Fitzgerald to meet the convoy,

OPENING OF THE MYSORE WAR

taking with him two companies of Europeans, a battalion of sepoys under Captain Baillie, and two field-pieces, and Hyder, not having learnt that the reinforcement had joined the convoy, promptly attacked in person. His horse was shot under him, his cavalry was very severely handled, and he was driven off with heavy loss, while the convoy, having been lodged during the action in an adjacent mud fort, was in no way disturbed.

Immediately after this failure Hyder moved up the ghats into Mysore with the bulk of his force, leaving a body of cavalry to watch the movements of the British. The Nizam had already retired in the same direction consequent on the advance from the Northern Circars, of a column of Bengal troops which had been sent thither under a Colonel Peach, the Madras Government in their extremity having asked Bengal for assistance. Colonel Smith now, with his whole force, made several marches towards the dominions of the Nizam, who at once endeavoured to treat with Smith. For some time his overtures were declined, but at last, on **1768** February 23rd, 1768, peace was signed at Madras between the Nizam and the Company, the Circars being ceded to the latter as an indemnification for the expenses of the war.

Colonel Smith then made preparations to march into Mysore territory, taking with him the 1st and 2nd European Regiments, a detachment of artillery, the Foreign Legion, a Bengal battalion, and seven battalions of Madras sepoys. At the same time Colonel Wood was detached to undertake operations against certain petty forts in Southern Baramahal, in Salem, Coimbatore, and Dindigul; he had under his command the 3rd Madras Europeans, some artillery, four battalions of sepoys, and five companies drawn from other Madras sepoy regiments.

Colonel Smith's operations were very successful; the fort at Caveripatam was abandoned on his approach at the end of February, while on May 2nd the hill fort at Kistnagherry surrendered to him. Smith then sent on Colonel Donald Campbell with detachments drawn from the 1st and 2nd Europeans and from four sepoy battalions, by whom the forts of Vencatagherry and Colar were captured, while Captain Mathews took that of Mulwagul by stratagem. Campbell then rejoined the main force, and the whole moved against the fort of Oossoor, which fell on July 11th, while a few days later Captain Cosby secured the surrender of the forts of Anicul and Dencanicottah.

Colonel Wood had enjoyed at least equal success; commencing in February with the capture of Tingerycottah, by the end of the first week in August he had made himself master of no fewer than twelve other forts of varying size and importance, and then, leaving small garrisons in these places, he set out to rejoin Colonel Smith in Mysore, reached Kistnagherry on September 1st, and moved up the pass towards Bodicottah. Hyder, however, had returned from the western coast of Bangalore early in August, and now marched to cut Wood off; but Colonel Smith effected a junction with him on September 6th, when Hyder fell back, followed up by the English for some distance until want of supplies induced Smith to retire upon Colar.

About the end of September Hyder Ali made proposals for peace, but these were not accepted and hostilities again commenced, Hyder re-capturing in October the fort of Mulwagul. Colonel Wood marched to attempt its recovery, and finding the main enemy body had retired he stormed and captured the lower fort, but failed in an attack on the upper work. On October 4th Colonel Wood was surprised by Hyder in person with a large body of troops and a very obstinate action resulted which ended in Wood remaining in possession of the field through narrowly escaping defeat. Fortunately for Wood, Colonel Smith joined him in the course of the afternoon whereupon the enemy disappeared. Wood's detachment had 20 Europeans and 28 sepoys killed, 56 Europeans and 125 Indian soldiers wounded.*

On October 5th the army moved to Vellore where the sick and wounded were left; from here Colonel Smith was summoned to Madras ostensibly to advise the Council on the future conduct of the

* Thus Wilson; another account gives the casualties in the Europeans as 2 ensigns and 17 other ranks killed, 3 lieutenants and 53 other ranks wounded.

COLONEL WOOD'S OPERATIONS

war, but the real reason being that the authorities were led by Colonel Wood's earlier successes to attach an undue importance to his military capacity, and were therefore anxious to give him further opportunities for distinction by removing his superior officer; they quickly found reason to repent their ill-advised action.

On November 4th Hyder appeared before Colar, but Colonel Campbell's defence arrangements were so good that no attack was made.

At this time an evil practice had been instituted by the civil authorities in Madras of causing their commanders in the field to be accompanied by so-called Field Deputies whose presence—as later in similar manner in the wars of revolutionary France—had a most prejudicial effect on the operations against the enemy. These field deputies constantly interfered in military arrangements of which they were naturally profoundly ignorant; they frequently thwarted the plans of the commander, causing on several occasions defeat and loss; and while not affording any assistance whatever in the collection of supplies and carriage, which they might appropriately have made their natural and special province, they actually hindered Colonels Smith and Wood in the efforts they themselves made in this direction. Further, these deputies insisted on being provided with a standing escort of 200 Europeans, several guns and five battalions of sepoys!

On November 16th Colonel Wood, now in command of the forces in the field, having been reinforced by the arrival of a battalion of sepoys under Captain Cosby, marched to the relief of Oossoor, then besieged by Hyder. Wood had with him the 2nd and 3rd Madras Europeans, about 700 strong, and five native battalions, averaging 800 men apiece. He was at Baugloor, a small walled town, on the 17th and here he left his baggage and two 18-pounders, continuing thence his march to Oossoor, which was some ten miles distant. Hyder, however, had received notice of his approach and evading him marched on Baugloor, whence he succeeded in carrying off the two guns and a large number of draught cattle, before Wood could retrace his steps. Hyder then, having placed all his plunder in a secure place, returned on the 22nd and surprised Colonel Wood's force while on the march towards Colar and inflicted upon it a loss of 7 officers, 20 Europeans and 200 sepoys killed and wounded. He only drew off on the approach of a body of troops from Vencatagherry under Major Thomas Fitzgerald.

Fitzgerald now urged Wood to march to the relief of Baugloor, but Wood, not considering his force equal to the task, Baugloor and its garrison under Captain Alexander was left to its fate. The Madras Government, hearing of this affair and its consequences, directed Colonel Wood to hand over command to the next senior officer, Colonel Ross Lang, and return to Madras, where some months later he was tried by court-martial for, among other charges, the misappropriation of stores, etc., and misconduct in the field.

Hyder now organized a strong force at Seringapatam under his general, Faiz-Ullah Khan, for the recovery of the several places taken by Colonel Wood in Coimbatore and elsewhere, while he himself prepared to descend through the ghats into the Carnatic. The dispositions which had been made for the defence of the forts and passes in the Coimbatore country were very faulty; the garrisons were all weak and isolated, of five detached companies under Captain Faizan not one was within ten miles of another, while three were twenty-five, forty and fifty-five miles from all support. The first post attacked was commanded by a brave sergeant of the Corps, named Hoskan, at the head of a company of sepoys; he repulsed the first attack, and, in reporting it to his officer, said: "I expect them again to-morrow morning in two parties with guns. I will take the guns from them with the help of God." Next day, as he anticipated, he was attacked by a force of 700 horse, 5,000 infantry and 7 guns, and held out until his post was reduced to ruins, when it was carried by assault and nearly all its gallant defenders put to the sword.

Whether Sergeant Hoskan was slaughtered with the rest of his garrison or lingered for a time in the dungeons of Seringapatam, history does not relate.

The other posts in the Gujalhathi Pass fell as rapidly; one of these after two assaults, in the second of which the commandant, Lieutenant Andrews, was killed, surrendered, while the garrison of Coimbatore, composed for the most part of Muhammad Ali's troops, massacred Lieutenant McCutcheon and Mr. Hamilton, the paymaster, and gave up the place to the enemy. In the course of a very few days every post and garrison, whether from treachery or want of supplies, had fallen to the enemy, with the exception of Caveripooram, where Captain Faizan commanded, and Erode held by troops under Captain Orton.

The following are the names of officers and non-commissioned officers holding some of those many small posts :—Captains Faizan, Orton, Hegue, Lieutenants Andrews, Rouse, Knightly, Byrne, McCutcheon and Johnson, Sergeant-Major Johnston and Sergeant Hoare.

When Colonel Lang heard of Hyder's movements he sent after him a mobile force of some 5,000 men under Major Fitzgerald ; this contained 500 cavalry, European and native, 300 of the 3rd Madras Europeans, 150 of the grenadiers of the 1st and 2nd Regiments, about 4,000 sepoys in five battalions and 14 guns. Fitzgerald marched on December 10th, but finding himself unable to overtake the enemy, he made towards Trichinopoly which he had been ordered to safeguard, while Hyder entered the Carnatic laying waste the country he passed over.

At Erode Captain Orton was unaware that the enemy was so close to him, or that the fort at Caroor had already surrendered, and he sent a detachment of 50 Europeans and 200 sepoys, with two 3-pounders, under Captain Nixon, to escort a supply of stores from Caroor to Erode, some forty miles of road. Nixon had proceeded about half-way when six guns suddenly opened on his little column at point blank range ; he at once fell back behind a small embankment, where he was charged upon by two bodies of Hyder's troops. The Europeans with Nixon stood their ground firmly until the enemy had arrived within twenty paces, when the little band of fifty heroes rushed forward with the bayonet causing their opponents to fall back in confusion and fly. But while the English were still in some disorder, the enemy cavalry charged down upon them from all sides. All were at once ridden over, and not an officer or man remained unwounded with the exception of Lieutenant Gorham, who was saved by the interposition of a Mysore officer. A summons to surrender Erode was now sent to Captain Orton who complied next day, considering the place unable to stand a siege. Under the terms granted, the garrison was to have been permitted to proceed to Trichinopoly, but Hyder violated his promise and all were sent captives to Seringapatam.

Captain Faizan, after a gallant and protracted defence, also surrendered Caveripooram; he obtained the same terms as Orton and in his case too they were shamefully broken.

The only officers left by Colonel Wood in these many small posts who succeeded in bringing away their men were Lieutenants Johnson from Darapooram and Byrne from Sunkerrypooram; the former fought his way to Trichinopoly, though closely followed up and harassed by superior numbers, while Byrne made his way to Trichinopoly through the Travancore country without loss.

The year 1768 closed with these unfortunate events. A gallant and devoted body of European troops, artillery and infantry, and a faithful army of well-disciplined sepoys, were frittered away and sacrificed by an inefficient government and corrupt civilian subordinates; while the energy and ability of Colonel Smith, an officer of approved worth, were paralysed and thwarted by those to whom he rightly looked for support.

1769 Colonel Smith resumed command of the army in the field on February 1st, 1769, at Chittapet, 70 miles southwest of Madras, and, having been at last furnished with sufficient carriage, he began to press Hyder hard. The Madras Government, however, being weary of the long-enduring war, made several overtures for peace, and a cessation of arms for twelve days was agreed upon, commencing on February 22nd. The rival parties could not agree upon terms, and on March 6th hostilities recommenced, when the whole of the Carnatic was once more in flames.

In a series of masterly movements between Gingee and Madras, when Colonel Smith, from his vicinity to the Presidency, was able to move with as great rapidity as was Hyder, the Mysore chief was more than once out-manœuvred, and was only saved from serious defeat by the superiority of his cavalry. He now was also desirous of peace, and resolved by a bold stroke to bring the war to an end without risking a general action. He accordingly sent off his main body, guns, and baggage to Mysore, and marched, with 6,000 horse and a very small body of infantry, towards Madras. He covered the intervening distance of 130 miles in three days and a half, appearing before the Presidency on March 29th. Arrived here, he at once demanded that Mr. Du Pré, member of Council, should be sent to him at St. Thomas's Mount to discuss terms of peace. This was done, and a treaty was signed between the two parties early in April. Colonel Smith had, by March 31st, arrived within 12 miles of the Mount, but Hyder was so greatly disquieted at the presence of the British force that he insisted on Smith being directed to withdraw to a distance of 25 miles until matters were finally settled.

Hyder Ali at all times spoke in the highest terms of the military qualities of Colonel Smith. The conduct of this officer throughout the war gained him the reputation of being one of the best officers of his day, particularly when we take into consideration the difficulties he had to encounter from his own government. Hyder showed himself to be the first Indian general of his time, and to the honour of the Madras European Regiment be it said that he declared " the British officer of whom he had the highest opinion, and who was the only officer he ever avoided encountering, was Colonel Smith," an officer who had risen in the Corps and had studied his profession under Lawrence and Clive.

Before Hyder left the Mount he begged for an interview with his " preceptor," as he styled Colonel Smith. Circumstances prevented the gratification of this wish, so he asked for a portrait, which was later sent him. After the capture of Seringapatam this was found in the palace, and was sold by auction with other prize property, eventually reaching England and coming into the possession of the late General David Smith, of Comet Row, Somersetshire.

During the campaign now closed the losses sustained by the army from death, sickness, and desertion had been very heavy, as is seen by the "state" of Smith's force on April 4th, 1769, when the effective cavalry, European and Native, had been reduced to 68 men, the two regiments of Europeans with him to 379 all ranks, while the battalions of sepoys had been reduced to less than half their establishment of 1,000 men each.

The Madras Government, in their report on the result of the campaign to the Court of Directors, attempted to lay the blame for failure anywhere but on their own action—or inaction; especially did the Council seek to justify their appointment of Field Deputies to the army in the field; but they were not upheld by the Court of Directors, who wrote out saying: "We cannot but disapprove of their original appointment, which could have no other tendency but to impede the operations of the campaign, and give rise to very mischievous disputes betwixt the Commander-in-Chief and the Deputies, by which we fear the public service has suffered essentially. . . . Our opinion is that when the Company has made choice of a proper person to be Commander-in-Chief, all trust and confidence should be reposed in him to direct the plans and operations of the campaign."

1770 In July, 1770, Major-General Coote arrived in Madras, having been appointed their Commander-in-Chief in India by the Honourable East India Company, and he immediately commenced to carry out certain reforms in accordance with instructions given him by the Court of Directors; but a difference of opinion having arisen as to the manner in which orders should be promulgated to the army, it was ruled by the whole Council, Brigadier-General Smith alone dissenting, that the commission held by Mr. Du Pré as Governor and Commander-in-Chief of the fort and settlement at Madras was superior to that of General Coote. This decision caused the resignation of that officer, who returned home, and was succeeded by General Smith.

AFFAIRS IN TANJORE

The Governor and Council of Madras were severely censured by the Court of Directors, who pronounced their conduct wholly unjustifiable.

By August, 1770, the Madras European Infantry Corps had been reorganized, and now consisted of two regiments, each of two battalions; each regiment was commanded by a full colonel, and each battalion was officered by 1 lieutenant-colonel, 1 major, 9 captains, 12 lieutenants, and 16 ensigns.

1771 Nothing of special military importance occurred in the Madras Presidency from the signing of the Treaty with Hyder in April, 1769, up to September, 1771, when a force was sent against the ruler of Tanjore to enforce the payment of his share of the expenses of the late war. The troops were assembled at Trichinopoly under General Smith, and contained the following units:—Captain Tonyn's troop of European cavalry, 300 artillerymen, the 1st Battalions of the 1st and 2nd Europeans, the Grenadier Company of the 2nd Battalion, 2nd Regiment, 6 battalions of Carnatic Infantry, 2 regiments of the Nawab's cavalry, and 2 battalions of his infantry; Captain Baillie was Brigade-Major, and Captain Kennedy was Quartermaster-General with the force.

The army proceeded to Tanjore, invested the place, and by the end of October had made a practicable breach, upon which the Rajah came to terms and the troops marched back to Trichinopoly. Though the operations did not last long, the casualties incurred were disproportionately heavy, amounting to 158 of all ranks killed and wounded; of the Madras Europeans, Lieutenant Weld, 1 sergeant, 2 corporals, and 25 privates were killed, while Lieutenants Darrell and Bonnevaux, 4 sergeants, 5 corporals, and 81 men were wounded. Of the British officers serving with the sepoy battalions, Lieutenant Henry Nicoll was killed, Captain Mackenzie, Lieutenants Barton, Campbell, Davis, and Stuckey, and Ensign Dixon were wounded.

1772 In April, 1772, a field force was again assembled under General Smith for service against the Marawar chiefs of Ramnad and Caliacoil at the instance of the Nawab. The force contained a detachment of artillery, the 1st Battalion 1st

European Regiment, the grenadier company of the 1st Battalion 2nd Regiment, three Carnatic battalions, and some of the Nawab's cavalry. At the storming of Ramnad the grenadiers of the Regiment, under Captain Robert Godfrey, particularly distinguished themselves, and Lieutenant Burr, one of the subalterns of the grenadier company, was among the first to mount the breach. After the reduction of Ramnad the force marched on towards Caliacoil, Lieutenant-Colonel Bonjour, with the greater part of two sepoy battalions, being detached to make a détour and fall back upon the enemy's rear. This he successfully effected, Caliacoil fell, the enemy was dispersed, and the country subdued.

The Nawab had long been desirous of possessing himself of the town and province of Tanjore, and in June he succeeded in prevailing upon the Government of Madras to assist him in a second attack* upon the rajah, under pretext of non-payment of arrears of tribute; and some time in July Colonel Smith got a force together at Trichinopoly. It contained 35 European cavalry, 298 artillery, 1,069 European infantry, 7 sepoy battalions, and some of the Nawab's horse and foot; Major Horn was Quartermaster-General with the force, and Captain Cosby was Adjutant-General.

The Nawab made certain promises as to prize-money to the army, varying in amount from 6,000 pagodas for a lieutenant-colonel to 20 pagodas for a British private, which no doubt went far to make these and similar expeditions very popular with the troops!

The column left Trichinopoly on July 31st and after some sharp skirmishing arrived on August 6th within a short distance of Tanjore. The same night the European grenadiers attacked the camp of the enemy's cavalry and completely surprised and routed them, inflicting much loss. On August 20th approaches were made to within 500 yards of the city wall. Four days later the enemy made a very determined sortie, but were driven back with many casualties, the European grenadiers again as usual doing excellent service. By

* All those expeditions were later strongly condemned by the Court of Directors.

September 16th the breach was practicable and seven volunteers of the Regiment, under the superintendence of Lieutenant Alexander McGregor Murray, made with fascines a passage over the wet ditch; all but one of the seven were killed at their work. About noon on the 17th the troops advanced to the assault, and the place then fell almost without resistance.

During the operations about sixty of the Madras Europeans were killed and wounded, Lieutenant-Colonel Fletcher being among the latter.

The conduct of the Army met with the approbation of the Court of Directors who resolved :—"*That the thanks of this Court be given to Brigadier-General Joseph Smith for his long, faithful and meritorious services to this Company in the government of their forces on the coast of Coromandel, and more especially for his late able conduct in the reduction of Tanjore, in which service the officers and troops under his command have manifested the most exemplary discipline and resolution.*"

1775 Early in the year 1775, on the outbreak of the First Mahratta War, two companies of European Infantry under Captain Myers were ordered on service to Bombay and joined a force of Bombay troops under Colonel Keating; these companies were actively employed in Gujerat and took part in several actions, amongst others in that near Arras on May 18th, when Captains Myers and Serle were killed and Lieutenant Turing wounded; this officer was afterwards again wounded and taken prisoner in Colonel Baillie's defeat, and finally fell in a later action.

In March of this year the news was received in India of the death of the great Lord Clive, formerly of the Madras European Regiment, on November 22nd of the year previous.

In the words of his biographer, Sir John Malcolm : " India has produced many illustrious men, both in his time and since; but none of them has yet obscured or equalled the fame of Clive, as one of those extraordinary men who give a character to the period and country in which they live. His name cannot be erased from the history of India, nor from that of Britain. Born in the rank of a private gentleman and launched out early in life into the wide sea of Indian adventure, he soon far outstript all his competitors in the race of fortune and fame. He was trained in the best of schools—a state of danger, of suffering, and activity. Those who would lessen his fame by representing him as victorious over Indian armies only, forget his successes over the French and Dutch, at that time the bravest nations in Europe. But it was not at the head of armies alone that his talents were conspicuous; he was a remarkable man in all the circumstances of life."

The Army of India owes much to Lord Clive, and his princely gift of £70,000 for the support of invalid soldiers and the widows of officers and soldiers of the East India Company's Service " must rank among the noblest of living benefactions."

1776
1777
During the years 1776 and 1777 the headquarters of the four battalions of the two regiments of Madras Europeans appear to have been stationed at Fort St. George, Trichinopoly, Vellore and Poonamallee respectively, with a detachment at Tanjore.

The war, which for some considerable time England had been waging with her rebellious colonies in America, had been progressing none too favourably, and in October, 1777, the disastrous capitulation of General Burgoyne at Saratoga had provided England with two new foes in Europe in addition to those of her own family that she was facing in America, for the news of Saratoga was the prelude to an alliance between France and America, which left England no alternative to war. The example of France was soon followed by Spain, while England was also threatened by the hostility of the Dutch. War was declared in London against France on March 18th; the news reached Calcutta via Cairo on July 7th, and Warren Hastings, now Governor-General, at once sent orders to Fort St. George to prepare for an immediate attack upon Pondicherry.

The Commander-in-Chief in Madras at this time was Major-General Hector Munro, who had only arrived from England in the month of February in the *Lord North*. This officer was, however, no stranger to India, having served there with the 89th Foot in

1761 and following years in the rank of major, and when in command of the troops at Patna he fought and won the decisive action of Buxar.

Munro lost no time in assembling a substantial force and by August 8th he had arrived at the Red Hills with the following troops: all the available artillery from the Mount and from Trichinopoly, the four battalions of European Infantry, eleven battalions of Madras Infantry, six battalions of Grenadiers—four of these formed from the grenadier companies of the Carnatic battalions and two from those of the eight Circar battalions raised for service in the Northern Circars,* a company of marksmen, and some of the Nawab's troops of each arm, but of the numbers of these no details seem to be to hand.

On July 29th Commodore Vernon had sailed from Madras with a squadron of five ships to blockade Pondicherry, where he also arrived on the 8th, but a French squadron of equal strength now making its appearance, Vernon gave chase and a smart action resulted on the 10th, when the French made their way back to Pondicherry roads with their hulls seriously injured, followed slowly by Vernon, whose ships had been damaged, chiefly in the rigging. The French declined further action and sailed away leaving Pondicherry to its fate, and on the same day Munro took possession of the "bound hedge," so often mentioned in connection with sieges of this place, cutting off all communication with the surrounding country, while Vernon effectually blockaded Pondicherry from the sea

It will be remembered that after the capture by Coote in 1761 the fortifications had been wholly destroyed, but on the rendition to the French at the peace, these had been greatly restored and improved, and were defended by a garrison of close upon 3,000 men commanded by a M. Bellecombe, a very skilful, brave and resolute soldier.

On September 18th the British opened batteries armed with 28 guns and 27 mortars; but the activity and courage of the

* At this date each sepoy battalion had two grenadier companies.

besieged, coupled with the rainy season which now set in, retarded the operations to such an extent that it was October 15th before a passage was formed across the ditch. The actual assault was to have been made on October 17th, but on the 16th the Governor, convinced that he could not hold out much longer, offered to capitulate, and his proposals were accepted on the 18th, very liberal terms being granted in consideration of the gallantry shown and the honourable manner in which the defence had been conducted; the garrison was permitted to march out with all the honours of war and the Regiment of Pondicherry was allowed to retain its Colours.

The losses among the defenders amounted to 200 killed and 480 wounded. The casualties in the force under General Munro were, Europeans: *killed*, 2 officers and 66 other ranks, *wounded*, 8 officers and 114 non-commissioned officers and men; Sepoys: *killed*, 5 British officers and 148 other ranks, *wounded*, 14 British officers and 482 other ranks. The Madras European Regiment had 1 captain—Captain D. Thomson—2 sergeants, 2 corporals and 44 privates killed; 1 captain, 5 lieutenants, 2 ensigns, 4 sergeants, 3 corporals and 107 privates were wounded. Among the captures were 265 guns and over 6,000 stand of small arms.

In General Orders of October 8th the following appeared relating to an officer of the Madras European Regiment:—

"*The Honourable the President and Select Committee have been pleased to appoint Lieutenant James O'Hara, who stands next for promotion, to be a captain in consideration of his gallant behaviour in the attack on the north-west ravelin at Pondicherry, which has been mentioned to them in a particular manner by General Munro, and for which they have thought proper to confer on him the mark of their approbation.*"

In February, 1774, General Clavering had been appointed Commander-in-Chief of the Company's forces in India, but some three and a half years later he died at Calcutta, and thereupon Eyre Coote, now a lieutenant-general and a K.B., had been **1778** nominated to succeed him. Coote sailed from England in May, 1778, intending to proceed in the first instance to Calcutta, but on touching at Cape Town he received news that hostilities with the French had already broken out in Coromandel and in Bengal, and he therefore decided to proceed at once to Madras where he landed on December 28th.

1779 On New Year's Day, 1779, General Coote reviewed the troops in Fort St. George, and issued the following General Order :—

"*Lieutenant-General Sir Eyre Coote, on his return to the command in India, felt himself particularly happy in the recollection that he should have the honour of once more leading those troops, whose military firmness and intrepidity he has been an eye-witness of during former wars. But on his arrival here he begs leave to address the Army on this establishment with the overflowings of a heart replete with gratitude to them as an Englishman, as King's and Company's officer, for the essential services they have so lately rendered the English nation, its allies, and more particularly their Masters, the Honourable East India Company. The service they have been employed on during the siege of Pondicherry required leaders of approved abilities, and soldiers in the highest sense of the word, and as such the Army on the Coromandel Coast have signalised themselves to all the world.*"

While Coote was in Madras the project was discussed in full of proceeding to the capture of Mahé, the only French settlement now remaining to that nation in India. When first proposed, Hyder Ali had viewed the prospect with alarm and indignation, since if Mahé fell into English hands not only would the source be closed whence he drew his military supplies from France, but his allies, the French, would lose their last remaining possession in India. He therefore caused it to be made known to Rumbold, the Governor of Madras, that he considered *all* the European settlements on that coast to be equally under his protection, and he warned the Madras Council that in the event of any attack being made upon Mahé he would not only aid in its defence, but would retaliate either by laying waste the province of Arcot or by invading the Carnatic.

Although the Court of Directors had issued orders for the reduction of Mahé, Rumbold now, in view of the threats of Hyder, proposed that the project be abandoned, but he was overruled by

Coote, who was upon the point of proceeding to Calcutta,* and an expeditionary force was accordingly assembled; it was placed under the command of Lieutenant-Colonel Brathwaite, and consisted of 3 companies of artillery, 1 battalion of European Infantry from Tanjore under Lieutenant-Colonel George Brown, and 3 Carnatic battalions. The expedition arrived before Mahé on March 14th and on the 19th the place surrendered; the works were destroyed in November, when Colonel Brathwaite returned to Pondicherry, taking most of the troops with him, and a detachment moved into Tellicherry, then threatened by the Nairs, instigated by Hyder; Major Cotgrave commanded this detachment, in which were included 5 officers and 52 other ranks of the Madras European Regiment.

1780 In February, 1780, Lieutenant-Colonel Brown, with 100 gunners, the 1st Battalion 2nd Regiment of Europeans, 500 strong, and a Carnatic battalion, embarked at Madras for Surat, and joined Colonel Goddard near Pawungarh for service against the Mahrattas, being engaged at Bassein and at the forcing of the Bor Ghat in February, 1781. At the conclusion of the war the greater number of the surviving privates of the Madras European Regiment were transferred to the Bombay Regiment, only the officers, three non-commissioned officers, and a few men rejoining headquarters at Madras.

Already in January, 1780, it was well known to everybody in India, except apparently the majority of the members of the Madras Council, that Hyder Ali, angered by the capture of Mahé, was preparing a large army for the† invasion of the Company's territories. No steps were taken to meet the emergency; the usual garrisons remained at Poonamallee, Vellore, Trichinopoly, Pondicherry, Guntur, Tanjore, and Masulipatam; no attempt was made at concentration, and the Madras Council remained supine until July 24th,

* He actually embarked on the 13th, and reached the Hooghly on March 23rd, 1779.

† Wilks and Innes Munro give the numbers as 2 troops of French cavalry, 500 European infantry, 100 guns, 28,000 Mysore cavalry, 15,000 regular and 40,000 irregular infantry, 5,000 pioneers, and 2,000 rocket-men.

when the sight of burning villages and the appearance of crowds of terrified natives flocking to Madras announced that Hyder Ali was actually at hand. Then only was any action taken, but even now were counsels divided. The Madras Government resolved to assemble the army near Conjeveram, and ordered Colonel Lang to send thither the European battalion from Vellore. Lord Macleod, commanding the 73rd Highlanders* at Poonamallee, protested, and urged the concentration of all available troops near Madras before embarking upon operations. He was in a measure overruled, and General Munro decided to move himself on Conjeveram; but Colonel Brathwaite was ordered in to Madras from Pondicherry, bringing with him the garrison of Trichinopoly, eventually arriving with 1 battalion European Infantry, some artillery, a regiment of the Nawab's cavalry, and 4 sepoy battalions; on August 6th Colonel Cosby was sent south with a detachment of native troops, cavalry and infantry, to endeavour to intercept Hyder's convoys; and small garrisons were maintained at the following places in the Carnatic: at Wandewash, under Lieutenants Flint and Parr; at Gingee, under Ensign Macaulay; at Thiaghur, under Lieutenant Roberts and Ensign Higginbotham; and at Permacoil, under Lieutenant Bishop.

On August 26th Sir Hector Munro marched off with a force estimated by himself at 5,209 of all ranks, and containing 35 European cavalry, 315 artillery, 73rd, 628, 2nd Battalion 1st Europeans, 351, Grenadiers of the 2nd Battalion 2nd Europeans, 105, Cadet Company, 32, a company of marksmen, 111, and 5 battalions of sepoys numbering 3,391. With these troops Conjeveram was reached on the 29th, but the march had shown the defects of the newly-arrived, unacclimatized regiment of Highlanders, who suffered terribly and even fatally from the heat.

Among the detachments which had been ordered to return to Madras was one at Nellore, under Colonel William Baillie, composed as under :—

    Artillery : 4 officers and 77 non-commissioned officers and men.

* The 73rd arrived at Madras in January, 1780, in fourteen ships after a year's voyage.

European Infantry: 7 officers, 2 cadets, and 104 non-commissioned officers and men.

Sepoys: 36 officers, 24 sergeants, and 2,606 non-commissioned officers and men.

This body of troops reached Goomerapandy, 27 miles north of Madras, on August 24th, and here received orders diverting it to Conjeveram, and in compliance with these the route was changed, and on the 27th the detachment arrived at Vungal on the Corteliar River; the river was, unfortunately, not at once crossed, and during the night the stream became impassable, and consequently Baillie could not move forward again until September 3rd, on which day Hyder Ali took up a position 6 miles west of Conjeveram, containing Munro, while sending off a force of 30,000 cavalry, 8,000 infantry, and 12 guns under his son Tippoo to fall upon Baillie.

Tippoo came upon Baillie near Perambaucum, 14 miles north of Conjeveram, on the 6th, and there was heavy fighting from eleven to two, but Baillie not only beat off all attacks, but inflicted severe losses on the Mysore army; he also managed to get through a message, which Munro received on the 8th, stating that he could not advance further, and asking Sir Hector to move to his help. The General decided, however, that he could not leave his stores at Conjeveram, but he sent to Baillie on the night of the 8th what in his report to the Government he describes as "a strong detachment," under Lieutenant-Colonel Fletcher: this contained the grenadier and light companies of the 73rd, the latter commanded by Captain (afterwards General Sir David) Baird, 2 grenadier companies of the Madras Europeans, under Captains Phillips and Ferrier with 11 other officers, a company of sepoy marksmen under Lieutenant Muat, and the 10 grenadier companies of 5 sepoy battalions under Captains Rumley and Gowdie, with 10 other officers. The total strength of this reinforcement was 301 Europeans and 706 natives, or a total of 1,007 of all ranks; they had with them nine camel-loads of ammunition.

Fletcher, in spite of the fact that his guides were in the pay of Hyder and did their best to mislead him, made a very successful

BAILLIE'S DISASTER

night march, and brought his party safely into Baillie's camp early on the morning of the 9th September. The united party marched off at 8 p.m. that night, being fired on soon after starting; but this died down, and then, having arrived within 9 miles of Conjeveram, Baillie decided to halt until daylight—entirely against the orders of Munro and in disregard of the protests of Fletcher.

During the night Munro remained stationary; his tents were struck and his men remained under arms; firing was heard in the distance about midnight, but it soon ceased and occasioned no disquiet.

Hyder sent off his guns and infantry towards Perambaucum, and at 4 a.m. on the 10th followed to take command in person, entertaining but a low opinion of the military capacity of his son.

At dawn on the 10th Baillie again set forward, but near the village of Pollilore Tippoo appeared on the left of the column and opened a cannonade which obliged it to halt, when the sepoy grenadiers, under Captains Rumley and Gowdie, were ordered to storm the guns; this they did with conspicuous gallantry, and having driven the enemy back were in the act of seizing the guns, when they were charged and forced back in turn by a large body of cavalry, the advance of Hyder's army masking the movement of his infantry and cannon, all pushing forward to the attack. In a very few minutes from 50 to 60 guns opened a heavy and destructive fire at short range, two of the English ammunition tumbrils blew up, and the camp followers, rushing in for protection, caused increased confusion. Fletcher, apprehensive for the safety of the rear, took the grenadiers of the 73rd in that direction—and was never seen again.

The detachment moved forward, formed in square, with the wounded, sick and ammunition in the centre, attacked on all sides by thousands of Hyder's soldiers, who were invariably repulsed; but the ammunition beginning to fail, the enemy charged down on the sepoy battalions and soon completely destroyed them. And now the Europeans of the little column, reduced to 400 in number, Baillie himself wounded, were drawn together in a square occupying some slightly rising ground; repeatedly charged, the enemy were as often repulsed, and even when the musket ammunition was exhausted the struggle was maintained with the bayonet, with which no fewer than thirteen separate charges were repelled. The enemy guns were now brought up close on all sides while the cavalry and infantry of Hyder's army formed for another attack, when Baillie, seeing no sign of any advance to his relief, about 10 a.m. tied his handkerchief to his sword as a flag of truce and ordered Baird, now second in command, to cease fire. Finding the signal was unseen or disregarded, the men were ordered to ground arms, when the enemy rushed in and a scene of dreadful slaughter ensued, and but for the humane interposition of some of the French officers, like the younger Lally and Pimoran, not an officer or man would have been saved.

Of 86 European officers, including those on the staff and the surgeons, 36 were killed or died of wounds and 34 were wounded, while of the European privates 160 were killed and nearly all the remainder severely wounded. Very few of the sepoys escaped—practically all were killed or captured; the total loss was about 508 Europeans and 3,312 sepoys killed, wounded and missing.

There were 22 officers of the Madras European Regiment present, and of these Lieutenant-Colonel Fletcher, Captain Phillips, Dr. Wilson, Lieutenant Wade, Ensigns Clarke and Galway were killed; Colonel Baillie, Captain Monteith, Lieutenants Massy, Bowser, Halliburton, Hope, Nash and Turing and Cadet Baillie, junior, were wounded; Captain Ferrier and Lieutenant Knox died of their wounds; while Captain Wragg, Lieutenant McNeal, Cadets Gorie and Baillie senior, and Volunteer Latham were taken prisoners. A few days after the action the wounded were sent off, some to Seringapatam, others to Arnee—exposed to the sun in bullock-carts, taunted and abused in every Mysore village through which they passed. But few lived through the years of captivity, nearly all died of starvation and want of proper medical attention, while some were poisoned or otherwise made away with.

At dawn on this disastrous day firing had been heard at Conjeveram, and Munro marched a few leisurely miles in the direction of Perambaucum, meeting on the way a wounded sepoy-fugitive who brought news of the defeat of Baillie's detachment. It is possible that even then the action was not over and that by pushing quickly on Munro might have been able to save the remnant of the force, but in spite of Macleod's remonstrances Munro turned about and fell back on Conjeveram. Arrived here at 6 p.m., the heavy guns and stores were thrown into a large tank and early on the 11th the army was in full retreat on Madras, so closely pressed by the Mysore cavalry that the rear guard lost 500 men before arrival at Chingleput at dawn on the 12th. Camp at Marmelong, near the Mount, was finally and gratefully reached at 1 a.m. on the 14th.

On Friday, September 22nd, the *Nymph*, " a swift ship flying before the south-west monsoon," arrived from Madras in the Hooghly, and the news she brought from the south convinced the Supreme Council at Calcutta that it was faced by so powerful a combination of enemies, so serious a military disaster, as might well, had less resolute leaders been at the head of the Government, have made the years 1780 and 1781 as fatal to our power in Asia as they were to our rule in America.

Warren Hastings at once grasped the situation and acted with decision; he abandoned all idea of engaging the Mahrattas, he disregarded the dangers threatening Bengal, he saw where the real trouble lay, and announced, " while I have a soldier or a rupee I will never abandon the Carnatic; for if we do not fight Hyder Ali in that country, we shall have to fight him here."

But he at once took active measures; he laid an embargo on the shipping in the Hooghly, with directions for every vessel to be ready to proceed to Madras in five days; and he ordered fifteen lakhs of treasure to be packed ready for transmission to the south. Then on Monday, September 25th, the great Pro-Consul met his Council and read to them a forceful minute which he had prepared; he described all that had lately happened in the Carnatic, and dwelt on the danger to which our domination there was exposed; suggested that treasure and a large detachment of European infantry and artillery be at once sent to Fort St. George, and that " the Commander-in-Chief be requested, and I do for my part make it my most earnest and particular request, that he will proceed himself immediately to the coast and take the command of the army in that establishment."

These proposals were carried, Lieutenant-General Sir Eyre Coote joyfully accepted the responsibilities thus laid upon him, and he sailed for Madras on October 14th, taking with him the 2nd Battalion 1st Bengal European Regiment, four guns and two companies of artillery with three battalions of lascars, leaving orders for a further reinforcement of five battalions of Bengal sepoys to follow by land, under Colonel Pearse, so soon as the necessary transport could be provided.

Sir Eyre Coote reached Madras on November 5th, and was received, alike by soldiers and civilians, with demonstrations of joy and relief.

CHAPTER VIII

1781.

THE BATTLES OF PORTO NOVO, POLLILORE AND SHOLINGHUR, AND THE RELIEF OF VELLORE.

ON the retreat to Madras of the army under General Munro, Hyder broke up his camp near Conjeveram and returned to Arcot to **1780** prosecute the siege, which was conducted under the direction of French officers until November 3rd, when it surrendered—two days prior to the arrival of Coote in Madras. The capitulation of Arcot was signed by Captain Dupont—Captain Prendergast, the actual commandant, having been severely wounded. The garrison, composed of 157 men of the 1st Battalion 1st European Regiment, a company and a half of sepoys under Lieutenant Leighton, and a party of the Nawab's infantry, was allowed to depart on condition that the Europeans did not serve again during the war, and this was one of the only two occasions on which the terms were observed by Hyder.

Nearly all the remaining forts fell much about the same time.

On November 13th all the troops, except those actually comprising the garrison of Fort St. George, were formed into three divisions as under:—

The 1st, or Right Division, under Major-General Sir Hector Munro, was stationed at Vepery and Egmore and was composed of:—

    1st Regiment Nawab's Cavalry.
    The Bengal Detachment.
    Six Companies of Grenadiers from the Northern Circars.
    The 2nd Battalion of Sepoys.

The Centre Division, under the Commander-in-Chief, was at or near the Choultry Plain and contained :—

    The 73rd Regiment.
    2nd Battalion 1st Madras European Regiment.
    The 15th, 17th and 21st Battalions of Sepoys.

The 2nd or Left Division, under Colonel Lord Macleod, was quartered at the Luz and St. Thomé; it consisted of :—

    Troop European Cavalry.
    Three Regiments of the Nawab's Horse.
    The Tanjore Grenadiers.
    The 16th Battalion of Sepoys.

The posts at the Mount were occupied by what was known as "the Trichinopoly detachment," a name given to the force which had been sent south in the previous August under Colonel Cosby to endeavour to intercept Hyder's convoys, and this, with some artillery, was placed under the command of Captain Bilcliffe.

General Coote early perceived that the Madras Government had made little or no provision for the needs of a serious campaign, that the field guns required were not ready, since the construction of carriages and tumbrils had only now been taken in hand, while probably the most pressing want of all was a body of efficient cavalry. The mounted troops maintained by the Company in Madras consisted of a weak troop of Europeans, only thirty-three in number, under Lieutenant Young. Dependence had hitherto been placed on the Nawab of Arcot, who had maintained several cavalry regiments, officered by Europeans, some of the Company's and some of the Nawab's service, but these regiments appear to have been very irregularly paid with the natural result that when needed for service they declined to march. Coote now arranged for four of these regiments to be taken into the Company's service and they formed a brigade—only some 800 strong, however, commanded by Colonel Cosby; the commandants of two of these regiments were Company's officers—Captains Edward Jourdan and John Macalister.

In November General Coote published an order of far-reaching importance—*that all corps should in future parade two-deep, unless particularly ordered otherwise*—a formation not unusual this year in the British Army in America, but now for the first time adopted in India.

The want of European troops was greatly felt, and Coote probably considered that in view of the heavy casualties incurred by the sepoy battalions in the late engagement under Colonel Baillie, and their consequent loss of *morale*, his Indian battalions required an even larger stiffening than usual of white soldiers—the more that the 73rd had suffered much from the climate and was greatly reduced in strength, while neither the Bengal nor Madras European Regiments were up to establishment. Warren Hastings at once opened negotiations with the Dutch East India Company for the hire of a force of 1,000 infantry and 200 artillery; but if these negotiations were ever seriously considered they became null and void when war broke out between England and Holland. General Coote then wrote to the Secretary at War on December 1st asking for "six battalions of Europeans and a large corps of artillery to defend and give permanency to our possessions"; and in 1781, and subsequently, something was done to comply with these demands, a regiment of light dragoons and two infantry battalions, numbered respectively the 101st and 102nd, being sent out and reaching India during 1782, while at the end of the same year two regiments of Hanoverians, numbered the 15th and 16th, which had been raised in Germany and handed over to the Company for service, also arrived in Madras.

At a Council of War held on December 30th, 1780, it was resolved that the army should proceed at once to the relief of the garrisons of Vellore, Wandewash, Permacoil and Chingleput, and

1781 the Commander-in-Chief having completed his arrangements he marched on January 17th, 1781, with the following force :—

Artillery: Madras and Bengal, 400 men and 44 guns.

Cavalry: the European troop about 50 strong, and four regiments of the Nawab's Horse, each 200 strong.

Infantry: 73rd Regiment, 600.
   Bengal Europeans, 350.
   2nd Battalion 1st Madras Europeans, 200.
   Seven Battalions of sepoys.
   The Trichinopoly Detachment.
   The Grenadier Battalion, eight companies from the Northern Circars.
   A company of Marksmen.
   A company of Pioneers.

The total effective strength was 7,450, of whom some 1,600 were Europeans.

General Stuart remained in command at Fort St. George with 200 Europeans, 50 artillerymen and 500 sepoys.

Chingleput was relieved on January 19th, and the following afternoon a detachment of about 1,000 men, including 12 European artillerymen under Captain Tanner with six guns, the whole commanded by Captain Davies, was sent on ahead from the camp on the Palar River to capture the fort of Carangoly, eight miles distant. The place was not taken without considerable opposition and some loss, 3 Europeans and 8 sepoys being killed and 4 European officers and 59 other ranks being wounded. In his remarks on the action in his orders of the 21st, General Coote specially mentioned Captains Davies, Moorhouse, Tanner and Pringle, and expressed the relief with which he had learnt from the surgeon that the wounds received by Captain Moorhouse, Lieutenant Anderson, Ensign McAlister and Lieutenant-Fireworker O'Brien were not dangerous.*

On the 22nd Coote, leaving five companies of grenadiers, 300 levies and some guns in Carangoly, marched on Wandewash, 23 miles to the west. Early in the preceding August Lieutenant Flint had been sent to take over command of this important post and had arrived there just as the native commandant was arranging to deliver it up to Hyder Ali. Flint established himself here, re-awakened the martial zeal of the original garrison, and, ably supported by

---

* The Captain Pringle here mentioned appears to have been Coote's Intelligence Officer, and he signs his reports as "Captain, Corps of Guides."

Ensign Moore, the only other European, repaired the works, built carriages for his guns, made his own powder and trained his sepoys as gunners, and not only held the place for the Company, but made it a base of supply for the whole army. Hyder's principal officer, one Meer Sahib, had now been besieging the fort since December with a powerful train of artillery, 11,000 foot and 22,000 horse, and by the time of Coote's arrival two approaches had been advanced close to the counterscarp of the ditch. The advance of the main army, however, caused the Mysore General to raise the siege, and Coote was able to encamp his force on the very ground where he had set up his tents, when, twenty-one years before to a day, he had fought the battle and raised the siege of Wandewash.

The order which he issued, dated Camp Wandewash, January 23rd, 1781, runs as follows:—

"*The Army is now encamped on the field where a glorious victory was achieved over the French on the 23rd January, 1760, and the Commander-in-Chief directs that an extra dram and biscuit be drawn for the Europeans and dry batta for the native troops.*"

General Coote also gave great praise to Flint and Moore for their gallant conduct in holding the place, granted every man of the garrison a month's pay, and promoted Flint captain and Moore lieutenant—promotions subsequently cancelled by the Court of Directors as being contrary to the rules of their service, which awarded promotion in rank by seniority only—like Lord Melbourne and the Garter, they probably considered there was " no damned merit about it " !

On January 28th the army marched towards Permacoil, leaving Flint in command of Wandewash with ample supplies for standing a prolonged siege, but had only proceeded a few miles when an express arrived from Madras announcing that a French squadron had appeared off that place, and the army now marched first to Carangoly, then raised the siege of Permacoil, defended by Lieutenant Bishop and one company of sepoys, and finally moved on Pondicherry, camping on the Red Hills on February 5th. Steps were at once taken to destroy all the surf boats and so prevent any communication between the French ships and the shore, and all military stores and provisions found in the town were seized.

Hyder Ali had been at Arcot, but on the evening of February 8th he suddenly made his appearance with his whole army within a very few miles of the English camp, when Coote moved off towards Cuddalore. The French fleet left the coast on February 12th, but the army remained for some months at Cuddalore, receiving grain from Madras but having to forage for beef and mutton, a work of great labour and difficulty, since Meer Sahib lay at Trivady, only fifteen miles distant, with an army of observation, from which he constantly detached parties of horse in all directions to prevent supplies from the surrounding country passing into the British camp. At the same time Tippoo had been detached to besiege Thiaghur, while the younger Lally had marched to seize Nagore.

In April, however, Coote personally led a force of several battalions of sepoys to the capture of Trivady, and about the same time the army received a small but doubtless very welcome reinforcement of two companies of the Madras Europeans and a battalion and a half of sepoys who had been serving under General Goddard against the Mahrattas, and who were brought round from the Malabar Coast in the ships of Admiral Hughes's fleet; and also of two sepoy battalions under Captain Lamotte from Nagore, which had left that place by sea just before the troops under Lally entered the town.

Coote had strained his resources in the endeavour to relieve Thiaghur, but his efforts were in vain, and Lieutenant Roberts, his ammunition having been expended, found himself obliged to surrender on June 7th.

The next enterprise to be attempted was the reduction of the fortified pagoda of Chillambrum, 3 miles south of the River Vallaar, and about 26 miles in the same direction from Cuddalore. This pagoda, one of the first of Hyder's conquests in the Carnatic, had been fortified by him for the dual purpose of arresting his enemy's progress to the south, and of serving as a depot or magazine for provisions for the use of his own army, as well as of such French troops as might be thrown ashore on the coast. The Bengal troops, marching under Colonel Pearse, had by this time reached the Carnatic and were moving rapidly southward, and the Commander-in-Chief, to prevent Hyder from attacking them on the march, proceeded towards Chillambrum on June 16th, crossing the Vellaar River on the 18th.

He had hoped to take the place by a *coup de main*, and advanced in the evening of this day with four battalions to achieve his purpose. A gun was brought up to the outer gateway and blew it open, and was then run forward to the inner gate; but the European gunners were here all killed or wounded, and Captain Moorhouse and Lieutenant Taafe only were left to keep the gun in action, the last round being fired by Moorhouse, who " rammed home the charge with his fuzee and fired the gun with the lock." The enemy opened a particularly deadly fire on the column, which had to fall back, having experienced a severe loss. The *pettah* had, however, been thoroughly searched, and the large quantity of grain found in it was brought away. On the 24th the army retired towards Porto Novo, some 6 miles distant, to land guns from the ships and prepare materials for reducing Chillambrum by a regular siege.

The casualties in this unsuccessful assault were serious: 2 Europeans and 7 native ranks were *killed*, 8 officers, 1 volunteer, 8 European rank and file, and 112 natives were *wounded*, while 1 officer and 2 Europeans and 34 native ranks were *missing*.* Another account gives the casualties among the officers as follows: *Killed*, Lieutenant Bruce, Assistant Engineer; *wounded*, Captains Hussey, Shaw, and Lamotte, Lieutenants Younge, Montgomery, Ford, North, Clark, and Collins.

Sir Eyre Coote had himself a narrow escape, a cannon ball breaking the leg of Lieutenant Younge, upon whose shoulder he was at the moment leaning.

The repulse here sustained had been so greatly magnified to Hyder that he now resolved to risk the battle Coote had for long been offering him; his own Mysore officers cordially supported

* The casualties in this and in some other of Coote's actions are in the P.R.O.: W.O. 40/5.

Hyder, only Lally urged delay or at least caution, but Hyder hoped to drive the English into the sea or to cut up the army as he had cut up the unfortunate detachment under Baillie. Coote was equally determined to do something to restore the spirits of his men and to check the presumption of the enemy, and he now directed the continuance of the preparations for the siege of Chillambrum, embarked the heavy guns and impedimenta on the ships of the fleet, and issued four days' grain to be carried by each soldier during the operations necessary to bring on a general action; while Hughes was asked to cover Cuddalore with a portion of his fleet, holding the remainder ready to embark the army should the need for such action unfortunately arise.

Early on the morning of July 1st Coote moved out on to the wide plain, already dotted with bodies of Hyder's cavalry, having at his disposal an army no more than 8,476 strong, containing 830 cavalry, 598 artillery, and 7,048 infantry; his order of battle was formed in two lines: the first, under Sir Hector Munro, was composed of 2 regiments of the Nawab's cavalry, the 73rd Highlanders, the Madras and Bengal Europeans, 5 battalions of sepoys, and the Trichinopoly detachment; the second line, commanded by General Stuart, contained 4 battalions of sepoys, and with it were 26 guns, while 30 accompanied Munro.

Coote's unwieldy and slow-moving baggage train, with its huge host of camp followers, was placed between the right of the army and the sea, and was protected by the two remaining regiments of the Nawab's Horse, by a battalion of sepoys, and 7 guns.

Coote's own estimate of the numbers of the army of his opponent placed them at 47 guns, 630 Europeans, 1,100 Topasses, 40,000 cavalry, 18,400 infantry in 23 battalions, and 120,000 irregulars, besides a horde of fighting men of the armies of the petty chiefs who had joined Hyder Ali since his entry into the Carnatic.

The army advanced for rather more than a mile in a direction slightly west of north, when the enemy's position was clearly discernible; it lay across the road to Cuddalore, and extended from commanding ground on the right to some sandhills near the sea, and was strengthened by earthworks and gun emplacements; and so soon as the army came within range of the Mysore guns it was greeted with a warm cannonade, to which Coote did not permit his artillery to make reply. The Commander-in-Chief wrote:—

"It was necessary to explore, if possible, the ground on our right, in hopes of its admitting to advance from that point, by which we should avoid the enemy's direct fire from their batteries, and have a chance of gaining the left of their posts or other ways to command them. The principal force of their army was drawn up in the rear of their works, extending further on the plain than either eye or horizon could command, with large bodies of cavalry in every direction, and their rockets were thrown in numbers to impede and harass our movements. During this interval of unavoidable inaction, thoroughly to examine their position, we were obliged to suffer a warm cannonade. Their guns were well served and did execution; we could not afford to throw away any shot to answer them, having occasion for every round we had for more decisive service."

"Coote," says Fortescue, "was 55 years old and prematurely aged by hard work, sickness, and long residence in unhealthy climates; but he had not forgotten how to fight a battle."

It was clear to the British leader that an attack upon the enemy's right would involve the troops in broken ground—a network of low hills and steep ravines; an advance against the centre under the concentrated fire of the Mysore guns was not to be thought of; but there seemed a chance of turning the left of the position by an advance northwards of a mile or more, followed by a wheel to the west to bring the British down on the extreme flank of Hyder's huge but unwieldy force.

The rain which had delayed Coote's advance, had also prevented the completion of his enemy's dispositions; his arrangements on the right and centre were perfected, but a full day's work was yet to be done on the extreme left near the sea, where a well-designed redoubt remained half-finished and unarmed. Between this redoubt and the Cuddalore road, and parallel to the sea, were some low sand hills, and Coote's practised eye saw that these would help to conceal his movements to this flank, while the existence of the redoubt made it more than likely that a road had been made whereby guns and material might reach it. "At 9 o'clock Sir Eyre Coote had determined on his measures; and without any previous movement among his troops that should indicate a change of disposition, he ordered both his lines to break into column, by the simple tactic of that day, by facing to the right, a battalion from the left of each line changing their front, for the purpose of protecting that most exposed flank and covering the whole interval between the lines."*

Arrived at the cover afforded by the sand hills, Stuart halted and faced to the west, while Coote moved Munro's column further to the north, where presently was found the expected road. This pass was seized and held, and Munro, pushing through, deployed in the plain beyond, his right protected by a thick hedge. Stuart, in echelon on the left, was to drive the enemy from his immediate front before the troops with Coote could advance further.

Hyder's position was turned, and he was obliged to leave his entrenchments, but the day was not yet won. He moved his guns to a fresh position, massed a huge body of infantry in front of Munro, and sent a strong force of infantry and cavalry against Stuart. This officer behaved admirably; he seized the position which had been pointed out to him, repulsed all attacks upon it, and so established himself as to make possible Munro's further advance. *He*, however, could only move very slowly forward, fighting every inch of his way under a very heavy cannonade, the British artillery struggling manfully against the powerful and numerous ordnance of the enemy; and Hyder now, seeking by heroic measures to bring the battle to a close, poured down his best horsemen, European and Native, under Lally and Pimoran, on both British divisions. Those who attacked Munro withered away before the steady volleys of the two-deep line, while the cavalry body which made for Stuart's rear came unexpectedly under the fire of a light-draught schooner, the *Intelligence* (Captain Murray), which had come close in-shore.

* Wilks, Vol. II, p. 311.

Meer Sahib was slain by this fire, and his followers fell back in confusion.

It was now 4 p.m., and Hyder refused for some time to believe that the day was lost and that his career of conquest was checked; but his friends and advisers urged him to fly and finally forced him from the field, his army melting away behind him and nowhere rallying until it reached Chillambrum.

"It is impossible to describe the awful magnificence of the scene that our army beheld from the heights upon which it halted. The space as far as the eye could reach was entirely covered by multitudes of horse, foot, artillery, and heaps of baggage, all intermingled in the greatest confusion, flying in the utmost consternation, galloping across each other over an extensive plain, and raising such clouds of dust as almost to obscure the sky."*

Admiral Hughes's fleet could not take any part in the action, except so far as the *Intelligence* was concerned, but the masts and yards were throughout covered with sailors anxiously awaiting the issue of the battle in which the sister service was engaged.

Coote's cavalry was too few in numbers to pursue, and the army camped on that night and the two following days at Mootypollam, moving on July 4th to the neighbourhood of Cuddalore.

The General gave unstinted praise to his troops for their conduct in battle:—"*The behaviour of the whole army . . . was uniformly steady and worthy of the highest commendation. . . . Every individual of our little army seemed to feel the critical situation of our national concerns. . . . The only difficulty was to restrain the ardour of the troops within prudential bounds. . . . The spirited behaviour of our sepoy corps did them the greatest credit; no Europeans could be steadier; they were emulous of being foremost in every service it was necessary to undertake.*"

The victor put the enemy's loss at about 3,000—Lally was amongst the wounded; the British casualties were, all things considered, astonishingly light, amounting to—Europeans, 1 officer and 18 killed, 5 officers and 31 other ranks wounded; Natives,

* Innis Munro, *Operations on the Coromandel Coast*, p. 250.

64 killed and 198 wounded, while 1 European soldier and 18 sepoys were missing.

The casualties in the Madras European Regiment—or "Coast Infantry" as Coote styles them in his despatch—were Lieutenant and Quartermaster Francis Baillie, 2 sergeants and 1 man killed; Ensign Charles Thewles and 5 rank and file wounded.

"The victory," as Fortescue says,* " was not in the ordinary sense a great one, for Coote had no trophies to show of guns and prisoners taken nor of the enemy's army destroyed; but it was the salvation of Southern India."

Sir Eyre Coote was very anxious to move northwards, for already two days previous to the battle of Porto Novo he had heard from young Flint at Wandewash that Tippoo Sahib " with 7,000 infantry, a large body of cavalry, and 12 guns had arrived within 6 miles of Wandewash with intent to besiege it," and the general was desirous of effecting the relief of this stronghold and of forming a junction with Colonel Pearse's Bengal detachment now close at hand.

Leaving, then, his wounded and sick at Cuddalore, and having been joined by some recovered convalescents who had been placed there when the army moved on Chillambrum, Coote, taking such meagre supplies as were procurable and as his weak transport could carry, moved on Wandewash, and on July 15th came in sight of the camp of his enemy, who at once hurried off to the westward. On the 18th Tippoo was repulsed in an attempt to carry Wandewash by storm, and was then obliged to raise the siege. Coote, arriving before the place on the 20th, Tippoo now, strongly reinforced, moved off to try to intercept Pearse, whose march had been delayed by many things, but mainly, of course, by the length of the journey of nearly 1,000 miles, mostly through unsurveyed country, and also by an epidemic of cholera. To join Pearse and save him from attack, Coote made a forced march of 150 miles, practically without transport and supplies, finally effecting a junction with him at Pulicat on August 2nd.

* Vol. III, p. 454.

The combined army now returned to St. Thomas's Mount, and on August 8th it was reorganized in one cavalry and four infantry brigades. In the 1st Brigade was all the European Infantry —the 73rd Highlanders, the Bengal European Infantry, and the 2nd Battalion 1st Madras European Infantry, and both the brigadier and brigade-major belonged to the 73rd. The commands and staff appointments of the other four infantry brigades were tolerably equally distributed among the officers of the two Presidencies of Bengal and Madras, Colonels Ross Lang and Brown, Lieutenants Richardson and Oliver being the commandants and brigade-majors of the 2nd and 5th Brigades, and belonging to the Madras Europeans, while Colonel Pearse commanded the 3rd Brigade, the brigade-majors of this and the 4th Brigade being also Bengal officers. To the 4th Brigade General Coote appointed Colonel Owen, his military secretary, as brigadier, an appointment which seems to have given much umbrage, Major Thomas Breton and Captain Henry Harvey, of the Madras Europeans, declining to serve under Owen, and being consequently placed under arrest.

The cavalry brigade was, as before, composed of four regiments, and was still commanded by Colonel Cosby.

Colonel Lang was at this time at Vellore, and therefore did not at once take over command of his brigade, which seems to have been temporarily in charge of Major Edmondstone, a Bengal officer.

Preparations were now set on foot to march and lay siege to Arcot and to relieve Vellore, but before the army could attempt either of these projects it was necessary to take Tripassore, 33 miles to the westward, a post lately greatly strengthened and garrisoned by some 1,500 men. The army accordingly marched on the 16th, and arrived before Tripassore on August 19th, when Hyder, who was at Conjeveram and was informed of Coote's movements, at once advanced to harass the British. On the 22nd a breach was made in the walls, and the garrison thereupon demanded terms, but by this Hyder and his army were close at hand, so orders were given to storm, when the commander of the fort surrendered at discretion and Hyder drew off.

The losses of Coote's army here were 6 killed and 10 wounded, Ensign Carey, of the 8th Battalion of Sepoys, being killed by the bursting of one of the 18-pounders.

The supplies found at Tripassore and a convoy from Poonamallee enabled Coote to secure enough rice for six days' use, and with this scanty store he marched 17 miles west on the 26th in the hope of bringing Hyder to action; and at 9 a.m. on the 27th the advanced guard discovered the Mysore army in force in its front and extending towards both flanks, strongly posted in rear of the woods and village of Pollilore, nearly on the ground where Colonel Baillie's detachment had met disaster scarcely a year previously, and where Hyder had been assured that the fates would be propitious to him.

The advanced guard, moving along the tree-shaded road, was fired into by four 18-pounders posted in a grove on the left of the line of march; it was thereupon halted, and Coote, riding forward, found the enemy's position to be one of great strength, Hyder occupying three villages, the ground in front and on the flanks of these being in every direction cut up by water courses and nullahs, while the guns behind the banks of the ditches were fired through embrasures. The main Mysore army was massed in rear. As the strong land wind dropped for a moment and permitted distant objects to be seen through the dust it had raised, Coote's practised eye saw a small and thick grove of trees on a slight eminence some 800 yards to the front and nearly encircled by a water-course; this he at once sent a battalion of sepoys to occupy. A heavy fire, rapidly increasing in intensity, was opened on this battalion, whereupon another was sent forward in support.

The first line—three brigades—under Sir Hector Munro, was deployed in advance of the tree-crowned hillock facing south-west, fronting what then, in the broken and wooded country, seemed to be the main body of the enemy; while the second line, under Stuart, formed in support of Munro. This latter officer had scarcely completed his deployment, however, when he found his line enfiladed by eight or nine guns from a somewhat distant wooded village to the west. Hyder had in fact, as at Porto Novo, drawn up his main body on the left flank of Coote's advance, with the left resting on Pollilore and its right on another village further to the east, and had sent no more than a detachment under his son Tippoo to check the British in front.

Munro now changed front to the right, his line covered to some extent by the jungle in front; this was found to be penetrable and the British first line, moving through it and lining a bank beyond, brought up their guns and soon obtained the mastery over the enemy's artillery.

This movement unfortunately had the effect of widely separating the two divisions of the army. The grove and eminence first occupied were so hotly cannonaded by the enemy that Stuart found himself obliged to deploy every man at his disposal to strengthen and extend the position against which the chief efforts of the enemy seemed to be directed. Nowhere was the outlook reassuring—here it assumed an almost desperate appearance. The irregularities of the ground broke up the battalions into confused and scattered bodies; a newly-raised Circar battalion, enlisted for local service only, fell back in disgraceful flight from an attack upon a village; and Sir Eyre Coote now hurried from the right to the left of his line to see how best to restore the fortunes of the day.

He recognized that the village of Pollilore was the real objective, but also that, before attempting to capture it, a connected line must be re-formed, and he therefore ordered Munro to change position once more—to face south with his left some 1,300 yards more to the west than it had been originally, and with his right exactly opposite the village of Pollilore. The right brigade of the first line, supported by the fire of every British gun that could be brought to bear, moved directly upon the village, turned out the defenders, and plied them with the fire of two light guns which had accompanied the advance.

The battle had now been eight hours in progress; the rest of the first line supported the right brigade; while the second line drove back the enemy in its front and gained some high ground, whence its guns cannonaded the enemy now everywhere in retreat.

The enemy fell back that night on Conjeveram and next day to Arcot, the British in no position effectively to pursue, since on the 29th there was not one single day's supplies in hand for the soldiers, while the followers had been fasting for forty-eight hours. The victory was scarcely more than a drawn battle; the native portion of the army does not seem to have fought as stoutly as at Porto Novo; while the ground was quite unsuited to the rigid formations of those days.

Coote estimated the strength of the enemy's forces on this day at 150,000 men with 80 guns, and their losses in killed and wounded at nearly 2,000. In his army there were 129 killed, 261 wounded and 63 missing, 24 Europeans being killed and 54 of all ranks wounded. General Stuart lost his leg, and Colonel Brown, of the Madras Europeans, was mortally wounded, while Captain Hislop, the Commander-in-Chief's aide-de-camp, was killed, as was also Assistant-Surgeon Ranken; Ensigns Gould, Watson and Hazlewood died of wounds, and Captains Bridges and Herbert were also hit.

The following order was published after the action by General Sir Eyre Coote:—

"*The Commander-in-Chief takes the earliest opportunity of returning his thanks to the whole army he has the honour to command for their very steady and gallant conduct throughout the action of yesterday, and which alone ensured the success of the operations of the day. . . . The spirited conduct of our troops must strike the enemy with that awe and respect for our arms, which cannot fail to be of essential service to our national cause, and, it is hoped, will eventually be the means of shortening the confinement and suffering of our brother soldiers in the enemy's miserable prisons. The Commander-in-Chief takes this opportunity of mentioning that he will set forth to His Majesty and to the Company the very essential services this army has rendered. . . .*"

On the 29th the army moved to Tripassore, arriving there next day, and from here General Munro went into Madras preparatory to going to England, as he was in a bad state of health, and Coote seems also to have had some idea of resigning his command, being disgusted at the very meagre support his army was receiving from the Government of Fort St. George.

Some scanty supplies having been with much difficulty collected, the army marched on September 21st into the country of the Poligar Chiefs, the object being to obtain regular supplies from them, and, by defeating Hyder, to attach them definitely to the British cause. The general's efforts were only partially successful ; the chiefs were afraid openly to assist the British ; and the army lived from hand to mouth by the discovery of the hiding places wherein grain had been stored and by means of a small magazine of supplies found in the little fort of Pollore, captured on September 23rd.

The state of the garrison and fortress of Vellore had for some time occasioned Coote no little anxiety, Colonel Lang, the commandant, having declared he must shortly surrender unless relieved ; while it was now reported that Hyder Ali was only ten or twelve miles distant, holding a pass in the Sholinghur Hills on the direct road between Pollore and Vellore and some thirty miles due west of Tripassore. Coote at once decided to endeavour to bring his formidable opponent to action, and, leaving some of his heavy guns and the greater part of his baggage at Pollore, he moved on September 26th some seven miles down the Arcot road, intending to pursue his march early on the following morning. During the night, however, rain fell very heavily, and Hyder, knowing well the inefficiency of Coote's transport, decided that his enemy would for a time make no further movement, and sent out his own cattle to graze far afield while allowing his men to disperse in search of food and plunder. Such carelessness was, however, almost criminal when so tried a commander as Eyre Coote was in the field, and Hyder was to pay the penalty usually demanded of those who affect to despise their enemy.

Early on the 27th Coote rode forward to reconnoitre and saw in his front a long rocky ridge, a spur from the Sholinghur Hill, and of which the enemy was in possession. Sending for the 2nd Brigade, the enemy was dislodged from this position, and the General, pushing on, presently descried Hyder's army encamped to the south and within not more than three miles of him. The main body was now ordered up, and moving to the right, passed almost along the foot of the Sholinghur Hill nearly parallel to the enemy's camp, until the centre of the first line was opposite Hyder's main body. The first line then advanced, its flanks covered by small rocky hillocks, while the second line broke into echelon of corps, the left thrown back, with the dual object of supporting the baggage guard placed near the hills, and of watching and keeping in check large enemy cavalry bodies hovering on the flank. Coote's object was obviously to force the unwieldy mass before him to change position and so take such advantage as might offer of the superior manœuvring power of his own troops.

Up to this Hyder seems to have regarded Coote's movements as of the nature of a reconnaissance only, but he now realized that he was about to be seriously attacked, and sent out horsemen in every direction to call in his soldiers, cattle and drivers, drawing up his main body in rear of a gentle rise of ground where the bulk of his artillery was posted, the front covered by swampy rice fields; Lally commanded on the right, Tippoo Sahib with a numerous cavalry directed the left, while Hyder himself was in the centre. The Mysore army numbered 150,000 men with 70 guns. Coote commanded at most 11,500, of whom 1,500 only were Europeans.

It had been intended that Edmondstone's brigade, moving well round to the right with its front protected by a large tank on the enemy's left front, should endeavour to cut Hyder's communications with Arcot, while Coote's main body advanced directly to the attack. The Second Brigade, however, seems to have gone rather further to the right than had been intended, and Hyder opened fire upon the British line from all his guns, hoping to throw Coote's troops into confusion while Edmondstone's error was being corrected. The English General, wholly unmoved, bade the Second Brigade incline to its left to close the interval, maintaining at the same time the general advance, the little army appearing, as

Fortescue describes it, " to be moving into the midst of a huge circle of enemies."

The nature of the ground, partly rocky, partly swamp, caused occasional gaps to appear in the British line and into these Hyder sought to pour his cavalry. In the centre Colonel Pearse and his staff fought hand to hand with the Mysore Horse; some of Coote's guns had to be turned about and trained on the cavalry as they charged through to the rear; similar attacks were made upon the left, and here one of the battalions of Bengal sepoys came upon an abandoned gun which proved to be one of the eight lost with Colonel Baillie's detachment a year previously.

There was a moment of intense anxiety, almost indeed of crisis, when Tippoo opened fire with several guns on the British left, enfilading the line. The tumbrils were not immediately at hand, the limber ammunition with Coote's guns was running short and some of the fuses failed to act. There arose now a shout that the gun ammunition was expended, and the report reaching the ears of Coote he halted the line and galloped to the left to ascertain the real state of affairs. The delay, slight as it was, afforded Hyder an opportunity of drawing off, his retreat covered by Tippoo's horsemen, while the retiring enemy was cannonaded by Edmondstone's guns and harassed until darkness came on by the persistent attacks of Cosby's cavalry brigade.

A contemporary historian tells us that "the Mysoreans uniformly describe the battle of Sholinghur as a surprise and admit it to have been a severe defeat, in which their loss probably exceeded 5,000 men"; but in a note written from the field the General stated that he would have willingly exchanged the trophies he had won, together with the credit of the victory, " for five days' rice ! " Of his troops his despatch says :—

" I am at a loss for words to do justice to the behaviour of the whole army on the late occasion. . . . Nothing could exceed the approved firmness and intrepidity of our troops on these very trying occasions ; opposed to attack a well-posted line of infantry, with a numerous train of artillery covered by large bodies of cavalry, the most active zeal and

cool deliberate military steadiness was successfully exerted, and, to the honour of the British arms, the enemy assaulted and repelled in all quarters."

The losses in Coote's army were extraordinarily slight—only one British officer, Ensign Deakin, one European gunner, and 21 native ranks were killed, 5 European gunners, 56 sepoys were wounded, and 9 native ranks were missing; there do not appear to have been any casualties of any kind in the brigade containing the three European regiments—an astonishing result in an action of such magnitude.

The Poligar chiefs of North Arcot and Nellore now showed themselves more friendly to the British after their recent victory, upon which Hyder Ali, furious at their defection, determined upon punishing them, and on October 12th news came to Coote that a select body of Hyder's troops had entered the Pollams and was harrying the country. Coote was at the time in indifferent health, but he acted with his usual decision, and placing himself at the head of a body of troops, he marched on October 14th and returned after an absence of thirty-eight hours, of which thirty-two were spent in the saddle, having surprised, discomfited and dispersed the enemy, who fled leaving his plunder, tents and equipment behind him.

To ensure further supplies required for the force about to march to the relief of Vellore, a considerable detachment, mostly composed of native troops, was pushed on in advance some twenty miles under Colonel Owen to collect provisions from the country and, if possible, to intercept the enemy's convoys. On October 23rd Owen was attacked at daylight by a very large army commanded by Hyder in person; Owen was obliged to retire and suffered considerable loss, indeed, had it not been for the steadiness and gallantry of the troops with him, it might easily have been a similar disaster to that which overtook Colonel Baillie's party. The British casualties numbered 317 killed and wounded, Captain Walker and Ensign Maclean being killed, while Lieutenant Price, Ensigns Dods, Hall, Symons and Darley were wounded, but the enemy's casualties were estimated at 3,000 and Hyder Ali was much disheartened at the failure of his attempt to destroy the detachment under Colonel Owen.

Towards the end of October the state of affairs at Vellore was approaching a crisis; there was not a single day's reserve of supplies in the magazine, and the garrison was entirely dependent on such provisions as could be smuggled in by night from distant and friendly villages. From the very commencement of the war, Vellore had been continually besieged or blockaded, and a large portion of the Mysore Army with battering train had been constantly before it. The fort was a very ancient one, constructed before the days of cannon, and, being close to a range of hills, it had in later days become necessary for its effective defence to push out from the *enceinte* and fortify the summits of the hills which commanded it. The actual ramparts of the fort were of solid masonry, while the ditch was broad and deep and filled with water. The siege now in progress was conducted with great skill and judgment by French officers; one attack was carried on against the hill defences for five weeks, the enemy's artillery being well served, his guns numerous, and his infantry in overwhelming strength, but the fine defence made by the garrison under Lieutenants Champneys and Parr foiled and repulsed every assault. On one occasion the ladders were placed in position and ascended by the enemy, but they were hurled back with great slaughter, and Parr and his men pursuing fell upon them with the bayonet and drove them from the breach.

At this time the lower fort was garrisoned by the headquarters of the 1st Battalion Madras Europeans and these one night made a sortie, entered the enemy's trenches and spiked his guns.

It was not until November 1st that General Coote was able to set out for Vellore, carrying with him such supplies of rice as he had been able to collect, loaded up on some 700 bullocks captured from Hyder's raiding parties. So rapid was his march that Coote, accompanying the advance with his bodyguard, came suddenly upon a small body of Mysore cavalry, posted to prevent supplies or messengers getting through the hills to Vellore. Coote at once ordered his bodyguard to charge; "the European troop, about 30 men, chiefly did the business as they were better mounted than the native cavalry"*; all the staff seem to have taken part, Lieutenants Dallas and Rollestone particularly distinguishing themselves; and "the gallant old General himself exchanged a pistol-shot with a horseman."†

On November 3rd Vellore was finally relieved, and the magazines were filled up with thirty-six days' supplies for the reduced force it was proposed to leave there when the army moved off again. The General published a very complimentary order on the gallant defence made by Colonel Lang and his subordinates—and the names of the following are specially mentioned in accounts of the siege—Captain Sale,‡ Lieutenants Champneys and Parr, Sergeants Lantwein and Johnston.

The main army remained only two or three days at Vellore and the General then, taking with him Colonel Lang and the Grenadiers of the 1st Battalion 1st Madras Regiment, under Champneys, so as to reduce the number of Europeans to be provisioned, fell back towards Chittore, the command of Vellore being entrusted to Captain Cuppage. The army arrived on November 7th before Chittore which capitulated on the 10th, but the supply of grain here found was disappointingly small.

Hyder was still very active; he sent part of his army to lay siege to Tripassore, while he himself attacked a post at Paliput where Captain Temple, with a sepoy battalion, had been left to guard the sick and stores. Temple withdrew on the approach of the Mysore Chief, abandoning guns and stores, and was able to rejoin the main army, while the small fort of Pollore also fell to Hyder, who failed to capture the garrison, but secured four 18-pounders which, for want of gun-bullocks, Coote had been obliged to leave there when he marched to meet the enemy at Sholinghur.

Coote was now in some difficulty; Hyder must be checked, but

* *Naval and Military Magazine*, Vol. I, pp. 406, 407.
† *Ibid.*
‡ Father of the General Sale of Jellahabad fame.

if Tripassore was to be relieved a garrison must be left in Chittore at the risk of capture by the enemy; the army was much weakened, Coote's chief object was the defeat of the main Mysore body, and there seemed no object in exhausting the British force further in minor operations, but the Madras Council was pressing for the relief of Tripassore, so, leaving a small garrison in Chittore under Captain Lamotte, Coote marched to the relief of Tripassore. Lamotte well knew the risks of his situation and it is said that he or some other wag chalked on the main gate of Chittore fort—" the high road to Seringapatam!"

On the 17th the army set out, but on the 19th, when the gun-fire at Tripassore could be distinctly heard, heavy rain storms began, the rivers, three in number, came down in spate, the transport—elephants, camels and carts—stuck fast in the mud and had to be abandoned, while the fighting men struggled on. The last river was just fordable when the army came up to it on the 21st, and that evening the force camped near Tripassore with no more than two days' supplies in hand. Tippoo had already made a breach in one of the sides of the fort, but drew off on Coote's approach, leaving the fort which had been admirably defended by its garrison under Captain Bishop (of Permacoil fame) and Lieutenant Oram.

Of the trials of this march Coote wrote on the 29th to Fort William :—

"Such was the distress to which the army was reduced for provisions that in the march from Chittore to the relief of Tripassore, one-half was three successive days alternately without rice. The followers of the army from the last time of their leaving Madras until they came back to Tripassore had had two seers (4lbs.) of paddy served out to them. Numbers have died by hunger and the inclemency of the weather, from which causes in the course of two marches we lost nearly a hundred cavalry; likewise bullocks, elephants and camels, both public and private. In short the scene exhibited was more like a field of battle than a line of march."*

* Forrest, *Selections from State Papers*, Vol. III, p. 827

Towards the end of the month the army returned to Madras, the Commander-in-Chief so prostrated by illness that he had to be carried in his palanquin; and on December 3rd the force was distributed in cantonments, the sepoy brigades at the Mount and the remainder on the Choultry Plain and in other places near Madras.

The last event of the campaign of this year was the recapture of Chittore by Hyder, this place being surrendered about Christmas Day on condition that the garrison should be permitted to return to Madras. Again did Hyder Ali fail to keep faith; Lamotte and his officers were sent to join those previously taken and already in captivity at Seringapatam, while the bulk of the rank and file were marched to Bednore.

While two battalions of the Madras European Regiment had been engaged in the field under Coote and in the defence of Vellore, the remaining battalions had been employed during this year in other arduous and important services in different parts of India.

Something has already been said of the work of that part of the Corps, 346 strong, in company with the Bombay troops under General Goddard, and of the subsequent incorporation of many of the rank and file of this detachment in the Bombay European Regiment.

Then in Tanjore, and in Southern India, the 2nd Battalion 2nd Madras European Regiment, under Colonel Brathwaite, had helped in the defence of Tanjore, with the exception of which city the whole Tanjore country was possessed by Hyder and the strong forts garrisoned by his well-found troops. Brathwaite's force was small and largely composed of native troops; two attacks he made upon enemy posts were repulsed with severe loss, and in one he was himself wounded, the command then for a time devolving upon Lieutenant-Colonel Nixon of the Corps, who, reinforced by a draft of the Regiment, attacked two other forts in enemy possession; he carried these but suffered many casualties, particularly in his Europeans. The rule of the Raja of Tanjore had by these operations been to some extent re-established, and the British force in these territories was now directed to move against Nagore as a preliminary to the reduction of Negapatam, an operation now much favoured by the Madras Council.

In June, 1781, Lord Macartney had arrived at Madras as Governor and was determined to prosecute with the utmost vigour the war which had just been declared with the Dutch, and to this end was specially desirous of capturing Negapatam and Trincomallee. At the time—July—Coote was greatly opposed to any dispersion of his small force, but Macartney, whose complete ignorance of military matters was no bar to his powers of interference, determined to attempt at least the capture of Negapatam with the help of the fleet under Admiral Hughes and of such land forces as might be drawn from Tanjore. On October 31st Coote sent Macartney a final protest, but by that time the Governor had already made his preparations for the expedition and nominated the commander. This was to be General Sir Hector Munro, who had left the Army in bad health after Pollilore and was at Madras awaiting an opportunity to return home. He was inclined to refuse the command pressed upon him, and seems to have finally accepted mainly from a sense of duty, but loyally refused to move until he had obtained Coote's sanction. He then left Madras in the fleet under Hughes and arrived off Nagore, four miles to the north of Negapatam, about October 20th. Here Colonel Nixon appeared with the Company's troops on the next day, upon which General Munro landed and assumed command. On the same day Admiral Hughes put ashore and placed at the disposal of the military commander all the Marines of the squadron, amounting to 443 all ranks, and on the 22nd he further landed a battalion of seamen 827 strong. From a return of the army present and dated November 19th, the sum of the besiegers was 4,215, but of these the Europeans, exclusive of the sailors and marines, appear to have numbered no more than 99, while the strength of the garrison of Negapatam on the same date was 6,551, with a European infantry battalion 288 strong, besides artillery.

The lines in front of the works were carried by storm on October

29th, ground was broken in front of the north face on November 3rd, and the batteries opened two days later; while the squadron, anchored close in shore, kept up a heavy cannonade until the 12th, when, the garrison having made two very desperate sorties which were repulsed, the Governor, Reynier Van Vlissingen, demanded a parley, and articles of capitulation were signed.

Two Colours, over 200 serviceable guns, iron and brass, and all the troops that had not already deserted, were surrendered with the town and citadel.

The casualties in the besieging force were very small, amounting to no more than 133 Europeans and sepoys, killed, wounded and missing, and were distributed as under:—

Navy: 1 sergeant, 11 men killed; 2 officers, 1 sergeant, 17 men wounded.

Marines: 1 corporal, 3 men killed; 1 sergeant, 20 men wounded.

Cavalry: 5 sepoys wounded.

Artillery: 1 officer, 1 sergeant, 11 other ranks wounded.

European Infantry: 4 men wounded.

Sepoys: 12 men killed; 1 British officer and 33 men wounded; 8 men missing.*

---

* Hughes' and Munro's despatches are in the *London Gazette* of May 18th, 1782; I have nowhere else found the strength and casualties given.—H. W.

CHAPTER IX

1782–1793.

BATTLE OF ARNEE—THE SIEGE OF CUDDALORE—THE FIRST WAR WITH TIPPOO SULTAN.

VELLORE had been provisioned up to December 15th, 1781, and Captain Cuppage, the commandant, had by various means managed to collect supplies sufficient to last him until January **1782** 11th, 1782; but the matter of the relief of Vellore seeming urgent, Coote assembled the army on January 4th near Tripassore, whence it was to commence its forward march next morning. On the 5th, however, when the troops were upon the point of breaking camp, Coote was discovered to have had a stroke of apoplexy and Colonel Lang was hurriedly summoned from Madras to take his place. The general made, however, an astonishing recovery and was well enough on the 6th to accompany the army in his palanquin. Marching via Sholinghur the force was cannonaded while crossing the Poonee River on the 9th, but, pressing on, Vellore was reached on the 11th and some three or four months' supplies having been thrown in, the army started on its return march on the 13th. When passing through some swampy ground Coote was again attacked, but the advance was not seriously impeded and Coote led his force back safely to Tripassore.

In these two operations Lieutenant Greenwell and 4 European infantrymen were killed, 2 officers and 8 rank and file were wounded while 1 man was missing; of the sepoys 24 were killed, 66 were wounded and 9 were missing.

Early in February a French fleet appeared off the Coromandel Coast and in March the French landed a considerable body of troops at Porto Novo, but before this latter date our troops had experienced a serious disaster in the south. On February 18th Colonel Brathwaite, with some 1,700 men (including 50 of the Madras Europeans under Ensign Fenwick)* and 9 guns, was encamped at a place called Annagudi, about six miles north-east of the town of Combaconum and three miles south of the Coleroon River. Brathwaite's intelligence service was defective, and he had no idea that the enemy was in his immediate neighbourhood, while the concealment of the movements of Tippoo, who had a force of 6,000 horse, 12,000 infantry and 20 guns, was favoured by the existence of several large and deep rivers. On February 18th Brathwaite suddenly found himself practically surrounded, and at first endeavoured to fall back upon Negapatam, but after fighting desperately for twenty-six hours, during which Lieutenant Eastland and Ensign Stuart were killed and all the other officers except the surgeon were wounded, the force surrendered and its European officers were sent to join Hyder's earlier captives at Seringapatam. But for the presence of some 400 Frenchmen under Lally, who cut down some of his savage allies with his own hand, the whole force would have been massacred after surrender.

This was to prove the beginning of a recrudescence of success to Hyder and the French; on April 4th Cuddalore, which had been partly dismantled and was garrisoned by a force of sepoys, too small for the perimeter to be defended, under Captain James Hughes, was surrendered, and the French and Mysore forces, having effected a junction, then appeared before Permacoil early in May. Coote, after some unavoidable delay due to want of supplies, moved on the 17th to its relief, but only arrived on the 21st at Carangoly where he learnt that Permacoil had that day capitulated, the enemy then advancing on Wandewash, where, after several days spent in vain attempts to reduce that place, held by young Flint, they fell back

* The following European Infantry officers were also present :—Lieutenant Cameron, brigade major; Lieutenants Sampson, Bowles, Gillon, Lind, and Eastland; Ensigns Graham, Thewles, Loy, Holmes, Stuart, McAlly, Gahagan, Haywood, and Kennet; and Surgeon White.

towards Pondicherry on hearing of the approach of the army under Sir Eyre Coote.

There were now two courses open to the General—to attack an enemy strongly entrenched and in greatly superior strength, or to try to draw him from his ground and force him to accept battle upon more equal terms. Coote, then, turned away from Permacoil, marched fifteen miles to the west and encamped near Chittapet, making as though he proposed to attack it. This movement had the desired effect, for Hyder no sooner heard of the course Coote had taken than, leaving his French allies behind him, he marched rapidly to relieve Chittapet. In continuance of his plans the English leader now struck off towards Arnee, 17 miles south of Arcot and 74 south-west of Madras. This occasioned further alarm to the Mysore chief, for Arnee was his principal depot in this district and was somewhat feebly garrisoned, and he followed Coote at speed, marching 43 miles in 48 hours.

On June 2nd, about three miles from Arnee, his advance came up with the British rear guard just as the army was about to encamp. This rear guard—two cavalry regiments and two native infantry battalions—was commanded by Lieutenant-Colonel Elphinstone of the 73rd, and was at once cannonaded by 20 guns, but Elphinstone stood his ground until Coote had deployed his troops, posting the 2nd Brigade and some cavalry under Colonel Owen to protect the baggage. The cannonade now became general and warm on both sides. The British line was no sooner formed than it made a rapid advance upon the enemy's artillery, when Hyder, always fearful of losing any of his guns, immediately ordered these to retire some distance and then again open fire. There was a river in the enemy's rear, and it seemed at one time as though the rapid advance of the British would drive the army of Mysore into it, but a large body now threatening the baggage, Coote was obliged to halt his army until he could draw Colonel Owen nearer to him.

This being done the army advanced again at a brisk pace towards the enemy, who now fell back across the river and were pursued for a mile beyond it. Some tumbrils and a gun—a long brass 6-pounder—were seen to have stuck fast in the sandy bed of the river, while a party of the enemy worked hard to extricate it. The Grenadiers of the 73rd under Captain Lindsay and those of the Madras Europeans commanded by Captain Brown, charged down and captured the tumbrils, while a battalion of Bengal sepoys took the gun by a dash upon Lally's men who were covering the retreat.

The usual want of cavalry prevented any real pursuit, and while the action was in progress—the last in which Coote and Hyder were to meet—Tippoo had marched on Arnee, removed all treasure and reinforced the garrison. Coote summoned the place, but there appearing to be small hope of its early reduction, the army, on June 6th, began to retrace its steps to Madras.

Of the conduct of his men the General wrote :—"*Considering that the first movement of the army commenced at 4 in the morning, and that its most laborious operations were performed during an intensely hot day, and with the most unparalleled courage and cheerfulness, the praise due to every rank in it, both officers and men, is far beyond what can be expressed—at least such is the sense I entertain of their exertions as to place their merits infinitely above the reach of any encomiums of mine. I have in General Orders paid them the tribute of my hearty thanks and applause, and I am happy in this opportunity of recommending them as highly deserving of every attention or indulgence in the power of your Government to bestow on them.*"

The loss again was happily very small, only 13 being killed and 53 wounded, but the 73rd suffered terribly from the heat, an officer and 7 rank and file dying from its effects.

On June 23rd news was received that peace had been declared between the English and the Mahrattas, and a Royal Salute was fired from the guns on the ramparts of Fort St. George on confirmation of the news being announced.

On July 1st General Coote moved off with his army towards Wandewash and made an attempt to get into communication with Hyder Ali with a view of arranging terms of peace, but nothing resulted from these overtures, and the army then marched to Cuddalore with the intention of attempting its recovery, but returned to Madras early in September, the Mysore Horse hanging on the flanks and rear of the column and Coote so ill and prostrated that he had been obliged to hand over command to Major-General Stuart. Coote left for Bengal at the end of the month and though he did return to Madras at a crisis in the affairs of the Southern Presidency, he never again took the field and died within a few hours of landing.

On November 20th 2 captains, 4 subalterns and 2 companies of the 2nd Battalion 1st Madras European Regiment, under command of Major Cotgrave, embarked as reinforcements to Colonel Macleod at Ponniani, on the Malabar Coast, the investment of which place by Tippoo was only raised on the receipt of the intelligence of the death of Hyder Ali, which occurred on December 7th, 1782, and on the 11th Tippoo and his army were in full march to the eastward.

For a good two months after the death of Hyder Ali the army made no move; General Stuart does not seem to have possessed the *driving power* of Coote, and was possibly less fitted than his predecessor to cope with the interference of Lord Macartney. The time which should have been employed in action was wasted in idle discussion, and it is more than probable that had a spirited and immediate advance been made upon the late ruler's camp, prior to the arrival there of Tippoo, the Mysore army might have been dispersed and Tippoo's succession endangered or even prevented. Ignorance cannot be pleaded in excuse for inactivity since the news of Hyder's death reached Vellore on the day following his demise and positive intelligence of the event was at once transmitted to Madras by the commandant. Nor can it be said that the army was too weak to undertake any serious operations, for during the latter part of the year 1782 very considerable reinforcements in European troops had been landed at Madras, and the following distribution of the army under General Stuart on January 5th, 1783, shows in part this substantial increase.

1783

The army was now formed in two lines; the first, under Colonel Reinbold, of the 15th Hanoverians, consisted of three brigades, viz.:

1st Brigade: Under Lieutenant-Colonel Stuart, 78th Highlanders, contained the 73rd, 78th and 101st Foot, a detachment of the 15th

Hanoverians, and the Madras European Infantry—this last had in the previous October received a draft of 500 men from England.

2nd Brigade: Commanded by Major Edmondstone, contained two regiments of Bengal and one of Madras sepoys.

3rd Brigade: Under Major Blane, consisted of one regiment of Bengal sepoys, the Trichinopoly detachment, and a Madras battalion.

The second line, under Colonel Pearse, contained two brigades only.

4th Brigade: Under Lieutenant-Colonel Kelly, Madras Army, contained one Bengal and three Madras sepoy battalions.

5th Brigade: Commanded by Lieutenant-Colonel Elphinstone, 73rd, was made up in the same way as the 4th.

On February 7th the following slight modification of the above organization was announced in orders :—" The Madras European Regiment, with two 12-pounders from the 1st Brigade, is to be considered the centre of the second line as soon as the Army encamps to-morrow, but to move in the morning as usual with the 1st Brigade."

On February 13th the army came within sight of the combined forces of the French and Tippoo, but these retired, and General Stuart then, having demolished the works at Wandewash and Carangoly, moved to the relief of Vellore, and it was not until April 21st that he commenced his march towards Cuddalore, meaning to try to recover that place from the French; his movements were, however, so slow that he took 48 days to cover 126 miles and consequently did not reach the banks of the river, five miles west of the boundary hedge, until June 7th. The north and west faces of Cuddalore appearing to be very strong, Stuart crossed the river, passed over the Bandapollam Hills and encamped in a strong position, the right on the sea and the left on the hills, about a mile and three-quarters from the south face of Cuddalore. De Bussy then, who was in command of the garrison, drew 3,000 European infantry, 3,500 sepoys, and 2,000 of Tippoo's cavalry from the north side and took up a position facing Stuart.

The British were now for some days busy landing stores and

preparing for the siege, and on the 11th the grenadier companies of all the European regiments were formed into a grenadier battalion under the command of Major the Hon. Charles Cathcart, of the 98th Foot, part of which regiment had landed at Madras the previous autumn, the remainder having been embarked on the fleet to serve as marines. The grenadier company of the 1st Battalion 1st Madras Europeans was commanded by Captain Daniel Burr, and contained 4 lieutenants, of whom Lieutenant Robert Mackay was one, and 57 other ranks. The battalion was of a strength of 5 captains, 18 subalterns and 297 rank and file, and had two 12-pounders attached to it.

By this time the command of the Second Line had been given to Colonel Gordon, of the 101st, *vice* Colonel Pearse.

The enemy's lines had been thoroughly reconnoitred on the 12th by Lieutenant-Colonel Kelly, who penetrated through the thick jungle on the Bandapollam Hills and managed to obtain a complete view of the interior of the entrenchments on the right. The attack was fixed for the next day when the following arrangements were made :—

Lieutenant-Colonel Kelly, with the Madras Europeans, three Madras sepoy battalions and a party of pioneers, was ordered to march over the Bandapollam Hills before daylight in order to turn the extreme right of the enemy's position, held by one French regiment and some Mysore troops.

The 78th Highlanders and two sepoy battalions under Major Edmondstone were on the right.

Cathcart's grenadier battalion, supported by the 73rd and two native infantry regiments formed the left attack, while the centre attack, under Major-General Bruce* and Colonel Gordon, was composed of the 101st Foot, detachments of the 15th and 16th Hanoverians—these last only quite lately arrived at Cuddalore—and three, or portions of three, sepoy battalions.

Kelly reached his destination at daybreak, assaulted and captured a battery posted on a hill on the extreme right of the

* This was the C.O. of the 102nd, who had been given the local rank of Major-General.

enemy's position, and turned the guns on the Mysore troops who at once dispersed, when the position these had vacated was seized by the troops of the left attack. The centre division assailed a large redoubt in their front but were repulsed and followed up by the French regiment, but the troops under Kelly and Cathcart now advancing, occupied the ground the French had left and opened so heavy a fire that the French retired in great confusion towards their left. The British continued their advance along the line of entrenchments, driving the enemy before them, but sustaining many casualties from the fire of several batteries. When they arrived within range of the guns on the ramparts of Cuddalore they were halted, and eventually ordered to take possession of a large redoubt, which commanded the whole range of works.

This bloody conflict continued until 5 p.m., when firing ceased and both sides lay on their arms waiting to renew the struggle at daybreak. During the night, however, the enemy retired within the walls of Cuddalore, leaving behind them 17 guns and 50 unwounded prisoners. The loss on both sides was very great; 1,030 of Stuart's men were killed and wounded, of whom 8 killed and 31 wounded belonged to the Madras European Regiment.* The losses of the enemy were uncertain, but they acknowledged to 850, exclusive of 14 officers killed, 25 wounded and 6 taken prisoner.

General Stuart had intended to storm the enemy's lines before daylight next morning, but the enemy having withdrawn, a parallel on the south face was at once commenced and work on it carried on with vigour.

On the 15th it was given out in General Orders that the grenadier company of the 2nd Battalion 1st Madras European Regiment should join the Grenadier Battalion under Major Cathcart.

By this time the French admiral Suffren, with 15 ships of war, had appeared off Cuddalore, to which the English fleet of 17 vessels had dropped down to prevent the French landing reinforcements. There was an indecisive naval action on the 20th, but after some

* Actually wounded were 1 lieutenant, 1 ensign, 3 sergeants, 1 drummer, and 25 privates.

three hours' fighting at long range the French admiral brought his ships into port and landed a welcome reinforcement for de Bussy of 2,400 men.

About 3 a.m. on the 25th, while Colonels Gordon and Cathcart were commanding in the trenches, the enemy attacked at three points, but were everywhere repulsed. "This attack," writes one who witnessed it,* "was conducted by the Count de Damas, and consisted of two columns of 500 choice troops each. Our lines were occupied at the two points attacked by the 24th Regiment of Bengal Sepoys, which made a gallant resistance, and also by one of the Madras battalions under Lieutenant Wahab, which behaved nobly. Lieutenant Greuber, of the former corps, was killed, and Captain James Williamson, commanding it, wounded; Lieutenant Ochterlony wounded and prisoner and the Colours of the Regiment taken. This was desperate work. A column of men must succeed when they first penetrate, but a steady corps will at length repulse them; the attack was on the centre—the flank companies stood firm and kept up a severe fire, the reserve of European Grenadiers, under Lieutenant-Colonel Cathcart, were in motion to support the troops in the trenches, and as the other column had not succeeded and our great guns began to ply them with grape, the French troops who had penetrated laid down their arms, and their comrades on the outside scampered off to relate the story of their repulse. The Count de Damas surrendered to Lieutenant Wahab."

Another historian† writes: "The loss of the English was surprisingly small. Major Cotgrave, who commanded the Madras sepoys in the trenches, was killed; 3 other officers wounded and missing; and 20 rank and file killed and wounded, chiefly sepoys. Among the wounded prisoners was a young French sergeant, who so particularly attracted the notice of General Wangenheim, commandant of the Hanoverian troops in the English service, by his interesting appearance and manners that he ordered

* Lieut.-Colonel R. Scott's Diary, in the *Naval and Military Magazine*, Vol. II, pp. 55, 56.
† Wilks, Vol. II, pp. 442, 443.

the young man to be conveyed to his own tents, where he was treated with attention and kindness until his recovery and release. Many years afterwards, when the French army under Bernadotte entered Hanover, General Wangenheim, among others, attended the levée of the conqueror. " You have served a great deal," said Bernadotte on his being presented, " and as I understand in India." " I have served there." " At Cuddalore ? " " I was there." " Have you any recollection of a wounded sergeant whom you took under your protection in the course of that service ? " The circumstance was not immediately present to the general's mind, but on reflection, he resumed—" I do indeed remember the circumstance and a very fine young man he was. I have entirely lost sight of him ever since, but it would give me pleasure to hear of his welfare." " That young sergeant," said Bernadotte, " was the person who has now the honour to address you, who is happy in this public opportunity of acknowledging the obligation, and will omit no means within his power of testifying his gratitude to General Wangenheim."

Bernadotte, as we all know, became a marshal of France under Napoleon and later Crown Prince and King of Sweden.

The following is an extract from the General Order issued by General Stuart on June 25th in regard to the action of the 13th and the repulse of the sortie :—

" The Commander-in-Chief having taken time minutely to investigate the conduct and execution of the orders and plan in attacking the enemy's outposts, lines and redoubts on the 13th instant, with the comparative strength in number and position of the enemy, composed almost entirely of the best regular troops of France, takes this occasion to give it as his opinion to this brave army in general, that it is not to be equalled by any he knows or has heard of in modern history, whether we look to the extent and entire success, or to the national importance of that day's complete victory. He takes this occasion to return his thanks to Major-General Bruce, Lieut.-Colonel Cathcart, Major Moore and the Corps of Grenadiers . . . and to Lieut.-Colonel Kelly, who, with the brigade led by the second grenadier company and the rest of the Honourable Company's European Infantry, under the command of

Captains Collins, Bonnevaux and Sale, so ably and opportunely possessed himself of the enemy's post upon the hills. . . . In general, the Commander-in-Chief takes the present occasion to acquaint the Army that he has already informed Government of their particular merit in the attack of the 13th, and that he will endeavour to represent it as it deserves to our most gracious Sovereign and Country.

"*It has so happened that on the very day when the Commander-in-Chief thought it his duty to return his thanks to this army for the important victory of the 13th, an occasion offers to express his satisfaction for a new and recent display of their steadiness and undaunted courage—the successful repulse of the enemy's best regular and veteran troops this morning, in sight too of their admiral and whole fleet, taking the colonel who commanded prisoner, with the loss of their principal officers. The General can only repeat his most sincere acknowledgment and admiration on this occasion, with his particular thanks to Colonel Gordon and Lieutenant-Colonel Cathcart, to Captain Williamson and the 24th Bengal Regiment.*"

The position of the English was now somewhat critical, since their numbers had been seriously diminished by casualties in action and by disease, while the enemy had received no inconsiderable reinforcements. However, on July 1st a British frigate arrived in Cuddalore roads with the news that peace had been concluded with France; hostilities then at once ceased and the siege of Cuddalore came to an end, and now General Stuart, who had for some considerable time past been on the worst possible terms with Lord Macartney and his Council, was directed to make over command of the army to Major-General Bruce and to proceed at once to Madras.

Before the operations of the army at Cuddalore had commenced, and during their progress, a battalion of the Madras European Regiment was serving with the southern army under Lieut.-Colonel Ross Lang, and, entering the Mysore country, took a conspicuous part in the reduction of Caroor, where, on March 21st, 1783, the breach was attacked by four grenadier companies of Europeans and four of sepoys under Captain Thomas Maitland, while the wall was escaladed by two other parties, each of twenty Europeans and five companies

[Vol. I.

of sepoys, under Captain Gardiner and Lieutenant Wharton respectively, when the enemy retired into the fort. On the night of April 2nd the enemy was driven out of the covered way by a storming party of forty Europeans and four companies of sepoys, and on these effecting a lodgment on the glacis the enemy abandoned the place during the night. At Caroor sixty of the Madras Europeans were killed and wounded.

Again on April 10th the fort of Avaracoorchy was taken by storm, while on May 4th Dindigul surrendered without opposition.

A few days after this Colonel Lang was superseded by Colonel Fullarton, of the King's service, recently promoted Colonel and who thus became senior to Lang, and he had just signalized his assumption of command by the capture of Dharapuram and was about to march on Coimbatore, when an express arrived from Stuart directing him to join him at once at Cuddalore. Fullarton had arrived within three marches of this when he heard that peace had been concluded with the French, and at once returned to the southern country and conducted some very successful operations. In September he was reinforced by two detachments from the main army, one, of the 78th, some Hanoverians and a large party from the 1st and 2nd Battalions of the 1st Madras Europeans with two complete sepoy regiments and the grenadier companies of three others, under Colonels Stuart and Kelly; the other, under Colonel Elphinstone, and containing 500 men from the 101st and 102nd Foot and two native battalions.

These accessions brought Fullarton's force to a strength of some 13,600 men, of whom over 2,000 were Europeans, and he formed these into two lines, the one of three, the other of two brigades, under Colonels Stuart, 78th, and Forbes, 102nd; all the European Infantry were in the 1st Brigade commanded by Lieutenant-Colonel Elphinstone, 73rd.

With this powerful force Fullarton proceeded towards Madura and Tinnevelly, which districts he thoroughly subdued and then again advanced into Mysore. After a most trying march through dense jungle he reached Palghat early in November and was in possession of it by the 13th; he then moved against Coimbatore and captured it on the 26th, and was preparing to move thence on Seringapatam hoping either to seize it in the absence of Tippoo, then besieging Mangalore, or to force him to hurry back to defend Seringapatam, raising the siege of Mangalore. But on November 28th Colonel Fullarton received instructions from the Madras Government to suspend hostilities, to restore all the strong places he had captured, march his troops back to Trichinopoly, and there place them in cantonments.

Fullarton strongly protested, pointing out the great strategic advantages of his position, but without avail, and he accordingly made his preparations for cantoning his troops, when, **1784** towards the end of January, 1784, the Madras authorities, beginning belatedly to doubt whether Tippoo was sincere in his desire for peace, cancelled their previous orders to Fullarton and directed him to reassemble his army and retain or regain possession, until the conclusion of the negotiations, of all the places he had taken.

A treaty of peace was finally signed with Tippoo on March 11th, when all the troops were withdrawn from the field into their usual garrisons. The 1st Battalion 1st Madras Europeans had its headquarters at Vellore with detachments at Masulipatam and in the south; the 2nd Battalion 1st Regiment garrisoned Trichinopoly and Tanjore; while the 1st and 2nd Battalions of the 2nd Madras European Regiment were stationed respectively at Ellore and Fort St. George.

On October 6th a large detachment from the St. Helena Regiment arrived at Madras and was taken on the strength of the 2nd Battalion 2nd Madras European Regiment.

On March 1st, 1784, Lieutenant-Colonel Cosby was appointed to the command of the 1st Battalion 1st Regiment, and was employed in a small campaign in the Tinnevelly district with the grenadier company of his battalion, some guns, a regiment of native cavalry and three sepoy battalions.

In the year 1785 the European Infantry on the Madras
1785 Establishment was reorganized, and under an order issued
on August 23rd :—

The 2nd Battalion 1st Regiment became the 1st Regiment.
The 1st Battalion 2nd Regiment became the 2nd Regiment.
The 1st Battalion 1st Regiment became the 3rd Regiment.
The 2nd Battalion 2nd Regiment became the 4th Regiment.

This arrangement, however, only lasted for something less than
a year, for on May 20th, 1786, the following changes were
1786 made. The four regiments became the 1st, 2nd, 3rd and 4th
Battalions respectively, the number of companies in each was
fixed at eight, two of which were to be grenadiers, and the establishment of a battalion was to consist of 1 colonel, 1 lieutenant-colonel, 1 major, 8 captains, 10 lieutenants, 6 ensigns, 24 sergeants, 32 corporals, 16 drummers and fifers and 544 privates, with a staff of 1 chaplain, 1 adjutant, 1 quartermaster, 1 surgeon and 1 surgeon's mate.

It was determined about the same time that a European battalion should be attached to each of the four senior native brigades, and the following arrangements were accordingly made :

The 1st Battalion at Trichinopoly was attached to the 1st Brigade.
The 2nd Battalion at Ellore was attached to the 4th Brigade.
The 3rd Battalion at Vellore was attached to the 2nd Brigade.
The 4th Battalion at Madras was attached to the 3rd Brigade.

In General Orders of March 11th, 1787, the following field-officers were appointed to the European corps :—Lieutenant-Colonel William Russel, and Major George Oldham, to the 1st Battalion; Lieutenant-Colonel Robert Chesshire, and Major John Patterson, to the 2nd Battalion; Lieutenant-Colonel Edward Collins, and Major Thomas Prendergast, to the 3rd Battalion; Lieutenant-Colonel James Edington, and Major George Clarke, to the 4th Battalion.

The officers commanding the four European battalions, Colonels Horn, Brathwaite, Nixon and Kelly, now became brigadiers.

In the same month the army was formed into four divisions, the headquarters of which were stationed respectively at Fort St. George, Wallajabad, Ellore, and Trichinopoly, and the native battalions were at the same time formed into five brigades, it being ordered that any European regiment, whether of the King's or Company's service, stationed at the headquarters of a native brigade, should form part thereof—the senior officer present to command.

During this year the East India Company began to evince an unusual solicitude for the well-being of the families of its soldiers, and an asylum for boarding and educating the sons of the European soldiers was founded at Madras, and placed under the management of the Vestry-men of St. Mary's Church, Fort St. George. The number of boys was at first fixed at 230, and the cost per boy per mensem was estimated at Rs10 of which government paid half, the balance being raised by subscription. This institution continued to exist under the title of " The Madras Military Male Orphan Asylum " until 1871, when it was amalgamated with the Lawrence Asylum at Ootacamund.

The following order notifying the grant of Royal Commissions to the officers of the Honourable East India Company's service was published at Madras on August 29th of this year :—

"*Resolved that it be published in General Orders to the Army that His Majesty by a warrant under his sign manual, has been graciously pleased to authorise the Commander-in-Chief to grant brevet commissions of King's local rank in India to all the officers in the service of the Honourable Company of the same degree which they now hold in the Company's service. but the commencement of that rank is not to extend in any case whatever beyond the publication of the cessation of hostilities between England and France at Cuddalore, viz., the 9th day of July, 1783, and in all instances within that period is to correspond with the date of their present commissions. The Commander-in-Chief is also empowered to grant similar brevet commissions to all the Company's officers who may in future attain appointments on promotion in the regular line of their own service. . . "*

1787 About the end of 1787 more European troops being required for service in India, four regiments were raised for that purpose—the 74th, 75th, 76th and 77th, and commissions in these new corps were given to 78 officers of the Company's service, viz., 1 lieutenant-colonel, 3 majors, 14 captains, 44 lieutenants and 16 ensigns—a certain number being allotted to each Presidency. In conformity with this arrangement 2 captains, 1 lieutenant and 4 ensigns of the Madras Establishment were transferred to the King's service.

1789 The following " state " for November, 1789, shows how large was the number of King's regiments then in the Madras Presidency :—

19th Light Dragoons	324 Rank and File.
36th Foot	792 ,, ,, ,,
52nd ,,	798 ,, ,, ,,
71st ,,	762 ,, ,, ,,
72nd ,,	774 ,, ,, ,,
74th ,,	694 ,, ,, ,,
76th ,,	390 ,, ,, ,,
14th Hanoverians	558 ,, ,, ,,
15th ,,	571 ,, ,, ,,
Total	5663 Rank and File.

Of this number 678 were either invalids or time-expired men.

1790 The war of 1790–92 with Tippoo was occasioned by his attack upon the Raja of Travancore, who was an ally of the British. In 1789 the Dutch East India Company sold to the raja certain towns and forts which, being situated near the western extremity of the general line of defence known as the Travancore Lines, seemed to Tippoo to constitute, if not a menace, at least a security against his designs of conquest, and he demanded their surrender. This demand was refused by the raja under the expectation of British support; this was, however, not immediately forthcoming, and on December 29th, 1789, Tippoo attacked the lines and was repulsed with much loss. The Madras Government remaining still curiously inactive, Tippoo, having been reinforced from Mysore, attacked again and carried the lines by storm on April 15th, 1790, and some three weeks later had made himself master of nearly the whole of the province; then, hearing that the English were making at last preparations for war, he demolished the lines and withdrew his forces into Mysore.

Major-General William Medows was by now Commander-in-Chief in Madras and by May 24th he had assembled at Trichinopoly an army of some 15,000 men disposed in two British and four sepoy brigades of infantry, with a powerful artillery, and a cavalry brigade of one British and three native regiments. The 1st Battalion Madras European Regiment was in the Second European Brigade of the Left Wing of the Army, the Wing being commanded by Lieutenant-Colonel Stuart of the 72nd, and the Brigade—in which were also the 71st and 72nd Regiments—by Lieutenant-Colonel Clarke, Madras Army.

The plan of campaign was as follows :—The southern or grand army was, as in Colonel Fullarton's recent campaign, after reducing the Coimbatore country, to ascend the Gujalhathi Pass; a Bombay army was to act on the western side; while Colonel Kelly, with a small but effective force, was to watch the passes leading into the Baramahal.

It was on May 26th when the march towards Mysore commenced, but so defective were the supply arrangements in the main army that it was June 15th before Caroor, the frontier station and 50 miles from Trichinopoly, was reached. Caroor was found abandoned, but the monsoon now setting in heavily the army was not able to move forward again until July 3rd and had to leave a large number of sick behind. On the 5th and 10th the forts of Avaracoorchy and Dharapuram were taken and four companies of the Madras Europeans left in garrison in the latter place. The cavalry and a mobile body of infantry then moved against one of Tippoo's subordinate generals and drove him over the ghats, while Colonel Stuart marched on Dindigul, before which he arrived on August 16th, with the 52nd, two companies of the Madras Europeans

—one of these being a grenadier company under Captain Bowser—one cavalry regiment and three sepoy battalions, with a detachment of artillery and pioneers.

The fort of Dindigul, situated on the summit of a high, precipitous rock, was only accessible at one point; the fortifications had been greatly improved since its earlier capture; while the garrison was numerous and well provided. Fire was opened on the 20th from two 18-pounders, two 12-pounders and two mortars and from some field-pieces, and before night the enemy's fire was silenced. The breach was, however, not yet practicable, but Stuart had run out of shot and therefore determined to storm. The grenadiers of the Madras Europeans, under Captain Bowser and Lieutenant Ogilby, led the stormers up the so-called breach studded with pikes. The assault was pressed with the most determined gallantry but with no success, but the enemy had had enough and shortly surrendered at discretion. Ensign Davidson of the Madras Army and six Europeans were here killed, 19 Europeans and 11 sepoys wounded.

Lieutenant Ogilby was appointed Fort Adjutant at Dindigul and while here he did much good service, capturing the strong fort of Ootampollam at the head of the Dindigul Valley, garrisoned by 1,200 Mysore troops, and accomplishing this feat with a party of one ensign and 23 men of the Madras Regiment, 27 sepoys and 200 irregulars; while, scouring the neighbouring country by dangerous and devious tracks, he brought in some 14,000 bullocks to the main army then at Coimbatore.

After the reduction of Dindigul, Stuart was sent against Palghatcherry, a place of some strength, having been reinforced by the 71st and 72nd, and a sepoy battalion. On fire being opened the place almost at once surrendered and 60 pieces of ordnance were here taken.

During these operations under Colonel Stuart, other detachments had reduced Satyamangalam and taken Erode and established a line of depots through the country; but the English Army was thus now divided into three parts—one under Colonel Floyd, about sixty miles in advance, near the foot of the Gujalhathi Pass; the main army was at Coimbatore; while the third portion under Colonel Stuart was near Palghat and was thus open to separate attack by Tippoo's mobile hordes.

Early in September the Mysore Army descended into Coimbatore territory by the Gujalhathi Pass, on the 12th crossed the River Bawany, and advanced on Colonel Floyd, hoping to cut him off. A severe action ensued and though the enemy was repulsed Floyd was obliged to retire during the night, leaving two of his guns behind him, and closely followed up by Tippoo, who so continually harassed him that when Floyd rejoined the main army on the 16th he had lost nearly 450 men killed and wounded, many Europeans among them.

In the meantime the centre division of the army, under Colonel Kelly, had been joined at Arnee on August 1st by considerable reinforcements, and was now composed of the 74th, the 3rd and 4th Battalions of the Madras Europeans, and a formidable train of artillery, and totalled, including natives, some 10,000 men. On the death of Kelly on September 23rd, Colonel Maxwell, 74th, assumed command. Maxwell had a good deal of skirmishing with Tippoo's forces in the neighbourhood of Caveripatam during the first half of the month of November, but failed to bring him to serious action. On the 17th the centre and southern divisions of the British Army joined forces and followed the enemy as far as Caroor and Trichinopoly, and then received orders to return to Madras from Lord Cornwallis, who had now arrived at Madras to take command of the operations in person.

1791 The army commenced its march towards the Presidency on December 30th, and encamped at Vellout, some 18 miles from Madras on January 27th, 1791, Lord Cornwallis taking over from General Medows two days later.

The new commander had brought certain useful, if not especially substantial, reinforcements with him from Bengal, amounting to some 50 European artillerymen, a regiment of cavalry and 1,400 sepoys, and the army that on February 5th left Vellout and marched for Vellore is described in the *Madras Courier* of the day as " a force certainly unequalled ever in this country, and perhaps never surpassed in Europe"; but while it consisted of some 18,000 men it was accompanied by ten times as many followers! It appears to have consisted of the following corps :—

Cavalry : 19th Dragoons and 4 regiments of native cavalry.
Artillery : 20 guns.
Infantry : 36th, 52nd, 71st, 72nd, 74th and 76th Foot, the 4th Battalion Madras Europeans, 6 battalions of Bengal and 14 of Madras sepoys.

The Madras Europeans, with two regiments of Madras sepoys, formed an independent brigade which moved usually in support of the cavalry and was commanded by Major Gowdie; of the other battalions of the Regiment the 1st was at this time holding Trichinopoly and the southern provinces, the 2nd, under Lieutenant-Colonel Collins, had just arrived at Fort St. George from Ellore, while the 3rd was in Vellore. Both the 2nd and 3rd had recently been augmented by a reinforcement from the St. Helena Garrison and the recruits arrived from home that season.

By February 11th the grand army under Cornwallis was concentrated near Vellore, by the 17th a brigade had ascended the Mugli Pass near Chittore, and by the 21st the army, with its artillery and baggage, had entered Mysore territory without opposition and was encamped within 90 miles of Bangalore.

The march, slightly harassed by the Mysore Horse, was continued until March 4th, when the enemy was met with in greater force and an unsuccessful attack was made upon the British baggage column, and late on the 5th the force was close to Bangalore. Next day a stronger position for investment was sought, and while this movement was in progress Colonel Floyd* with his cavalry attacked and routed a body of the enemy's horse, but, pursuing too far, was severely handled, Floyd himself being wounded and unhorsed, and being saved from disaster by the advance, contrary to

* This officer had fought at Emsdorff in 1760 in the 15th Light Dragoons, then known as Eliott's Light Horse, as a boy of 12, having his horse killed under him!

orders, of Gowdie's brigade, which completely checked pursuit, enabling the cavalry to reform and retire to camp in good order. Major Gowdie and his brigade received great praise from Lord Cornwallis for their conduct on this occasion.

Early on the morning of the 7th an assault was made upon the pettah of Bangalore and in this, and in the subsequent street fighting, the Madras Europeans participated, having some twenty casualties. On the next day batteries were erected against the fort and operations were continued until the 21st when, a practicable breach having been made, it was assaulted and carried after a very desperate resistance. The storming column was made up of the flank companies of all the European corps available, and these, as they gained the ramparts, swept along the defences to right and left, and then, meeting near the Mysore gate, descended into the *enceinte*, upon which all opposition ceased. This great success was gained at comparatively small cost to the British, only 129 being killed and wounded, but the losses among the defenders were terribly heavy—the number of the wounded of the enemy was never known, but next day the victors buried 1,000 dead, the majority of whom had fallen by the bayonet.

On the 12th the army was joined by 10,000 of the Nawab's cavalry.

Lord Cornwallis marched for Seringapatam on May 4th and on the 13th arrived at Arakere on the north bank of the Cauvery, meaning here to cross the river; but the stream was at the moment impassable by reason of recent heavy rain, so he halted on the 14th when he learnt that Tippoo with his whole army was encamped some five miles from him, his right on the river and his front protected by rocky ground and a deep ravine. On hearing this Lord Cornwallis determined to try to turn the enemy's left so as to cut him off from Seringapatam, now some three or four miles distant. The European regiments and 12 sepoy battalions marched at midnight, but the way was long, the roads heavy, and the march delayed by a severe storm, so that day broke before the force had proceeded more than a very few miles.

All hopes of surprise were now at an end, but the Commander-in-Chief was resolved to bring the enemy to action if possible and continued his advance. On his approach, Tippoo changed front to his left, his right being covered by the ravine already mentioned, while his left rested on the lower slopes of the Karighatta Hill.

The crossing of the ravine by the British Army took nearly two hours, and it then deployed into line, the engagement being commenced by Maxwell's division on the right, which attacked and carried a hill in front, when the whole line advanced and the action became general. The Mysore infantry fought well but was gradually driven back, finally retreating to a position covered by the guns of Seringapatam whence they could not then be dislodged.

The enemy loss was considerable, that of the British, 420 all ranks.

On the 18th the British force marched to a place some eight miles from Seringapatam with the object of effecting a junction with the Bombay troops under General Abercromby; but supplies had been so short and the condition of the transport cattle was so wretched that Cornwallis was obliged for the present to abandon any attempt against Seringapatam. He therefore destroyed his heavy guns and impedimenta and had marched some few miles on his return journey to Bangalore, when he was joined by a Mahratta army of 40,000 men with 20 guns, of whose coming no intelligence had reached him; but the destruction of his guns and stores had nullified any advantage which might have accrued from this reinforcement, and the march was resumed on Bangalore where the army arrived on July 11th.

Lord Cornwallis marched again on the 15th to effect the reduction of the numerous hill forts to the west of Bangalore, and to establish a line of posts to protect his convoys in the coming campaign. Major Gowdie's brigade was instrumental in the capture of Oossoor and Royacottah, Captain Oliver leading the stormers at the taking of the latter; and several other forts were seized or submitted.

The approaches to the Carnatic being thus secured, Gowdie

was sent on to endeavour to capture Nundydroog and other forts to the north of Bangalore, and about daybreak on September 22nd he attacked and carried the pettah of Nundydroog; operations for besieging the place commenced at the end of the month, and by the middle of October the rest of the army came up under Lord Cornwallis, who, having inspected the breach, directed that the assault should commence at moon-rise on the night of the 17th.

The fort of Nundydroog is situated on a precipitous granite rock nearly 2,000 feet high, inaccessible on three sides, and on the fourth defended by two strong walls and an outwork that covered the gateway. An attempt had in the first instance been made to bombard the fort from a hill adjoining the rock, but the range was found to be too great. Approaches were then carried up the steep face of the rock to within breaching distance of the outwork, and after immense exertions batteries were erected and the guns to occupy them brought up by elephants; the fort was defended by one of Tippoo's ablest lieutenants.

On the night of October 18th the stormers were all lodged in the foundations made for a wall that for some reason had never been raised, and the arrangements for the assault were as follows:—The grenadiers of the 36th and 71st Foot were to carry the breach in the curtain; the light companies of those regiments were to storm the outwork; while the flank companies of the 4th Battalion Madras Europeans, under Captain Doveton, were to escalade the inner wall. On the signal being given the storming parties rushed forward, but they had no sooner left their cover than they were at once discovered, the walls were instantly lit up by blue lights, and a heavy fire of guns, musketry and rockets was opened, while large fragments of rocks were hurled down upon the attackers. Both breaches were, however, soon carried and the enemy was so closely followed as he fell back, that the flank companies under Doveton forced the gate of the inner fort and were the first to enter and take possession of the body of the place.

Some of the garrison escaped by ropes over a low part of the wall, of the remainder nearly 600 were killed or wounded or made prisoners. The British casualties numbered 120 and of these some 30 were among Doveton's men.

On October 19th Lord Cornwallis published the following General Order :—

"*Lord Cornwallis having been witness of the extraordinary obstacles, both of nature and art, which were opposed to the detachment of the army that attacked Nundydroog, he cannot too highly applaud the firmness and exertions which were manifested by all ranks in carrying on the operations of the siege, or the valour and discipline which was displayed by the flank companies of His Majesty's 36th and 71st Regiments, those of the Madras 4th European battalion, the 13th Bengal battalion of Native Infantry, and of the 3rd, 4th, 10th, 13th and 27th Battalions of Madras Native Infantry, that were employed in the assault of last night; and which, by overcoming all difficulties, effected the reduction of that important fort.*

"*His Lordship is highly sensible of the zealous and meritorious conduct of Major Gowdie in the command of that detachment, both at the attacks of Roymanghur [sic], and in carrying on the arduous operations of the siege of Nundydroog, for which the Major will be pleased to accept his best acknowledgments. The whole of the officers and soldiers who composed that detachment appear likely to be justly entitled to the strongest expressions of his approbation. . . .*"

Almost exactly fifty years later the 1st Madras European Regiment, as it had then come to be called, received permission to bear the name of this fort as an Honour upon its Colours, together with a badge in commemoration of its gallant services in the Mysore War, as the following testifies :—

"*General Order by the Right Hon'ble the Governor in Council.*

"FORT ST. GEORGE,
12th March, 1841.

"*No. 48 of 1841. The Right Hon'ble, the Governor in Council having had under consideration the many honorable services of the 1st Madras European Regiment, whose career is to be traced through the most eventful periods of the military history of British India, has been pleased to order that, in commemoration of its victories under Lawrence,*

Reduction of Savendroog an impregnable Hill Fort of Tippoo Said.
by the Marquis Cornwallis.

Clive, Sir Eyre Coote, Lord Cornwallis, and other distinguished Generals, it shall bear emblazoned upon its Colours the motto ' Spectamur Agendo ' and the names of the following battles and expeditions in which it has borne part :—

* * * *

" Nundy-Droog, which it assisted to capture in 1791, and for which His Lordship in Council is pleased to permit it also to bear a Royal Tiger on the Colours and appointments :

* * * * "

Before advancing upon Seringapatam it was found necessary to reduce certain forts lying between it and Bangalore ; one of these, Savandroog, was carried by assault without the loss of a man on December 21st, Ramgherry and Shivanagherry on the 22nd, and Ootradroog on the 24th. The Madras Europeans were not engaged as a regiment in any of these minor operations, but while the siege of Savandroog was in progress the brigade in which the 4th Battalion was serving was employed in protecting the besieging force from interference from Seringapatam, while both here and at the capture of Ootradroog the European pioneers of the army, who were men belonging to the Madras European Regiment and were temporarily officiating as engineers, particularly distinguished themselves.

1792 On February 1st, 1792, the British, the Mahratta and the Nizam's armies, having all united near Savandroog, marched towards Seringapatam in three parallel columns ; the British force was contained in two wings, a right and a left under Colonels Stuart and Maxwell respectively, and each containing one British and two native infantry brigades ; the 4th Battalion Madras Europeans and one Madras sepoy battalion were in the Reserve or Seventh Brigade under Major Gowdie.

The advance was continued until February 5th when the army took up a position within six miles of Seringapatam ; this position was behind the French Rocks and was divided by the River Lokany, the right of the line passing to the north of the Rocks, its front being partly covered by a large tank ; the left rested on the hills to the north-east of Seringapatam ; the allies were some few miles in rear.

The position of Tippoo's army could be seen from the English camp the right was secured by the Karighatta Hill which was strongly fortified, and his line extended to the west and was enclosed by a wide hedge of prickly-pear, while the river, a canal and a considerable extent of wet rice fields covered the greater part of his front. One large redoubt, known as the Eedgah, stood at the north-west angle close to the hedge, two other redoubts were in the centre about 600 yards apart, and a second line of three redoubts was in rear nearly equi-distant between the hedge and the river; all these were armed with heavy guns. Tippoo's infantry, computed at 40,000 men with 100 field-pieces, was drawn up between the two lines of redoubts with 500 cavalry in rear.

Tippoo himself commanded the centre and right, his headquarters being in the so-called Sultan's Redoubt in the second line; two other of his generals, supported by the French battalion and Lally's brigade under M. Vigie, commanded on the left; another subordinate leader on the Great Karighatta Hill; and a fourth the actual garrison of Seringapatam.

On the night of February 6th the British Army moved forward in three divisions to the storm of the Mysore lines; Major-General Medows led the right, Lord Cornwallis himself the centre, and Colonel Maxwell the left division, the brigade, in which was the 4th Battalion Madras Europeans, forming the reserve. The right division attacked and carried the left of the enemy's line after overcoming a determined resistance at the Eedgah Redoubt; the centre stormed the main enemy front eventually penetrating into the island of Seringapatam; while the left division under Maxwell ascended Karighatta Hill, carried the redoubt on the summit and entered the boundary hedge on the right, joining up with the centre column on the island.

At daylight on the 7th the action was renewed, the enemy endeavouring by repeated attacks to drive the British from the positions gained, but they were invariably repulsed with loss, and night again brought the operations to a close. When day dawned on February 8th it was found that the enemy had fallen back from

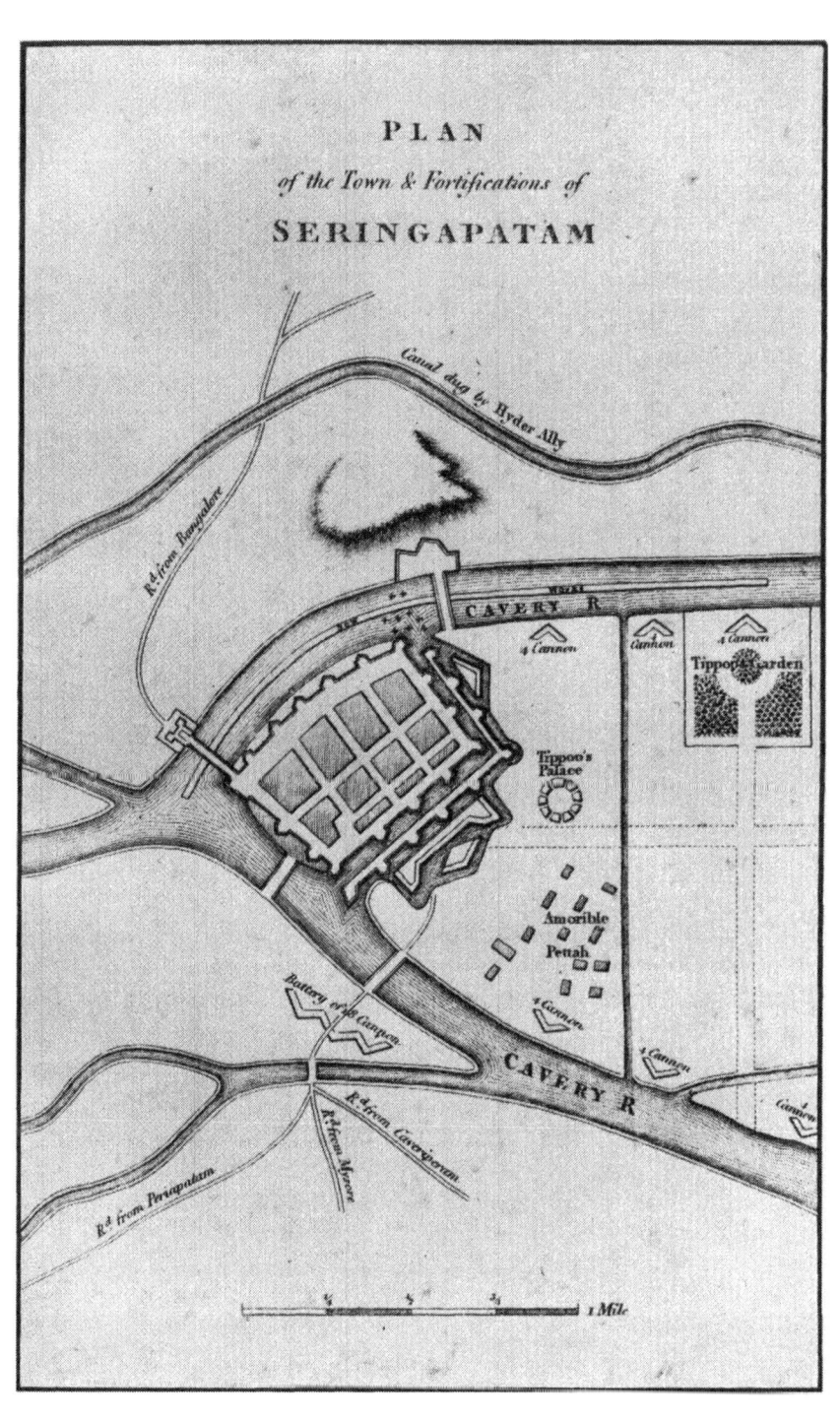

ATTACK ON SERINGAPATAM

all his posts within the hedge; these were occupied by the British and the fort was now closely invested on all sides. This night Major Gowdie's brigade took post at the foot of the Karighatta Hill in readiness to pass over into the Island on the first alarm.

On the evening of the 7th Lord Cornwallis issued the following order :—

"*The conduct and valour of the officers and soldiers of this army have often merited Lord Cornwallis's encomiums; but the zeal and gallantry which were so successfully displayed last night, in the attacks on the enemy's whole army in a position that had cost him so much time and labour to fortify, can never be sufficiently praised; and his satisfaction on an occasion which promises to be attended with the most substantial advantages, has been greatly heightened by learning from the commanding officers of divisions, that this meritorious behaviour was universal throughout all ranks to a degree that has rarely been equalled.*

"*Lord Cornwallis, therefore, requests the army in general will accept of his most cordial thanks for the noble and gallant manner in which they have executed the plan of attack. It covers themselves with honour and will ever command his warmest sentiments of admiration.*"

On the morning of the 8th it was found that the enemy had wholly withdrawn from the fortified camp, and the army occupied all posts not within range of the fort. This evening two British officers, Lieutenants Chalmers and Nash, prisoners of Tippoo, were released in order to carry to Cornwallis overtures of peace, but nothing coming of these the preparations for a siege were pushed on. Already the British had captured some 80 guns, iron and brass, and had inflicted upon the enemy casualties estimated at 4,000 at a cost to themselves of no more than 535 killed and wounded,* while the Mysore chief had sustained still more serious loss by desertion.

On the 16th a Bombay force, composed of several European regiments and seven sepoy battalions, under General Abercromby, arrived and joined the army before Seringapatam.

Three days later an attack was made upon that portion of the Mysore Army camped north of the river, the object being to distract

* The Madras European Regiment does not figure in the Casualty Return.

his attention from the siege preparations now in active progress; this attack created much "alarm and despondency" and the parallels were advanced to within 800 yards of the citadel.

On the 22nd Tippoo attempted to dislodge Abercromby from the position he had taken up, and an action ensued which lasted until sunset. By the same night the works had been greatly advanced, while the allied Mahratta Army was daily drawing near, and Cuppage's brigade, composed of the 1st Battalion Madras Europeans and three sepoy battalions, after capturing two forts, had ascended the Gujalhathi Pass and was escorting large supplies to the besieging army.

Such was the very favourable situation of the army when it was announced on the morning of February 24th that preliminaries of peace had been settled and orders to cease fire were issued. The conditions of peace were ratified on March 19th and under these it was settled that:—

1. One-half of the Mysore dominions was ceded to the allies.
2. An indemnity of 3 crores and 3 lacs of rupees was to be paid.
3. All prisoners were to be released.

The prize-money realized amounted to £93,584, and from this sum, and additional grants made by the Company, the army benefited in varying degree—a colonel receiving £1,161 12s. and a European private £14 11s. The shares of Lord Cornwallis and General Medows amounted to over £62,000, but both these officers generously resigned their shares in order that the army generally might more materially benefit.

The army now returned to the Carnatic, the 1st Battalion of the Madras Europeans proceeding to Vellore, the 2nd and 3rd to Fort St. George, and the 4th to Arnee. During the campaign now concluded the 2nd and 3rd Battalions had secured the west of the Carnatic and protected the convoys passing to the grand army; the 1st had protected the southern provinces, eventually entering Mysore territory, and, as part of Colonel Cuppage's brigade, advancing upon Seringapatam; while the 4th Battalion had served throughout the war against Tippoo with the main army.

Colonel Thomas Bruce, Lieutenant-Colonel G. Conningham, and Major W. Malcolm, were the field-officers of the 1st Battalion. Colonel Brathwaite, Lieutenant-Colonel E. Collins and Major Alex. Wynch of the 2nd; Colonel James Bridges, Lieutenant-Colonel R. Tolson, and Major Cuppage, of the 3rd; and Colonel Charles Fraser, Lieutenant-Colonel Thomas Prendergast, and Major F. Gowdie, of the 4th.

Among officers of the corps who were on the general staff of the army were the following:—Colonel Brathwaite commanded the centre division; Colonel Fraser and Lieutenant-Colonel Prendergast, at Vizagapatam; Major Malcolm was Adjutant-General of the Army, and eventually Military Auditor-General; Captain Barry Close, Deputy Adjutant-General, and afterwards Adjutant-General; Captain Gabriel Doveton, in charge of Tippoo's sons; Lieutenant William McLeod, intelligence department with the Grand Army; Captain Alexander Agnew, Deputy Adjutant-General of the Army.

The following is from the returns of the Regiment from May—October, 1792 :—

1st Battalion.

Average strength.—1 colonel, 1 lieutenant-colonel, 1 major, 8 captains, 9 lieutenants, 7 ensigns, 1 surgeon, 4 cadets, 24 sergeants, 16 drummers, 605 other ranks.

Deaths.—1 ensign, 240 other ranks.

Prisoners of war at Ellore.—1 lieutenant, 2 ensigns, 4 sergeants, 2 drummers, 49 other ranks.

2nd Battalion.

Average strength.—1 colonel, 1 lieutenant-colonel, 1 major, 8 captains, 10 lieutenants, 6 ensigns, 2 surgeons, 1 cadet, 24 sergeants, 16 drummers, 576 other ranks.

Deaths.—1 lieutenant, 23 other ranks.

Received from other corps.—3 captains, 5 lieutenants, 2 ensigns, 1 cadet, 7 sergeants, 2 drummers, 246 rank and file.

3RD BATTALION.

Average strength.—1 colonel, 1 lieutenant-colonel, 1 major, 7 captains, 9 lieutenants, 8 ensigns, 1 surgeon, 9 cadets, 31 sergeants, 18 drummers, 706 other ranks.

Deaths.—1 major, 1 sergeant, 15 other ranks.

4TH BATTALION.

Average strength.—1 colonel, 1 lieutenant-colonel, 1 major, 8 captains, 10 lieutenants, 8 ensigns, 2 surgeons, 9 cadets, 24 sergeants, 17 drummers, 638 other ranks.

Deaths.—4 sergeants, 51 other ranks.

Recruits and released prisoners.—9 cadets, 1 sergeant, 52 other ranks.

Average total strength of Regiment.—4 colonels, 4 lieutenant-colonels, 4 majors, 34 captains, 44 lieutenants, 33 ensigns, 6 surgeons, 33 cadets, 115 sergeants, 71 drummers, 2,972 other ranks.

Total deaths.—1 lieutenant-colonel, 1 major, 1 lieutenant, 1 ensign, 5 sergeants, 113 other ranks.

During these campaigns no fewer than 67 forts and 801 guns had been taken from the enemy; of which 56 forts and 656 guns had been captured by the British forces, the remainder by their allies of the Mahratta and Nizam's armies.

One may well surmise that to the soldiers of the army led by Lord Cornwallis one of the most welcome results of the peace wrung from Tippoo Sultan was the release of those unfortunate comrades of theirs who had languished for so many years and in such large numbers in the dungeons of Seringapatam. In March and April of 1784, prisoners to the number of 1,146 British soldiers, sailors and civilians and 3,000 sepoys had been released, but over 200 men were not even then set free and some of these did not regain their freedom until 1791; while when the captured survivors of Colonel Baillie's detachment arrived at Seringapatam in 1780 they found two British soldiers there who had been taken prisoners in 1768!

CHAPTER X

1793–1819.

THE MYSORE, MAHRATTA AND PINDARI WARS.

1793 WAR having been declared by the National Convention of France against England and Holland on February 1st, 1793, preparations were made at Madras for the capture of Pondicherry, and towards the end of July a well-equipped force of about 10,500 men, of whom 3,200 were Europeans, was assembled on the Red Hills near Pondicherry under the command of Colonel Brathwaite. Among the European troops were the 3rd Battalion Madras Regiment, 538 strong, the flank companies of the 1st and 2nd Battalions, 364 all ranks, and the European Pioneers, 2 officers and 80 men. The 3rd Battalion, the 36th and 52nd Regiments, composed a brigade under command of Lieutenant-Colonel Nesbitt of the 52nd Foot.

No opposition was expected since the French garrison was very small, amounting to no more than 512 Europeans and 884 sepoys, but, as the French refused to surrender, siege operations were commenced on August 10th, fire was opened on the 20th, and on the evening of the 22nd Pondicherry capitulated and was taken possession of next day. The British loss in killed, wounded, and missing totalled 248, of which the Madras European Infantry and Pioneers had 5 men killed, 3 wounded and 1 man missing.

Six stand of Colours, 166 guns, 74,000 rounds of shot and shell and a considerable quantity of small arms and stores fell into the hands of the army under Brathwaite, and in October of this year the work of razing the fortifications and works was taken in hand by Lieutenant Dowse and the Pioneer Corps and was completed in June of the year following.

The thanks of both Houses of Parliament to the troops engaged in the war with Tippoo were published to the Army in July, and during the following month those of the Court of Proprietors of the East India Company were received at Madras. The following is the text of the latter :—

"*Resolved unanimously that it is the opinion of this Court that the most Noble Marquis Cornwallis, Knight of the Most Noble Order of the Garter, has displayed uncommon zeal and ability in the management of the affairs of the East India Company during the time he has been Governor-General and Commander-in-Chief in India and particularly in conducting the late war with Tippoo Sultan and also in concluding the late Treaty of Peace with Tippoo Sultan on terms so honorable and advantageous to the interests of the Company and their Allies.*

"*That the thanks of this Court be given to Marquis Cornwallis for the very gallant and important services he has thus rendered to the East India Company; also—*

"*That his statue be placed in this Court Room that his great services may be ever had in remembrance.*

"*Resolved unanimously that the thanks of this Court be given to Major-General Sir William Medows, Knight of the Most Honorable Order of the Bath, for his gallant and meritorious services during the late war in India.*

"*Resolved unanimously that the thanks of this Court be given to Major-General Sir Robert Abercromby, Knight of the Most Honorable Order of the Bath, for his gallant and meritorious services during the late war in India.*

"*Resolved unanimously that the thanks of this Court be given to all the Officers of the Army, European and Native, under the Marquis Cornwallis for their gallant conduct during the late war in India, also—*

"*That this Court doth highly approve and acknowledge the services of the Non-Commissioned Officers and Private Soldiers, both Native and European, serving under the Marquis Cornwallis during the late war in India, and that the same be signified to them by the Officers of the several corps, who are desired to thank them for their gallant behaviour.*

"*Resolved unanimously that the thanks of this Court be given to the Members of the Supreme Council in Bengal, of the Council at Fort St. George, and of the Council of Bombay, for the zealous assistance and support which they have uniformly afforded to the Marquis Cornwallis and to the Army during the late war in India.*"

1794 In the latter part of the year 1793 the 4th Battalion Madras Europeans marched to Ellore, and in May 1794 its flank companies embarked at Masulipatam for Madras, they being intended for service in Mauritius, had not the expedition been later abandoned. The same month three companies of the same battalion embarked for Vizagapatam to crush a rising in that quarter.

In October the Reverend Mr. Owen joined the 3rd Battalion at Pondicherry as chaplain, and in December the Battalion changed quarters to Poonamallee.

1795 In the month of June, 1795, news of the outbreak of war with Holland was received at Madras, and in July an expedition sailed against Ceylon, while another, under Major Archibald Brown, of the Madras Army, proceeded at the same time against the Dutch possessions of Malacca, Amboyna, Banda and Ternate. Major Brown's force was a small one, containing only 3 officers and 134 other ranks of the Madras Artillery, and 14 officers and 340 non-commissioned officers and men from the flank companies of the 1st and 3rd Battalions Madras Europeans commanded by Captain Parr. The fort at Malacca surrendered to Major Brown on August 18th, and a small force which he there organized under Major Urban Vigors, and which contained, among other units, two flank companies of the 3rd and two battalion companies of the 2nd

1796 Madras Europeans, compelled the surrender of Amboyna on February 17th, 1796; and two companies of the Madras Regiment were employed also in the capture of the Spice Islands in March.

During 1796 the battalions of the Regiment were thus distributed:—The 1st and 3rd were on service in Ceylon and in the

Eastern Islands, the 2nd was stationed at Pondicherry and the 4th was at Masulipatam ; but in July the following General Order was issued by Government regarding the future organization of the European Infantry of the Madras Presidency :—

"FORT ST. GEORGE,
July 12th, 1796.

"*The Right Honourable the President in Council is pleased to publish, for the information of the Army, the following extracts of orders of the Honourable Court of Directors, under date the 8th January, 1796.*

"ORDERS OF THE HONOURABLE COURT OF DIRECTORS, 8TH JANUARY, 1796.

"*We have taken into our most serious consideration the state of the Company's military establishments at our several settlements, together with the memorials which have been addressed us from the respective corps of officers, and, having maturely considered the same, we have resolved that the peace establishment for your presidency shall be as follows :—*

"*European Infantry—Two Regiments.*

"*Having thus detailed the new peace establishment for your presidency, we have great satisfaction in acquainting you that in order to prevent the existence of jealousies between the King's and Company's troops :—*

"*The Right Honourable Henry Dundas, one of His Majesty's principal secretaries of State, has engaged to recommend to His Majesty to give every officer of the Company a King's commission of the same date with that which he receives from the Company, with a retrospect founded on the date of the General Brevet which has taken place in His Majesty's Army.*

"*Paymasters.*

"*That to each regiment or battalion one of the officers be appointed paymaster with proper allowances for the same ; such appointment to be made by the Colonel, or by the majority of the votes of the field officers and captains according to the practice in the King's service. If the* election be made by the Colonel, he is to be responsible for the conduct of the paymaster, otherwise the responsibility to rest with the captains and officers.

"*Pay and Allowances.*

"*As the promotions in the Company's army fully compensate for the diminution of certain allowances which have occasioned jealousies and discontentments between the establishments at different presidencies, we have resolved that the double full batta to officers be abolished, that the half batta as now allowed in Bengal, and at the same rate, be made generally to King's and Company's officers under the other presidencies, except to Colonels who are always to be allowed full batta ; and that full batta be the highest allowance of that kind to be granted in any situation whatever, except in the case of officers doing duty in the Vizier's dominions, who shall have such additional allowance as the Bengal Government may deem adequate to defray the extra charges incurred by the officers in that particular station.*

"*Furlough.*

"*That the following proportion of Company's officers at each presidency be allowed to be absent ; viz., one-third of the lieutenant-colonels, a major, and a fourth of the captains and surgeons to the troops, and one-sixth of the subalterns and assistant-surgeons to the Army.*"

In consequence of this alteration in the establishment of European Infantry the following order, dated "Headquarters, Choultry Plain, 13th July, 1796," was issued to all concerned :—

"*The 1st and 3rd battalions of Europeans ordered to compose the 1st Regiment of European Infantry being in a dispersed state on foreign service, will be gradually reduced to the new formation as circumstances shall permit. The 1st Battalion will compose the grenadier and four battalion companies of the 1st Regiment, and the 3rd Battalion the light and four battalion companies of the same. The six companies of the European Regiment in Ceylon to be reduced to three battalion companies, and the two battalion and flank companies on service to the eastward, to be considered for the present as a grenadier company. The detachment* of the 3rd European Battalion at Tripassore to be formed into two battalion companies, and the details from it on foreign service to be formed into a light and two battalion companies.

"The 2nd and 4th European Battalions to conform immediately to the new establishment, the 2nd Battalion composing the grenadier and four battalion companies, and the 4th the light and four battalion companies of the 2nd Regiment.

"Supernumerary non-commissioned officers, drums and fifes are not to suffer in their rank or pay.

"The flank companies under the new formation to be selected from the grenadier companies of the battalions respectively, as nearly as the present situation of these corps will admit; and so soon as the corps or regiments can be brought into a collected state, such exchanges may take place between men of the flank companies as may be necessary for giving the grenadier companies the men of the greatest bulk and stature, and the light companies those who from activity or make may appear best suited for the duties of the latter.

"The flank companies to consist of a captain and three lieutenants; the battalion companies of a field-officer or captain, two lieutenants and an ensign. The colonels' companies to have the lieutenant-captain in place of one of the lieutenants. The junior lieutenant-colonel and major are not to have companies.

"The Commanding Officer may post the companies in battalions and officers to companies, as he thinks proper, until the two divisions of each of the 1st and 2nd Regiments can join their companies, and they are to be considered as independent and returned accordingly. The division from the 1st European Battalion to be called the 1st Division of the 1st Regiment, and that formed from the 3rd European Battalion, the 2nd. The division of the 2nd Regiment at Pondicherry to be called the 1st Division of the 2nd Regiment, and that at Masulipatam, the 2nd; each division to retain the non-commissioned staff allowed to a complete Regiment as non-effectives until a junction takes place.

"Field Officers are appointed to European Infantry as follows:—

1st Regiment European Infantry :—

Colonel Eccles Nixon.
Lt.-Colonel Henry Malcolm.
Lt.-Colonel Robert Croker.
Major Thomas Parr.
Major Johnson Kennedy.

2nd Regiment European Infantry :—

Colonel John Brathwaite.
Lt.-Colonel George Wahab.
Lt.-Colonel George Waight.
Major P. A. Agnew.
Major Aldwell Taylor.

"*Establishment of the different corps of the Company's army on the Coast of Coromandel as fixed by the Honourable Court of Directors.*

"*European Infantry.*

"*The battalions on the present establishment to be formed into 2 regiments of 10 companies each to consist of :—1 colonel, 2 lieutenant-colonels (junior lieut.-colonel and junior major to be without companies), 2 majors, 7 captains, 1 captain-lieutenant, 21 lieutenants, 8 ensigns, 40 sergeants, 50 corporals, 22 drums and fifes, 950 privates, 20 puckallies. Staff: 1 adjutant, 1 quartermaster, 1 paymaster, 1 surgeon, 2 mates, 1 sergeant-major, 1 quartermaster-sergeant, 1 drill sergeant, 1 drill corporal, 1 drum major, 1 fife major. (1 adjutant and 1 quartermaster as on the old establishment, to be continued to each battalion until the battalions of each regiment are ordered to join.)*"

From August 1st, 1796, European women, the wives of soldiers who accompanied their husbands from England, were granted an allowance of one fanam and a half per diem, at the same time they were ordered to be regularly mustered. This appears to be the first instance of the soldier's wife receiving any allowance.

1797
On July 20th, 1797, the 2nd Madras European Regiment, 450 rank and file, then stationed at Pondicherry, was ordered to be held in readiness for foreign service on an expedition which had been projected against Manilla. Most of the troops had embarked before the end of August and part of the fleet had actually sailed when the expedition was suddenly abandoned in consequence of intelligence received from England; but three British corps, of which the Madras European Regiment was one, and a large body of sepoys, had arrived at Penang before they could be recalled.

1798
In the year 1798 five companies of the 1st Europeans in Ceylon composed the first division of that corps and had their headquarters at Point de Galle, the other five companies were serving in the Eastern Islands, and had their headquarters at Malacca. The 1st Division of the 2nd Regiment garrisoned Masulipatam and the 2nd Division of the same regiment Fort St. George.

On November 5th of this year details of a fresh organization of the European Infantry were published in orders:—

"*Establishment of European Infantry Corps.*

"*We have been apprised of His Majesty's intention to new model his regiments of infantry serving in the East Indies by forming them into 12 companies of 100 rank and file each, and in order to preserve a proper uniformity between His Majesty's and the Company's European Infantry we have resolved that our present establishment shall be formed also into regiments of the same strength. Each regiment is therefore to consist of:—1 colonel, 2 lieutenant-colonels, 2 majors, 7 captains, 1 captain-lieutenant, 25 lieutenants, 10 ensigns, 40 sergeants, 60 corporals, 26 drums and fifes, 1,140 privates, 24 puckallies, with staff, etc., as at present.*

"*The establishment which, on a due consideration of all the circumstances connected with this arrangement we have resolved on for your Presidency, is one regiment of European infantry of the foregoing strength.*

CHANGE OF TITLE

"*In obedience to the foregoing orders, the Commander-in-Chief* is requested to issue the necessary orders for drafting the non-commissioned officers and privates of the 2nd Regiment of European Infantry to complete the 1st Regiment to the new establishment, and to supply such vacancies in the corps of artillery as the number and the nature of the men may allow. The non-commissioned officers who may become supernumerary by this arrangement are to do duty with the 1st Regiment and to be brought on the strength of that corps as vacancies occur in their respective ranks.*

"*The Corps in future to be denominated 'The Madras European Regiment.'*

"*In order to carry into effect the arrangement ordered by the Honourable Court of Directors, for the future promotion of officers of infantry to the rank of Major, on the principle of regimental succession, the Right Honourable the Governor in Council has been pleased to resolve that the 15 senior officers of each rank shall be successively posted to the 15 regiments now on the establishment, that the next in seniority shall be posted in a similar manner, and that this operation shall be repeated until all the corps may be complete with officers.*"

1800 In consequence of the above-quoted General Order, instructions were issued on January 8th, 1800, by the Commander-in-Chief directing the organization of the European Corps into one regiment of 12 companies to be thenceforth known as "The Madras European Regiment," and that the 2nd Regiment of European Infantry should be drafted into the Madras Artillery and Madras European Regiment, 200 men going to the first-named corps.

The 2nd Division, 2nd Regiment, then in garrison at Fort St. George, was ordered to parade for this purpose on January 13th; these drafts joined the 1st Division of the Corps at Masulipatam, were formed into six companies, and designated "The 1st Division of the Madras European Regiment"; at the same time orders were sent to Amboyna, Malacca and Banda to transfer as many of the privates of the 2nd Regiment to these islands as were required, the

* Lieut.-General Harris was at this time C.-in-C. in Madras.

artillery and the remainder being drafted into the detachment of the 1st Regiment there serving, formed into six companies, and designated "The 2nd Division of the Madras European Regiment."

On January 11th, 1800, the following list of officers permanently posted to the Madras European Regiment was published:—Colonel, Major-General J. Brathwaite; Lieutenant-Colonels Thomas Leighton and Aldwell Taylor; Majors George Smith and John Munro; Captains John Dighton, Henry Webber, John M. Convenant, William Cunningham, Patrick Bruce, William King and Frederick Pierce; Captain-Lieutenant Thomas Tichborne; Lieutenants Sir John Cox, Bart., Francis Thompson, John Munro, Joseph Storey, Augustus Andrews, Henry Yarde, W. G. Waugh, Charles McDonald, John McDonald, Lovell William Hall, S. McDowall, Gilbert Waugh, Thomas Shute, Edward Fraser, Richard Phillips and David Forbes; Chaplain, the Rev. R. H. Kerr; Adjutant, George Custance; Quartermaster, Augustus Andrews.

The dispersed state of the 1st Madras Europeans in Ceylon, Malacca, Banda, Amboyna and Ternate, and the absence from India of a great part of the 2nd, prevented the employment of the Corps in the last Mysore War of 1799. The flank companies of the Division of the Regiment at Masulipatam did indeed embark from that place to join the army under General Lord Harris, but they were too late to take any active part in the campaign. A large detachment of the Corps, however, did duty with the Corps of Pioneers, and acted as sappers and miners in all the operations of the siege of Seringapatam, behaving with their customary gallantry.

The close of the eighteenth century brings the Madras European Regiment to the 154th year of its existence as a military body, or the 52nd since it was formed into a battalion by Major Lawrence shortly after the capture of Madras by La Bourdonnais, since which time it had been for forty-three years almost continuously on active service in all parts of India, the greater part of the time against the French; and during those years it had contained in its ranks some of the soldiers most distinguished in Indian history —Lawrence, Clive, Glass, Innes, Dalton, Kirk, Yorke, Cope, Preston,

MAJOR-GENERAL SIR THOMAS MUNRO, K.C.B.
Joined Regiment in 1780.
(From an oil painting by Reinagle, in the possession of the Oriental Club, Hanover Square)

EXPEDITION AGAINST THE SPICE ISLANDS

Polier, Campbell, Harrison, Holt, McKenzie, Knox, Caillaud, Forde, Kilpatrick, Fitzgerald, Orton, Nixon, Bonjour, Kelly, the two Smiths, Stewart, Brown and many others of earlier days, with Cosby, Lang, Gowdie, Bowser, Mackay, Brathwaite, Burr, Brown, Close, Munro and Malcolm of a later period, forming a roll of illustrious names which few, if any, corps have ever produced.

During its service since 1746 the Regiment, or detachments of it, had taken an active part in every military operation in Southern India, besides those in Bengal, Guzerat, Ceylon and in the Moluccas. It had participated and borne a prominent and distinguished share in 46 general actions, served at 74 sieges of places of the greatest importance, defended Tanjore, Fort St. David, Arcot, Vellore, Trichinopoly, Madras and Patna with the most determined resolution, captured all the Dutch islands in the eastern seas, and been engaged in innumerable minor affairs, defences of and attacks upon small forts and posts.

It was a matter of the keenest regret to the Regiment that it took no part in the last war with Tippoo Sultan, but the honourable mention made by Government of the names of Close, Malcolm and Agnew—all officers of the Madras European Regiment, shows that they well maintained the good name of the Corps to which they belonged. These officers were all serving in different posts on the staff of the Grand Army before Seringapatam.

1801 Early in 1801, at the instance of Mr. Farquhar, Resident at Amboyna, Colonel Burr, commanding the troops in the Moluccas, organized an expedition against Ternate, one of the Spice Islands belonging to the Dutch. The force employed only numbered 348 all told, 178 being Europeans and the remainder sepoys, and of the Europeans 83 non-commissioned officers and men belonged to the Madras Regiment and appear to have been commanded by a Captain Walker of the 4th Madras Native Infantry. Captain Astlé of the Indian Marine, had promised his assistance and it was considered that the force to be employed was sufficient for the purpose in view, as the strength of the Dutch was not thought to exceed 50 Europeans and 2,000 native soldiers.

The expeditionary force arrived off Ternate on February 10th and its surrender was demanded and refused; the troops were then landed, but the promised naval support was not forthcoming and an attack upon a strongly fortified post having proved unsuccessful, the force re-embarked on the 19th and returned to its base. On April 2nd another expedition sailed from Amboyna and arrived off Fort Orange on the 30th. By May 8th the troops had been landed and after some harassing service the island and its dependencies were surrendered to the British, the troops returning to Amboyna in July.

On June 21st of this year Major Dighton was, on promotion, appointed to the 1st Division of the Corps at Masulipatam, and Major Henry Webber at the same time joined the 2nd Division at Amboyna, Colonel Burr, in command at Amboyna, being transferred to Ternate, where he remained until the restoration of the island to the Dutch; he then brought the remains of the Regiment back to Masulipatam where the two divisions were united early in 1803.

1802 The flank companies of the Madras European Regiment had in 1802 been sent against certain hill rajas in the Ganjam district, continuing on service during the greater part of the year and losing a good many men from fever.

1803 On the departure from India of Major-General Brathwaite on January 4th and of Colonel Archibald Brown on February 18th, 1803, the Madras Government issued a highly complimentary order, regretting the loss to the Army occasioned by their departure, and conveying the strongest expressions of approbation of their long and distinguished services, as well as bearing testimony to their public merits and private virtues. General Brathwaite died in London in August of this year.

The dominions formerly constituting the Mahratta Empire had, for many years previous to this period, been divided into five separate states, governed in 1802 by the undermentioned chiefs :—

1. Baji Rao, the Peshwa, ruled over the Southern Mahratta country.

THE MAHRATTA WAR

2. Ragojee Bhonsla, ruled over Berar.
3. Scindia, possessed Candeish and the greater part of Malwa.
4. Holkar, lived at Indore and ruled over the remainder of Malwa, while
5. The Guickwar ruled in Guzerat.

Scindia, who was desirous of becoming the head of the Mahrattas, gained complete ascendancy over the councils of the Peshwa, and in October, 1801, inflicted a severe defeat upon Holkar, his principal rival; a year later, however, Holkar gathered his forces and defeated the combined armies of Scindia and the Peshwa under the walls of Poona. The Peshwa fled, landed at Bassein and made to the British certain overtures which resulted in the Treaty of Bassein concluded on December 31st. Under this treaty a subsidiary force over 6,000 strong was to be stationed in the dominions of the Peshwa who was to cede certain districts to the Company, the annual revenue of which was to be devoted to the expenses of the upkeep of the force. For the protection of the Company's territories, and the eventual establishment of the subsidiary force at Poona, an army nearly 20,000 strong was assembled on the north-western frontier of Mysore, but the Supreme Government decided that only some 10,000 men, under Major-General Wellesley, should advance into the Mahratta country.

With the main events and the chief actions of the Mahratta War the Madras European Regiment had no concern, but during August and September, 1803, an expeditionary force was got together in Ganjam for the purpose of taking possession of Cuttack, then belonging to the raja of Berar. The force was placed under the command of Lieutenant-Colonel Harcourt, 12th Regiment, and contained some 2,700 troops, British and native, the European portion being represented by 200 men of the 22nd Foot and 300 of the Madras European Regiment.

On September 8th the troops advanced from Ganjam, on the 14th Manikpatam was abandoned by the Mahrattas and occupied by the British; and then, having crossed the Chilka Lake, Nursinga-patam was entered on the 17th and Jagarnat occupied on the following day. On the 20th the advance was resumed in the direction of Ahmedpore through a country rendered almost impassable by heavy rain, and by October 4th Mukandpore was reached. There had been repeated skirmishing, and near Mukandpore there was a sharp action between the advanced guard and the enemy who was repulsed with loss, and a few days later the force arrived on the banks of the Katjuri River. On October 10th Cuttack, the capital of the province, was surrendered, and Colonel Harcourt then commenced preparations for the siege of the fort of Barabati, about a mile distant from Cuttack.

This fort, strongly built of stone and surrounded by a deep wet ditch varying from 25 to 135 feet in width, had only one entrance by a very narrow bridge across the ditch. On the night of October 13th batteries were completed 500 yards from the south face of the fort and these opened fire early next day. By 11 a.m. the fort guns had been silenced and a storming party, of which men of the Madras European Regiment formed part, with a 6-pounder to blow open the gate, advanced to the attack. The bridge was quickly passed under a heavy fire from the walls, but it was nearly forty minutes before an opening sufficient to admit one man at a time had been made. The Europeans charged in one by one and so quickly that, in spite of a stout resistance at the inner gate, they entered with the retreating garrison, who now abandoned the fort, the capture of which was followed by the submission of the whole province of Cuttack.

The storming party evinced rare gallantry and the bravery of Captain Francis Thompson of the Corps was specially noticeable, and in an order issued by the Governor-General on receiving Colonel Harcourt's despatch, we read that, " His Excellency in Council expresses the satisfaction with which he has noticed the zealous and efficient services of Major of Brigade Thompson of the Madras European Regiment."

Immediately after the capture of Barabati a detachment of the three arms and containing a company of the Regiment, the whole under Major Forbes, was sent to force the pass of Bermuth, the only passage through the hilly country separating the province of Cuttack from the Berar country. This pass was seized on November 2nd, the enemy escaping into Berar.

Colonel Harcourt was now approaching with the remainder of his force, in view of co-operating with General Wellesley, when news was received of peace having been concluded with the Nagpore raja consequent on the victories of Assaye and Argaum, and peace having then been concluded with Scindia the force in Cuttack was broken up and the Madras European Regiment returned to Masulipatam.

1804 In May, 1804, Lieutenant-Colonel Ross Lang was appointed to command the Corps; this officer, however, retired on
1806 April 26th, 1806, when Lieutenant-Colonel Innes assumed command of the Madras European Regiment.

It appears to have been in this latter year that messes were for the first time established in the different corps of the Company's army; the Court of Directors expressed an opinion in favour of the innovation and in consequence of their remarks the following order, dated May 15th, 1806, was issued by the Governor-in-Council:—

"*The Governor-in-Council, fully impressed with the important advantages to the public service and general discipline of the Army which will result from the establishment of messes of officers in the several Corps of the Army, as proposed in the thirty-second paragraph of the letter of the Honorable Court of Directors, desires that the Commander-in-Chief will adopt such measures as he may deem proper and necessary to obtain so desirable an object, to the extent which the nature of the service will admit, reporting his proceedings in this respect to the Right Honorable the Governor-in-Council.*"

Messes were accordingly introduced in June, 1806.

1809 In October, 1809, the frigate *Dover*, 38 guns, the *Cornwallis*, 44, and the sloop *Samarang*, 18, sailed for the Dutch settlements in the Eastern Islands, having on board a detachment of Madras Artillery and a large body of the Madras European Regiment under Captain Phillips, who had with him Lieutenants Forbes and Nixon and Ensign Roy; Captain Tucker, of the *Dover*, was in command of the whole naval and military force. The little armada was off Amboyna about February 14th, 1810, when it was seen that the defences consisted of a fort with a battery on each flank, the three mounting 215 guns, while on the hills behind the town were two more batteries about 1,500 yards apart, the one known as Wanitoo, the other as Battoo-Gantong; these were armed with 21 guns; the Dutch garrison was about 1,350 in number, Europeans and natives.

At 2 p.m. on the 16th a party, 400 strong and containing 130 of the Madras European Regiment, was landed under command of Captain Phillips, and covered by the fire of the ships' guns, proceeded to attack the two batteries on the hill. Captain Phillips with his own company, 30 gunners and 85 seamen advanced against Wanitoo and soon carried it, and was then proceeding to attack Battoo-Gantong, but found the approach barred by an impassable ravine. The other portion of the landing party—one company of the Madras Europeans under Lieutenant Forbes, 15 artillerymen and 140 seamen and marines, led by Captain Court, of the Madras Artillery, gained some high ground commanding Battoo-Gantong, when the enemy retired leaving it in our possession. In the morning two other batteries defending the anchorage were found to have been abandoned, and a heavy concentrated fire being then opened on Fort Victoria, this very soon surrendered, and terms of capitulation, involving the whole island, were signed.

In these operations the Madras European Regiment had two men killed and four wounded, and in the despatch describing the capture of the island, the officer-in-command wrote:—" I have already, I hope, done justice to the military conduct of Captain Phillips, to whom I am likewise under the greatest obligations for his advice—you are aware, Sir, how much the Service is indebted to that officer for the very important assistance derived from his knowledge of the Malay language. To Captain Forbes, of the Madras European Regiment, I owe every acknowledgment for the benefit of his judgment and his advice."

Some dispute arose between the Navy and Army, as well as

Capture of the ISLAND of BANDA, Augt 9th 1810.

between the captors and the Government of India, respecting the distribution of the property taken in Amboyna and other islands. The amount of spices captured—then of course of no insignificant value—totalled some 275 tons, the whole of which was claimed by the captors, but the Admiralty Court at Madras decided that this was the property of the Government. Two Dutch brigs captured by the Madras troops at the islands of Bouro and Laricque were seized by Captain Tucker as naval prizes, as were also two smaller vessels taken at Saperoua by Ensign Roy, of the Madras European Regiment.

In August, 1810, a detachment of the Regiment under Captain Forbes, with Lieutenants C. Forbes and Cursham, assisted in the capture of Ternate, and later in the same year another party of the Corps commanded by Captain Nixon was engaged in the successful attack on the island of Banda Neira. Several officers and a number of men of the Regiment died in these islands owing to the very trying nature of the climate; of the officers Lieutenant Davenant and Assistant-Surgeon Milne died at Banda in 1811, Captain Phillips at Macassar and Lieutenant Dacre at Banda Neira in 1814, while in 1815 Captain Forbes died at Banda and Lieutenant Carberry at Ternate.

In 1809 Major-General Gowdie, who had risen in and served with the Madras Regiment during a great part of the previous century and who had particularly distinguished himself in the Mysore wars, had succeeded General McDowall in command of the Madras Army, and when in March, 1811, General Gowdie finally left India, the Governor-in-Council issued a highly complimentary order recounting his past services.

At the end of this year news reached India of the death in Oxfordshire of Brigadier-General Caillaud.

1811 In 1811 the Regiment was under orders to take part in the expedition to Java, but the order was countermanded; though the Regiment did not actually embark, 1 subaltern, 3 sergeants, 3 corporals and 30 privates proceeded with the force under General Auchmuty, as pioneers, and were present at the capture of the Island of Java and the storming of Fort Cornelius.

1812
1813
In 1812 the Regiment was stationed at Vellore and in 1813 at Wallajabad, where in the year following the garrison was inspected by the Commander-in-Chief, Lieutenant-General Abercromby, who expressed himself about the Regiment in the following laudatory terms:—

"*The excellence and neatness of the appointments of the Madras European Regiment, as well as their performance in the field and their interior economy in barracks, leaves the Commander-in-Chief only to regret their want of numbers; but he trusts that at an early period they will be as complete in men as they are in that system and attention he has now with pleasure remarked.*"

In August, 1813, news was received in India of the death in England on April 18th of General Sir Barry Close, Bart. He had entered the army in 1772 and served with the Regiment in the early Mysore wars, held the appointment of Adjutant-General of the Madras Army and later was Resident at Mysore. In 1800 the Court of Directors presented him with a sword of the value of 300 guineas, and on his death erected a fine monument to his memory in St. Mary's Church, Fort St. George.

1815
The flank companies of the Regiment proceeded in 1815 as far as Trichinopoly, *en route* to Ceylon, in view of trouble which had broken out in Candy, but on the rebellion being suppressed, these companies returned and joined the army assembled in consequence of the outbreak of the Pindari War. When the army was broken up and about to return to quarters, General Sir Thomas Hislop, in a General Order, dated April 28th, 1815, expressed himself as "highly gratified at the excellent appearance of so large a force of the Madras Army; its high credit and reputation had led him to expect much, but its efficiency and discipline surpassed his utmost expectations."

The flank companies on return rejoined headquarters at Trichinopoly, and in October the whole corps marched and joined a force which had been collected near Kurnool under Colonel Marriott in consequence of some trouble with the local chief. On December 15th the fort of Kurnool surrendered and the Nawab was deposed, remaining for many years a state prisoner in the citadel of Bellary. Colonel Marriott reported in high terms on the " zeal, energy and efficiency of the troops under his command." After the surrender of Kurnool the Regiment marched to Hyderabad by way of Bellary, where the detachment of the Corps rejoined which for so long had been serving in the Dutch Islands now about to be restored to their former owners.

The Resident at Fort Victoria in a letter to the Government of Fort St. George specially eulogized the services of Lieutenants Kyd, Nelson, Gale and Dale. The officers who had commanded the detachment to the eastward at various times were Captain Phillips, Lieutenants David Forbes, Nixon, Charles Forbes, Carberry, Kyd, Cooper, Brown and Cursham ; Ensigns Roy, Gale, Dale, Williams and Clarke. Lieutenant, later Captain, David Forbes became Governor of Banda and while holding this post an insurrection broke out in the Island of Poran, where a body of Bengal troops sent to suppress it was defeated. Forbes then organized another expedition, largely drawn from his own Regiment, sailed to Poran and there defeated the rebels with great slaughter, capturing their chief.

During its stay in the Moluccas the detachment of the Corps was repeatedly engaged in various small affairs with insurgents or pirates ; many men died of disease and several were killed in action. Lieutenants Charles Forbes, Kyd, Gale and Dale were at various times on the personal staff of the Governor.

Before proceeding to the consideration of the events of the Mahratta-Pindari War of 1817, the following dealing with several matters of interior economy may be mentioned :—In November, 1812, the practice of distinguishing companies by letters of the alphabet was introduced into the Madras Army, but it did not apply to grenadier and light companies.

On December 20th, 1814, regimental canteens were established and regulations for their management were published to the Army.

1816 On October 11th, 1816, an order was published by the Governor-General to the effect, that all time-expired men belonging to the King's regiments in India should be allowed the option of volunteering into the Company's artillery and infantry. Men enlisting for a period of three years were to receive 15 pagodas (Rs52.8.0) each, those enlisting for five years 25 pagodas each (Rs87.8.0); while a bounty of three guineas per man was offered to volunteers from King's regiments returning home from India. Men over 32 years of age were, however, ineligible.

The Pindaris, against whom punitive operations were now to be undertaken, were not a tribe, still less a nation, but a military system of bandits of all races and religions. The origin of a Pindari has been aptly given by Sir Alfred Lyall*—

" . . . . I had no lands or wife,
" So I took to the hills of Malwa and the wild Pindari life."

They fluctuated in numbers, being augmented from time to time by military adventurers from every state and frequently amounted to as many as 30,000 men, and were thus continually receiving an accession of associates from the most desperate of mankind. They harried the countryside, resorted to torture to extract from their victims information as to concealed treasure. They sold their services readily to any chief who wished to revenge himself upon a neighbour, and during three years in succession—1814, 1815 and 1816—they raided the Madras Presidency, spreading consternation up to the walls of Madras itself. The British Government made every endeavour to enlist the aid of the States of the Mahratta Confederacy in the overcoming of these freebooters; but although these appeared to concur in the desirability of this measure, they took no action openly in this direction, while secretly encouraging the Pindaris and even sharing their plunder. In 1816 the Pindari ravages were specially extensive; their raiding bands

* *Verses written in India*—" The Old Pindari."

proceeded, some due south into the country of the Nizam, reaching the Godavery; others marched east into the Company's territory of Ganjam, killing and wounding 7,000 persons and carrying off or destroying property valued at £100,000; while others again crossed the Raptee and overran the dominions of the Peshwa to some distance beyond Poona.*

1817 In March, 1817, the Marquis of Hastings, then Governor-General, having received instructions from the Court of Directors to take action against the Pindaris, began to make preparations on a scale sufficient to deal with any hostility from one or more states of the Mahratta Confederacy, and at the same time ordered the governments of Madras and Bombay to have their several quotas of troops in readiness to move into the field.

For the forthcoming operations, the theatre of which was to extend over the greater part of Southern India, two armies were organized—the Grand Army to form at Cawnpore under the personal command of the Marquis of Hastings, and the Army of the Deccan under General Sir Thomas Hislop, this last containing seven and the Grand Army four divisions, each army having a complement of cavalry and guns. The Headquarters and five companies of the Madras European Regiment, under Major Augustus Andrews, formed, with the flank companies of the 1st Foot and the 1st Battalion 7th Native Infantry, the 1st Brigade, commanded by Colonel Thompson, of the 1st or Advanced Division; while the remaining five companies of the Regiment, the 1st Battalions of the 8th, 21st and 22nd Native Infantry, composed the Hyderabad Brigade of the 2nd Hyderabad Division; the brigade was commanded by Colonel Sir Augustus Floyer, K.C.B., and the division by Brigadier-General Doveton.

The Grand Army contained 43,687 fighting men, the Army of the Deccan 70,487, while the total strength of the native powers

* Burton, *The Mahratta and Pindari War*, p. 7.

eventually arrayed against the British forces was estimated as follows:—

Scindia	15,000 Horse.	16,000 Foot.	140 Guns.
Holkar	20,000 ,,	8,000 ,,	107 ,,
Peshwa	28,000 ,,	14,000 ,,	37 ,,
Bhonsla	16,000 ,,	18,000 ,,	85 ,,
Amir Khan	12,000 ,,	10,000 ,,	200 ,,
Pindaris	15,000 ,,	15,000 ,,	20 ,,
Making a total of ...	106,000 Horse.	81,000 Foot.	589 Guns.

For the destruction of the Pindaris it was proposed to close in from every side upon their headquarters on the Nerbudda River, and to assist this end the Army of the Deccan was ordered to advance into Malwa.

In the latter part of August, 1817, a detachment composed of a troop of Horse Artillery, a squadron of the 22nd Dragoons, a wing of the Madras European Regiment, a sepoy battalion and half a battalion of pioneers, all under command of Lieutenant-Colonel McGregor Murray, left Secunderabad and arrived at Nander on the Godavery River on October 16th. From here Sir Thomas Hislop, with the guns, cavalry and some native infantry, pushed on to Hurdah where he arrived on November 10th and here, three days later, Major Andrews joined him with the rest of the headquarter wing of the Madras European Regiment. Moving on as rapidly as possible the Headquarters of the Army of the Deccan was at Nemawar, on the right bank of the Nerbudda, on December 2nd, at Sundapore on the 3rd, on the 4th at Soankeir, on the 8th at Pipli, and on the 11th camped at Duttana Muttana, within eight miles of the 3rd Division at Ursoda.

On the 21st, moving before daybreak, the army had advanced some eight miles in the direction of Maheidpoor* before any sign of an enemy was met with, but on ascending a gentle rise a view was obtained of the town of Maheidpoor on the right bank of the Sipra

* This spelling has been preserved, as it is that on the Colours.

River with the enemy's army drawn up on the further side, the intervening plain on both banks covered with the Mahratta light horsemen who advanced to within a short distance of the column. As the advance continued the position of the hostile army was more clearly visible, while the British cavalry and light troops having driven in the enemy's horse, caused the position of the fords over the Sipra to be disclosed; one of these, and the most practicable, known as the Kuldee Ghat, was in front of the enemy's position, while the other, further down stream, was impassable by artillery. It was therefore determined to cross by the first-named of these fords, where, moreover, the banks being high, the troops would be able, after crossing, to form up under cover from enemy fire.

The army against which the British force was about to pit itself was mainly composed of Holkar's Indore troops, swelled by certain bodies of Pindaris which had been driven out of southern Malwa by the converging movements of the columns of the two British armies, now closing in upon them; the march of the Grand Army had, however, been slow, for cholera had broken out in its ranks and the line of march was strewn with the victims of the disease, while thousands of followers had deserted. The British force opposed here to Holkar was some 5,000 strong, all arms and all ranks, while the Mahratta infantry alone was of equal strength, and its front was covered by nearly 100 guns; beyond, a dense mass of 30,000 horse, forming a second line, crowded the plain as far as the eye could reach.

The Mahratta Army was drawn up about 8,000 yards from and facing the ford, its front nearly parallel to the river; the ruined village of Dooblee in the centre was on a slight eminence, the ascent of which was of the nature of a glacis; a ravine running down to the river and a ruined enclosure secured the right, while the left rested on the river bank, the stream here bending round to the rear of the position. The village was strongly held by infantry and guns and was flanked by the fire of heavy batteries.

Arrived within 600 yards of the ford arrangements were made for the safety of the sick and baggage, while the plan of attack was arranged as follows :—The light brigade was to cross at the ford and take up a position on the further bank followed by the cavalry and guns, the Europeans then crossing and forming on the right of the light brigade. The first and light brigades were under the immediate command of Sir John Malcolm, with Lieutenant-Colonel Robert Scott, of the Madras European Regiment, who also commanded the 1st Brigade, as his second-in-command.

The passage of the river was successfully effected, the two brigades being over by midday, " an extraordinary movement of countermarch being carried out during the passage in order to bring the right in front, a movement which exposed the " (first) " brigade to considerable loss " * ; while the British light guns on attempting to come into action were almost at once overwhelmed by the heavier metal of the hostile artillery.

" Arrived on the far side of the Sipra, the infantry was at once led to the attack which was carried out at the point of the bayonet. Launched against the enemy's batteries, and particularly against the ruined village in the centre, the advancing line," the Royal Scots led by Lieutenant-Colonel Murray, the Madras Europeans by Major Andrews, " was received with a discharge of grape, chain and round shot, which by its weight alone staggered the impetus of the charge. But with a cheer the British soldiers rushed straight at the enemy's guns. The onslaught was irresistible, and though the gunners stood manfully to their pieces, which were even turned by the survivors on the British line after it had passed, they could not withstand the assault and were nearly all killed, while the guns, 76 in number, fell into the hands of the victors."†

The enemy on the left of Dooblee fled along the bank of the river, the right and centre pressed towards the right, and went off pursued by the cavalry along the road to Allode. Malcolm's division, which was now re-forming some thousand yards in rear of the enemy's position, was ordered to move at once on the Mahratta camp standing in a hollow near the river bank beyond Dooblee,

* Burton, p. 51.
† *Ibid.*

THE FIELD

View of the Ground on which was fought the Battl

From an old Engraving.

REFE

- A.A. Avenue of Trees leading to Mehidpur.
- B. Fort of Mehidpur.
- C. Ruined Village of Dooblee.
- D. Ruined enclosure
- E.E. Fords of the Seepra, called Kuldee Gh
- a. Ravine in which the Light Brigade w posted.
- b. Ravine by which the European Brigad ascended

OF MEHIDPUR

Mehidpur, seen from the right bank of the Seepra.

NCES

- c   Horse Artillery Battery.
- d   Cavalry formed for Action.
- e.   Rocket Battery.
- 1.   Front of the Enemy's position.
- 2.   Enemy's Cavalry.
- 3.   Enemy's principal Batteries.
- 4.   Ravine by which parties of the Enemy's Infantry came down to annoy the British Cavalry.

but this was found to be deserted, and the troops then returned to the battlefield, while the British cavalry and two light infantry battalions kept up the pursuit of the fugitives until nightfall.

Young Holkar escaped, but his regalia and jewels were taken; the loss of his army amounted to not less than 3,000 men, and the country for many miles was strewn with Mahratta and Pindari dead. The British casualties numbered 174 killed and 621 wounded, while over 200 of the latter died for want of proper medical treatment. A contemporary writer says :—" At Mehidpur in the field hospitals there was scarcely a bit of dressing plaster for the wounded officers, none for the men; nor was there a single set of amputating instruments besides those belonging to individual surgeons, some of these (were) without them; and we have the best authority for saying that, of those amputated, from the bluntness of the knives and the want of dressing plaster alone, two out of three died in hospital."

Of the Madras Europeans seven, including one officer—Lieutenant Coleman—were killed and one officer—Lieutenant and Adjutant Hancome—and 52 other ranks were wounded, Lieutenant Hancome only surviving a very short time after the amputation of his leg. According to the regimental " Digest " Lieutenant Calder was also wounded, but was not entered in the return. It is said that a round shot fired by the enemy fell among the band when marching to the field, whereby five bandsmen were injured.*

The Battle of Maheidpoor was the last general action fought in Southern India on a large scale.

In a General Order, issued on September 22nd by Lieutenant-General Sir Thomas Hislop, he specially mentioned the services of the Madras European Regiment under Major Andrews, while Lieutenant Spankie, of the Regiment, employed as baggage-master with the Army, was also brought to notice as one to whom His Excellency's best thanks were due " not only for the manner in

---

* The actual detail of regimental casualties in the A.G.'s return is :—*Killed*, 1 Captain, 2 sergeants, 4 rank and file; *wounded*, 1 subaltern, 1 sergeant, 5 drummers, 45 rank and file. The strength of the Regiment in the battle was 9 officers and 314 other ranks.

which the department under his charge had been conducted, but particularly for his judicious arrangements and indefatigable exertions on the day of the action, to which the army was principally indebted for the safety of the baggage."

The army remained until December 28th at Maheidpoor, where a hospital and depot were established, and then marched to Taul on the Chambal River, where on the 30th a junction was effected with the Guzerat Division of the Deccan Army. On January 1st, 1818, overtures of peace were made by Holkar and on the 6th a treaty was concluded; ten days later the Headquarters and 1st Division marched, moving via Maheidpoor and Oojein, into Candeish, when all the baggage which had been left in Hindia at the beginning of the campaign, was ordered to be sent by February 10th to Korgaon, escorted by a company of the Madras Europeans and other details. The army moved on from Korgaon, and marched by the Sindevah Ghat, Punaghar and Kurrone, to Thalner, where the column was fired upon from the fort, situated on the Taptee River. The fort commandant, refusing surrender when summoned, it became necessary to storm the place, which was done by the Royals and Madras Europeans. Resistance was slight until the innermost gate was arrived at, when by a sudden attack two officers and several grenadiers were killed, but the remainder of the storming party charging in, the place was captured and the garrison put to the sword.

The army, now in pursuit of the Peshwa, Baji Rao, crossed the Taptee on March 3rd and on the 9th was joined at Pooltamba on the Godavery River by the 2nd Division under Brigadier-General Doveton. The divisions were now re-organized, the Army of the Deccan was broken up, and the 2nd and 4th Divisions were considerably reinforced, the flank and three battalion companies of the Madras European Regiment, with certain other units, joining the 2nd Division, under Brigadier-General Doveton, on transfer from the 1st.

On March 31st General Doveton marched, still in pursuit of Baji Rao, taking with him a portion of his force only—some horse

MASSACRE OF THE BRITISH OFFICERS IN FORT TALNEIR.

artillery guns, three cavalry regiments, three companies Royal Scots, the flank companies of the Madras Europeans and three sepoy battalions. Moving by Mekkar, Seiloo, Karinja and Deogaon, he was close upon Baji Rao, when that chief was surprised and defeated near Seoni by a Bengal column; on hearing of this General Doveton followed up the retreating Peshwa until April 23rd, when the exhausted state of the troops, and the fact that the fugitive had been driven from the Deccan, caused Doveton to retrace his steps to his starting point on the Godavery, where he arrived on May 11th.

In the meantime the remaining troops of the 2nd Division—some guns, two companies Royal Scots, three companies Madras Europeans, the greater part of three sepoy battalions and some irregular Horse—all under Colonel McDowall, moved into Candeish to reduce certain forts in the Chandor district. One of these named Rajdier proved a formidable task, being on a precipitous rock, while the approach to the summit was by a very narrow path defended by strong gateways, loopholes and embrasures. The outposts were soon driven in by some of the Regiment under Major Andrews and sepoys led by Captain Coombs, but the place was set on fire by the shells of the British guns, and on capture was found to be practically gutted, and in the course of the next few days some 18 forts in or about the Nerbudda Valley were easily taken.

The column then moved on towards Chandor, and on May 15th had arrived near Malegaon, a quadrangular fort with two lines of works, built of solid masonry, flanked by towers, and having three sides washed by the river. On the night of the 18th, batteries were constructed and opened fire next day; that night the enemy made a very determined sortie, the British covering parties were driven in, and the enemy were almost upon the working parties, when Major Andrews, with a few men of the Regiment, counter-attacked and drove back the assailants; but in the fighting Major Andrews was wounded, and Malegaon was not finally captured until June 13th after very hard fighting, in which the attack had 209 killed and wounded, of which one officer—Major Andrews—and 26 men of the Regiment were wounded and 2 killed.

Sergeant William O'Brien and Corporal Thomas Tate, of the Regiment, were specially conspicuous for their gallantry during these operations.

Space does not permit to recount the many minor operations in which Companies of the Regiment were engaged during the remaining months of this year, and it may be sufficient to say that towards the end of February, 1819, the Madras Europeans formed part of a force under General Doveton which marched against the fortress of Asirghar, whither many of the harried remnants of the Mahratta and Pindari bodies had fled for shelter. Asirghar stood in an almost inaccessible position on a western spur of the Satpura range of hills. It consisted of two forts, an upper and a lower. The upper crowned a detached hill, 750 feet in height, scarped and precipitous, and accessible only at two places, both of which were very strongly defended; under and to the west of the hill was the lower fort known as Mallyghar, commanded by the upper and surrounded by a strong wall, but no ditch. Beyond all was the pettah, partly surrounded by a wall.

1819

By March 17th General Doveton had taken up a position before the fortress, his troops consisting of the Royal Scots, 30th Foot, 67th Foot (8 companies), Madras European Regiment (8 companies, 409 strong), 3 regiments of cavalry, and some 12 battalions of sepoys and pioneers; but these units all varied greatly in strength, the 1st Foot being only 279 all ranks, while the numbers of the native infantry battalions were one as low as 167, and another as high as 832.

Sir John Malcolm's division was also present, and was of much the same numbers.

Early on the morning of the 18th a column of attack was got ready to attack the pettah; it was divided into two parties—the one drawn from four British and one native battalions, and including the flank companies of the Regiment; the other, a reserve, containing one or more companies from several regiments, British and native, and containing one company of the Madras European

Regiment. The attack was entirely successful, and the troops established themselves under cover. Before the day closed a battery of five howitzers was ready, and by daylight on the 20th a heavy gun battery was completed, had opened fire, and by the same evening had nearly effected a practicable breach, despite the interruptions caused by two very determined sallies made by the garrison. On the 21st the defenders evacuated the lower fort, but this could not be occupied, as it was wholly commanded by the upper fort. Many fresh batteries were opened, and the siege proceeded until April 7th, when the garrison asked for and accepted terms, and firing then ceased.

The loss of the enemy was trifling—only 43 killed and 95 wounded—while the casualties among the besiegers amounted to 11 officers, 95 European soldiers, and 117 native ranks killed and wounded, of whom the Madras Europeans had one man killed (Lieutenant d'Esterre) and 9 men wounded.

With the fall of Asirghar the Mahratta wars came to an end, the force under General Doveton was broken up, and the troops dispersed to their several peace stations. Six companies of the Madras European Regiment remained in Asirghar as part of the garrison, while the rest of the Regiment proceeded to Nagpore.

During the whole campaign a detachment of the Regiment had served as sappers and miners, being present at many sieges and operations, and in December, 1817, a party of 24 men employed as pioneers at the battle of Nagpore had 2 sergeants and 12 privates out of their number killed and wounded.

In Government Orders of September 27th, 1819, it was announced that—

"*The Governor in Council is pleased to permit the undermentioned Corps to bear on their appointments, or similarly embroidered on their regimental standards, the words* "*Maheidpoor, 21st December, 1817*" *in commemoration of the splendid victory achieved by these corps or detachments of them over the army of Mulhar Rao Holkar on that day:—*

* * * *

Madras European Regiment.

* * * *"

While on October 2nd the Governor-General in Council published to the armies of the three Presidencies the resolutions of both Houses of Parliament conveying their thanks to the officers and troops concerned for " their conduct, discipline, and bravery during the late Pindari and Mahratta Campaigns."

NOTE TO CHAPTER X.

DISCONTENT IN THE MADRAS ARMY.

From the beginning of 1807 there were symptoms of unrest and discontent among the officers of the Madras Army, due, among other causes, to the disproportion in allowances of the Bengal and Madras services, the larger number of commands given to officers of the Royal Army, the abolition of certain monetary allowances, and the discontinuance of others. Early in 1808 a considerable number of officers put their names to a memorial setting forth their grievances; this was submitted by the Commander-in-Chief to the Madras Government, and was replied to by the Court of Directors justifying their various decisions and making certain observations on the subject of the memorial. The Madras Government, at the head of which was at the time a very unpopular and injudicious governor, one Sir George Barlow, then informed the Commander-in-Chief that no officer who had signed the memorial was to be appointed to the staff.

In January, 1809, a further memorial, chiefly signed by officers commanding corps, was addressed to the Commander-in-Chief and forwarded by him, but was returned by Government, and this action

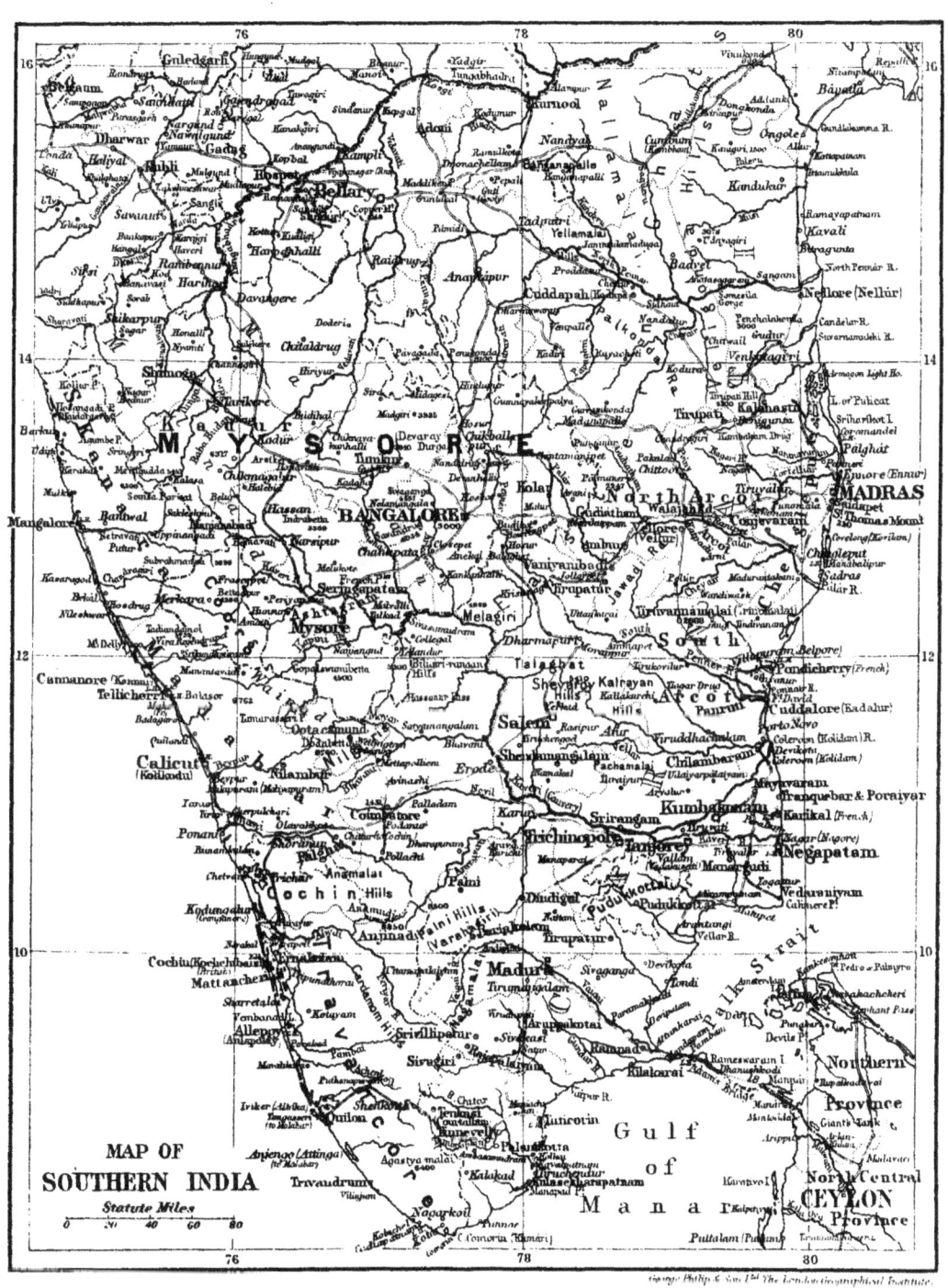

by Sir George Barlow seems to have given great umbrage to General Macdowall, the Commander-in-Chief, who, having expressed himself in somewhat unusual terms on the action of Government, was, on applying to retire, dismissed from his appointment. The abovementioned memorial was then forwarded to the Supreme Government, which pronounced it disrespectful in tenor, and expressed their approval of the initial refusal to forward it of the Madras Government.

In February, 1809, a third memorial was drawn up and extensively signed by officers of the Madras Army, but though all idea of forwarding it was within a very few weeks abandoned, Sir George Barlow by some means obtained a copy and a list of those who had put their names to it, and thereupon determined to punish those concerned, finally recommending to Council the suspension, removal, suppression, or dismissal of some fourteen officers ranging in rank from captain to lieutenant-colonel. These recommendations were agreed to, and the suspensions and removals published in a General Order of May 1st, 1809, in spite of the fact that some of those thus punished denied having had anything whatever to do with the memorial. No sooner had this order become public than the great majority of the Madras officers placed themselves in opposition to Government, and in certain garrisons this attitude became one almost of actual mutiny.

One of these garrisons was that of Masulipatam, where at this time there were quartered six companies of the Madras Europeans, a native regiment, and a detachment of artillery. On May 7th Lieutenant-Colonel Innes, recently appointed to command the Madras Europeans, dined for the first time at mess, on which occasion Lieutenants Forbes and Maitland, of the Regiment, proposed the toast "The Friends of the Army," and as this followed on remarks which had passed condemning the recent orders of Government and praising the attitude of the different memorialists, Colonel Innes objected and left the room, when the toast was proposed and drunk with enthusiasm. Colonel Innes reported the matter to H.Q., but particularly asked that no action be taken pending further report from him. This request was ignored, and Forbes was ordered to be sent to an especially unhealthy station, while Maitland was removed from his office of quartermaster. The excitement occasioned by these measures was increased by a sudden Government order—the legality of which was more than questionable—directing 3 officers and 100 men of the Madras Europeans to be held in readiness for service as marines. The officers determined to disobey this order, and, receiving no support from Colonel Innes, they placed him in confinement, Captain Andrews assuming command of the Regiment in his place.

Government now appointed Colonel John Malcolm to command the Regiment and garrison, and he arrived early in July at Masulipatam, where he found matters in a very disturbed state; he strongly advised the Government to give way to the demands of the officers and to grant a general amnesty, but the Government declined to accept his recommendations, complaining of his " unreasonable forbearance." Ultimately, however, a general pardon was offered to all offenders, and discipline among the troops at Masulipatam was thus finally restored, the Madras European Regiment being ordered in from there to Madras in September.

Ultimately every surviving officer who had been suspended, cashiered, or dismissed was, with very few exceptions, restored to the Service, but in at least one case such restoration did not take effect until October, 1811.

MAJOR-GENERAL SIR JOHN MALCOLM, K.C.B.
Joined Regiment in 1781.
(From an oil painting by S. Lane, in the possession of the Oriental Club, Hanover Square)

CHAPTER XI

1821–1826.

THE FIRST BURMA WAR.

1821 IN June, 1821, General Hislop returned to England when the command of the Madras Army was temporarily assumed by Lieutenant-General Bowser, formerly of the Madras European Regiment; and in October of the same year Sir John Malcolm went home after the completion of many years of honourable service in the Regiment, on the staff of the Army, and in several high civil appointments.

1822 Early in the following year all the Madras troops which had composed the Nagpore Subsidiary Force were relieved by Bengal Regiments, and the Madras Europeans, under Major Amos Kelly, marched to Masulipatam, and remained in that garrison during the years 1822 to 1824. At the commencement of this latter year the Corps was upwards of 1,200 strong, and was composed of a very fine body of men, the flank companies being of especially good stamp and appearance. The barracks at Masulipatam were not sufficiently large to accommodate more than two-thirds of the Regiment, and the remaining third was consequently quartered in the native lines and in some large houses inside the fort.

1824 When in 1824 war was declared against the Kingdom of Ava, the Madras European Regiment was naturally one of the first of the corps warned to take part in the expedition to Rangoon, and some account must now be given of the progress of the events which had forced the Government of India to undertake operations against this new enemy.

British and Burman interests first came into collision at the end of the eighteenth century, when the people of Ava, having liberated themselves from the yoke of Pegu and having waged tolerably successful war during some fifty years, began to consider fresh conquests, and turned their eyes to Arakan, Assam, and even Bengal. Disputes arising over the surrender of certain Burman subjects who had sought British protection, the then Governor-General, Lord Wellesley, sent a mission to Ava, and a treaty was drawn up, the beneficial results of which were, however, only of a very temporary character. Other missions followed, but achieved even less success, and in 1811 the King of Ava laid an embargo on all British ships then in Rangoon. Under ordinary circumstances war would probably have at once resulted, but the various campaigns undertaken by the Marquis of Hastings for the security of India had excited so much adverse and ignorant criticism in England, that his successors were unwilling to risk similar reproaches, and contented themselves with sending yet another mission to Ava.

The effect of this course of action upon an Eastern people may readily be understood; the Burmese imagined that the English were not only afraid, but powerless, and the attention of the East India Company being at the time occupied with troubles in Nepal in the north and the states of the Mahratta Confederacy in the south, a Burmese General invaded the country between Burma and Bengal, conquered Assam and Manipore—then an independent state—threatened Cachar, and, invading British territory, actually captured a party of British sepoys. The Burman General then began levying taxes on British boats trading on the river forming the boundary between Arakan and Chittagong, and finally, landing an armed party on the island at the mouth of the river, killed and wounded six of the British garrison.

At this juncture Lord Amherst arrived in India as Governor-General, and at once turned his attention to Burma; a demand for explanation and satisfaction merely elicited insolent replies, and the patience of the Indian Government being at last exhausted, war was declared against the Kingdom of Ava on March 5th, 1824.

The plan of campaign was to be as follows :—Brigades were to be formed and stationed at Chittagong, Jemalpore, and Goalpara for the security of the eastern frontier, with a strong reserve at

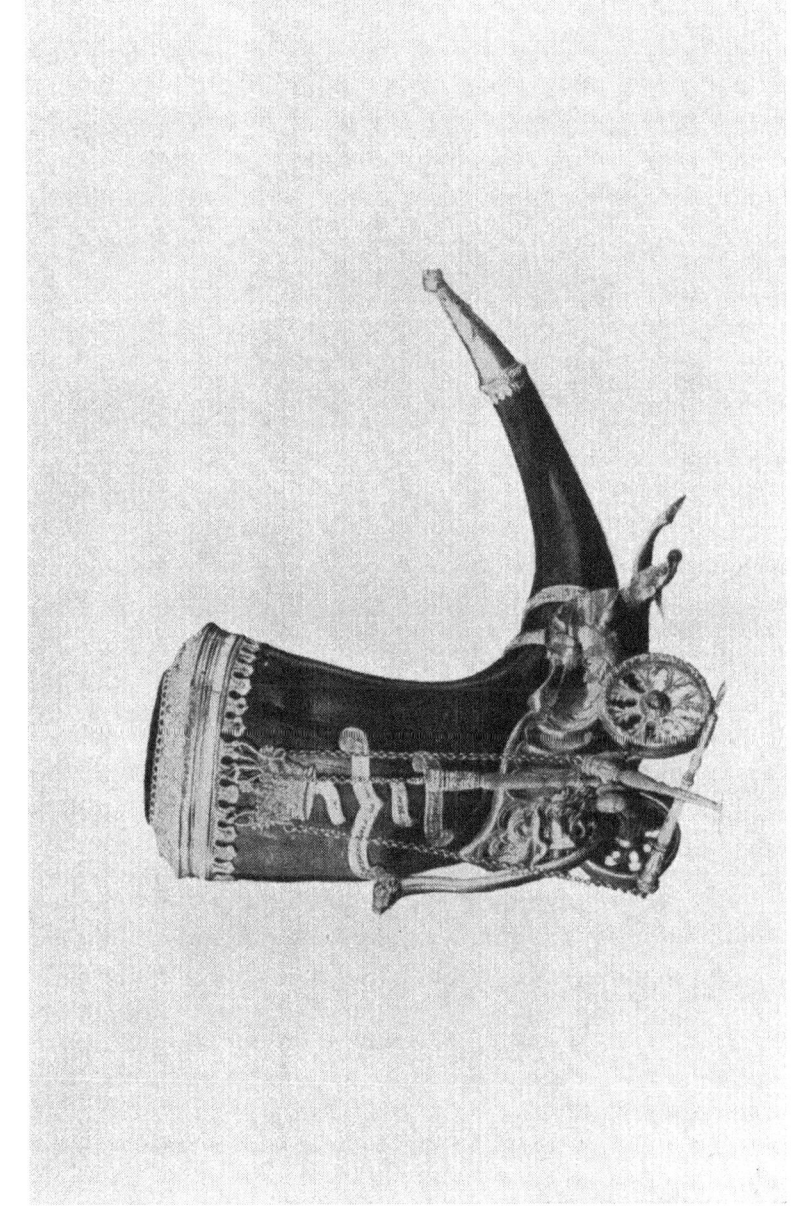

HORN SNUFF BOX.

Presented to the "Blue Caps" by General Sir J. Malcolm in commemoration of Maheidpoor

Dinajpore and an efficient river flotilla on the Brahmaputra in the vicinity of Dacca. The frontier operations were to be restricted to the defensive or, at most, to the re-conquest of the countries recently taken possession of by the Burmese, while the offensive was to be conducted by means of an overseas expedition against Burma and selected portions of the enemy coastline. For the Rangoon Force a body of 10,655 troops, including nearly 4,000 Europeans, was detailed, and was placed under the orders of Brigadier-General Sir Archibald Campbell, K.C.B.; it contained one Bengal and four Madras infantry brigades, and the Madras European Regiment was posted to the 2nd Madras Brigade, containing one other battalion only—the 1st Battalion 9th Madras Native Infantry, the brigade being commanded by Lieutenant-Colonel Hodgson, of the last-named corps.

The expeditionary force included five British and eight native infantry battalions, with the usual complement of artillery and administrative services, but it was wholly destitute of cavalry; this deficiency was remedied by the dispatch later of some 300 men of the Governor-General's Bodyguard and two squadrons of a regiment of Madras Cavalry, while before the war ended considerable reinforcements were found necessary, amounting, in infantry, to four more British and eight more sepoy battalions.

The naval portion of the expedition was composed of 11 vessels of the Royal Navy or of the Company's Marine, with 19 armed brigs and schooners, and a flotilla of 20 row-boats, each armed with an 18-pounder.

On the Madras European Regiment being warned for service, 863 out of the 1,300 men then composing it were selected as the most efficient and healthy, the remainder being left behind, under Lieutenant Manning and Ensign Saxon, as a depot, which was eventually marched to and stationed at Kamptee. The Regiment, under command of Lieutenant-Colonel Hastings Kelly, with 6 captains, 15 lieutenants, 4 ensigns, 1 surgeon, and 3 assistant surgeons, embarked in the transports *Bannerman*, *David Clarke*, and *George IV*, and sailed from Masulipatam on April 13th for

Port Cornwallis in the Andaman Islands, where the Bengal troops and the first portion of the Madras contingent were assembled by May 3rd. The following were some of the officers who accompanied the Regiment to Burma:—Lieutenant-Colonel Kelly; Captains Cursham, Hooper, Kitson, Kyd, Maxwell, and Roy; Lieutenants Boyce, Butler, Chambers, Charleton, Doveton, Duke, Greene, Grubb, Hopper, Howden, Kerr, Marshall, Robertson, Simpson, and Stenton; Ensigns Hill and Weir; Surgeon Dean, and Assistant-Surgeons Richardson and Johnson. Two days later the fleet sailed, entered the Rangoon River on the 10th, and on May 11th anchored off the town. A small battery on shore opened an ineffective fire upon one of the ships, but it was quickly silenced, and the troops then landed and took possession of Rangoon, which was found to be abandoned.

Two companies of the Madras European Regiment landed on the opposite or southern bank of the Irrawaddy, and established themselves in the town of Dallah without resistance, while their presence had the further useful effect of preventing the enemy from assembling and attacking one of the vessels of the fleet which had here run aground. Next day these two companies rejoined the Regiment, which was now comfortably quartered in some priests' houses on the road leading from Rangoon to the Great Pagoda. The duties, especially at night, were very harassing; the long grass in many places not only hid the sentries from one another, but enabled the enemy to creep close up unperceived, hurl their spears at a sentry, and disappear. Several men were killed and wounded in this way, and the knowledge of the presence of an active enemy, coupled with the uncertainty of his exact whereabouts, caused at first a good deal of firing, thus breaking the rest of the troops.

It was, unfortunately, not long before the troops commenced to suffer severely from the incessant rain, the heavy duties, the unhealthy climate, and, more especially, from the insufficiency and bad quality of the rations supplied, and the hospitals began to fill up and the flower of the European soldiery of the force in Rangoon was daily carried off.

ATTACK ON KEMMENDINE

Early on the morning of June 3rd two columns marched to attack certain stockades in the direction of Kemmendine, the exact situation of which was not known. The one column, under Lieutenant-Colonel Hodgson, contained a portion of the Madras European Regiment and the 9th Native Infantry, while the other, commanded by Lieutenant-Colonel Smith, was made up of some companies of the Regiment, two native infantry battalions, and three guns; three companies of the 41st Foot also proceeded up the river in boats to co-operate.

Marching by separate tracks through the jungle for some five miles, the columns, that of Colonel Smith leading, came upon a strong stockade about 14 feet high; the guns opened upon it, and the grenadiers of the Madras Europeans, led by Captain Kyd, of the Corps, and supported by a native battalion, carried the place by storm, the men mounting upon one another's shoulders. Colonel Hodgson's party moved round to the rear to cut off the retreat of the enemy, but was too late. After an hour's halt the march was resumed, and Colonel Smith soon reached the formidable stockade surrounding Kemmendine itself. The guns were ineffective, the stockade in the absence of ladders was too high for escalade, while since the party had no axes all efforts to destroy it proved fruitless. Both columns were engaged, but after persevering for nearly two hours, and having suffered some loss from the ill-directed fire of the British flotilla in the river, Colonels Smith and Hodgson then decided to retire. The Regiment had lost 2 sergeants and 7 men killed, and 2 sergeants and 30 men wounded—2 officers, Captain Kyd and Lieutenant Stenton, among the latter—while there were 25 native casualties. Among other fine soldiers of the Madras Europeans who fell on this occasion was Sergeant Morrison, of the Light Company; he had been sent back to bring up a gun which had been left at the first stockade on account of the difficulty experienced in dragging it along the muddy road, nearly the whole country being under water. On his way back he was shot dead from the thick jungle bordering the path.

On June 10th the attack on Kemmendine was renewed by a

force of some 3,000 men and eight guns, under the personal command of General Campbell, while two divisions of armed vessels were to be employed at the same time to attack the river face of the stockade. There were three columns of attack, and 25 men of the Madras Europeans were in No. 1 Column and 5 companies of the Regiment in No. 2.

About 10 a.m. a small stockade was reached, nearly a mile from Kemmendine, the ground in front covered with water and the remaining sides surrounded by jungle. The guns had made a breach, and General Campbell now rode up to one of the battalion companies of the Regiment and called for volunteers to storm, when several men at once stepped forward. One of these was Corporal Thomas Freer, who was at once promoted sergeant; while another was Colour-Sergeant O'Brien, who later became drill-sergeant in the Regiment and ultimately an Ordnance store sergeant.

The storming parties now advanced with ladders, and though the enemy made a determined resistance, leaving 300 dead on the field, the stockade was successfully carried, with a loss to the Madras European Regiment of 1 sergeant killed, Lieutenant Robertson, 2 sergeants, and 6 rank and file wounded.* Lieutenant Robertson died shortly afterwards of his wounds.

The enemy having dispersed, the column marched on, and at nightfall arrived in torrents of rain at Kemmendine; the batteries opened on the stockade, and the storming parties rushed forward at daybreak on the 11th; but the stockade was found abandoned, the enemy having escaped on the uninvested side.

Four companies of the Regiment were left here in garrison, and part of the grenadier company, under Lieutenant Grubb, was sent to occupy the stockade first captured, while the rest of the force returned to Rangoon. In a complimentary order issued next day

* In Hayman's *Documents Illustrative of the Burmese War*, p. 60, it is stated that, "Two men of the Madras European Regiment were missing soon after the arrival of the army at Rangoon, and have not been included in any of the returns, having been taken whilst straying from their line, and not whilst engaged with the enemy."

THE FIGHTING AT DALLAH

General Campbell specially mentioned Captain Kitson, Madras European Regiment, for " the undaunted manner in which he led his men into the enemy's works."

From this time on the enemy became very bold, coming close up to our posts, and cutting down sentries, and so annoying did these attacks become that it was considered desirable to drive the enemy parties from the vicinity of Rangoon; for this purpose, on July 8th, a large force, containing 250 of the Madras Europeans, was got together under Brigadier-General McBean to attack certain stockades near Kemmendine, while the Commander-in-Chief proceeded up the river with the gunboats to engage the enemy in position at Pagoda Point. The conjoint operations were singularly successful, General McBean's party capturing seven stockades in succession, while three fell to the river column; the enemy left 800 dead on the ground, and 38 guns of various kinds and 300 muskets were captured. The casualties in the two columns numbered under 40, and of these the Regiment counted 1 man killed and 4 wounded.

On August 3rd a strong detachment containing 300 men of the 41st Foot and Madras Europeans, with parties drawn from three native regiments, under Lieutenant-Colonel Kelly, attacked and carried by storm the strongly stockaded Syriam pagoda on the Pegu River, when the Regiment had one man wounded. A few days later Colonel Kelly was given command of a detachment made up of men from his own corps, some seamen, and native artillery and infantry, and was sent to dislodge some Burmese who had collected in strength at Dallah on the bank of a creek. Proceeding two miles up the creek, a heavy fire was suddenly opened on the boats from a high stockade at the water's edge; the native boatmen became panic-struck, threw down their oars, and lay prone in their boats, and thus time was lost until the boats could be run ashore under the heavy fire. The European soldiers of the force then jumped out, some up to and some above their waists in mud and water, their ammunition being thus rendered useless; but they erected their ladders, swarmed up them, and carried the stockade in very gallant style, but with very considerable loss, especially in

Europeans, of whom 3 officers (one being Lieutenant J. Grubb, of the Regiment) were wounded, with 36 private soldiers. The conduct of Lieutenant Kerr, of the Regiment, was on this occasion particularly conspicuous; his boatmen, when the firing began, let fall the anchor, thus leaving the boat exposed to fire within a very few yards of the stockade, when Kerr cut the cable, and he and his men ran the boat ashore and joined in storming the position.

The Regiment remained at Rangoon, finding guards, picquets and fatigues, having occasional petty skirmishes, and providing part of the garrison of Kemmendine, varied by taking part at the end of November in an expedition to occupy Pegu. On returning to Rangoon on December 2nd, it was found that the town was now closely invested by the whole Burmese Army under their chief general, one Bandula; Kemmendine was also besieged, and communication between that place and Rangoon, except by river, was wholly cut off. The enemy force was estimated at some 60,000, more than half armed with muskets, the remainder with swords and spears; there was also a small body of mounted men; the guns were represented by *jingals* throwing a ball of from 6 to 12 oz. in weight, while a large number of fire-rafts accompanied the war boats down the river.

Among the small garrison of Kemmendine were 58 rank and file of the Madras European Regiment, and in order to give greater confidence to the sepoys of the defence, these were distributed among the different posts—Ensigns Hill and Weir of the Regiment being stationed on the front and north faces of the stockade.

The night of December 1st had passed off quietly, but just before dawn a huge mass of blazing fire rafts, followed by a large fleet of war boats, was seen drifting down the river; these rafts were made of large logs of wood so joined together that, on coming in collision with a vessel, they would swing round and encircle her, while they carried every kind of combustible, including oil. As these approached the cruiser stationed off Pagoda Point for the protection of the river front of Kemmendine, she was obliged to slip her cable and drop down stream. However, the fire of the fort guns obliged the war-boats to draw back out of range, but the enemy on shore gathered round the stockade, and during the day made several determined attempts at escalade; these were all repulsed, but the Burmans entrenched themselves a short distance away, and at 8 p.m. again attacked on three sides simultaneously, getting up to the very foot of the stockade before the steady and well-directed fire of the defence drove them back. There was spasmodic firing throughout the night, and in the morning another fire-raft was sent down the river; attacks were renewed on the north and east faces, and it was now seen that the enemy had advanced his trenches to within 50 yards, and from these he kept up a heavy and well-aimed fire.

The better to reply to this, the defence mounted a small carronade on the top of a pagoda within the stockade; the gun crew were, however, here so much exposed, that two of the detachment were almost at once very severely wounded, and the commandant gave the order for firing of the carronade to cease. But, at the urgent request of Sergeant Bond of the Regiment, it was decided to fire one more round, and the sergeant, mounting the platform, was immediately killed beside the gun. Sergeant Bond had particularly distinguished himself while on detachment at Kemmendine, and was greatly respected by all ranks. In his report the Commandant wrote of him as follows :—

"*I had the painful mortification of seeing Sergeant Bond, of the Madras European Regiment, shot dead; a braver or more willing soldier never graced the British uniform.*"

The enemy kept up his attacks during the whole of this day and the following night, but early on the morning of December 3rd a reinforcement of eighty men of the Madras Europeans joined by water, and the wounded were evacuated to Rangoon; one of the new arrivals in landing missed his footing and fell into the river, and was drowned by reason of the weight of his accoutrements.

During the fighting on the 4th several Burmese had established themselves in trees whence they commanded the interior of the stockade, but Corporal Lucas, of the Regiment, an excellent marksman, was posted behind the top of a pagoda to reply to these, and not only kept down their fire, but did considerable execution; he was honourably mentioned in the Commandant's report, and recommended for the promotion vacant by the death of Sergeant Bond.

On the 5th the fire from a small gun became so annoying, that it was resolved to try to effect its capture. A party of 40 of the Madras Europeans and 40 sepoys was mustered, under command of Captain Page, 48th Native Infantry, who was at the time attached to the Regiment, with Ensign Weir of the Madras Europeans and 2 British officers of a native corps, and sallied out through a very narrow gateway admitting of the passage of only one man at a time. Twenty Europeans having emerged, these formed up and charged the gun from which the enemy was driven; but the Burmans rallied, their very superior numbers prevented the gun being removed, and the party had to fall back, having had 2 men killed and 3 wounded.

And so the attack continued actively until the morning of the 9th, when the enemy at last retired and the siege came to an end; while it lasted no man had been able to leave his post, the garrison was quite worn out, and every wounded or sick man who could handle a musket did his duty manfully.

It was mentioned above that the Regiment had returned to Rangoon from Pegu on December 2nd, and on arrival found that a large Burman army was about to attack the city. During the 3rd the enemy displayed great activity, attacking the British outposts, and since, on the 4th, the Burmans were seen to be strengthening their entrenchments, orders were issued in the evening for the storming of their lines next day. Two columns were detailed for the attack; the one fell in at the Great Pagoda, was commanded by Major Sale, 13th Foot, and contained 1,100 bayonets, some of which were furnished by the Madras Europeans; the other, 600 strong, and also including a detachment of the Regiment, collected at the Whitehouse Picquet, under command of Lieutenant-Colonel Walker.

Both columns arrived at the same time at the enemy's entrenchments: that under Walker was met by a very heavy fire which caused the death of its leader, but, forming line, the men charged forward and drove the Burmans from their position. The line being then enfiladed by heavy fire from a battery on the left, the light company of the Regiment wheeled in that direction, charged, and captured it. The enemy then rallied behind a breastwork in rear, which was at once stormed and carried by a party led by Lieutenant Butler, of the Regiment, who was here wounded. The enemy in front of Major Sale was also completely routed, and the whole were dispersed and followed up some distance. Unfortunately, some of the enemy's mounted men came round in the rear of the British hoping to cut up stragglers, and Butler and some others of the wounded had very narrow escapes. An old soldier of the Regiment was very nearly cut off; being wounded and having fallen behind, he was surrounded by the mounted enemy, who hurled their spears at him, but he was able to keep them off until help reached him.

In spite of their defeat, the enemy rallied and assembled in large numbers in front of the British posts; and there was further fighting on the 6th and 7th. On the evening of this day the General resolved to attack the Burman lines in four columns, a fifth under Major Sale making a diversion in their rear, the Madras European Regiment proceeding up the creek with one of the columns to attack a stockade at Dallah. The operations were entirely successful. Brigadier-General Campbell wrote:—" The defeat of Bandula's army was now most fully accomplished. His loss in killed and wounded, from the nature of the ground, it is impossible to calculate, but I am confident I do not exceed the fairest limit when I state it at 5,000 men. In every other respect the mighty host which so lately threatened to overwhelm us, now scarcely exists"; while of the behaviour of his troops the General wrote:—" I cannot say enough; their valour was only equalled by the cheerful patience they bore long and painful privation. My Europeans fought like Britons, and proved themselves worthy of the country that gave them birth."

The loss in the Madras European Regiment from December 1st to 7th was :—*Killed*, 1 sergeant and 3 other ranks ; *wounded*, Captain J. Roy and Lieutenant C. Butler, 3 sergeants, 1 drummer, and 16 privates; while Lieutenant Glover, of the Regiment, attached to the 8th Native Infantry, was severely wounded in the arm, which had to be amputated at the shoulder.

In spite of their defeats on the 5th, 7th, and 8th, about 2,500 Burmans assembled under another of their leaders, and took up a position at Kokien, four miles from the Great Pagoda. General Campbell, having resolved to dislodge them at once, marched on the morning of December 15th in two columns ; with the left column, which was made up of 100 of the Body Guard and some 800 men drawn from four British regiments (including the Madras Europeans) and five native battalions, was the General in person. There was a scarcity of ladders, and some of these broke down, but the stockades were carried with great gallantry and the enemy driven headlong from them. Corporal Thomas Tate, the man who had before distinguished himself at Malegaon, was here again to the fore, and was promoted for gallantry. The result of this fresh defeat was that the enemy wholly disappeared from the neighbourhood of Rangoon and fell back on Donubyu ; the character of the war was now completely changed, the enemy no longer attacked in force, but confined himself to the defence of his posts on the river, and the road to the walls of his capital was now open to the British.

1825 By the middle of January, 1825, the sickness, which had so long continued in General Campbell's force, commenced to abate ; but, like other corps, whether British or native, the Madras European Regiment had suffered much, and was now only a skeleton of the fine battalion which had sailed from Masulipatam. It had lost 317 men killed in action, or died of wounds or disease, 25 had been sent back sick to Madras, 125 convalescents were gone or were on the point of departure for Mergui for the benefit of their health, leaving only about 390 non-commissioned officers and men, including those sick in hospital at headquarters, actually present with the Regiment.

The inadequacy of the transport and the deficiency of supplies had led General Campbell to doubt the expediency of any attempt to move into the heart of the country by the line of the Irrawaddy, and he had proposed two alternative schemes; neither of these, however, met with the approval of the Supreme Government, and the result was, that the line of advance by the river was decided upon, and preparations were accordingly made for an advance in two divisions—one, 2,400 strong, by land; the other, composed of 1,170 men, by water. General Campbell marched with the land column, and Brigadier-General Cotton proceeded with that which moved by the river. This second party contained the 47th and 89th Foot, part of the Madras European Regiment, and two native battalions. The European Infantry in this column numbered 799, of which 281 belonged to the Madras Europeans, who were commanded by Captain Hooper.

A small column of 800 men was sent against Bassein, while a force of 4,000 men remained at Rangoon with orders to follow the Commander-in-Chief whenever transport could be provided.

The river column proceeding up the Irrawaddy arrived on January 19th at Panhlaing, where the enemy had built two strong stockades, but they evacuated these on the approach of the British force. No onward movement was made until the 25th, when, leaving a native battalion and 25 men of the Regiment in garrison under Major Ross, the troops re-embarked, entered the main stream on the 27th, and next day came in sight of Donubyu, where Bandula, with some 15,000 men, was strongly entrenched in a number of formidable stockades extending for a mile along the river bank, with a main work situated on a height and enclosed by abatis. Some delay now occurred in getting the guns and supplies up the river, and it was March 5th before General Cotton was ready to attack. On the 6th he sent in a summons to surrender, which was refused, and next day the troops, less 100 of the 89th Foot, were landed to attack the so-called " White Pagoda Stockade."

The attacking party—650 bayonets—was formed in two columns, the 89th on the right, the 47th and the Madras Europeans on the left. Both parties assaulted with conspicuous gallantry, and the enemy made a very determined resistance. The left column reached the objective the earlier, and Sergeant Gwyn, of the Light Company of the Regiment, was the first to enter the stockade, immediately followed by Captain Roy. There was severe hand-to-hand fighting, and of the enemy 230 were killed and 374—nearly all more or less wounded—were captured, with many *jingals* and muskets. The enemy had, however, a second line of defence, and this was attacked by the 89th; but the stockade was not to be forced, and the attack fell back, the 89th having lost nearly 70 officers and men. During the night General Cotton re-embarked his troops and retired to his former position, there to await further orders from the Commander-in-Chief.

General Campbell, however, had unwisely marched some twenty-six miles beyond the arranged rendezvous, and did not hear of his subordinate's reverse until March 11th, when he retraced his steps, meaning to attack Donubyu with his whole force. It took him some time to pass his troops across the Irrawaddy, and it was the 25th before he arrived in front of Donubyu, when he concerted measures with Cotton, opened trenches, erected batteries, and began to bombard the position on April 1st. One of the first shells fired killed the Burman general, Bandula, upon which his followers at once lost heart, abandoned the place, and fled precipitately. A large amount of grain, ammunition, and guns here fell into the hands of the British.

On the 3rd and 6th the two divisions, under Campbell and Cotton, moved on towards Prome, the Regiment being left in garrison at Donubyu under Lieutenant-Colonel Conry, who, on March 30th, had assumed command from Captain Hooper. On April 12th, consequent on a reorganization of the Regiment which will be dealt with later, Captains Maxwell and Roy, Lieutenants Kerr, Stenton, Duke, and Simpson, and Ensign Hill returned to Madras from Burma.

The Regiment remained at Donubyu until September 5th, when it returned by river to Rangoon; while at Donubyu the men's health had very materially improved with rest and good and abundant food, but none the less the death-rate had been heavy; in January 28 men died; in February, 15; in March, 5; in April, 6; in July, 1; in August and September, 2—or a total of 57; while 64 men had been invalided, and nearly 100 had been sent away to different places for the recovery of their health. It is not matter for surprise, therefore, that scarcely 200 men remained with headquarters. One officer—Lieutenant Grubb—died at Donubyu on June 3rd.

On August 18th, 1825, a "Present State of the Army" under General Campbell shows the strength of the Madras European Regiment as—at Rangoon, 1 subaltern, 1 surgeon, 1 sergeant, 1 drummer, and 29 privates, with "sick present" 2 sergeants and 10 men; and at Donubyu, 1 field officer, 1 captain, 6 subalterns, 1 assistant surgeon, 2 staff sergeants, 25 sergeants, 15 drummers, and 227 privates, with 10 privates "sick present."

There had seemed to be some likelihood of the establishment of peace during this year, but the overtures made came to nothing.

The temporary inaction of the Regiment subsequent to the fighting at Donubyu seems to furnish a good opportunity for describing the steps which had been announced, and which had for some time past been in progress, for the reorganization of the Madras European Regiment.

On June 1st, 1824—when the Regiment had already proceeded on active service to Burma—the Madras Europeans, in conformity with instructions from the Court of Directors, were formed into two separate regiments, designated the 1st and 2nd European Regiment, each of which was to be officered in the following manner, the number of captains being increased, while that of lieutenants was diminished—viz., 1 colonel, 1 lieutenant-colonel, 1 major, 5 captains, 10 lieutenants, 5 ensigns.

That part of the Regiment then in Burma now became automatically the 1st Regiment, but arrangements for forming the corps into two separate regiments were not actually completed until

August, 1825, as may be seen by the following General Order, dated Fort St. George, August 5th, 1825 :—

"*The Honourable the Governor in Council is pleased to direct that the 1st and 2nd European Regiments shall each consist of the following establishment formed into five companies—viz., one grenadier, one light and three battalion companies. With reference to the establishments assigned to them, the complements of each company to be 6 sergeants, 7 corporals, 3 drummers, and 100 privates.*

"*The following staff is allowed to each regiment :—1 adjutant and 1 quartermaster, 1 surgeon, 1 assistant surgeon, 1 sergeant-major, 1 quartermaster-sergeant, 1 drill-sergeant, 1 drill-corporal, 1 drum-major, 1 fife-major, 5 pay-sergeants, and 5 colour-sergeants.*"

In consequence of the above, the companies were designated as follows :—Grenadier, "A," "B," "C," and Light, and were made up from the Regiment as it stood, while the officers of the 1st European Regiment were posted as under :—

Grenadier : Captain Cursham, Lieutenants Charlton and Doveton.

"A" : Captain Fenwick, Lieutenants Butler and Manning.

"B" : Captain Calder, Lieutenant Boyce.

"C" : Captain Gordon, Lieutenants Greene and Weir.

Light : Captain Hooper, Lieutenants Howden and Chambers.

The 2nd Regiment had already been partially formed at Masulipatam from some 430 men left behind on embarkation of the Corps for Burma and from the season's recruits ; the headquarters of the 2nd Regiment were provisionally fixed at Nagpore. The 1st Regiment retained facings of French grey, while white facings were assigned to the 2nd.

In October of this year 3 colour-sergeants, 6 sergeants, 9 corporals, and 89 privates of the Regiment, who were at that time on sick leave from Burma at Madras and Masulipatam, were transferred to the 2nd European Regiment.

The 1st European Regiment, as that in Burma must now be called, remained at Rangoon until October 28th, and then embarked —only 206 rank and file—for Pegu, where it joined a small brigade formed of the Regiment, some details of artillery and pioneers, the 3rd, a wing of the 12th, and the 34th Native Infantry, under Colonel Pepper, of this last corps. This small force was intended to be employed to dislodge the enemy from his positions on the Sittang River, ultimately proceeding north as far as Tonghoo, so as to clear the right flank of the main army during its advance on the capital. Colonel Pepper did not start until December 22nd, and by then the strength of the 1st European Regiment had been still further reduced, seven men having died during its stay at Pegu. The order of march was as follows :—The advance guard was composed of 1 subaltern, 1 sergeant, 2 corporals, and 15 privates of the Regiment, followed by 100 of the 12th Native Infantry ; then came the artillery—two 6-pounders, two 5½-pounders, and two camel howitzers, and in rear of these came the 1st Europeans, the 3rd and 34th Native Infantry, the park, baggage, and rear guard.

The account which follows of the remainder of the campaign in Burma will be supplemented by extracts from the published narrative of an officer who served with the Regiment in those strenuous days.

"After traversing about 70 miles of alternate swamp and jungle in a N.N.E. direction, we reached the large stockaded town of Shwegyin, pleasantly situated on a bend of the Sittang River, which here is about 200 yards broad, very rapid, but generally shallow. . . . Though the nature of the country, thickly clothed with jungle and intersected by ravines, afforded every facility to an enterprising enemy for harassing our line of march, the Burmese contented themselves with merely sending a party of 100 men to watch our movements."

This stockade the enemy abandoned after firing a few shots, and the troops camped there for the night. The next day Shwegyin was reached after a trying march, and from here also had the enemy fled, though the works were strong and surrounded by abatis. A force wholly composed of native troops was now detached from the little column under Colonel Conry to capture the fortified post of Sittang on the same bank of the river ; this attack failed with the loss of Colonel Conry, another British officer and 10 native ranks killed, 2 British officers and 18 sepoys wounded. The only unwounded British officer left, after several fruitless attempts at escalade, finally withdrew his men and re-embarked for Mekyo some 15 miles up the river.

"No sooner had the official account of the disaster reached us than prompt measures were taken to retrieve our lost honour. It was my lot to be attached to the grenadier company of the 1st Madras European Regiment, a company any soldier might have been proud of; and well we knew that by the morrow's dawn many of us would be *en route* to reinforce the detachment at Mekyo. We were not deceived; that day's orders detailed who were to partake in the honour of a second attack upon this redoubtable stockade."

Some time was unavoidably lost in collecting and preparing a sufficient number of boats, but the relieving force was in motion by 3 a.m. on January 11th, 1826, and the Brigadier and two guns landed at Sittang on the same morning at 9 o'clock, while a party which had started earlier by land arrived there much at the same time. This land party contained the flank companies of the Regiment, 78 other ranks, and 225 sepoys. Later some 160 sepoys of the 3rd Native Infantry joined the force. The same afternoon Colonel Pepper prepared three columns of attack; in the centre column was the Light Company of the Regiment containing only 36 rank and file, while the Grenadier Company—42 non-commissioned officers and men—was in the left column, led by Captain Cursham of the Regiment. The officer from whose account extract has already been made, describes the stockade as being on "an elevated ridge, with a very abrupt and rocky ascent, resting upon the river, on which it looked down from an almost perpendicular height of 100 or 200 feet. . . . Describing it as a military position, I should say it was a strongly stockaded height, with its right and rear protected by a dense and impracticable jungle, its left resting on the River Sittang, and having its front protected by a deep creek, only fordable at low water, at about musket-shot

CAPTURE OF SITTANG.

distance, while it was further strengthened by the steep and rugged nature of the intervening ground. Beyond this creek was a bare plain of some extent. . . .

"At length, about half-past two p.m., the creek being reported fordable, we moved off to the assault; each party was supplied with two escalading ladders, carried by pioneers. The left column, in which my lot was cast, was accompanied by Colonel Pepper. This was destined to surprise the enemy's right face by a long *détour* to the left through some dense jungle, which effectually concealed the stockade from view, and which was here only approachable by a narrow winding path much overgrown. The column, on issuing from the jungle, which reached to within 60 or 80 yards of the position, was to dash at and escalade it; whilst the centre column, by a simultaneous movement, was to effect an entrance in the centre face about 200 yards or so to our right. The small column on the right was to attack the enemy's left, but, being weak in numbers, its main duty, I conceive, was to distract the enemy's attention, thereby making a diversion in our favour. . . .

"The creek was about 40 or 50 yards wide, and was forded with some difficulty, for our shortest men were up to their necks in water; the men kept their ammunition dry by carrying their pouches on their bayonets. As for myself, I well remember being up to my shoulders in water, with my sword in one hand and my watch held up high in the other. We were permitted to cross over without any molestation from the foe . . . and from an unaccountable stillness that prevailed in the works we began to feel fully persuaded that the enemy had vacated them. Having emerged from the creek, the column began to thread its way through the jungle by a narrow and tortuous pathway, that was to bring us suddenly upon the right face of the stockade. Our progress was slow, for the jungle was dense, but we had not advanced many paces before the stillness was broken by the ring of a musket; another and another report followed, and one shot lodged in the pouch of a grenadier by my side, who, poor fellow, was killed a few minutes after; his name was Pollock, a lad of twenty. . . . At length the column was halted ... a section of European grenadiers was ordered to the front, then came the two scaling ladders, carried by the Madras Pioneers, while the main body was to follow. ... When we first showed ourselves all was still as death, but in a moment the scene was changed : a deadly stream of flame burst from the works, whilst the din of fire-arms, thick clouds of smoke, and the whistling of the musket balls were most convincing evidences of the garrison of Sittang being at home and in regular fighting order. ...

"The effect of such a concentrated fire was as severe as it was instantaneous, and before we could return a shot a considerable number of the leading men were prostrate. ... The enemy never fired with better effect or showed a bolder front ; we were literally muzzle to muzzle with them, both sides firing alternately through the same loopholes. ... Though the column staggered for a moment from the effects of the first volley, it as quickly recovered itself ... and, in spite of a heavy fire from front and flank, the summit of the steep ascent on which the stockade stood was gained and the ladders planted ; calling to 'the Lambs' to follow, in I jumped, coming down on all fours, the men following as best they could. The stockade was now virtually won."

The other columns had by this equally effected their entrance, but the bulk of the enemy escaped, while the attackers were too few and too exhausted to pursue.

In the centre column the Light Infantry Company of the Regiment, commanded by Lieutenant Howden, led the assault, and Lieutenant Chambers, of that company, was the first man of the column into the stockade.

The bodies of upwards of 3,000 dead Burmans were found in the stockade, while many of their dead had been thrown or had fallen into the river ; further, the toll of their wounded was very heavy. The attacking columns had 80 killed and wounded, including 7 officers, while of the flank companies of the Regiment that were engaged Captain Cursham and 6 men were killed, Lieutenant Charlton, 4 sergeants, 5 corporals, and 11 men were wounded—some 33 per cent. of those engaged !

In his report on this action Colonel Pepper—who was himself wounded—said of the Regiment :—" The conduct of the flank companies of the 1st European Regiment (both officers and men) has been such as nobly to sustain the high character of British soldiers. . . . The unremitting attention and humane consideration and care of the sick and wounded by Assistant-Surgeon Richardson, 1st European Regiment, is such that I feel it is my duty to bring his name likewise to your favourable notice."

The day of the 12th was passed in burying the dead and in burning and destroying the stockade, and, prompted, no doubt, by recollection of the manner of the conduct of the funeral rites of his dead comrades, the above-quoted historian wrote :—" I cannot refrain here from adverting to the great neglect shown by our Government to the spiritual wants of the British troops while on service in the field. During the Burmese war which occupied nearly two years and a half, there was no such person as a chaplain attached to the troops, nor do I remember there being any provision for the performance of Divine service, though at Rangoon alone there were no fewer than nine English regiments, besides artillery. In my own corps the Sabbath was observed by officers commanding companies reading the ' Articles of War ' to their men. By the performance of this duty, and hoisting the British colours on the flagstaff, we thought we sufficiently honoured our Maker !"

Re-embarking again on the morning of the 13th, the troops were back at Shwegyin forty-eight hours later, and then on February 24th a Treaty of Peace, known as the Treaty of Yandabo, was signed between the representatives of the British and Burmese Governments, and by the end of April the British force, with the exception of those troops remaining in Rangoon until the whole of the demanded indemnity had been paid, was on its way to Madras and Bengal.

On March 25th the 1st European Regiment marched to Mekyo, and from there to Pegu, where it arrived on April 7th. Here the Regiment remained in garrison until June 8th, when it marched to Rangoon and embarked in the *Argyll*, sailing on the 13th for Masulipatam. During the voyage the vessel was discovered to be on fire in the hold, the tents having presumably been stowed while damp and having in some way become ignited. The fire was prevented from spreading by the exertions of the men of the Corps, who assisted in getting up the tents and throwing them overboard. The *Argyll* arrived in Masulipatam Roads on July 23rd, and the Regiment landed on the following day. Out of the 863 gallant soldiers who had embarked for Burma in April, 1824, only about 100 came back, and these were broken by hard service, climate, and privation; nearly all the remainder died in Burma, the majority rather from disease and starvation than at the hands of the enemy. The officers had suffered almost equally with the men: Captain Cursham and Lieutenant Robertson had been killed; Captains Forbes and Roy, Lieutenants Greene, Grubb, and Charlton had died either in Burma or immediately after leaving that country; Lieutenants Butler, Doveton, and Chambers had been sent home dangerously ill; while Lieutenants Boyce, Hopper, and Marshall all died in 1827, mainly from the effects of the war.

A very cordial expression of thanks for services rendered by all the regiments engaged in the war was published by the Supreme Government, and on May 9th, 1826, a General Order of the Governor-General in Council, dated May 11th, was republished at Madras. By this order the several regiments employed were permitted to bear the words " Ava " or " Arrakan " on their Colours and appointments; consequently the Madras European Regiment became entitled to the Honour of " Ava."

In the same General Order it was announced that medals for the campaign would be struck for the *Native Troops* which had taken part; and it may here be mentioned as a very remarkable fact, that up to the year 1851, when the General Service " Army of India " medal was instituted and made, to some extent, retrospective, the Honourable East India Company, on the occasions when it granted a medal for war service, issued it to the native ranks only, with the single exception of the Seringapatam medal for the final and second storming by Lord Harris, at which the Madras European

Regiment had the ill-fortune not to be present. So that it was not until the year 1851, when the Madras European Regiment had been in existence for considerably more than a century, during which it had been almost continuously on active service of some kind or another, as a whole corps or in detachments, that individual officers and men of the Regiment had anything to show for their war services; while the medals even then granted were commemorative of no more than the actions or campaigns of the last quarter, at most, of the Regiment's stormy life.

APPENDICES

Note to Chapter III

Memorandum by the late Colonel R. S. Wilson, concerning Certain Services of the Bengal and Madras European Regiments, now H.M.'s 101st and 102nd Regiments.

In 1751 a detachment of the Madras European Regiment, with some sepoys under the command of Captain Clive, defeated a superior force of French and sepoys at Condour, near Tanjore, in the Southern Carnatic.*

2. In 1758 a detachment of the Bengal European Regiment, with some sepoys under the command of Colonel Forde, defeated a superior force of French and sepoys at Condore, near Rajahmundry, in the Northern Circars.†

3. By G.O., dated March 12th, 1841, the Madras European Regiment was permitted to bear on its Colours the names of the actions in which the Corps had been present. Amongst them was the following :—

"Condore. Where it greatly distinguished itself under Colonel Forde in December, 1758."

4. The above statement is erroneous. No portion of the Madras European Regiment was present in the action of 1758. One officer of the corps, Captain Callender, was attached to Colonel Forde's detachment, but it cannot be supposed that this circumstance can give the Regiment a right to share in the honours of the victory. The error no doubt originated in a confusion between the Condour of 1751 and the Condore of 1758.

5. Whilst the Madras Regiment thus bears on its Colours the name of a battle in which it was not present, the Bengal Regiment, by which the battle was won, is not privileged to bear any memorial of it.

* Orme's *History*, Vol. I, p. 182.
† Broome's *History of the Bengal Army*, p. 220 ; and Orme, Book X, p. 377.

6. It is submitted that the error might be remedied by causing the Madras Regiment to carry the date "1751" in addition to the word "Condore," and by granting to the Bengal Regiment the right to carry the badge "Condore, 1758."

7. It is not necessary to say that the regiments in question are now H.M.'s 101st and 102nd Regiments.

* * * * * *

8. The first battle of Condore was, as regards numbers, a mere skirmish, but it was a gallant and well-contested affair, and had important results. The English detachment was in charge of a convoy for Trichinopoly. Had it been defeated, that place must have been lost.

9. The second battle was a very brilliant affair, and had important results. It is strange that it should have received so little notice.

10. After winning it, Colonel Forde laid siege to Masulipatam. His means for a regular siege were insufficient, and a force was advancing to the relief of the place. He resolved to attempt a *coup de main*, and succeeded. The place was taken by assault. There is no more brilliant feat of arms anywhere on record, but no memorial of it is borne by any portion of the troops engaged.

11. In Captain Broome's *History of the Bengal Army** it is mentioned in connection with the above subject that the Bengal European Regiment bears the word "Guzerat" on its Colours without being entitled to do so. If this is the case, which I do not doubt, and if it is thought desirable to grant the corps the privilege of bearing the words "Condore, 1758," and "Masulipatam," to which its claim is indisputable, it would be a good opportunity of cancelling the other badge. The impropriety of a regiment bearing a distinction to which it is not entitled is obvious. The thing is wrong, not only as regards the corps itself, but because it tends to throw a doubt on all other similar badges. Nevertheless, when a distinction has been borne for a long time, the removal of it is

---

* Broome, p. 220.

disagreeable. But if in lieu of a false badge two true ones are granted, the justice of the measure is so apparent that there can be no ground for dissatisfaction.

12. In the *History of the Madras European Regiment** it is stated that all the European infantry employed under Colonel Forde belonged to the Madras Presidency, and that they had formed a portion of the expedition which left Madras for Bengal under Clive at the end of 1756 for the recovery of Calcutta. By the subjoined extracts from Captain Broome's *History*,† it will be seen that the above is incorrect. In September, 1758, all the Madras Europeans who remained alive of the detachments which went to Bengal in 1756 were transferred to the Bengal Establishment. They were probably not many, for the climate of Bengal, aided by a period of intemperance which followed the Battle of Plassey, had carried off a great number of them. Of one party numbering 230 in 1756, only 5 remained alive in 1758. The above is corroborated by all the information I have collected from the Madras Records. There can be no doubt of its accuracy.

13. In connection with the above, the following is submitted for consideration :—The first battle of Condore was fought during the war which the two East India Companies (English and French) carried on as auxiliaries of the two rival Nawaubs of the Carnatic. The war lasted from 1750 to 1754. A great many gallant actions were fought in the course of it, of which two are pre-eminent for merit and importance. These are the defence of Arcot by Clive in 1751, and the victory of Bahoor gained by Lawrence in 1752. Of the first it is not necessary to speak ; the 102nd already bears the name on its Colours. The other, though less known, was equally important. It was *the* battle of the war. I cannot but think it to be desirable that the Regiment should carry its name instead of that of Condore. This would be more correct historically, and more to the honour of the Regiment. The action of Condore was, as above stated, a mere skirmish in point of numbers, and though it was a gallant affair, and had results, the same may be said of

* Page 143. † Broome, p. 185.

many of the actions which took place round Trichinopoly and elsewhere during the war. At Bahoor, on the other hand, the numbers engaged were considerable; both armies were commanded by their respective Commanders-in-Chief; the manœuvring was skilful; the battle was well contested, and was decided by the bayonet; out of a strength of 400 men, the Madras European Regiment had 4 officers and 78 men killed and wounded; the enemy were totally defeated, losing all their guns, ammunition, and stores; their Commander-in-Chief was taken prisoner, with a number of officers and men, and they could not appear again in the field that year. The battle was the counterpart of the Condore of 1758, and of all the many actions fought between 1750 and 1754 best deserves to be commemorated. It is described in Orme, Vol. I, page 256; and in Cambridge, page 36.

Extracts from Broome's "History of the Bengal Army."

"Colonel Clive, finding it impracticable to send back the detachments belonging to Madras and Bombay to their respective Presidencies, determined also to incorporate the men composing them into the Bengal battalion, which was accordingly done as far as the Europeans were concerned."*

* * * * * *

"The option was given to the Officers of returning to their own Presidencies or entering the Bengal Service, which latter alternative appears to have been generally adopted, and they were accordingly brought on the strength of the Bengal Army from the 1st September (*i.e.*, of 1758), retaining the rank they held in their own services."*

* * * * * *

"Clive hastened his preparations, and dispatched a force under the command of Colonel Forde, consisting of five companies of the European Battalion and the second company of Artillery, with 100 lascars attached, and one-half of the Sipahis at the Presidency. The total number of the Europeans, including the Artillery,

* Pp. 204, 205.

was 500, and of the Sipahis 2,000, consisting of the 1st and 2nd Bengal battalions, and the remnant of the Madras Sipahis that had come round in 1756 forming a third battalion."*

* * * * * *

"Thus ended the Battle of Condore, one of the most brilliant actions on military record, which, however, is generally little known or mentioned in the service, and by a strange chance not one of the corps employed have ever received any distinction for this important victory, whilst the 1st Madras European Fusiliers, of which not an officer or man, excepting Captain Callender, was present, have the word "Condore" emblazoned on their Colours and appointments."†

* * * * * *

"The Madras Presidency assumed the direction of the newly-acquired province, and restored the factory at Masulipatam, which they placed under the charge of Mr. Andrews. They also directed Colonel Forde to proceed to Madras, with the European portion of the force under his command, to aid in the contemplated hostilities against the French; but that officer had received peremptory orders from Colonel Clive, who had anticipated that such a requisition would be made, not to comply, as the state of affairs in Bengal rendered it absolutely necessary that the troops should be at hand to return there when required. The Colonel, however, sent the remnant of the Madras Sipahis who had come round with Colonel Clive in 1756, and who were desirous of returning to their homes; these were now reduced to between 400 and 500 men."‡

Remarks

With regard to the word "Condore" carried by Her Majesty's 102nd Foot or Royal Madras Fusiliers as an honorary distinction for service under Colonel Forde in 1758, it is noted that there were two distinct actions at places named Condore, or Condour. The first was fought in 1751 near the village of Condour about 10 miles

* Pp. 210, 211.   † Page 220.   ‡ Page 224.

north of the town of Tanjore, by Captains Clarke and Clive, with 100 Europeans, 50 sepoys, and one small field-piece, against the French, with 30 Europeans and 500 sepoys.*

The only French officer having been desperately wounded, and ten of his Europeans killed, the rest broke and fled, and the English detachment, by making a détour, reached Trichinopoly in safety.

The second action was fought in December, 1758, near Condore in the Northern Circars, about 40 miles north-east of Rajahmundry, and 12 miles north of Samulcottah. The force under Colonel Forde was composed of 470 men of the Bengal European Regiment, six guns, the 1st and 2nd Bengal Native Battalions, and a 3rd Battalion composed of the surviving Madras sepoys who had gone to Bengal in 1756. Besides these, there were 500 horse and about 5,000 foot belonging to the Rajah of Vizianagram, but of a very inferior description. The French troops, under the Marquis de Conflans, consisted of 500 Europeans, 13 guns, 500 horse, and 6,000 sepoys.

The victory on the part of the English was complete, and has been described as a very brilliant action.

When granting to the 1st Madras European Regiment in 1841 permission to carry the word "Condore" on the Colours, Government made use of the following words:—"Condore, where it greatly distinguished itself under Colonel Forde in 1758." It is therefore manifest that the battle in the north was the one meant, and it seems unlikely that any honorary distinction would have been conferred for the affair near Tanjore, where the enemy had only 30 Europeans against 100 on the part of the English at a period when the sepoys on either side were of little account in the open field, as they were badly disciplined, and not officered by Europeans.

The application for Honours which was preferred by Colonel Bell in behalf of the 1st Madras European Regiment in 1840 did not contain any mention whatever of the action at Condore, and nothing has been found to show how it came to be included amongst

* Orme, Vol. I, Book VII, p. 182.

the honorary distinctions granted in 1841. It is remarkable that the fact of the presence at the defence of Fort St. George of both battalions of the Regiment at the very time when the battle at Condore was fought by Forde should have escaped the attention of the authorities to whom the matter was submitted, more especially as other claims made at the same time were rejected as untenable.

The expediency of attempting to remedy the mistake by now adding the date 1751, in the face of the order in which the year 1758 and the name of Colonel Forde are mentioned, appears to be very questionable, and in these days of critical inquiry and research the true character of the action of 1751 is sure to become known; but by the substitution of the words "Fort St. George" a really important service would be commemorated on the Colours of the regiment which took the most prominent part in the defence of that place.

Broome, after pointing out that the Bengal Fusiliers are entitled to carry the word "Condore," makes the following observation regarding an honour borne by that regiment to which it is not entitled :—" A similar anomaly is to be found in the honorary badges of the Bengal Fusiliers, amongst which is the word 'Guzerat,' whilst no European infantry from Bengal were attached to General Goddard's Division, for the services of which force that badge was accorded."*

This statement is borne out by the official returns of General Goddard's force, but the Madras Fusiliers were fully entitled to participate in any distinction granted for the campaign in Guzerat during 1780-81, as a detachment of about 500 men of the Madras European Battalion served therein under Lieutenant-Colonel George Brown. Their services, as well as those of the 8th Carnatic Battalion (8th Regiment M.N.I.), were acknowledged by General Goddard in very handsome terms in a letter to the Madras Government, dated at Bombay, July 5th, 1781.

H.M. 101st Regiment represents the battalion engaged at the Battle of Condore in 1758, and at the storm and capture of Masuli-

* Page 220.

patam in 1759. H.M. 102nd Regiment represents the two battalions of Madras Europeans which defended Fort St. George against the French in 1758-59, and the half-battalion which served in Guzerat under General Goddard in 1780-81; should, therefore, any or all of these services be considered worthy of being commemorated by any honorary distinction, the words "Condore" and "Masulipatam" might very properly be carried by the 101st, and "Fort St. George," and "Guzerat" by the 102nd, in lieu of those names to which their claim cannot be established.

W. J. W.

APPENDICES

NOTE TO CHAPTER IV.

A list of officers doing duty on the Coast of Choromandel in the service of the Honorable the United East India Company, January 1st, 1756.

	Date of Brevets.	Date of Commissions.	What Corps.
Major:			
James Kilpatrick	July 20th, 1754	—	—
Captains:			
George Gardner	—	Sept. 28th, 1750	Eng. Inf., Coast.
Francis de Vareilles	21st July, 1751	—	Do.
Edmund Pascall	—	Oct. 30th, 1751	Do.
John Henry Schaub	—	Nov. 21st, 1751	Swiss Inf., Coast.
Paul Polier De Bottens	—	Dec. 18th, 1751	Swiss Inf., Bay.*
Edmund Maskelyne	—	Feb. 17th, 1752	Eng. Inf., Coast.
George Frederick Gaupp	—	Aug. 3rd, 1752	Swiss Inf., Coast.
Lewis D'Illins	—	Dec. 20th, 1752	Train, Coast.
John Brohier	—	May 11th, 1753	Do.
John Caillaud	May 12th, 1753	June 26th, 1753	Eng. Inf., Coast.
William Lin	May 13th, 1753	June 27th, 1753	Do.
John Howes	July 3rd, 1753	Feb. 17th, 1755	Do.
William Lee	Aug. 4th, 1753	June 16th, 1755	Do.
Charles Campbell	—	Nov. 19th, 1753	Do.
John Innis	—	Mar. 25th, 1754	Do.
Joseph Smith	—	Mar. 26th, 1754	Do.
James Spears	—	April 22nd, 1754	Do.
George Beaver	May 10th, 1754	Aug. 27th, 1754	Do.
Alexander Callender	May 11th, 1754	Oct. 17th, 1754	Do.
Timothy Bridge	Aug. 17th, 1754	June 17th, 1755	Do.
Captain-Lieutenants			
John Stephen Bilhock	—	Nov. 15th, 1754	Do.
Lieutenants:			
Frederick Gurtler	—	Nov. 21st, 1751	Swiss Inf., Coast.
Alexander Peyer Imhoff	—	Dec. 18th, 1751	Swiss Inf., Bay.
Rodolph Wagner	—	Aug. 3rd, 1752	Swiss Inf., Coast.
Edward Davis	—	Dec. 6th, 1752	Eng. Inf., Coast.
Benjamin Godwin	—	May 11th, 1753	Train, Coast.
John Seaton	—	May 12th, 1753	Do.
Christian Fisher	—	June 25th, 1753	Eng. Inf., Coast.
Achilles Preston	—	June 26th, 1753	Do.
Arthur Nelson	—	June 27th, 1753	Do.
Stephen Augustus Monchanin	—	Nov. 1st, 1753	Do.
Richard Smith	—	Nov. 2nd, 1753	Do.
John Perceval	—	Nov. 5th, 1753	Do.
Thomas Rumbold	—	Nov. 19th, 1753	Do.
William Rumbold	—	Nov. 20th, 1753	Do.
John North	—	Mar. 25th, 1754	Do.
Donald Campbell	—	Mar. 26th, 1754	Do.

* The Presidency of Bengal.

	Date of Brevets.	Date of Commissions.	What Corps.
John Fraser	—	Mar. 27th, 1754	Eng. Inf., Coast.
Andrew Greig	—	April 22nd, 1754	Do.
Robert Campbell	June 10th, 1754	Nov. 15th, 1754	Do.
Thomas Newton	June 11th, 1754	Nov. 16th, 1754	Do.
John Hume	Aug. 29th, 1754	—	Eng. Inf., Bay.
Richard Black	—	Nov. 17th, 1754	Eng. Inf., Coast.
Dugald Campbell	June 6th, 1755	June 17th, 1755	Do.
Edward Frith	June 7th, 1755	June 18th, 1755	Do.
Samuel Samson	June 8th, 1755	Oct. 27th, 1755	Do.
John Reith	June 9th, 1755	—	Do.
Henry Tripsack	June 10th, 1755	—	Do.
John Dickenson	—	July 21st, 1755	Train, Coast.
Thomas Blagg	Aug. 10th, 1755	—	Eng. Inf., Bay.
Second-Lieutenants :			
John Francis De Beck	—	Nov. 21st, 1751	Swiss Inf., Coast.
Robert Barker	—	Nov. 7th, 1753	Train, Coast.
Claud Philip Lutin	—	April 8th, 1754	Swiss Inf., Coast.
John Francis Paschoud	—	July 21st, 1755	Train, Coast.
Conrad Ziegler	—	Oct. 13th, 1755	Swiss Inf., Bay.
Ensigns and Fireworkers :			
John Donavan	—	Nov. 3rd, 1753	Eng. Inf., Coast.
John Wood	—	Nov. 4th, 1753	Do.
John Ogilvie	—	Nov. 6th, 1753	Do.
John Vouga	—	Nov. 7th, 1753	Do.
Francis Flaction	—	Dec. 24th, 1753	Do.
John Clarke	—	Mar. 25th, 1754	Do.
George Airey	—	Mar. 26th, 1754	Do.
Daniel Frischman	—	April 8th, 1754	Swiss Inf., Coast.
Bryan Scotney	—	April 22nd, 1754	Eng. Inf., Coast.
Simon Hart	—	April 23rd, 1754	Do.
Ferdinand Jarger	—	June 10th, 1754	Swiss Inf., Coast.
John Henry Mayers	June 13th, 1754	June 17th, 1754	Eng. Inf., Coast.
Joseph Darke	June 14th, 1754	June 18th, 1754	Do.
William Jennings	June 15th, 1754	July 21st, 1754	Fireworker, Coast.
David Blake	June 16th, 1754	Nov. 17th, 1754	Eng. Inf., Coast.
Randfurlie Knox	June 17th, 1754	June 16th, 1755	Do.
Robert Bannatyne	June 18th, 1754	June 17th, 1755	Do.
Richard Burk	June 19th, 1754	June 18th, 1755	Do.
Robert Lister	June 20th, 1754	—	Do.
John Charles Erdman	June 21st, 1754	—	Fireworker, Coast.
Nicholas Bonjour	June 22nd, 1754	—	Do.
John Dyer	Oct. 31st, 1754	—	Eng. Inf., Coast.
Charles Kerr	June 6th, 1755	—	Do.
Charles Todd	June 7th, 1755	—	Do.
Jonathan Brook	June 8th, 1755	July 21st, 1755	Fireworker, Coast.
William Elliott	June 9th, 1755	—	Eng. Inf., Coast.
John Lamb	June 10th, 1755	—	Do.
Richard Geers	July 1st, 1755	—	Eng. Inf., Bay.
John Francis Raillard	July 22nd, 1755	—	Fireworker, Coast.
Henry Spellman	Aug. 10th, 1755	—	Eng. Inf., Bay.
Leonard Parrot	—	Oct. 13th, 1755	Swiss Inf., Coast.

Ordered that the above officers, when joined with troops not belonging to the Coast of Choromandel, take rank according to the dates of their brevets, but when doing duty with such only as belong to this coast, they are then to rank according to the dates of their commissions.

(*Signed*) GEORGE PIGOT
AND COUNCIL.

APPENDICES

Uniform, 1672 to 1822.

There appears to be singularly little forthcoming about the uniform worn by the officers and other ranks of the Madras European Regiment during the early years of its existence. The first reference to a desire on the part of the Directors of the Honourable East India Company to dress their soldiers in anything of the nature of a uniform has already been mentioned in Chapter I of this History, when in the year 1672 the Court of Directors wrote to their representatives at Fort St. George a letter stating that, " It being found here in Europe very necessary and convenient for the soldiers to have coates of one collour, not only for the handsome representacion of them in their exercise, but for the greater awe to the adversary, besides the encoragement to themselves, wee have thought requisite that our Soldiers with you should bee put into the like habitt, for though it bee hott in the daytime, yet the night being coole (and in times of raine) it may bee a meanes to preserve their healthes . . . or if you judge cloth may be too thick, you may make use of perpetuanoes* and cause the turning up of the coate sleeves to be faced with something of a different coler. . . ."

The authorities at Fort St. George do not seem whole-heartedly to have approved this suggestion, for they replied in September, 1673:—
" The bestowing of coates upon your Souldiers would be very creditable, and so we understand it is allready in practise at Bombayn; but the proportion of English being so small in respect to the Portuges and Mestizos, unless we gave the same to all it would rather show our weakness than our strength. . . ."

The proposal was, however, evidently carried out, for in July, 1679, there is an entry in the Fort St. George books stating that, " it is thought fitt to cloath the Soldiers with the Redd ones " (perpetuanoes) " at 7 anams per yard, and line the said Cloathes with Callico Dyed green, and the Mony for the said Cloathing to be stopt out of their pay, the English in 4 months and the Portuguez in six months."

* A durable woollen cloth made in England.

From certain commissions issued in 1724 it seems that the three European Companies then in existence were distinguished by facings of different colours:—" Sign'd the following commissions for the Military: To John Roach, Captain of the Blue Company and Major of the Troops under the command of this Presidency: To Alexander Sutherland, Lieutenant of the Yellow; To Thomas Ogden, Lieutenant of the Green; To David Wilson, Lieutenant of the Blue."

In June, 1748, the Court of Directors drew up and sent out voluminous directions for, "forming, disciplining and governing the Military of Fort St. David," and from paras. 22 and 23 of these it seems that at this time, when the European Infantry in Madras was contained in seven companies only, considerable license was permitted the commanders as to the pattern of the uniform worn by their subordinates. Para. 22 runs:—
"That each captain have the cloathing of his own company, and that for regularity, the Major or Officer Commanding the Companys, shall appoint a pattern coat and hat or cap suitable to the climate to be approved of by the Governour, and to which every Captain shall conform at the first making new cloaths, and that the Major shall appoint the uniforms for the commission officers, to be approved of by the Governour, but great care is to be had by the Governour and Majors that the cloathing be not too expensive either to the officers or private men, and that the stoppages from the non-commission officers and private men be no more than is reasonable, and that it be made gradually, and in such equal parts as to reimburse the captain from new cloathing to new cloathing for his first cost and a moderate profit thereon, making an equitable allowance for the losses he may sustain by deserters carrying away their cloathing or from other accidents.

23. "That the Governour and Major or Officer Commanding the Companys, shall take care that the Captains do justice to their non-commission officers and soldiers in their cloathing and pay, that they be new cloathed once in 2 years out of the Company's warehouses, and that they nor the subaltern officers do not oppress them. . . ."

By a general order, dated Choultry Plain, October 20th, 1775, the facings of the Madras Europeans were determined as follows:—" In consequence of the frequent scarcity of cloth for facings, and the inconvenience subaltern officers are in particular often put to when exchanged from one corps to the other, it is now ordered that in future there shall be only three infantry regimentals on the coast, and they are to be without lapels, each brigade to have its distinct uniform, and the officers are to be distinguished only by embroidery on their epaulets. The 1st Regiment of Europeans to be turned up, or faced with buff; the 2nd with black."

In 1776 Colonel James Stuart was in temporary command of the Army, and on December 11th he issued certain sumptuary directions from which the following are extracted: "The Acting Commander-in-Chief has thought proper to diminish the quantity of necessaries formerly ordered to be provided by every soldier, which are now to be 4 shirts made full and long, 3 black neck cloths, and 1 white ditto, to clasp, 3 waistcoats made to button low down, 2 pair breeches made full, to come up well upon the belly and to cover the knees, 2 pairs of pantaloons, 2 pair of stockings, regimental uniforms, 1 pair of black gaiters to button, 2 pair of shoes.

"The Commander-in-Chief takes this occasion to say that in respect to the dress of the soldier he does not expect all the precision and exactness of a Europe parade, he knows the climate will not admit of it, but he expects a uniform soldierlike appearance in the whole army, answerable to the means afforded by the Honorable Company which are very ample; for the condition of a private soldier, here in their service, is to his knowledge better than in any other service in the known world."

In 1777 the facings of the two regiments of Madras Europeans were again changed as appears from an order dated Fort St. George, July 7th: "The uniform now to be seen at the Adjutant General's quarters is to serve as the pattern to the officers for the next year's clothing, with this difference only, that all the officers of the European regiments are to have narrow lapels sewed down. The 1st Regiment is to be faced with blue, and narrow gold button-holes. The 2nd Regiment with white, and gold button-holes the same. The grenadier officers to be distinguished as at present."

On May 11th, 1785, the Commander-in-Chief ordered a new uniform for the Army, to be made up, from a pattern deposited at the A.G.'s office, by September 1st; under this the facings of corps were to be as under:—" Cavalry, blue; European Infantry, blue; native infantry battalions, green, yellow or buff; Corps, faced with blue or green, to be embroidered with gold, the rest with silver. The officers commanding the different regiments of Europeans to fix upon regimental hats for their various corps ; the European corps to have an epaulette on the right shoulder." On the issue of clothing on December 3rd, 1786, the 1st Regiment Madras Europeans was faced with blue with gold looping, the 2nd with green and yellow looping, the 3rd and 4th with yellow and white looping ; while the officers of the corps had the number of the Regiment on their epaulettes, and also on the buttons of the commissioned and non-commissioned officers.

In an order issued by the Commander-in-Chief on February 29th, 1788, the following appears about the dress of the European Infantry :—

"Officers' Regimentals.—A short jacket, yellow lapelles, silver embroidery, nine button-holes placed three and three at equal distances, on cuffs and collar three each, one epaulette on right shoulder.

"Hats, round, white, turned up close on left side, black feather.

"Stock, black leather with a false white linen collar to overtop about a quarter of an inch. Waistcoat, white linen, cut short, as worn at present. Pantaloons, white linen, to be made long enough to overlap the hind part of the shoe and to cover the place of the buckle, and to be fitted to the ankle by 7 buttons from the swell of the lower part of the calf to the quarter of the foot to which the pantaloon is to be kept close by a strap coming from the inner side under the shoe, and fixing to the lower button.

"Sword-belts for officers of battalion companies black leather, worn across the body with an oval plate, on which is to be engraved the Company's crest and motto and the number of the battalion.

"Officers attached to the flank companies are distinguished by their King's arms and accoutrements. Scarlet shoulder straps instead of epaulettes. The hats of flank companies to be ornamented as commandants of battalions may direct, but both companies must be uniform.

"Officers to have jackets without embroidery for common duties, the pattern the same as now ordered for the full regimentals.

"Shoe and knee-buckles not to be considered part of an officer's dress on duty ; but when off duty breeches, silk stockings and buckles may be worn if preferred.

"It is recommended having waistcoats and pantaloons made of nankeen when field service is ordered. Half-boots uniformly made for officers in the field.

APPENDICES

"The arms of the officers in flank companies are either a spontoon or a fuzil, the former for grenadiers, the latter for light companies.

"Non-commissioned officers and privates :—

"The agent is furnished with patterns of their jackets and white hats.

"Stocks the same as officers with brass clasp.

"Breeches, white linen with gaiters to be placed under the knee-band, the same as stockings; the gaiters to be kept close to the quarter of the foot by a strap coming from the inner side under the shoe and fixing to the lower button; shoe-buckles to be discontinued."

At the end of 1799 the uniform of the Regiment was as follows :—
"A uniform jacket, with light blue facings and gold embroidery ... black leather stock with false linen collar one-third of an inch deep; white linen waist-coats, single-breasted, and cut round with metal regimental buttons, the same as those on the jacket; white nankeen pantaloons with half boots, and black round hats ornamented in such manner as the officer commanding the Regiment thought proper. Swords according to the present pattern to be worn with a buff shoulder belt, the breast-plate to be of whatever pattern the commanding officer might deem proper. The officers of the European Regiment, when off duty, are permitted to wear uniform coats with the same facings, epaulettes and embroidery as directed for the uniform jacket."

On June 17th, 1804, further regulations as to dress were promulgated, when the Regiment was ordered to wear white pantaloons, black gaiters, and the hair to be powdered and tied with a black leather thong; while the following was the revised list of necessaries for the soldier, artillery and infantry :—

Shirts	4	Shoes, pairs, ...	3
White sleeved waistcoats of Nankeen with red and green wings to distinguish the flank companies ...	3	Stock, clasp brass	1
		Hair leather	1
		Foraging cap	1
		Knapsack	1
White pantaloons	3	Cumley watch-coat	1
Linen false collars	3	Clothes brush	1
Cloth, half gaiters, black, prs.	2	Shoe brushes	2
Black leather stock	1	Combs	2

Pipe clay, whiting, black ball, grease and powder for the hair, and powder bag and puff, in such proportions as regulated by regimental standing orders.

About the end of the year 1807 it was ordered that the pattern of forage cap worn by the officers of the 59th Foot should be adopted by the European officers of the Company's infantry, including those attached to native corps. In October, 1810, the following alterations, among others, were ordered:—Clubs and Queues were abolished in all ranks and the hair was to be cut close to the neck—no powder to be worn on duty.

All field officers were to wear 2 epaulettes.

Captains of flank companies, who were brevet majors, to wear epaulettes in addition to wings.

Captains and subalterns to wear one epaulette on the right shoulder, but those of flank companies to wear a wing on each shoulder with grenade or bugle-horn on the strap, according as they belonged to the grenadier or light company.

Wide trousers or gaiter-pantaloons might be worn by company officers in lieu of pantaloons and half-boots.

Officers were strictly forbidden to appear outside their quarters without uniform and swords.

The non-commissioned officers and men of European infantry were to wear white trousers and white gaiters.

The Dress Regulations of October, 1810, were modified by an order of July 1814, from which the following are extracts:—

"Wellington pantaloons and half-boots are to be worn by all officers —except cavalry.

"Black kid-skin caps* of the same muster in every respect as in use in the Madras European Regiment, to be worn by all officers—except cavalry and artillery.

"For bad weather and cold climates Wellington pantaloons of dark-grey cloth are permitted to be worn—quite plain without trimming or ornament. Plain greatcoats of the same colour are also established, made single-breasted with regimental buttons and distinguishing epaulettes or wings for all regimental officers. Sword belts and sashes to be worn above the greatcoat."

In June, 1816, a new regulation cap, as prescribed for H.M.'s regiments of infantry, was ordered to be adopted by the officers of the Madras European Regiment; and in September a uniform shell jacket for

---

* These were abolished two years later as unsuited to the Indian climate.

infantry officers, to be worn at drills, fatigues, on the march and in the lines, was introduced. Four years later another general order dealing with dress was published, and concluded with the following remarks :—

" The deviations which regimental officers have, for some time past, made from their established dress, have not failed to draw the attention of the Commander-in-Chief at the Presidency. His Excellency notifies his determination of abolishing forage caps altogether if officers continue to wear them in public. They were established for the comfort of officers in common regimental duties, drills, and in their own lines, and not to appear in on the public roads."

It was no doubt with the view of suppressing the forage cap by the introduction of something specially becoming—if perhaps hardly suited to the climate of Madras—that on February 21st, 1822, all infantry officers were required to provide themselves with uniform caps made of beaver !

INDEX

ABERCROMBY, Gen., 236, 241
Adaire, Ensign James, 15
Adlercron, Col., 39th Foot, 85, 88, 92, 110; slowness of his movements, 115, 116
Agnew, Capt. Alexander, 243
Airey, Lieut., 127, 132; Captain, 157
Aix-la-Chapelle, Treaty of, 30
Ali Verdy Khan, 90, 91
Anderson, Lieut., 192
Andrews, Lieut. Augustus, 254; Major, 265, 268, 271
Andrews, Capt. Thomas, 24
Andrews, Lieut., killed, 171
Angria, Pirate, 89
Annagudi, action at, 216
Arcot, Siege and Defence of, 42-49, 122; Coote moves on, 135, 136; surrenders to the French, 189
Arms, bad quality of, 4
Army, under Coote, composition of, 189, 190
Ariancopang Redoubt, 150, 151
Arnee, action of, 49-50; battle at, 217, 218, 233
Asirghar, capture of, 273
Astlé, Capt., Indian Marine, 255
Astruc, Mons. 73-75, 78, 80
Ava, history of Kingdom of, 277 et seq.
Axtile, Capt. Thomas, 4

BAHOOR, action of, 67, 68
Baillie, Capt. William, 162, 167, 175; Colonel, disaster to, 183-187, 202, 244
Baillie, Cadet, 186
Baillie, Senior Cadet, 186
Baird, Capt. David, 184, 186
Battoo-Gantong, 260
Bandinel, Lieut., 160
Bangalore, storm of, 235
Bannatyne, Capt., killed, 131
Barnes, Ensign, killed, 127, 129
Barton, Volunteer, 159; Lieut., 175
Bates, Lieut., 112, 129
Battalion, two formed, 111

Beaver, Ensign, 111; Capt., 111, 125, 126, 129
Bellingham, Ensign, 111; Lieut., 134
Belton, Ensign, 129
Bengal, Military unrest in, 159
Bernadotte, Marshal, 224
Bett, Lieut. James, 4, 8, 10; Capt.-Lieut., 12
Bilcliffe, Lieut., 159
Bilhock, Capt.-Lieut., 112; Capt., killed, 126, 129, 190
Bishop, Lieut., 183, 193; Capt., 211
Black, Capt., 112, 129
Black Hole, Tragedy of, 90
Blair, Lieut., 111, 129, 134
Blake, Capt., 134
Blakeney, Ensign, 146
Blane, Major, 220
Bombay, service of Regt. in, 177
Bond, Sergt., 285
Bonjour, Ensign, 112, 127, 129, 145; Major, 161; Lieut.-Col., 176
Bonnevaux, Lieut., 175; Capt., 225
Bonus, Ensign Nathaniel, 8
Boscawen, Admiral, 27, 28; raises siege of Pondicherry, 30, 35
Bowles, Lieut., 216
Bowman, Lieut., 162
Bowser, Lieut., 186; Capt., 232; Lieut.-Gen., 277
Boyce, Lieut., 280, 292, 298
Boyd, Lieut. Hugh, 15
Bradford, Surgeon Philip, 4
Brathwaite, Col., commands Mahé force, 182, 183, 212, 216, 228, 243, 245; Maj.-Gen., 254, 255; leaves India, 256
Brereton, Major, 124, 125, 127, 131-134, 138
Breton, Major Thomas, 201
Brewster, Ensign Benjamin, 15
Brodie, Surgeon James, 27
Brooke, Ensign John, 23, 25; Capt., 129
Brown, Capt. Archibald, 218; Major, 247; Colonel, leaves India, 256
Brown, Capt., 162; Lieut.-Col., 182, 201; Col., mortally wounded, 204

INDEX

Brown, Lieut., 131, 263
Brown, Capt. William, 24, 30
Bridge, Capt., 93; killed, 98
Bridges, Capt. James, 204; Col., 243
Briggs, Capt., A.D.C. to Clive, 93, 95
Briggs, Surgeon-Gen., 143
Bruce, Capt., 29
Bruce, Ensign, 157, 158; Lieut., killed, 195
Bruce, Capt. Patrick, 254
Bruce, Col. Thomas, 243
Bruce, Maj.-Gen., 221, 225
Buckley, Ensign Philip, 25
Bulkley, Lieut., 43-45, 50; killed, 51
Budge Budge, 94
Bullock, Capt., 157, 158
Burma War, 277 *et seq.*; Regt. leaves, 297
Burr, Lieut. Daniel, 176; Capt., 221; Col., 255, 256
Butler, Lieut., 280, 287, 288, 292, 298
Byrne, Lieut., 171, 172

CAILLAUD, Capt., 79, 83; Major, 111, 114, 115, 121, 123, 130-134; sails to Bengal, 148; Brig.-Gen., death of, 261
Calcutta, state of affairs at, 90 *et seq.*; Regt. embarks at Madras for, 93; action at, 98
Calder, Lieut., 269; Capt., 292
Caliacoil, Fall of, 176
Callender, Capt., 93, 108, 114
Calvert, Lieut. Mathias, 162; Capt. 166
Campaign, Coote's plan of, 190, 191
Campbell, Brig.-Gen., Sir Archibald 279 *et seq.*
Campbell, Capt. Charles, 111, 126, 129; Major, 157, 158; Col., 159
Campbell, 1/Lieut. Colin, 27
Campbell, 2/Lieut. Daniel, 27
Campbell, Capt. Donald, 112, 129; Col., 167, 169
Campbell, 1/Lieut. Dugald, 27, 91
Campbell, Capt., 66; killed, 96
Campbell, Lieut., 175
Campbell, Lieut. Robert, 93
Campbell, Lieut. & Qr.Mr., 108
Cameron, Lieut., 216
Canteens established, 263
Carangoly, 135, 193, 216
Carberry, Lieut., 261, 263
Carey, Ensign, killed, 202

Caroor, reduction of, 225, 226, 231, 233
Carr, Lieut.-Fireworker, 159
Carty, Ensign, 145, 146
Casualties at Wandewash, 141; at Pollilore, 204; at Sholinghur, 208; at Arnee, 218
Cauvery River, 52, 60
Cauverypauk, action at, 57, 58, 136, 142
Caveripatam, 161, 233
Ceylon, expedition to, 247
Chabbert, Capt. John, 56
Chalmers, Lieut., 241, 280, 292, 296, 298
Champneys, Lieut., 209, 210
Chanda Sahib, 15, 35, 38, 39, 42, 45, 52, 53, 61, 66, 121, 122
Chandernagore, surrender of, 99
Changama, action of, 161
Charlton, Lieut., 280, 292, 296, 298
Chase, Capt., 73
Chase, Ensign, mortally wounded, 126, 129
Cheeseman, Lieut. Francis, 4
Chesborough, Lieut. Joseph, 24, 27
Chesshire, Lieut.-Col. Robert, 228
Child, Lieut., 10
Chillambrum, 194, 195
Chingleput, 70, 122, 123, 127, 134
Chisholm, Lieut., 137
Chittore, 211; fate of, 212, 234
Clark, Ensign Ralph, 15
Clarke, Ensign John, 25; Capt., 60
Clarke, Lieut., 111, 195
Clarke, Ensign, killed, 186
Clarke, Ensign, 263
Clarke, Maj. George, 228; Lieut.-Col., 231
Clive, Robert, reaches India, 17; taken prisoner, 19; Ensign, 20, 25, 29, 33; at Arcot, 42-49; given sword of honour, 85, 89; to command expedition to Calcutta, 92; death of, 177; his benefactions to the Army, 178
Close, Capt. Barry, 243; Gen. and death of, 262
Coilady, fort of, 42
Coleman, Lieut., killed, 269
Coleroon, River, 41, 52
Collins, Lieut. Edward, 195; Capt., 225, Lieut.-Col., 228, 234, 243
Coke, 2/Lieut. George, 27
Condore, victory of, 131
Conjeveram, 131; enemy retreat on, 204
Conningham, Lieut.-Col. G., 243

INDEX

Convenant, Capt. J. M., 254
Cope, Ensign James, 23, 25; Capt., 31, 34, 37, 38, 39; death of, 55
Cook, Ensign, 129; Capt., 162
Coombs, Capt., 271
Cooper, Lieut., 263
Coote, Capt. Eyre, 93, 95; Major, 105; Col., 118, 134; at Pondicherry, 149 *et seq.*; superseded, 151; goes to Bengal, 155; at Madras, 174; C.-in-C., 181, 182, 188, 215; death of, 219
Cornish, Admiral, 147
Cornwallis, Lord, 233, 235
Cosby, Ensign, 151, 152; Capt., 161, 162, 169, 176; Col. 183, 190, 201, 227
Cossimbazar, 90, 99
Cotgrave, Major, 182, 219, 223
Cotsford, Lieut., 141
Council of War at Plassey, 100 *et seq.*
Cox, Lieut. Sir John, 254
Crew, Ensign Arthur, 15
Croley, Ensign, 111, 123, 127, 129; Capt., 157
Crompton, Lieut. John, 20; Capt., 24
Crow, Lieut., 69
Cuddalore, 26; surrenders to Lally, 119; surrenders to Hyder, 216; Stuart marches on, 220
Cunningham, Capt. William, 254
Cuppage, Capt., 210, 215; Major, 242, 243
Custance, Lieut. and Adjt., 254
Cursham, Lieut., 261, 263; Capt., 280, 292, 294; killed, 296, 298

Dacre, Lieut., 261
D'Aché, Admiral, 117, 118
Dale, Ensign, 263
Dallah, attack on, 283
Dallas, Lieut., 210
Dalton, 1/Lieut. John, 27; Capt., 32-35, 39-41, 52, 54, 55, 59, 60-62, 65, 66; at Trichinopoly, 68, 72, 77; leaves India, 81
Dalrymple, Capt. James, 27
Darke, Lieut., 111
Darley, Ensign, 208
Darrell, Lieut., 175
D'Auteuil, Mons. 36, 63, 64, 66, 115; captured, 150
Davenant, Lieut., 261

Davies, Capt., 192
Davis, Lieut., 175
Dawson, Ensign, 43, 45, 50
Day, merchant, 1
Dyson, Sergt. John, 109
Deakin, Ensign, killed, 208
Dean, Surgeon, 280
De Beck, Lieut. J. F., 56,; Capt. 112, 129, 146
De Bussy, Baron, 120; at Wandewash, 137-140; captured, 220, 223
De Damas, Count, 223
Deegman, Ensign, 111
De Gingins, Lieut. Rudolph, 16, 20; capt., 24, 38-40, 53, 57, 60, 67
De la Bourdonnais, Mons., 17
De Mainville, Mons. 82, 83, 84
De Morgan, Lieut. John, 19; Capt., 24
Desplan, Ensign, 111
D'Esterre, Lieut., killed, 273
Devicotah, siege of, 31-34, 66, 83
Dickinson, Sergt., 70
Dighton, Capt. John, 254; Major, 256
Dindigul, 231
Dixon, Ensign, 175
Dods, Ensign, 208
Donaldson, Ensign Lawrence, 23, 25
Donubyu, 290, 291
Doveton, Capt., 237, 243; Brig.-Gen., 265, 270, 272
Doveton, Lieut., 280, 292
Dowse, Lieut., 245
Draper, Col., 118; leads a sally, 124, 125, 131
Duke, Lieut., 280, 290
Duncanson, 2/Lieut. Robert, 27
Duncanson, Lieut., 159
Dunn, Volunteer, 159
Dupleix, Mons., 17, 26, 28, 82; recalled, 85
Dupont, Capt., 189

Eastland, Lieut., killed, 216
Eckman, Lieut. Peter, 15, 18, 22
Edington, Lieut.-Col. James, 228
Edmundstone, Major, 201, 206, 220
Elivy, Lieut., 111
Elliot, Lieut., 111, 113, 114, 125, 126, 129
Elphinstone, Lieut.-Col., 217, 220, 226
Erdman, Lieut., 91
Evans, Ensign, 141

INDEX

FACINGS, of corps, original, 9
Faizan, Ensign, 111, 145; Capt., 170, 172
Felix, Lieut., 55
Fenwick, Ensign, 216; Capt., 292
Ferrier, Capt., 184; dies of wounds, 186
Field Deputies, 169, 174
Fischer, Lieut., 93; Capt., 108
Fitzgerald, Lieut., 160
Fitzgerald, Capt. R. V., 157, 158, 160, 166
Fitzgerald, Major Thomas, 159, 162, 166, 170, 171
Fitzpatrick, Ensign, 112, ; Lieut., 133
Flaction, Ensign Francis, 91
Fletcher, Lieut., 111; Capt., 159; Col., sent to reinforce Col. Baillie, 184-186
Flint, Lieut., 111, 131; Major, 159
Flint, Lieut., 183; at Wandewash, 192, 193, 200; Capt., 216
Floyd, Col., 233, 234
Forbes, Lieut. C., 261, 263
Forbes, Lieut. D., 254, 259, 260; Capt., 261, 263, 298
Ford, Lieut., 195
Forde, Major, 113; Col., 116, 128, 130
Fort St. David, 14; surrenders to Lally, 120
Fort St. George, beginnings of, 1; surrenders to French, 19; description of, 21; defence of, 123 *et seq.*
France, war declared with, 178, 245
Fraser, Col. Charles, 243
Fraser, Lieut. Edward, 254
Fraser, 2/Lieut. Hugh, 27, 93, 108
Freer, Cpl. Thomas, 282
French, rivalry with, 15; fleet in Madras waters, 117
French Rock, 53, 60
Frischman, Lieut., 111, 129
Fullarton, Col., 226-231
Fullerton, Capt. Alex., 15
Fulta, 90, 94

GAHAGAN, Ensign, 216
Gale, Ensign, 263
Galway, Ensign, killed, 186
Gardiner, Capt., 226
Gardner, Capt., 111
Gaupp, Lieut. G. F., 56; Capt., 95, 98, 105; at Plassey, 109
Gillon, Lieut., 216
Gingee, 8, 67, 183

Gingen, 3/Lieut. Adolphus, 18
Glass, Ensign, 43-46, 50
Glover, Lieut., 288
Godeheu, Mons., relieves Dupleix, 89
Godfrey, Lieut. R., 159, 160; Capt., 176
Godwin, Capt.-Lieut., 91
Golden Rock, 53; action at, 74-79
Gordon, Major R., 132, 138
Gordon, Major W., 138, 140
Gordon, Capt., 292
Gorham, Lieut., 172
Gorie, Cadet, 186
Gould, Ensign, dies of wounds, 204
Gowdie, Capt., 184, 185; Major, 234-239, 241, 243; Major-Gen., 261
Graham, Ensign, 216
Grant, Capt. A., 27; Major, 105
Grant, 2/Lieut. J., 27
Gravely, Lieut., 159
Greene, Lieut., 280, 292
Greenwell, Lieut., 215
Greig, Capt., 111, 129, 133
Grenvill, Ensign, T., 25; Capt., 82
Greuber, Lieut., 223
Griffin, Commodore, 26, 28
Grubb, Lieut., 280, 282; death of, 291, 298
Gwibal, 2/Lieut. P., 27
Guard and sentries at Fort St. George, 6
Gujalhathi Pass, 170, 231, 233, 242
Gujerat, Regiment serves in, 177
Gurtler, Lieut. F., 56; Capt., 111, 129

HALIBURTON, Lieut. J., 29
Haliburton, Lieut., 186
Hall, Ensign, 208
Hall, Lieut. L. W., 254
Hamilton, Ensign F., 25
Hamilton, Ensign, 133; Lieut., 134
Hamilton, Paymaster, 171
Hammond, Ensign, 159
Hammond, Surgeon J., 27
Hancome, Lieut. and Adjt., dies of wounds, 269
Harcourt, Lieut.-Col., 257-259
Harden, Ensign J., 25
Harper, Ensign, 111; Capt., 157
Harrington, Ensign Jas., 15
Harrison, Lieut., 81
Hart, Lieut., 111; Capt., 134
Harvey, Capt. H., 201
Hastings, Marquis of, 265 *et seq.*
Haywood, Ensign, 216

Hazlewood, Ensign, dies of wounds, 204
Hegue, Capt., 171
Heidigger, Lieut. J. C., 56
Herbert, Capt., 204
Heron, Lieut.-Col. A., 87, 88
Higginbotham, Ensign, 183
Hill, Ensign, 280, 284, 290
Hislop, Capt., killed, 204
Hislop, Gen. Sir T., 262, 265, 266, 277
Hitchcock, Lieut., deserts to Hyder Ali, 162
Hoare, Sergt., 171
Holland, 2/Lieut. J., 18, 20; Capt., 24, 29
Holland, Ensign M. S., 16
Holland, war with, 247
Holmes, Ensign, 216
Holt, Ensign Tilman, 8; Lieut., 81
Honours, Battle, for Arcot, 49; for Ava, 298; for Nundydroog, 238; for Maheidpoor, 273
Hope, Lieut., 186
Hooghly, fort of, 97
Hooker, Lieut., 162
Hooper, Lieut., 134; Capt., 280, 289, 292, 298
Hopper, Lieut., 280, 298
Horn, Lieut., 145; Major, 176; Col., 228
Hoskan, Sergt., 170
Hospital, first established for soldiers, 5
Howden, Lieut., 280, 292, 296
Hughes, Admiral, 196, 199, 213, 214
Hughes, Capt. Jas., 216
Hume, Capt., killed, 126, 129
Hunt, Capt., 114
Hurter, Ensign, killed, 131
Hussey, Capt., 195
Hyder Ali, 74, 84; allied with Lally, 147; war with, 160; his many successes, 170 et seq., 173

ILDERTON, 2/Lieut. T., 27
Indiamen—*Chandos*, 12; *Chesterfield*, 91; *Defence*, 12; *Discoverie*, 2; *Durrington*, 81; *Exeter*, 32; *Fox*, 155; *Hardwicke*, 110; *Harwich*, 32; *James*, 12; *Lord North*, 178; *Marlborough*, 94, 95; *Nymph*, 187; *Shaftesbury*, 128; *Thames*, 127; *Wager*, 42; *Walpole*, 91; *William*, 2; *Winchelsea*, 23, 24; *Winchester*, 17
Innis, Lieut., 37, 47, 49; Capt., 111; Lieut.-Col. to command Regt., 259

JACOBS, 2/Lieut. E., 27
James, Commodore, 110
Java, expedition to, 261
Jermin, Lieut., first C.O. of Corps, 3
Joecher, Lieut., 93, 108
Johnson, Asst.-Surgeon, 280, 298
Johnson, Lieut., 171, 172
Johnston, Sergt., 210
Johnston, Sergt.-Major, 171
Jourdan, Capt. E., 190

KARICAL, 121
Karrighatta Hill, 236, 240
Katwa, Coote sent to attack, 100
Keene, Ensign W., 23, 25; Lieut., 58
Kelly, Major Amos, 277
Kelly, Lieut.-Col. H., 220, 221, 228, 231, 233, 279-283
Kelsey or Kelsall, deserter, 65
Kemmendine, 282; defence of, 284 et seq.
Kennedy, Capt., 175
Kennet, Ensign, 216
Kerr, Rev. R. H., 254
Kerr, Ensign, 93; killed, 95
Kerr, Lieut., 280, 284, 290
Kilpatrick, Capt. Jas., 35, 41, 49, 57, 59, 75-78, 81; Bt. Major, 85, 90, 94, 96, 97, 105-108
Kilpatrick, Ensign, 112
King, Capt. W., 254
Kinneer, Major, disaster to, 67
Kirk, Ensign, 68; Capt., 75, 76; death of, 78
Kirker, Lieut., 150
Kirkpatrick, Capt., 157, 158
Kistnagherry, attack on, 160
Kistnaveram, 55
Kitson, Capt., 280, 283
Knightly, Lieut., 171
Knipe, Major C., 16, 22
Knox, Ensign, 93; Lieut., 108, 159; dies of wounds, 186
Knuttall, 2/Lieut. G., 27
Kuhn, Cornet, 141
Kyd, Lieut., 263; Capt., 280, 281

LALLY, Count de, 117 et seq.; arrives at Pondicherry, 118; at Wandewash, 137-140; sent to England, 155
Lally, Gen., 198
Lamotte, Capt., 194, 195, 211, 212
Landey, Lieut., 10

INDEX

Lang, Lieut. R., 111, 112, 134, ; Capt. 157, 170, 171 ; Col., 201 ; at Vellore, 204-210, 215, 225, 226 ; commands Regt., 259
Langford, Lieut. T., 24, 25
Lantwein, Sergt., 210
Latour, Ensign, killed, 133
Law, Mons. 61-63, 65, 66, 99
Lawrence, Stringer, 11 ; previous services, 22 ; commands at Madras, 24 ; captured at Pondicherry, 29 ; resigns, goes home and returns, 38 ; returns to India, 59 ; relieves Trichinopoly, 61, 62, 73 ; receives Sword of Honour, 85, 91 ; again C.-in-C., 116 ; defence measures, 123, 127 ; goes home ill, 131 ; returns with rank of Maj.-Gen., 155 ; leaves India, 163, 164
Leighton, Lieut. T., 189 ; Lieut.-Col., 254
Lesley, Lieut., 10
Lewis Ensign E., 25
Lewis, 2/Lieut. W., 27
Lin, Capt. W., 91, 108
Lind, Lieut., 216
Lindsay, Capt., 218
Little, Lieut., 112, 129
Loy, Ensign, 216
Lucas, Cpl., 285
Lyon, Capt. Patrick, 27

MACALISTER, Capt. J., 190
Macartney, Lord, Gov. of Madras, 213, 219
Macaulay, Ensign, 183
Macdonald, Ensign, 157, 158
Mackay, Lieut. R., 221
Mackenzie, 2/Lieut. E., 27
Mackenzie, Ensign, 81 ; Capt., 175
Maclean, Ensign, killed, 208
Macleod, Col. Lord, 183, 187, 190, 219
Macleod, Lieut., W., 243
MacMahon, Ensign, killed, 152
MacPherson, 1/Lieut. L., 27
McAlister, Ensign, 192
McAlly, Ensign, 216
McCutcheon, Lieut., 171
McDonald, Lieut. C., 254
McDonald, Lieut. J., 254
McDowall, Lieut. S., 254
McDowall, Gen., 261
McKain, Lieut., 186
McNeal, Lieut., 186

Madge, Lieut., 162
Madras, beginnings of, 1, 2 ; Lally besieges, 122 ; siege raised, 128
Madura, investment of, 37
Mahé, projected attack on, 181
Maheidpoor, battle of, 266-269
Mahratta War, outbreak of, 257
Mahratta-Pindari War, 265 et seq.
Maitland, Capt. T., 225
Malcolm, Major W., 243
Malcolm, Gen. Sir J., 268, 277
Malegaon, capture of, 271
Manilla, expeditions to, 155, 156, 252
Manning, Lieut., 279, 292
Marchand, Sergt. R., 145 ; Capt., 159
Marriott, Col., 263
Martin, Capt., succeeds Jermin, 3
Martin, Ensign Claud, 156
Marshall, Lieut., 280, 298
Maskelyne, E., 19 ; Ensign, 25 ; Lieut., 41 ; Capt., 93, 108, 111
Massy, Lieut., 186
Mathews, Ensign W., 25 ; Capt., 168
Maxwell, Capt., 280, 290
Maxwell, Col., 233, 236, 239, 240
Medals, 298-299
Medows, Major-Gen. W., 230, 233, 240
Messes, established, 259
Meyers, Lieut., 111
Milne, Asst.-Surgeon, 261
Minns, Lieut. & Adjt., 112 ; killed, 133
Minors, Commandant, 3
Mir Jaffier, 100, 109
Monchanin, Capt., 129, 145
Monson, Major, 138, 143, 147-149 ; wounded, 151 ; Col., marches against Madura, 156, 157
Montgomery, Lieut., 195
Monteith, Capt., 186
Moorhouse, Capt., 192, 195
Moore, Carpenter, 33
Moore, Ensign, 159, 193
Morari Rao, 48, 71, 74
Morrice, Ensign, 43, 50
Morrison, Sergt., 281
Muat, Lieut., 184
Munro, Lieut. J., 254
Munro, Major J., 254
Munro, Gen. Sir H., marches on Pondicherry, 179 ; moves against Hyder Ali, 183 ; retreats to Madras, 187, 189, 196 ; at Pollilore, 202, 204, ; at Negapatam, 213, 214
Murray, Lieut. A. McG., 177 ; Lieut.-Col., 266, 268
Murray, Capt.-Lieut., 59
Murry, Lieut. D., 24

INDEX

Murry, Pte. D., 108
Muhammad Ali, 36, 37, 38, 48, 54, 55, 71, 171
Myers, Capt., 177
Mysore, operations in, 160 *et seq.*; war in, 166
Muzaffar Jang, 35

NAGORE, 194
Nairne, Ensign, 159
Nangle, Ensign P., 15
Nash, Lieut., 186, 241
Negapatam, 133; operations against, 213
Nellore, 8, 113, 183
Nelson, Sergt., 68
Nevinson, 2/Lieut. S., 27
Nicoll, Lieut. H., killed, 175
Nield, Lieut., 159
Nixon, Capt., 171; Lieut.-Col., 212; Col., 228
Nixon, Lieut., 259; Capt., 261, 263
Noble, Capt. J., 27
North, Lieut., 195
Nundydroog, assault upon, 237

O'BRIEN, Lieut.-Fireworker, 192
O'Brien, Sergt. W., 272; Clr.-Sergt., 282
Ochterlony, Lieut., 223
Ogden, Lieut. T., 15
Ogilby, Lieut., 232
Ogilvie, 2/Lieut. J., 27; Capt., 112
O'Hara, Lieut. J., 180
Oldham, Major G., 228
Oliver, Lieut., 201; capt., 236
Oosoor, 236
O'Neale, Capt. P., 8
O'Neill, Capt. E., 15
Oram, Lieut., 211
Orphan Asylum established, 229
Orton, Lieut. & Adjt., 112; Capt., 159, 171, 172
Oswald, Ensign, 93, 108
Owen, Col., 201; attacked by Hyder Ali, 208, 217
Owen, Lieut., 157, 158

PAINTER, Lieut., 162
Palar River, 43, 70, 136

Parker, Ensign H., 25
Parliament, thanks of, to Army, 246
Parr, Lieut., 183, 209, 210; Capt., 247
Parrott, Lieut., 111
Pascall, Ensign E., 23, 25; Capt., 111, 126, 129
Paschoud, Lieut., 91
Patterson, Major J., 228
Patterson, Qr.Mr., 159
Pearse, Col., 188, 200, 201, 207, 220, 221
Pegler, Dmr. P., 108
Pegu, advance to, 293
Perambaucum, casualties at, 186
Permacoil, 145, 183, 193, 216
Phillips, Ensign, 111; Capt., 184; killed, 186
Phillips, Lieut. R., 254; Capt., 259, 260, 263
Pierce, Capt. F., 254
Pigot, Gov. of Madras, 127
Pigou, Ensign B., 25; Capt., 83, 84
Pimoran, Gen., 198
Pindaris, account of, 264
Pitt, Thomas, 9; governor, 14
Plassey, description of field, 104; battle of, 105-107; casualties at, 107, 108
Pocock, Admiral, 130
Polier, Capt., 83; Major, 111, 119, 120; mortally wounded, 126, 129
Pollock, Pte., 295
Pollilore, 202; battle of, 203, 204
Pondicherry, 8, 14; French attack upon, 115, 134; Coote advances to, 143; description of, 146, 147; surrenders, 153; restored to French, 159; losses at siege of, 180; surrenders to Munro, 180, 193; capture of, 245
Poonamallee, 9, 11, 47, 123, 202
Porto Novo, battle of, 197-199
Powlett, Captain, 32, 33
Prendergast, Capt. T., 189; Major, 228; Lieut.-Col., 243
Preston, Volunteer, 58
Preston, Capt. A., 111, 127, 130, 134; Major, 148; captures Thiaghur, 154, 157; killed, 158
Provost, Ensign J. L., 56
Price, Lieut., 208
Pridmore, Sergt. D., 109
Pringle, Capt., 192
Pringle, Sergt. J., 109
Prisoners of Tippoo, 244
Prize money for Seringapatam, 242
Puckle, Major W., 7

Pulicat, 200
Pybus, Lieut., 43
Pye, Capt., 93, 95; killed, 98

Raison, Cpl. John, 108
Ramnad, storming of, 176
Ramsay, Capt. J., 27
Rangoon, occupation of, 280; fighting near, 287
Ranken, Asst. Surgeon, 204
Raworth, Surgeon J., 27
Regiments, British, 19th Light Dragoons, 230, 234; 1st Foot, 265, 272; 12th, 257; 30th, 272; 36th, 230, 234, 238, 245; 39th, 85, 92-94, 110, 113; 41st, 281; 47th, 289; 52nd, 230-234, 245; 67th, 272; 71st, 230-234, 238; 72nd, 230-234; 73rd, 183, 190, 192, 196, 201, 217-220, 226; 74th, 230, 233, 234; 76th, 230, 234; 78th, 219, 221, 226; 79th, 118, 121, 153, 156, 162; 84th, 118, 132, 153, 162; 89th, 150, 162, 163, 178, 289, 290; 96th, 162, 163; 98th, 221; 101st, 219, 221; 102nd, 221, 226
Regiments, French, Lally, 124, 125, 130, 139, 151, 154; Lorraine, 124, 125, 130, 139, 140, 151, 154; India, 124, 130, 139, 154; Volunteers of Bourbon, 154
Regiments, Hanoverian, 15th, 219, 220, 221, 230; 16th, 221, 230
Reorganization of Regiment, 228, 248, 252, 291, 292
Repington, Ensign, 68; Lieut., 77
Revel, Lieut., 43-46, 50, 83
Richards, Capt. W., 59
Richardson, Asst. Surgeon, 280, 297
Richardson, Lieut. W., 8, 10
Richardson, Lieut., 201
Ridge, Capt., 79
Roberts, Lieut., 159, 183; surrenders Thiaghur, 194
Robertson, Lieut., 280, 281; dies of wounds, 282
Robinson, Lieut., killed, 131
Robson, Lieut., 111, 129
Rollestone, Lieut., 210
Ross, Major, 289
Rouse, Lieut., 171
Roy, Ensign, 259, 261, 263; Capt., 280, 288, 290, 298
Royacottah, 236
Rumbold, Lieut., 93, 98; Capt., 108
Rumley, Capt., 184, 185
Russel, Lieut.-Col. W., 228

St. Thomé, 3, 5
Sale, Capt., 225
Sampson, Ensign E., 25
Sampson, Lieut., 216
Samson, Lieut. S., 91
Saubinet, Mons., 115
Sauhojee, 31, 35, 121
Saunders, 2/Lieut. J., 27
Saunderson, Capt. R., 24
Saxon, Ensign, 279
Schaub, Capt. J. H., 56, 111
Schomberg, Ensign, 129
Scotney, Ensign, 93; Lieut. and Adjt., 108
Scott, Lieut.-Col. C. F., 87
Scott, Lieut.-Col. R., 268
Scrimsour, Lieut. J., 24; Capt., 32
Seaton, Lieut. F., 12
Seringapatam, siege and capture of, 240-242
Seringham, island of, 52 et seq., 61, 73, 115
Serle, Capt., 177
Shaw, Lieut., 159; Capt., 195
Shawlum or Shaulur, Sergt., 58
Ships, R.N., *Bridgewater*, 92, 97; *Cornwallis*, 259; *Cumberland*, 92; *Dover*, 259; *Intelligence*, 198; *Kent*, 92; *Revenge*, 110; *Salisbury*, 92, 94, 95; *Samarang*, 259; *Tiger*, 92, 99
Ships, French, *Bien Aimé*, 119; *Harlem*, 127
Sholinghur, Battle of, 205-208
Shute, Lieut. T., 254
Simpson, Lieut., 280, 290
Sittang, operations near, 294-296
Sinclare, Lieut. H., 12
Sivajee, 8
Smith, Major George, 254
Smith, Ensign Joseph, 18; Capt., 86, 111, 115, 137, 144; Major, 148, 151; Colonel, 160; operations in Mysore, 166 et seq.
Smith, Capt. Richard, 111, 114, 122, 129
Smith, Ensign Samuel, 25
Smith, Lieut. Stephen, 111, 125; Capt., 143, 145; captures Gingee, 154
Southby, Capt. W. H., 24
Spankie, Lieut., 269
Speed, 2/Lieut. J., 27
Spice Islands, expeditions to, 247, 255, 256
Stables, Ensign, 134
Stenger, Ensign, 93, 108
Stenton, Lieut., 280, 281, 290

INDEX

Stewart, Capt., killed, 131
Storey, Lieut. J., 254
Stuart, Ensign, killed, 216
Stuart-General, 196, 204; succeeds Coote, 219
Stuart, Lieut.-Col., 219, 231, 232, 239
Stuckey, Lieut., 175
Stukeley, Surgeon W., 27
Suffren, Admiral, 222
Sugar Loaf Rocks, 53, 60, 77
Surajah Dowlah, 90; marches on Calcutta, 97, 98; death of, 109
Sutherland, Capt. A., 15
Swiss Companies, raising of, 56
Symons, Ensign, 208
Syriam Pagoda, attack on, 283

Taafe, Lieut., 195
Tabby, Ensign, 93, 108
Tait or Tuite, Ensign, 93; Lieut., 108
Taishan, Lieut., 55
Tate, Cpl. T., 272, 288
Tanjore, operations in, 175, 176, 212
Tanner, Capt., 192
Taylor, Lieut.-Col. A., 254
Temple, Capt., 210
Thalner, capture of, 270
Thewles, Ensign, 216
Thiaghur, 183, 194
Thompson, Lieut., F., 254; Capt., 258; Colonel, 265
Thomson, Capt. D., 180
Tippoo Sahib, 200, 230, 235
Tichborne, Capt.-Lieut. T., 254
Title of Regiment, changes in, 253
Todd, Lieut. C., 127, 129
Tolson, Lieut.-Col. R., 243
Transports, *Argyll*, 297; *Bannerman*, 279; *David Clarke*, 279; *George IV*, 279
Treaty, of Paris, 159; with Hyder Ali, 173
Trenwith, Lieut., 43, 45, 46
Trichinopoly, 15; description of, 52 *et seq.*, 60, 134, 233
Tripassore, surrenders to Coote, 201; defence of, 211
Trivady, 70, 71; action near, 81, 194
Trivatore, 47, 131, 136
Troughton, Lieut. Z., 12
Trusler, Ensign or Lieut., 42
Turing, Lieut., 177, 186
Turnbull, Ensign J., 25
Turner, Ensign, 43, 50, 148

Uniform, first worn, 9
Usgate, Capt. J., 24
Uttramalur, 115

Van Francken, Ensign, 18
Vashon, Ensign, 157; killed, 158
Vasserot, Lieut., 129, 138, 140, 143
Vaughan, Capt., 131
Vaughan, Ensign, 134
Vellore, 43, 49, 201, 215, 233, 242
Vellout, 233
Vernon, Commodore, 179
Vigors, Major U., 247
Villeret, Ensign, 112, 145
Villenore Redoubt, capture of, 151
Vizagapatam, 12
Volconda, 39, 40, 67
Vouga, Ensign J., 91

Wade, Lieut., killed, 186
Wagner, Lieut. Rudolph, 56, 93; Capt., 108
Wahab, Lieut., 223
Walker, 1/Lieut. M., 27
Walker, Capt., killed, 208
Walker, Capt., 255
Wandewash, 115, 122; Brereton repulsed at, 133, 134; Battle of, 137-141, 183; defence of, 216
Wangenheim, Gen., 223, 224
Wanitoo, 260
Wardlow, Ensign R., 25
Ware, Lieut., 157, 158
Warren Hastings, his great decision, 187
Watson, Rear-Admiral C., 85, 89, 91, 95, 107
Watson, Ensign, dies of wounds, 204
Waugh, Lieut. Gilbert, 254
Waugh, Lieut. W. G., 254
Webber, Capt. H., 254; Major, 256
Weir, Ensign, 280, 284, 286; Lieut., 292
Weld, Lieut., killed, 175
Wharton, Lieut., 226
White, Surgeon, 216
White Pagoda Stockade, 289
Whitman, Lieut., 133

INDEX

Wiecks, Ensign, 93, 108
Wilkey, Lieut., 69
Williams, Ensign, 263
Williams, Lieut. J., 24
Williamson, Capt. J., 223, 225
Willson, Ensign, 111
Wilson, Surgeon, killed, 186
Woman, enlistment of a, 13, 14
Wood, Lieut. J., 69; Capt., 112, 142, 143, 144, 156; Major, 157; Colonel, 161, 166-170

Wragg, Capt., 186
Wynch, Major A., 243
Wynn, Ensign, 111

YANDABO, Treaty of, 297
Yarde, Lieut. H., 254
Young, Lieut., 190
Younge, Lieut., 195

www.ingramcontent.com/pod-product-compliance
Lightning Source LLC
Chambersburg PA
CBHW080541230426
43663CB00015B/2664